W9-DCF-704

WITH CHRIST IN GOD

WITH CHRIST IN GOD

A Study of Human Destiny

by

SHIRLEY C. HUGHSON,
O.H.C.

LONDON
S · P · C · K
NEW YORK
HOLY CROSS PRESS
1947

241.45
H874

112769

MADE IN GREAT BRITAIN

TO
THE NAME

WHICH IS ABOVE EVERY NAME,
IN HUMBLE THANKSGIVING
FOR THE LOVING-KINDNESS AND MERCY
WHICH HAVE FOLLOWED ME
ALL THE DAYS OF MY LIFE

CONTENTS

CONTENTS

PREFACE

The author does not presume to offer this book to scholars. He has a good hope, however, that there may be not a few who, although they do not possess theologically trained minds, are sufficiently instructed in the fundamentals of Christianity, and have a good enough mental equipment, to enable them to think seriously on great religious subjects if they will but apply themselves industriously to the task. It is amongst this group that he ventures to hope to find a hearing, to the help of some souls, as God may will.

One of the main purposes in view is to seek to disabuse certain minds of the erroneous idea that is so widespread, that the Christian Life consists in accepting certain articles of belief and conforming to a certain code of conduct. This is, indeed, an indispensable part of it, but the life " in Christ," as our Lord repeatedly teaches, is personal union with God, and without this union, no amount of intellectual acceptance, or mere following of codes of behaviour, will suffice for that progressive sanctification which is necessary for attaining the ultimate destiny which God has prepared for every soul He creates. Love is the essential factor in Christianity, and love, whether human or divine, is the unitive virtue. It binds friend to friend in the human and natural sphere, it binds man to God in the supernatural sphere. One fears from actual observation that only a small proportion of practising Christians have any vivid realization of what union with God means, and therefore they give little thought to it. One has found those who appear never to have heard of it. They read the many passages in the New Testament which testify to this without glimpsing the obvious truth. They are conscientious in following certain practices, but God is too often a Being quite apart from their consciousness.

The author offers no apology for this book being repetitive. He has been at some pains to make it so. He conceives reiteration to be one of the soundest of pedagogical principles. He who would teach must reiterate. This principle was followed by the greatest of all teachers. On a single occasion He gave the parables of the lost sheep, of the lost coin, and of the lost son, all of them conveying substantially the same lesson.

The quotations from Scripture follow, in most cases, the familiar Authorized Version, but there has been no hesitancy, in many instances, in re-translating, where the A.V. was weak in its emphases, or where a better text has been produced by modern scholarship.

Acknowledgements are due to the Rev. Dr. Leicester C. Lewis for his kindness in reading the MS. and for offering much valuable criticism; and to many other friends and fellow-workers who have assisted in bringing the work to completion.

Soli Deo gloria.

S. C. H.

Holy Cross Monastery,
   West Park, N.Y.,
      Epiphany, 1947.

PROLOGUE

THE destiny of the soul, its call to be "partaker of the divine nature," [1] to participate in the essential holiness of Him who "only is holy," [2] may seem to some to be too lofty an objective for weak and sinful man. But it will seem so only to those who have failed to grasp the great primary principle of Christianity, that upon which every other principle depends, and without which there is no Christianity. Our purpose is to show that the culmination of man's development, of his evolution, both in body and soul, lies in finding his place "in Christ," and therefore, "with Christ in God." [3] Man, made one with Christ, is to be taken up with Him into the Godhead. He is to have his place amid the infinite and ineffable mysteries of the Holy and Indivisible Trinity. [4] These mysteries he cannot understand, but by the gracious and loving condescension of God, he can, and must, enter into them, and experience them. The apostle proclaims the duty of laying hold upon that "holiness without which no man shall see the Lord," [5] and there is but one holiness—"Thou only art holy." Of the holiness of God we must be partakers. There is no other destiny. He who fails to attain this, fails in all.

By the word evolution, we mean the unfolding, according to the will and purpose of God, of all man's spiritual potentialities and capacities, which have, through the divine creative omnipotence, either in nature, or by the special action of the Holy Spirit, been set in order within us. These gifts are in germ, so to speak, and are to be drawn out and developed under the power of the Holy Ghost, until they bring us to the highest level of the heavenly beatitude which, from eternity, God has ordained as our destiny.

The soul can attain to the required union with God only through our Lord Christ. "No man cometh unto the Father, but by me," He declared. [6] He said to His disciples, "I am the vine, ye are the branches." [7] In the sacrament of baptism we are grafted into Him

---

[1] 2 St. Peter i. 4.   [2] Rev. xv. 4.   [3] Col. iii. 3.

[4] The preference is given to St. Bernard's expression, "the Indivisible Trinity" (*De diligendo Deo*, Ch. iv), rather than to the English traditional "undivided Trinity." The latter declares only that the Trinity is not divided. The former declares the fundamental principle of the indivisibility of the Godhead. There is a difference between the mere fact of not being divided, and the impossibility of division.

[5] Heb. xii. 14.   [6] St. John xiv. 6.   [7] St. John xv. 5.

as a branch into the vine, and as the life of the branch is identical with the life of the vine, and is not merely a life like unto it, so our spiritual life is an actual participation in the life and holiness of Him who is both perfect God and perfect Man.

The destiny of man finds its beginning, is progress, and its fulfilment only " in Christ." This thought embraces the widest reach, and plumbs the profoundest depths, of the mystery of the relation between God and man. The expression " in Christ " occurs scores of times in the New Testament, and in connection with it are scores of precious promises and assurances which are given by the love and goodness of God. The consideration of a few of these passages will show that there is no phase of the Christian life, either in this world or the next, which is not conditioned by this abiding of the soul " in Christ." It began in the divine mind with the primeval creation, and extends to the ultimate consummation of God's work with and for man, in eternity.

Speaking of the purpose of God in creating man, St. Paul says, " He hath blessed us with all spiritual blessings in heavenly places *in Christ*: according as he hath chosen us *in him* before the foundation of the world, that we should be holy." [1] Again, he says, " He hath created us *in Christ Jesus* unto good works "; [2] and when we had failed of good works through sin, He made us " *in Christ Jesus* a new creature "; [3] " *In Christ Jesus* we who sometimes were far off are made nigh by the blood of Christ "; [4] " He hath accepted us *in the Beloved* "; [5] " *In Christ Jesus* God is made unto us wisdom and righteousness and sanctification and redemption " [6]—note the tremendous import of these four words. " *In him* we are also builded together for an habitation of God "; [7] God has given us grace to " press towards the mark for the prize of the high calling of God *in Christ Jesus*." [8] Again we are taught that it is the divine will that at the last " every man be presented perfect *in Christ Jesus* "; [9] " *In Christ Jesus* those who are his have fallen asleep "; [10] " *In Christ Jesus* they shall be made alive "; [11] " the dead *in Christ* shall rise first," [12] and as the final consummation, " He hath called us unto his eternal glory *in Christ Jesus*." [13]

Thus from His first choosing of us " before the foundation of the world," when we had no existence save in the thought of God, till the final resurrection and the eternal glory of the heavenly life, our destiny, in its various steps, is wrought out " in Christ."

---

[1] Eph. i. 3, 4.   [2] Eph. ii. 10.   [3] 2 Cor. v. 17.   [4] Eph. ii. 13.
[5] Eph. i. 6.   [6] 1 Cor. i. 30.   [7] Eph. ii. 22.   [8] Phil. iii. 14.
[9] Col. i. 28.   [10] 1 Thess. iv. 14.   [11] 1 Cor. xv. 22.   [12] 1 Thess. iv. 16.
[13] 1 St. Peter v. 10.

Christ is the normal man. We are not here employing the idea of the norm in its popular sense as indicating a mean or average. We are using it in its highest sense as an authoritative standard, and in this case the standard is a divine one, and can, therefore, be neither lowered nor revised.

Since the blight of sin fell upon the human race we are all sub-normal. Christ is the only normal Man, the only one since the fall of Adam who is conformed to the ideal which God had in mind when He planned the creation of man. Therefore, He alone can restore the race to normality, and this He does by incorporating the souls of men into Himself, and, therefore, into God, for He is also perfect God. In its ever-growing conformity to Him, the faithful soul moves forward to its splendid destiny, which is in the innermost sanctuary of the Holy Trinity in accordance with our Lord's promise, " Where I am there shall also my servant be." [1] In this promise lies the divine charter of our hope.

This life of union with God is not to be thought of as a vague, intangible thing, a condition belonging to some remote sphere into which it may be possible to enter in some dim future æon. This would be utterly fatal. It would be to miss the essential point of Christianity. " He that believeth on me hath "—not will have at some future time—" eternal life." [2] This union exists here and now, and here and now it is being made the more perfect, or is being the more violated, through every action of our daily life. It was no rhetorical exaggeration on the part of St. Paul when he said, " Whether, therefore, ye eat, or drink, or whatsoever ye do, do all to the glory of God." [3] It was the simple factual statement of the only method by which the Christian life can be lived adequately, the only way of securing the progress in the life of God which we must be continually making.

God is the only ultimate and absolute reality, and man will not attain to his normal status, as God ordained it to be, until he is made wholly one " with Christ in God." This is the supreme climax to be reached by every human soul. It is the profoundest of all historical realities possible in human life. It is the reality which for man will persist for eternity. The soul of man, the most complete and objective thing in God's creation, the only immortal earthly creature, is made one with God, and as God shall endure forever, so man's oneness with Him is to endure as long as God Himself endures.

[1] St. John xii. 26. [2] St. John vi. 47.
[3] I Cor. x. 31. See also Col. iii. 17; I St. Peter iv. 11.

Our dwelling in Christ is effected by Christ first taking up His abode in us. God always holds the initiative, but everywhere there must be a mutuality. It is His to begin the good work in us. It is ours to make the response. Without this co-operation, nothing can be accomplished. With it, all things that God has appointed for us will be fulfilled. In the end nothing will be lacking. Our Lord has declared, " He that eateth my flesh, and drinketh my blood, dwelleth in me, and I in him. As the living Father hath sent me, and I live by the Father: so he that eateth me, even he shall live by me." [1] In His final teaching the night before He suffered, He taught the same truth with emphasis and reiteration. " At that day ye shall know that I am in my Father, and ye in me, and I in you. . . . If a man love me, he will keep my words, and my Father will love him, and we will come unto him, and make our abode with him." [2]

In the great prayer with which He concluded His discourse in the upper room we find again the reiteration of these assurances in even stronger terms. He prayed " that they all may be one; as thou, Father, art in me, and I in thee, that they also may be one in us. . . . I in them, and thou in me, that they may be made perfect in one. . . . I have declared unto them thy name, and will declare it; that the love wherewith thou hast loved me may be in them, and I in them." [3] This mutual indwelling draws us into the innermost sanctuary of the Holy Trinity where Christ dwells.

This is the destiny which God has prepared for man, the only destiny. He offers no alternative.

---

[1] St. John vi. 56, 57.   [2] St. John xiv. 20 and 23.
[3] St. John xvii. 21–26.

The contemplation of our Lord is not only holy, but it makes us holy; even only to think of Him, to look at Him with faith and love, sanctifies us. For certain souls the life of Christ Jesus is one subject of meditation among many others; this is not enough. Christ is not one of the means of spiritual life; He is all our spiritual life. . . . Our holiness is of an essential supernatural order; God is not content, and never will be content (since He has resolved on making us His children), with a natural morality or religion. He wills us to act as children of a divine race. But it is through His Son, it is in His Son, and by the grace of His Son, that He gives us power to attain this holiness. All the holiness He has destined for each soul, God has placed in Christ, and it is of His fulness that we all must receive the graces which will make us holy. If Christ possesses all the treasures of wisdom and knowledge and holiness, it is that we may share them.

COLUMBA MARMION.

CHAPTER I

THE CALL TO HOLINESS

I

THE philosopher-poet has said that " the proper study of mankind is man." In a certain sense this is true, for it is indeed necessary to study man if we are to know how man is to attain his destiny. However, the study of man must always be secondary, nor can there be any real knowledge of man until we have learned something of God, for man is made for God. It has been said that every error concerning man has its root in some error concerning God. We cannot know our destiny, or the proper nature and direction of our powers, until first we have grasped something of the nature and character of God, by whom and for whom we were created, in whom we " live and move and have our being." [1] God has revealed Himself to us just in order that we may know something of the end and purpose of our being. In so far as we know God, we know ourselves. In so far as we know His will and purpose, we know our destiny.

The primary consideration in the study of God is His holiness. Scripture summarizes His infinite knowledge by calling Him " the Truth," His infinite perfection by calling Him " Holy." This revelation is repeated again and again. When He revealed to Moses His Name and character, He foreshadowed the fuller revelation which was to come through our Lord—namely, that the ground and cause of our holiness was to be His infinite holiness. No fewer than six times in the book of Leviticus does the Holy Spirit stress this condition of the covenant. In the eleventh chapter He declares twice that His people are to be holy because He is holy— " Ye shall be holy for I am holy." [2] The same injunction, and the same ground for it, are repeated in chapter xix. 2, in chapter xx, verses 7 and 26, and again in the eighth verse of chapter xxi. " Holiness is the fundamental virtue of God," [3] and He is the source of all holiness. His people can be holy only through partaking of His holiness. Of this holiness they must partake if He is

---

[1] Acts xvii. 28.   [2] Lev. xi. 44, 45.
[3] Pohle-Preuss, *Dogmatic Theology*, I, 437.

to be their God and they are to be His people.   In like sense this expression is found no fewer than twenty times in the Pentateuch, and is repeated again and again in various parts of the Bible.   In the great model prayer which our Lord gave and commanded to be used, the first petition is in honour of His holiness—" Hallowed be thy name."   In addressing His Father in the great High-Priestly prayer on the night before the Passion, our Lord used only two adjectives in describing Him—" O righteous Father," and " Holy Father." [1]

II

What is meant by holiness? Both the Hebrew and the Greek words employed in Scripture imply separation, a state of being set apart. God is infinitely separate from all that is imperfect. But this is only negative, and there is nothing negative in the essential Being of God. We do not say that He is holy because He is not, and cannot be, sinful. The mere absence of sin does not constitute holiness. Nor can God acquire holiness, for holiness constitutes the ultimate fulness of the divine Being, so that it is inconceivable that there could be anything in Him that could be other than absolutely holy. That which is infinitely perfect cannot grow or increase in any particular, and the conception of acquiring implies a lack, which is impossible where God is concerned.

We are not, however, to hesitate to use negative terms in referring to God. In discussing certain relationships, we are lacking in the power to speak of Him in any other way. We employ such expressions as infinite, immutable, incomprehensible, in describing Him, often forgetting, in our familiar use of such words, that we are merely saying that He is not finite, not changeable, not to be comprehended by the finite mind, or embraced in the limits of space. We can say what He is not; we have no ability to see and describe in any fulness what the infinite God is. We can say that He is good and kind, wise and merciful and loving, but when we come to see Him face to face, and to know Him, we shall be amazed to realize how these words were but a faint, linguistic gesture in comparison with the fulness of the knowledge of the beauty, and glory, and goodness, which shall stand revealed to us.

Although negative terms cannot be avoided in speaking of God, yet where it is possible to speak of Him in positive terms we should do so, since His life is wholly positive in its nature and operation. He declared His Name to be " I am that which I am." [2]   This

---

[1] St. John xvii. 11 and 25.   [2] Exod. iii. 14.

mysterious revelation of His Name is in no sense negative, but wholly positive, and it involves infinitely more in respect to holiness than being separate from all that is evil or imperfect. He is absolute holiness, and this is not to be thought of as a merely negative or even passive quality. God is pure activity; there is nothing passive in Him. His holiness is an infinitely active energy; it is the infinitely perfect expression of His infinitely perfect nature and being. We have our ideals, which are either revealed to us by God, or which we erect for ourselves, and one of the painful things in life is our constant manifest failure to reach that which our higher will desires. Strive as we may, succeed as we may, there is always some higher goal which we have not attained, and which beckons us on. Not so with God. What He wills to be, that He is.

III

In what we have been saying, however, we have dealt with the holiness of God rather as an ethical quality, and ethical perfection has a certain coldness about it. It is to be compared to an iceberg in the sunlight. Its glittering pinnacles may attract the eye, and awaken in us a sense of their beauty, but even the most intrepid investigator of the Himalayan glaciers feels no urge to negotiate their gleaming heights. The contemplation of ethical perfection creates no glow, it kindles no flame. We can find deeper levels of the divine holiness if we think of it in terms of love. " God is love," [1] says St. John, and in order to understand this, and to make that love the governing and effective law of our own nature, we must think of His holiness in relation to infinite love rather than as infinite ethical perfection. The latter we may admire; the former we can enter into with all the warmth and fulness of our being. When we consider Him in terms of love, He becomes to us not only the infinitely loving One, but also the infinitely lovable One.

We cannot explain these mysteries, but we are allowed to use human language, however inadequate, in discussing them, as our Lord did in delivering His revelation, and as the Spirit of God moved holy men of old to record His revelation in the Sacred Scriptures. Our wills are far, infinitely far, below the divine ideal; but this is the only ideal, and the nearer we approach to an equality between what He wills us to be and what we actually are, the holier shall we be.

St. Augustine tells us, " What God has, that He is." [2] As He is

---

[1] i St. John iv. 8.
[2] St. Augustine, *De Civitate Dei*, xi. 10; Migne, P. L., Tom. 41, Col. 325.

love, as He is wisdom, as He is power, as He is truth, so He is holiness. We do not speak of God as possessing His so-called attributes in the way in which we would say that a man possesses wisdom or love. I might have a heart overflowing with love to all, or I might be wholly devoid of it, but I would still be I. If I possess holiness and love, they are still something apart from my essential being. Not so with God. If He ceased to love or ceased to be holy, He would cease to exist, for His attributes are His very essence.

Holiness is the primary divine perfection which is unceasingly contemplated by the heavenly host. Twice in Holy Scripture are we given an account of the opening of the heavens, and of the vision of the celestial worship. This revelation was made to Isaiah, and is recorded in the sixth chapter of his prophecy; and to St. John the Divine as we read in the fourth chapter of the Book of Revelation. On both these occasions is heard the anthem of praise, " Holy, Holy, Holy." Not the praise of mercy or justice or power, not even of love; but holiness is the theme of the divine hymn. Since the sixth century in every liturgy throughout Christendom the faithful join in the hymn of the heavenly host; and on Good Friday the Church teaches us to cry, " Holy Lord, Holy and Mighty, Holy and Immortal." Whatever other attribute is named, holiness must be mentioned with it, for without holiness the attribute would fall short of perfection.

In all that He is, and therefore in all that He does, holiness is foremost, for His acts must be the perfect expression of His Being. When the angel announced to the Blessed Virgin Mary that she was to be the mother of the Messiah, he said—to quote the translation in our Authorized Version—" That Holy Thing which shall be born of thee shall be called the Son of God "; [1] but there is no word in the Greek of St. Luke which corresponds to the word " thing " in our English translation. The literal translation reads, " that Holy which shall be born of thee." Holy is not a mere descriptive adjective applied to the Son of God and Mary. The essential Holiness, the Eternal Son who is God Himself, the only-begotten, divine and infinite, was to become incarnate, and to be born of her. No wonder that, in her consciousness of the over-whelming honour done to her, Blessed Mary acknowledged that " He that is mighty hath magnified me," and then, bowing down in lowliest adoration, cried, " And Holy is His Name." [2] Originally the name given to a person signified the intrinsic character of its bearer, or some peculiar quality which he possessed. The primary

[1] St. Luke i. 35.　　　　[2] St. Luke i. 49.

intrinsic quality of Incarnate God is that of holiness. It was given by the Holy Spirit to the Blessed Mother to see this truth.

The Scriptures testify in many places to the holiness of God, and of how this holiness manifests itself. God is " holy in all his works " we are told.[1] This, of necessity, must be so, for since in His essence He is holy, it is impossible that the operation of His Being could be other than holy. We must be careful, however, not to get this truth in reverse. God is not said to be holy because He performs holy works; His work is necessarily holy because He is essential holiness. Since He is holiness, to fail to exercise holiness would be to fail to exercise His own life. This is one of the things impossible to God, for He cannot violate the law of His own Being. Such a course would indicate a deficiency in Him which would annul His very existence. If He ceased to be holy, He would cease to exist. All His acts are the expression of His intrinsic Being.

Holiness is not the sum of a series of good actions, even though that series be infinite. Good actions, whether in God or in man, are the expression of a life within, according to the maxim, *operatio sequitur esse*. The work is always consequent upon the nature of the worker. If the inner life, the *esse*, be good and holy, the expression of it in outward actions will be correspondingly good and holy. To refer once more to the Scripture authority, we find the psalmist declaring that " God hath spoken in his holiness." [2] Being what He is, He could speak in no other way, and His thus speaking is a promise, for the certain fulfilment and inviolability of which He pledges the holiness of His Being. The psalmist tells us further that " God hath sworn by his holiness." [3] This is the same as the statement made in the Song of Isaiah, " I have sworn by myself," [4] which is repeated in the sixth chapter of the epistle to the Hebrews. His holiness and Himself are identical. In giving His promise to Abraham, had God sworn by heaven and earth, the oath might perish, since heaven and earth were to pass away. But He swore by His own Being, by His holiness, which can never pass away. So His oath stands eternal, even as He is eternal.

Incarnate God, when He was upon earth, impressed men first and foremost by His holiness. St. Peter, seeing the miraculous draught of fishes, was overcome, not by the manifestation of His power, but by His evident holiness. " Depart from me, for I am a sinful man, O Lord," he cried; [5] and the centurion, pagan as he

---

[1] Ps. cxlv. 17.
[2] Ps. lx. 6.
[3] Ps. lxxxix. 35.
[4] Isa. xlv. 23.
[5] St. Luke v. 8.

was, was likewise moved, saying, " Lord, I am not worthy that thou shouldest come under my roof." [1]

Such titles as " Holy One of Israel," or " Holy One," occur some thirty times in Isaiah alone, the great Messianic prophet. Everywhere, in every part of the Scripture, written in various periods, ranging through some thousands of years, and in different parts of the world, by men of varying cultures, the idea of the holiness of God stands in the forefront.

IV

Not only is God holy, but there is no holiness apart from Him, and all holiness flows from Him. He is the only essentially Holy One. Again with St. John we look through the open gates of heaven, and hear the redeemed chanting the song of Moses and of the Lamb, saying, " Who shall not fear thee, O Lord, and glorify thy name? "—and why?—" for thou only art holy." [2] Primarily because of His holiness, the heavenly host glorifies God.

The Christian vocation is to a oneness with Christ, who is God the Eternal Son. Since, then, He, being God, is holy, we are called to holiness. This has ever been God's call. Holiness is always the central requirement. When our Lord came to seal the everlasting covenant with man, He said in the Sermon on the Mount, " Be ye therefore perfect, even as your Father which is in heaven is perfect." [3]

The word perfect is a relative one. Whenever we use it we have to ask, " Perfect in what? " and there can be no doubt as to the answer. If God appoints us to be like Him, He then appoints us to perfection of holiness, since holiness is His essential character. In all His dealings with men, God's unswerving purpose has been to bring man back to Himself, to renew in the creature the image and likeness which had been marred by sin. He has never been satisfied with anything less than that man should, to the utmost of his ever-expanding capacity, participate in the divine holiness.

We note in the series of covenants the ascending scale of demand as the divine helps and graces increase. " Unto whomsoever much is given, of him shall be much required." [4] First, to Abraham is revealed God's power. " I am the Almighty God," [5] and in the awed consciousness of His Almightiness men are to walk in His sight circumspectly. With Moses He goes a step further, and

---

[1] St. Matt. viii. 8.   [2] Rev. xv. 4.   [3] St. Matt. v. 48.
[4] St. Luke xii. 48.   [5] Gen. xvii. 1.

reveals His holiness as the model for His people. They are to be holy because He is holy.[1] Then in the final covenant which our Incarnate Lord offers to all mankind, He requires them to rise up to the perfection of holiness seen in God Himself, to be perfect in their finite sphere even as the Father is perfect in His infinite sphere.

The apostolic interpretation of the Christian vocation presents this ideal repeatedly. St. Paul returns to this thought again and again. He goes back to the beginning of man's vocation when he declares to the Ephesians, " Blessed be the God and Father of our Lord Jesus Christ, who hath blessed us with all spiritual blessings in heavenly places in Christ; according as he hath chosen us in him before the foundation of the world that we should be holy." He has blessed us " in Christ " because only in and through Him, the Holy One of God, can we be holy; only in Him, who is very God, can we share the holiness of God, which sharing is the supreme blessing given to us. Again St. Paul says that He hath sanctified His Church, " that it should be holy and without blemish." [2]

The epistle to the Colossians repeats the same teaching: He has " made peace through the blood of the cross, in order to present you holy and unblameable and unreprovable in his sight "; [3] and to the Thessalonians he reveals, " This is the will of God even your sanctification." [4] St. Peter repeats the teaching of our Lord—" As he which hath called you is holy, so be ye holy in all manner of conversation." [5]

Since the only life, the only enduring life, is in Him, and our life consists in a participation in His own nature, we must first have some knowledge of what His life is before we can know what ours ought to be. Therefore, to understand holiness, we must look not at men, not even at the saintliest of them, but we must with awe and reverence contemplate the source and origin, even the depths of the Godhead, the Holy Trinity, so far as the mystery of His Being and Nature are revealed to us.

When we consider His revelation of Himself, we discover God as the eternal Father eternally begetting the Son, and in this begetting communicating to Him all the infinite fulness of His own holiness without in any sense or degree diminishing His own possession of that holiness. The eternal Father and the eternally begotten Son are united in an infinite and substantial embrace of love (that is, united in the very substance and essence of their being), from which proceeds eternally the Third Person of the holy and

---

[1] Lev. xix. 2. [2] Eph. i. 4 and v. 27. [3] Col. i. 20 and 22.
[4] I Thess. iv. 3. [5] I St. Peter i. 15.

indivisible Trinity, to whom is assigned the mysterious title, the Holy Spirit. To the Spirit also, as to the Son, is communicated the infinite fulness of the divine holiness, and the fulness of all other divine attributes.

In saying this, we may save ourselves possible confusion of ideas if we remember that in the Godhead there is but one holiness, one love, one wisdom, one knowledge, one will, one power; and that each of the divine Persons partakes of the infinite totality of this one holiness, of this one love, this one wisdom, knowledge, will, power, and of all else that pertains to the Godhead. Likewise, if we are to be partakers of the Divine Nature in our finite and created measure, our will must be one with His all-holy will, even as the human will of Christ, the God-Man, is one with the divine will. Every advance in the Christian life consists in bringing our wills, by the help of the Holy Spirit, more and more in line with the divine ideal for us.

V

It is clear, therefore, that there was nothing new in this call to holiness in the Christian Covenant. God had of old set before His people the ideal of holiness as the only ideal, *but now, for the first time, is revealed the fulness of the method which man was to use in responding to the call.* The revelation of Jesus Christ is the clear declaration, in terms which men can know and follow, of the means and methods which have to be employed in order that they, by co-operation with the Holy Spirit, may approach nearer and nearer to a co-ordination of their wills with the ideal of the divine holiness.

After the long Old Testament preparation for the full revelation, Christ came " to make all men see what is the fellowship of the mystery which from the beginning of the world hath been hid in God." [1] Perhaps a better translation than *fellowship* is *dispensation.* Our Lord came that we might see and understand how this mystery is dispensed to man, how it is possible for him to lay hold of it. The word is οἰκονομία—economy. Webster defines economy as, " an orderly system regulating the distribution and use of parts, conceived as the result of wise and economical adaptation in the author, whether human or divine." It is this " eternal purpose which he purposed in Christ Jesus," [2] the purpose which was hid in the mind of God from all eternity, that Christ came to make us see; not only to reveal it to us, but to teach us how we were to

---

[1] Eph. iii. 9.   [2] Eph. iii. 11.

enter into and employ His divine system, in order to find our place and work in the kingdom for which God chose us " in Him before the foundation of the world."

Christ Himself is the personal revelation of the divine holiness, and He is also the way, and the only way, by which we can become holy. We are to note that not only has God given us the blessing " in Christ," but He " chose us *in Him* before the foundation of the world "—and to one end and purpose only, namely—" that we should be holy." From all eternity God contemplated each one of us, personally and individually, as receiving this holiness through being " in Christ." It was no afterthought.

What, then, is the method by which this mystery is dispensed to man? For an answer we must go back again into the consideration of the life of the Godhead. We have already pointed out that the essential holiness, which is the life of the Father, flows from Him in its infinite fulness into the eternally begotten Son, and into the Holy Spirit. So far as we can know it, this constitutes the inmost life and being of God, though we are able to perceive only a faint, dim reflection of the reality, which we cannot grasp, since it transcends all our powers of reason and spiritual vision.

God, as we have seen, was not content with this infinitely full and complete flow of the life of holiness within the mysterious cycle of His own Trinitarian Being. His life overflows from the secret place of His divinity upon the creatures He created out of nothing. But not yet was God satisfied. The creature must find union with the Creator. This was accomplished in the act of the Incarnation. In the Humanity of Christ, which is the supremest and most perfect of all things created, " dwells all the fulness of the Godhead bodily," [1] and His fulness, which is the fulness of the holiness of the Adorable Trinity, flows into us, and into all those who are made one with Him, into all those who are " in Him." This truth is of so tremendous a nature that any consideration of it staggers the intellect; but lest we, through a false humility, turn from the offer of His goodness and mercy, we dare not shrink from the full implication of what His love has revealed to us, namely, that " of His fulness "—that is, of the " fulness of the Godhead,"—" have all we received," [2] we who are sinners, we who have wounded and dishonoured Him, we who have deserved nothing at His hands save to be cast out of His sight. This is the blessing wherewith He " hath blessed us with all spiritual blessings in heavenly places in Christ." [3] It is the blessing of being made partakers of the divine

[1] Col. ii. 9.   [2] St. John i. 16.   [3] Eph. i. 3.

nature, of being given an objective participation in the holiness of
Him who only is holy.[1]

VI

All this would certainly seem enough to satisfy even the infinite
yearning of the divine Heart. But not so. He not only wills that
we partake of His holiness, but, He wills to exalt us to the highest
plane of that holiness possible to man. Therefore, He has decreed
that no man can maintain it unless he gives himself to the divine
leading so completely, that God will be able ever to increase in the
soul this endowment of divine holiness. This holiness must ever
abound, it must know no limit, either in time or in eternity. We
become holy not by anything we do, not through any gifts received
external to the Godhead, but only by sharing in the holiness of
Christ who is God, and, through Him, receiving the holiness of the
indivisible Trinity.

We know not how to express this truth. It is beyond the range
of human language, nor do we attempt to express it. We bow down
in awe and adoration before the ineffable mystery which God,
" who is rich in mercy, for his great love wherewith he loves us," [2]
has made known unto us. We do not inquire, we worship. We
accept it as a mystery of the Divine Being.

God reveals to us something of the processes of this communication of His divine holiness. It is communicated in the Godhead
from the Father to the Son by an eternal generation. It is communicated by the Son to the created Humanity to which He united
Himself in the Incarnation. It is then communicated to all souls
who are made one with that Humanity through the Sacraments.

The holiness which God predestined before the foundation of
the world to be received by men, He infused into the human nature
of Christ that it might be transmitted to them, for " of his fulness
have all we received." [3] He, in His Humanity, possesses all the
treasures of wisdom and knowledge and holiness, not for His own
glory and honour, for it is impossible that anything should be added
to Him, but in order that He might pour them out upon those who
were predestined to be holy " in Him." [4] The measure of our
holiness depends on our response to the leading of the Holy Spirit.
Note the prayer of the psalmist, " Teach me to do the thing that
pleaseth thee, for thou art my God: let thy loving Spirit lead me
forth into the land of righteousness." [5] The land of righteousness

---

[1] 2 St. Peter i. 4; Rev. xv. 4.   [2] Eph. ii. 4.   [3] St. John i. 16.
[4] See Marmion, *Christ the Life of the Soul*, p. 66.   [5] Ps. cxliii. 10.

is the state of union with God, of ever-deepening participation in the personal holiness of God. His tender, strong, and gentle urging within—how do we respond to it? God wills to promote us to ever greater honour, and gives the Spirit as our guide to the heights. Do we accept His guidance, do we follow His teaching? The issue is in our own hands. Our fulness of response is the measure of God's giving. He who wills to be holy is holy. This is the law.

VII

The holiness of which we are speaking is not, as we have seen, an ethical perfection, nor is it the development of our natural personality. The idea of the development of personality is one with which modern psychology is deeply engaged, but its mode of dealing with this important matter is often an evidence of a failure to realize the existence of the spiritual factor in human life; or, if that be recognized, it would seem to point to a deliberate purpose of divorcing life, as it must be lived by men and women every day, from God. Those who would make a so-called development of personality an approach to perfection, seek to find the *summum bonum*, " in a broad, nicely balanced human culture that is well informed on actual problems and careful to grasp those phases of Christianity which are most attractive to a lofty nature. But they have only a superficial knowledge of it, and they are given up to a practical naturalism devoid of any vivifying influence on souls." [1] It is in effect a materialistic philosophy which gives substantial denial to the desirability of preparing oneself for any life beyond this world. It is not only the ignoring of the creative power of faith without which all spiritual force is dead, but it eliminates morality, even as the world regards it, since it takes no account of God, who is the sole origin and fount of moral law. It follows the lead of those schools of philosophy which accept no standards or bases of conduct save those erected by public opinion, for the time being, which may reverse itself in another decade. It is above all a repudiation of the gift of holiness which God ordains to be received and cultivated if the soul is to attain to its divinely appointed destiny. Without the indwelling and ever-increasing holiness of God, there can be no development of personality.

As we have already seen, God performs holy acts because He is essentially holy. In like manner, the Christian life does not consist in merely doing holy things, but it is the expression of a holiness

[1] Garrigou-Lagrange, *Christian Perfection and Contemplation*, p. 131.

within, which, if it is in us at all, cannot help expressing itself. Bad men sometimes perform good actions, but through a merely natural instinct, not because the supernatural holiness of God dwells in them and is expressing itself in such action.

This seeking in the power of the Spirit to develop the divine gift is what the apostle meant by " perfecting holiness in the fear of God." [1] The " perfecting of holiness " requires the exercise of holiness, which means discipline. It means the warfare of the soul. Prayer, Holy Communion, good works, kindly loving thought, do not create holiness or impart it to us, but they more and more cultivate and perfect the divine holiness of which we were made partakers when we were grafted into Christ in baptism. The more we yield to the Spirit in allowing the holiness of God which resides in us to govern us in all things, the more deeply are we able to enter into His nature, and to become progressively holy even as He is holy.

Save as we impose limits upon ourselves through sin, there is no limit to our growth in holiness, because there can be no limit to the flowing of the infinite divine holiness into our souls. If we respond, there is an ever-richer partaking of the divine Nature in time and in eternity.

Let us note the divine simplicity of this holiness. Men shrink from the idea of living lives of holiness as though it were presumptuous. They regard it as a special privilege for the few, rather than as the normal life of grace for the many and as the vocation which is universal. Men think that the writings of the mystics are beyond them, but there is nothing in such writings which can compare for a moment in profundity with our Lord's teaching to the common people who heard Him gladly.[2] Take, for example, the Sermon on the Mount, or His discourse in the upper room, or what the apostles wrote to their converts. Read the eighth chapter of the Epistle to the Romans, or the First Epistle of St. John—inspired messages which were written to folk in all likelihood far less educated than our village congregations, the teachers themselves, St. Paul excepted, being in most cases " unlearned and ignorant men." [3] The early Christians were not of the intelligentsia, but they lived in the power of the Holy Spirit. They did not attempt to fathom the mysteries. They did not attempt to bring their powers of reasoning to bear upon these divine subjects; but they yielded themselves to the Spirit of God, and allowed Him to bring the power of these mysteries to bear upon

[1] 2 Cor. vii. 1.   [2] St. Mark xii. 37.   [3] Acts iv. 13.

them, and the accompanying grace to operate within them. They did not stop to consider anything except the love of God which reveals the existence of such mysteries. After all, if we try to solve the insoluble we shall find that it is the simple thing that baffles. It is God's simplicity that baffles those who would, in their pride, seek to understand Him. A highly complex organism is easy to analyze. The functions of the human body can be observed and charted, but science stands baffled before the simpler things. The amœba is a greater mystery than the courses of the stars.

VIII

In what manner do we receive this holiness? We receive it when we are adopted by baptism into the family of God. We then become, by grace and the undeserved favour of God, what Christ is by nature. " In him dwelleth all the fulness of the Godhead bodily, and we are complete in him." [1] In this passage the word " fulness " as applied to Him, and the word " complete " as applied to us, are merely different forms of the same word—πλήρωμα. This passage from St. Paul corresponds exactly with, and contains the same teaching as, that of St. John when he says, " The Word was made flesh . . . and of his fulness have all we received" [2] Through Him, and through union with Him, we are " filled with all the fulness of God," " the fulness of him that filleth all in all." [3]

To this end exists all the economy of the Church and all the work of the Holy Spirit. ".He gave some apostles, and some prophets, and some evangelists, and some pastors and teachers; " here we have " differences of administrations but the same Spirit," [4] and to what end?—" for the perfecting of the saints, for the work of the ministry, for the edifying of the body of Christ, till we all come in the unity of the faith, and of the knowledge of the Son of God, unto a perfect man, unto the measure of the stature of the fulness of Christ." [5]

This is the only objective, the only purpose in the will of God for us. The word which is repeatedly used in the New Testament, which we translate *fulness*, has a qualitative, not a quantitative, connotation. It means the permanent state of having neither lack nor void, " perfect and entire, wanting nothing." [6] The souls of men are like vessels small and great in the household of the heavenly Father. One may contain more than another, but they can all be

---

[1] Col. ii. 9.   [2] St. John i. 14 and 16.   [3] Eph. iii. 19; i. 23.
[4] 1 Cor. xii. 5.   [5] Eph. iv. 11–13.   [6] St. James i. 4.

equally full of the divine holiness. Such is the ideal that God has for every soul.

The adoption which effects our participation in the divine holiness begins, as we have seen, with baptism. This participation is accomplished once for all, but much needs to be done after we have entered into the state of holiness. As there are no fluctuations of holiness in the Godhead, so in us the life and holiness of God are to pursue a steadfast and continuous advance, ever deepening, ever increasing in their dominion over us and within us. It never entered into the divine purpose that there should be any cessation or diminution of the operation of this holiness in the souls of men. Nor yet any violation of it, any break or interruption of our participation in His divine nature. Where such violation occurs it is caused by our sin against the grace which is given to us in the purpose of God as a permanent and inviolable endowment which can be affected for evil only by our deliberate and serious rebellion against His all-holy will.

This is God's plan for each one of us from eternity. " He chose us in him before the foundation of the world, that we should be holy." [1]

O compassionate Trinity, Father, Son, Spirit : Enlighten me with Thine uncreated Brightness : Purify me with the fragrance of Thine ineffable Holiness which Thou dost shed abroad in the hearts of men of good-will.

[1] Eph. i. 4.

The mystics look upon our life as a holy pilgrimage, a journey whose end is the inner unity of God. The more a soul keeps itself open to God, abandons itself to the mysterious action of God, and lets itself be caught in His current, the deeper God draws it into the secret abyss where all springs rise. In grace, therefore, which contains every glory in germ, lie possibilities yet untold. God perfects the soul of him who gives himself up to God. The meaning of Christian perfection therefore lies not in mere development of personality, nor merely in the cultivation of all one's spiritual and moral faculties, nor even in the religious direction of our life alone— our aim, the end and summit of our evolution, lies in the interior of God, among the incomprehensible mysteries of the divine nature, which even now holds our being in its embrace.

JULIUS TYCIAK.

CHAPTER II

THE WAY OF PERFECTION

I

In order to understand what is involved in the fulness of our vocation to holiness to which we are called of God, we must look further into what is meant by perfection, whence its origin, and the means of its development. First, it must be recognized that God alone possesses absolute perfection, and since His perfection is infinite, it is not comparable to any perfection which might lie in the creature. The perfection of created things has to be regarded from a totally different point of view.

A thing is said to be perfect in so far as it attains the essential purpose for which it was made. Perfection has nothing to do with accidental beauty, or with any delicacy or skill of construction. A watch, for example, is made to keep time. It may be covered with precious stones, it may be enclosed in exquisitely chased gold, so as to excite the admiration of all as a work of art, but if it fails to record time correctly, it is lacking in perfection.

"What is it for?" This is the question which must be asked about everything, and the answer will show whether it be perfect, or is failing of perfection. It has been said that the ordinary needle which is found in every household, and which is one of the simplest and most primitive of the works of man, is the most perfect human invention. It has so perfectly fulfilled the purpose for which it was made that it has never been improved upon. The needle found in the dwellings of prehistoric man is our needle of to-day—a simple shaft of wood, or bone, or metal, sharpened at one end, and pierced with a hole in order to carry the thread. The simplicity of its design and construction has nothing to do with its perfection; it is well-nigh perfect because it does that for which it was made.

In order to test a man's moral and spiritual perfection, we have also to ask the question, For what was he made? Divine revelation gives us the answer: "Thou hast created all things, and for thy pleasure they are and were created"; [1] and it is the good pleasure and will of God that man reach his perfection by being made one

[1] Rev. iv. 11.

with Him in holiness and love. The progress of our union with Him is the progress of our perfection. Human perfection consists in a created participation in the nature of God. The profoundest revelation that God has made to man concerning his destiny is found in St. Peter's awed declaration that through the fulfilment of His great and precious promises we are made actual " partakers of the divine nature." [1] This means that we are partakers of the divine holiness, of the divine love, for the intrinsic nature of God is love and holiness.

The germ of our perfection lies in the gift of love. In the same measure in which our love increases, our perfection in holiness is developed. Love is a unitive virtue, and unites us to God. What we commonly call in this life a perfect soul is not one who has actually reached perfection, is really fulfilling completely the purpose for which he was made, but it is one in whom love dwells so habitually and intensively as to dispose the soul, under all conditions, to conform to the loving will of God promptly, easily, and sweetly. The souls of the saints in glory are completely conformed to the divine will, and this conformity is so fixed a state that it is impossible for them to act contrary to the will of God. In this mortal life no soul reaches the perfection of the saints in heaven. We are struggling against many obstacles, both within and without, but if we are persistently seeking, by the help of the Holy Spirit, to grow and increase in our possession of the divine nature of which we are partakers, and are using the means which the goodness of God has appointed to that end, eventually we, too, shall find ourselves in that fixed state which God has predestined for us all.

It is the power of God's love (which is His very Self, for " God is love ") [2] which works continually in the soul that responds to Him, and it is by this operation that He is able to subdue all things in us unto Himself. [3] The fire of His love burns continually in our souls, consuming all that is not of Him. St. Bernard says, " This fire which is God, consumes, indeed, but it afflicts not; it burns sweetly and lays waste happily, but it so exercises the power of fire upon all vices that it pours forth upon the soul the sweetness of its unction." [4]

II

Repeatedly the apostles in their writings give us an interpretation which shows that this call to the perfection of holiness was no thing

---

[1] 2 St. Peter i. 4.   [2] 1 St. John iv. 8 and 16.   [3] Phil. iii. 21.
[4] St. Bernard, *Serm. in Cant.* lvii, 7; Migne, P. L., Tom. 183, Col. 1053.

of vague and general terms. It was clear and definite and literal. They all understood it, and they all testified to it. St. Paul explicitly declares the objective of all the Church's work to be " for the perfecting of the saints, for the work of the ministry, for the edifying of the Body of Christ, till we all come in the unity of the faith, and of the knowledge of the Son of God, unto a perfect man, unto the measure of the stature of the fulness of Christ." [1] St. James puts it very succinctly—" That ye may be perfect and entire, wanting nothing." [2]

In dealing with man, God, in His infinite love, in His unswerving determination to bring man back to Himself, can be satisfied with nothing less than this perfection, for His eternal purpose is to make man like unto Himself. God's love for His creature can tolerate no lesser destiny. Love, from its very nature, can never be satisfied with anything less than the very highest for the beloved; and the highest that God can prepare for us is the gift of Himself in every divine attribute which the finite creature is capable of sharing with the infinite Creator. St. Bernard declares, " He is generous to those who call upon Him, but He can make to them no gift richer than Himself. He Himself is the end of all our deserving; He Himself is our reward." [3]

This demand for perfection is imperative. There is no qualification whatever. Ultimately, there must be perfection, or nothing. But the divine patience never ceases to be operative. Perfection is not required all at once. It is the goal towards which the soul, helped by divine grace, must be ever moving. The Christian life is commonly spoken of as the life of perfection, but this does not mean that those who are walking in the way of perfection are supposed to be perfect in any full sense of the word. Perfection is commanded not as that which we are to reach in this world, but as an end to which we are to attain eventually, and for which everyone must labour. Every command of whatever kind imposes nothing further than the obligation to make use of the known means which will lead to the required end. We cannot produce perfection in ourselves by a fiat; it is a gradual process, and God has not left us ignorant of the steps which must be taken in this process. The command is given to us in terms of perfection in order that there may be no question regarding the way in which we are to walk, or of the end we are to reach. As St. Augustine says, " No man can run aright unless he knows whither he is to run,

---

[1] Eph. iv. 12–13. [2] St. James i. 4.
[3] St. Bernard, *De diligendo Deo.*, ch. vii; Migne, P. L. Tom. 182, Col. 987.

and how can he know if no commandment is given?"[1] The perfection which is required of us in this life consists in a persistent endeavour to appropriate to ourselves the perfect holiness of God so far as the finite creature can lay hold of it; and this lies in the faithful and unceasing use of the revealed means of grace by which we shall be able to make His perfection our own.

Baptism, in which we are made one with Christ, inducts the soul into the state of perfection—that is, into a condition of life the normal operation of which leads on little by little to the inevitable fulness of perfection. This earthly perfection does not require us to be wholly free from faults which arise from infirmity. Venial sins retard the progress of grace, but do not destroy it. They are to be repented of and disavowed in our wills, as soon as we realize their presence; and we are continually to watch and pray against them. Those whom our spiritual masters so encouragingly call perfect souls in this life are they who have, by the help of the Spirit, freed themselves in their purpose and will, though they may fail from time to time, from all ill-regulated affections and desires. Those who have in the depth of their intention seriously renounced all that prevents them from giving themselves more and more to God, are the souls who possess the condition and essence of perfection. They have entered upon the way, and they are progressing in it. This is the state of perfection.

III

St. Thomas, with his invariable reasonableness, explains that there are two modes of fulfilling the divine service. One is the perfect, the other the imperfect, although both are to be accounted as faithful observance of the divine requirement, one better than the other, but both good. The perfection of service is attained only by the saints in glory. No soul on earth exercises it. The service of the faithful on earth is called the imperfect, not because there is any serious lack of consecrated purpose or of steadfast, loving endeavour, but because the time of consummation is not yet, though the required order, looking to that end and consummation, is being followed resolutely.[2]

St. Thomas Aquinas also gives us an explanation of the meaning of the expression, the way of perfection. He reminds us of our custom of calling children in school, scholars. The little child,

---

[1] St. Augustine, *De Perfectione Justitiae*, cap. viii, Migne, P. L., Tom. 44, Col. 301.

[2] St. Thomas, *Summa*, 2.2; q. 44; Art. 6.

he says, has not acquired any scholarship, but he has entered upon the way, and is using faithfully the appointed and well-proved means; and, if he perseveres, he may eventually attain to high scholarship. If he keeps on he will become well learned in the branches of knowledge he is pursuing.[1] Likewise, the Christian has entered upon a spiritual curriculum which, if pursued diligently, will inevitably lead him in the end to that perfection which God requires of those who would be one with Him. Therefore, we call the course he is following the way of perfection. But it is still only the way. Perfection is the end, and the end is not yet. It is a state of progress. St. Paul makes it clear that we are not to expect the fulness of perfection until we reach the goal which is the Beatific Vision of God. "When that which is perfect is come," he says, "then that which is in part shall be done away."[2] Then only shall we find the fulfilment of the command to love God with all our heart and soul and mind. The fulness of the precept is to be aimed at in this life, but can be attained only in the life to come. If we aim aright, in the end we shall attain aright.

St. Thomas gives us another comforting thought. He points out that we are not required in this life to reach any particular point of perfection at any particular time. It is only required that we make continual progress. This is the obligation that rests upon the Christian. He is "always to tend towards and labour for perfection."[3] Tendency is an interior habit or state, producing an inherent inclination towards the desired objective. A bent bow tends to spring back to its original straight position, but it is prevented by the bow-string. Let the string be cut, and the bow instantly snaps back to its natural place. I hold the steel away from the magnet in my fingers. Every atom of its structure is tense to fly to the magnet. I release it; instantly, swifter than the eye can follow, it projects itself to its natural object. God is the natural objective of the soul. "Thou hast made us for Thyself, and our heart can find no rest until it rest in Thee."[4] Remove the obstacles, and God instantly draws the soul to Himself, doing, through His infinite power and love, all that is necessary to lead the soul on to the ultimate perfection which is its normal destiny. The whole Christian course is so organized as ever progressively to remove impediments to the perfection of holiness within us. If the soul is faithful in doing what it can, God will do the rest, and the

---

[1] St. Thomas, *Summa*, 2.2; q. 186; Art. 2 ad 1.   [2] 1 Cor. xiii. 10.
[3] St. Thomas, *Summa*, 2.2; q. 186; Art. 2.
[4] St. Augustine, *Confessions*, i. 1; Migne, P. L., Tom. 32, Col. 661.

soul will actually move continually onward in the way of perfection. If, when my time comes, I am found making progress
Godward, though I may have gone but a little along the way, I
shall be safe for ever, and my crown of perfection will be secure.

The service may seem at times to be hard, but this is our duty,
or rather we would say, our privilege, for the apostolic injunction is
to " endure hardness as a good soldier of Jesus Christ." [1] Shame
were it upon us if we should be what St. Bernard calls " delicate
members of a thorn-crowned head." [2] Much less are we ever to
regard the service as impossible. God is working with us, and
within us, and with Him " nothing shall be impossible." [3] If we
would but allow the Holy Spirit to remove the obstacles, and by His
help cleanse our hearts from all that is contrary to God, easily
should we run the way of perfection.

This is consequent upon the fact that there is in every soul
an inherent, divinely ordained, law and principle of perfectibility.
Once the obstacles are removed, this principle operates to achieve
all that may be required in order to enter into the perfection of the
holiness of God Himself. But without prejudice to this principle,
which is perhaps the finest thing with which God has endowed the
natural man, we are not to conclude that this ability to go straight
to Him is inherent in us naturally. It is a gift from God, without
any claim or deserving on our part, and it would be more correct to
say that this going is the result of God's drawing us to Himself,
rather than our moving towards Him through any independent
will or power which we, of ourselves, possess. This principle of
perfectibility is that which makes it possible for us to respond readily
and perseveringly to the drawing of the divine love, once the
obstacles are removed. This drawing is along a way, the end of
which is the attainment of that wholly perfect state which will be
ours when we find at the last the place within His own Being which
His love has prepared for us as our final and only destiny.

All this revealed goodness of God is not, however, to put us at
so false an ease that we lose sight of the fact that the time is short,
and that we know not when the final bell will toll. " God who
gives us the morning does not promise us the evening," says the
wise author of The Spiritual Combat.[4] Surely, we cannot regard it
as a service of love and generosity to move with lagging steps along
the road which offers the soul so many and precious gifts and
blessings by the way, and a share in the heavenly glory at the end.

---

[1] 2 St. Tim. ii. 3.   [2] St. Bernard, Sermo v, in festo Om. SS., 9.
[3] St. Luke i. 37.   [4] Scupoli, The Spiritual Combat, chapter on " Sloth."

Is the divine Loveliness of so little attraction, has it so little lure for our souls, that it cannot spur us on to action made swift and resolute by love?

IV

St. Thomas's teaching regarding spiritual advance corresponds quite exactly with that of St. Paul in the remarkable spiritual autobiographical note which we find in his epistle to the Christians of Philippi. He makes his humble and holy boast of what God has done in him, but goes on to say, " Not as though I had already attained, either were already perfect; but I follow after, if that I may apprehend that for which also I am apprehended of Christ Jesus. Brethren, I count not myself to have apprehended, but this one thing I do, forgetting those things which are behind, and reaching forth unto those things which are before, I press toward the mark for the prize of the high calling of God in Christ Jesus." Then he adds the exhortation, " Let us therefore, as many as be perfect "—that is, as many as are walking in this way of perfection— " be thus minded." [1]

The apostle seems to be warning the Philippians against thinking the prize of the high calling to be too easy of attainment, or to be gained at a single stroke. The passage is taken to be a reference to his miraculous conversion on the way to Damascus, and he makes no claim that the prize was his in the moment of his conversion. That event only put his feet in the way of perfection. It only gave him a sure and good hope that in the end the prize would be his; and he now presses on to lay hold upon it even as he was then laid hold upon by Christ. He forgets the things that are behind; there is not time for congratulating himself even upon the manifold and gracious blessings bestowed upon him. There are greater and more precious gifts lying ahead, there is much and great labour necessary in order to claim them. So, he gives all his attention to reaching forth to the things that are before him, certain that the highest expression of gratitude for past graces is to concentrate wholly upon the further demands that the divine love makes upon him. The illustration is taken, of course, from the language of the athletic games, and describes the attitude of the runner in the races, with body thrust forward, and hand outstretched, in his eager straining for the goal.

As with a scholar in school, it is required that the Christian in this school of the Holy Ghost employ a definite method. Our

[1] Phil. iii. 12–15.

course has been worked out for us by the Spirit definitely and systematically. There are no haphazard methods in worldly affairs. If men seek to make their fortunes in any sphere of secular life, they go about it in a carefully prepared way. How much more should we follow the same principle in seeking to lay hold of the heavenly fortune which is laid up for those who love God. Well may we learn a lesson from men of the world who hesitate not to endure sacrifice and hardship in order to attain their sordid earthly aims. If the merchant who is seeking to accumulate a fortune which must perish with the using, were as neglectful of the approved means that he should use as we are of the course which leads to the heavenly reward, quickly would he become bankrupt; but he is guilty of no such neglect. As our Lord said, " The children of this world are in their generation wiser than the children of light." [1] " They hasten more quickly to death than we to life." [2]

V

In this curriculum two basic things are necessary: First, there must be grace and power from God; and second, there must be steadfast co-operation by us with what God is seeking to do in our souls. God's work is certain. There is no question but that He will perform His work perfectly. " He is faithful that promised." [3] But man's part is always uncertain, not only because of his natural perversity, his weakness and his sin, but also because what he does depends for its success on many fortuitous things. Let us, then, take God's part for granted, and consider what should be done to secure our own faithfulness.

First of all, we must keep in mind that without God we can do nothing. But, as St. Paul said, " I can do all things through Christ which strengtheneth me." [4] If I use the means which He has so lovingly provided, it will be impossible for me to fail in the end. If I am faithful in receiving the Sacraments, and in my life of prayer, and try, and, more than that, keep on trying, to do my duty day by day, there will be no question that I will be able to co-operate with Him to the end.

Let us consider three courses which we must continually pursue, faithfulness in which will most surely secure for us the fulfilment of this high vocation, and bring us victory and peace at the last.

First, there must be ceaseless labour to eradicate sin. When we

[1] St. Luke xvi. 8.
[2] St. Bernard, *Serm. De Divers*, xxxvi. 3; Migne, P. L., Tom. 183, Col. 639.
[3] Heb. x. 23.   [4] Phil. iv. 13.

make a survey of the plan of the Christian life, we find that there is only one thing that can possibly baulk the work of God in our souls. That one thing is sin. By sin we mean anything in the realm of thought, word, or deed which runs counter to what in our judgment and conscience we believe to be the will and precept of God for us. This may be what we do, or what we fail to do.

We must also take special note that this work is more than the mere breaking off of certain habits of sin which we may have acquired. This, of course, is necessary; but we must strive not only to eliminate certain acts of sin, but to go deeper, and dig out the very roots of sin. This is what the word *eradicate* means. It will avail but little to cut down the upper growth of a noxious weed in the garden. We have to dig down and tear out the roots. Everything out of which sin may grow—all circumstances, occasions, conditions and associations which experience and observation show us will lead to sin—is to be scrupulously avoided.

We have the apostolic teaching regarding this, which it were well for us to heed. The author of the Epistle to the Hebrews urges us to " follow peace with all men, and holiness, without which no man shall see the Lord." As we have seen, this holiness is the essential thing which we are seeking in our Christian life; it is our sole and all-inclusive vocation. The apostle reminds us of this, and then goes on to tell us of the vigilance which must be employed— " looking," he says, " diligently, lest any man fail of the grace of God; lest any root of bitterness springing up, trouble you." [1] Thus does he insist that he who would follow peace and holiness must tear out the very roots of sin, not being content to cut down from time to time the upper growth, but seeking so to change the whole interior condition that such sins will in time become practically impossible.

This will require self-study; but let us not make the mistake of thinking that self-study means self-centredness, or self-consciousness. It demands God-centredness, God-consciousness. In the covenant with Abram this was exactly what God commanded. " Walk before me "; [2] that is, be ever conscious of My presence, of My help, of My love. God-consciousness will produce the eradication of sin. It is rare that in the presence of one whom we love and reverence we do that which we know would wound and hurt him. We are likely to do such things if we forget his presence, but not when there is a consciousness of his presence, provided there be real love for such an one in our hearts. We shrink from

[1] Heb. xii. 14–15.   [2] Gen. xvii. 1.

hurting him, for we have an instinctive knowledge of what would wound those whom we love. We do not have to balance and weigh the question. As a rule, we decide with little or no argument with ourselves, that we must refrain from these hurtful things. Love's decisions are swift and intuitive.

But even the most complete eradication of sin is not enough. When we accomplish this, we have only arrived at zero. All the minuses have been eliminated, but we have now to go on with the positive work. There is a second course which must be followed with equal diligence, for the absence of sin, while necessary to a life of holiness, does not in itself constitute holiness. The absence of sin is a merely negative state, and holiness is essentially positive because following after holiness is the following of a course in which we are actually partaking of the holiness of God Himself; and there is nothing in God which is negative. We must keep this ever in mind. Growth in holiness is a continuous and ever-increasing participation in the intrinsic, essential holiness of God. This is what St. Peter meant when he said that we are " partakers of the divine nature," [1] for the fundamental attribute of the divine nature is holiness.

If this divine holiness is operating within us, then we not only refrain from sin, but we also " do the thing which is right." [2] We must " work the works of God." [3] Our daily examination of conscience should not be made to recall sin only, but there should be an examination of the day in order to make sure that we have, in our thinking, in our speech, and in our outward actions, responded to His incessant call of love by doing that which we know God wills us to do. It was a pagan emperor who cried, as he lay down to his night's rest, " I have lost a day "; and who explained to his inquiring courtiers that he could recall no good action that he had done. This truth has been expressed in a solemn manner in the familiar couplet:

> " Count that day lost whose low, descending sun
> Views from thy hand no noble action done."

If we are to work the works of God, we must proceed to our third course, and find an ideal of life to which we can seek to conform ourselves. Of course, there is, and can be, but one ideal, and that is the ideal presented in the earthly life of our Lord. There must be a strong and persistent effort to cultivate the virtues which Christ, in His nature as Man, exemplified to the full. But we must keep in mind that this following of the virtues of our Lord's Sacred

---

[1] 2 St. Peter i. 4.   [2] Ps. xv. 2.   [3] St. John vi. 28.

Humanity is not a mere imitation of Him. He is, of course, our example, but if that were all, He would be only one of many holy men whom we might seek wisely to imitate. We are indeed, as St. Peter exhorts us, to " follow his steps." [1] This is to be done through the action of our wills in co-operation with the divine will. It is an unhappy mistake which has been made by many, to think that Christian perfection can be secured by the mere repetition of acts of virtue, driven on by the will. We do not gain unity with God by the practice of the virtues. On the contrary, we are able to practise them at all only because we are, in some measure, already at one with Him. It is the indwelling God who enables us to do the things which lead on to an ever-deepening union with Him. "Without me ye can do nothing " [2]; "without thee we are not able to please thee." [3] We can take no step towards the casting out of sin, or the cultivation of the virtues, except through the power of Christ, who makes His abode in us.

VI

So, Christian perfection is infinitely more than the sum of a series of good and virtuous acts. Acts of virtue are necessary, but there have been certain schools of spiritual exercise which in their teaching bore so heavily on these acts of virtue, motivated by the human will, that their principles have been sometimes misunderstood by their followers. In some cases they seem almost to fall into the ever-persistent heresy of attributing to the unaided human will the power in itself of laying hold upon divine grace, which can be infused only by the Holy Spirit, unmerited and unpurchased by anything we can do save to yield ourselves to the divine leading. Such souls are in peril of becoming self-centred rather than God-centred.

If we are mindful of the warning given us by Richard of St. Victor, we are safe. " Virtue," he wisely tells us, " is nothing else but a well-ordered and measured affection, directed unto God for His own sake "; that is, centred upon Him, and upon nought else. And the great master, Père Berulle, throws a light upon this teaching when he says, " Our acts of virtue should result from our relation and homage to Christ Jesus rather than from the desire for the virtue in itself." [4] We are one with Him: these acts should be

---

[1] 1 St. Peter ii. 21.   [2] St. John xv. 5.
[3] Collect for XIX Sunday after Trinity.
[4] Berulle, *Oeuvres*, p. 1457. Quoted by Brémond, *Religious Thought in France*, III, p. 115.

made in and through Him, and the virtue cultivated through the ever-increasing transmission to us of the powers which inhere in His Sacred Humanity into which we are grafted. He dwells in us, and we in Him. We were made members of His Body when we were grafted into Him at our baptism. Just as the branch which has been engrafted into the vine receives the full life of the vine, so the very life of Christ dwells in us, and because life is activity, He must work in those in whom He dwells, and their progress in the perfection of holiness depends entirely on His work in them.

Therefore, the Christ-life to which we are called is nothing less than the operation of the God-Man in us, and this means that the Holy Trinity lives in us and we in Him. We live and move and have our being in Him, and we can truly say that He lives and moves and has His Being in us. Our Lord asks us to give Him our lives, and all our faculties, that He may use them for His own purposes. In the measure in which we surrender to Him is He able to do His work in and through us. Where He dwells the Holy Trinity dwells. All the occupations of His omnipotence take place in us. In our poor hearts His infinite omniscience reigns; there burns His perfect love; His goodness sits enthroned; eternal wisdom dwells within our gates.

Thus are we able to respond to the divine voice which cries to us, " This is the way, walk ye in it." [1] Thus are we able to go ever straight forward in the way, which is only another manner of saying that we walk in Him; we grow and increase in Him; for He has said, " I am the way," [2] and in that Way, and in that Way only, shall we find also the Truth and the Life. This Way is the Way of perfection in its fulness. If we walk with Him, it will prove true of us that " of his fulness have all we received." [3] If we yield to Him humbly and sweetly, there can be no question of what the end will be. We may seem to make little progress in acquiring the holiness of God, but be it little or much, we shall be fulfilling the call of love which God has given to us. As we have already thought, it is not a certain degree of perfection that God requires of us, but simply progress. There is an oft-quoted and most comforting saying: " Some run swiftly; some walk; some creep painfully; but everyone will reach the goal who keeps on."

O Dearest Lord : Remember me in Thy compassion. Leave me not lest I walk not with Thee. Slow, slow, my steps, halting and often turning back : Be not weary, Lord, of tarrying for one who keeps not pace with Thee.

[1] Isa. xxx. 21.   [2] St. John xiv. 6.   [3] St. John i. 16.

. . . that in the dispensation of the fulness of times he might gather together in one all things in Christ, both which are in heaven and on the earth; even in him: in whom also we have obtained an inheritance, being predestined according to the purpose of him who worketh all things after the counsel of his own will: that we should be to the praise of his glory.

SAINT PAUL.

CHAPTER III

THE DIVINE PURPOSE

I

THE apostle tells us that God's commands are never grievous.[1] We may further add that they are never arbitrary. They are designed for the sole purpose of carrying out, and that with a perfect and exact wisdom, not only the holiest and most loving purposes of the heart of God for His creature, but to secure in every case the practical end, which is that of bringing man back to the normal, back to his true nature in which God originally created him. This nature must be restored if man is to fulfil the purpose of his creation. This purpose in the eternal mind of God was that we should partake of the holiness of Him of whom it is said " Thou only art holy." [2] In this life of participated holiness the soul is to glorify God in all things, and so to reach the consummation of happiness which He has prepared for man from eternity. The glory of God is the sole aim. The salvation of souls, the work of the Church, the perfecting of the saints, and all else in the economy of the divine Kingdom as it affects the creature, are but means looking to this one great end. There is no mere altruism in anything that God does. He works out His purposes for His own glory and honour, and all that He does in the way of creation and redemption and sanctification of souls is instrumental to this end. The greatest manifestation of His love, and the highest honour He can show us, lie in choosing us as instruments of His glory.

Ever since the fall, in which man lost the holiness of God, all men are below normal through the effect of the disease of sin. Since the fall, only one normal man has been born in the world. This was Jesus Christ, who is both God and Man. In Him the entail of sin was cut off, and, therefore, in Him the normality of human nature was restored. All the rest of us have been, and are, sub-normal, sub-human, because of sin. Sin and all its effects must be eliminated before normality can be restored, before any child of man can again become fully and perfectly human. The ancient creed tells us that the Son of Mary was not only perfect

---

[1] 1 St. John v. 3.   [2] Rev. xv. 4.

God, but that He was also perfect Man. This means that He, in His human nature, was perfectly conformed to the ideal which God had in His mind when He created man in His own image and likeness. He is the absolute norm of humanity. The saying " To err is human," is a misstatement. It is not human, but sub-human, to err. The perfect Man did not err in anything. When we are finally perfected, error will no longer have any place in us. We shall then be like Him. There shall have been restored in us the norm according to which man was originally created, and in so far as we progress towards this norm we eliminate in the same measure all moral and spiritual error.

Man was created for union with God through love, which is the supreme unitive virtue, binding together those who have love one for another. Man, as originally created and endowed, was, through love, in union with God. Sin on the part of our first parents broke that bond of unity. Sin once committed, the breach was inevitable, for sin is the natural foe of love. I cannot sin against my friend and have at the same time purposes of love for him in my heart. Sin and love cannot dwell together in the same heart.

In the inspired account handed down to us we find that God, in His love, would not allow the curse which our first parents had invoked upon themselves to fall, without giving them a promise of hope; and so it was that at the gate of Eden He gave the first pledge of the redemption of mankind through the Passion of the Eternal Son who was to become Incarnate in human form in order to bring His banished ones home again. The seed of the woman was to bruise the serpent's head—sin and its power were to be crushed. Concurrent with the first sin was the first promise of the redemption. But not without the Agony and Bloody Sweat, not without the Cross and Passion of Incarnate God, was the great restoration to be wrought: the serpent was also to bruise His heel.[1]

II

The first transgression was an epitome of all subsequent sin in the manner of its inception, in its course, and in its consequence. Satan begins by throwing doubt upon the truth of God's revelation to them: " Hath God said? Is it not likely that you have mis-understood Him? " But there was no misunderstanding. Our first mother, in reply, declares quite exactly what the divine command had been. " Ye shall not eat of it, neither shall ye touch it,

[1] Gen. iii. 15.

lest ye die." Then follows the blasphemous denial of God's revelation: "Ye shall not surely die"; and the still more blasphemous suggestion of God's petty jealousy of His own creature: "God doth know that in the day ye eat thereof, then your eyes shall be opened, and ye shall be as gods, knowing good and evil." Eve parleys with the tempter, and, as will always be the case when one parleys with Satan, she loses. She does not turn herself swiftly from the evil, but she considers it in all its aspects. She looks upon the forbidden thing; she "saw that the tree was good for food, and that it was pleasant to the eyes, and a tree to be desired to make one wise." She deliberately enters into the occasion of three grave sins: gluttony, the lust of the eyes, and intellectual pride. After this, escape would have been almost a miracle. Then comes consent, and sin; but "no man dieth to himself." [1] She involves her husband, and the great tragedy is accomplished.

Even after this wickedness, God does not abandon His original purpose of making His creatures one with Himself. He comes to them to receive their act of repentance and to restore them to His favour. But there is no response in the heart of man to the loving advance of God, so terribly had sin wrought in so brief a time upon his nature. On the day of the great transgression which "brought death into the world and all our woe," [2] in the beautiful, idyllic, anthropomorphic story, as it is handed down to us, He, as it seems was His loving wont, comes, just as before, to walk with His children in the garden in the cool of the day. Theretofore, swiftly had they run to greet Him when that loving voice sounded through the aisles of Paradise; but now, guilty and afraid, they flee from Him, and hide themselves amid the trees of the garden. Man realizes himself to be in a condition which was never intended in the eternal purpose. He finds himself in revolt against his loving Creator, wholly out of harmony with the destiny of which he is conscious, in a state irreconcilable with the original purpose for which he was created. This heart-breaking story sets forth powerfully the truth that God does not forsake even the impenitent sinner. It is the sinner who forsakes Him. Man's reaction to his own sin is to flee from God in fear; God's reaction to man's sin is to draw near to man in love. The more we sin, the more do we need His love, and the more generously is that love offered to us. The vivid illustration of this is found in our Lord's first Word on the cross. "Then said Jesus, Father, forgive them; for they know not what they do." [3] The verb *said* is given in a form which implies continued action: "He

[1] Rom. xiv. 7.   [2] Milton, *Paradise Lost*, Canto I.   [3] St. Luke xxiii. 34.

D

kept on saying." As their blasphemies and mockings increased, He increased His cry that they might be forgiven. He would not let their sin outdistance His love. And so has He ever been. So will He ever be.

There is no spirit of repentance, no response to the call of love, on the part of our first parents. The man blames the woman, or rather, he first lays the blame on God Himself: " The woman whom thou gavest to be with me, she gave me of the tree and I did eat." It was as though he were saying, " I was not responsible for having her; Thou didst give her to me, and this is the consequence." The woman in her turn blames the serpent—in both, a futile effort to shift the awful burden of their guilt. But the eternal purpose still stands. God enters upon His work of repairing the breach made by the sin of man. Man is incapable of making any advance Godward, and therefore God Himself makes the advance, and the motive force behind this work of His is the infinite love with which He loves the sinner.

III

We see the long preparation through the ages, and how in the fulness of time it culminated in the Incarnation of God. The Incarnation was no symbolic thing, it is not something which comes to pass subjectively in the interior of any man's soul. It is a definite fact of the world's history, which occurred at a given moment of time, in a given place, and was the greatest event that has ever happened in human history, or that ever could happen. It was as real an historical event as the signing of the Magna Carta. Men may accept or reject it, they may deny that it ever occurred, but this cannot change, or in any way affect the objective fact of history.

Let us see just how this Incarnation was effected. God, the Holy Trinity, created miraculously out of the substance of the Blessed Virgin Mary, without the interposition of a human father, a human body to which He joined a human soul. The human being thus created was complete and perfect in every way, without sin, without any of the weakness of sin, or tendency to sin, incident to a fallen nature. In the moment of His conception in the womb of the Blessed Virgin Mother, the Holy Trinity united this perfect Humanity to the Eternal Son, the second Person of the Godhead, and by this union the God-Man came into being. He had both the divine nature and the nature of man, in their completeness, being, as the Athanasian Creed declares, " Perfect God and perfect Man, of a reasonable soul and human flesh subsisting." The same creed declares that this Incarnation was effected " not by conversion of the Godhead into flesh, but by taking of the manhood into God." He possessed, and will continue to possess through all eternity, the two natures, human and divine, in their perfection and fulness, distinct and unconfused, united in the One Person of the eternal and only-begotten Son of God. There is no human person in the God-Man. He is " God, of the substance of the Father, begotten before the worlds; and Man, of the substance of His Mother, born in the world."

Why, it may be asked, should the Son, the second Person of the ever-blessed Trinity, have become incarnate? Why not the Father, or the Holy Spirit? The answer is a plain and quite logical one. The purpose of the Incarnation was to make us sons of God. The purpose was not to make us Fathers or Spirits. Therefore, it was fitting that He who from eternity was the Son by nature, should take our nature, so that, by taking it, He might make us sharers in His quality as Son. He associated His divine Sonship with humanity in the act of Incarnation, in order that every member of the race might be associated with that Sonship. He partook of our human nature in order that we might become partakers of His divine nature.

The further question might be asked : Why, in order to become Incarnate, should the Eternal Son have taken humanity from a human mother? Why did God not create a body for His Incarnate Son as He created a body for the first Adam? Again we see the fitness of the mode of the Incarnation. The Eternal Son was Son from all eternity by an infinite generation; He was the " only-begotten Son of God." It was therefore fitting that, since He was Son of God by generation from the divine Father, He should become Son of Man by generation from a human mother. Being the only-begotten Son of God according to His Godhead, it was in keeping with the nature of things that He should become the only-begotten son of His Ever-Virgin Mother, according to the flesh.

At the moment when the Blessed Virgin yielded herself to the great purpose of God, and replied to the angel, " Be it unto me according to thy word," [1] in that moment the Incarnation was made complete. At that moment, as St. John expresses it, " the Word was made flesh, and dwelt among us." [2] She, by her consent to the holy leading of the Spirit, offset the dread consequences of the consent of our first mother to the evil leading of Satan. Eve was the human instrument in the hands of the tempter for the dis-

---

[1] St. Luke i. 38. [2] St. John i. 14.

honour of God, and for the overthrow of the race. Blessed Mary
became the human instrument in the hand of God for the accomplishment of the divine mystery of the Incarnation, whereby God's
honour was restored and the human race redeemed. At the
consent of a woman came the fall of man. At the consent of a
woman was set in motion the work of redemption and sanctification.
" By one woman, death; by another woman, life." [1] In the
Incarnation the primeval purpose was fulfilled. Man in Christ
Jesus was once more brought into perfect union with God.

As the ancient creed declares, the divine purpose was achieved,
" not by conversion of the Godhead into flesh, but by taking of the
manhood into God." Humanity was safe in the bosom of God,
even if not one soul beside the perfect human soul of Christ had
been affected by it.

IV

This fulfilment did not, however, satisfy the loving heart of God.
The Eternal Son came not merely to take to Himself a created
humanity like unto ours and give it a place in the bosom of Godhead, so that it could be said that in Him man the creature was in
reality united to God the Creator. The Incarnation was no mere
demonstration of what the omnipotent love of God could do. The
act of Incarnation was but the first step. Although complete in
itself, it was a means to a great end. The whole wide world
through all ages was to be the beneficiary of this supreme act of the
divine condescension. He took our nature in order to " save His
people from their sins "; [2] He came " to give his life a ransom for
many "; [3] " to give knowledge of salvation unto his people by the
remission of their sins "; [4] and all this to the end that we might be
" partakers of the divine nature." [5]

Christ willed that in the Incarnation not only should the
Humanity, Body and Soul, which He created and took to Himself,
be united to the Godhead, but He willed also, through the Incarnation, to " have all men to be saved, and to come unto the knowledge
of the truth." [6] This means that He willed that all men should be
taken up with Him into the Godhead, that, as He said, " where I
am there shall also my servant be." [7]

---

[1] St. Augustine, *Serm.* ccxxxii. 2; Migne, P. L., Tom. 38, Col. 1108. From
very early patristic times, Christian writers have set the antithesis between
Eve and Blessed Mary. See St. Irenæus, *Adversus Hæreses*, V. 19, Migne, P. G.,
Tom. 7, Col. 1175; and Tertullian, *de Carne Christi*, 17, Migne, P. L., Tom. 2,
Col. 827–828.

[2] St. Matt. i. 21.   [3] St. Matt. xx. 28.   [4] St. Luke i. 77.
[5] 2 St. Peter i. 4.   [6] 1 St. Tim. ii. 4.   [7] St. John xii. 26.

This destiny which God had prepared for men, and which our Lord came to make effectual, is not, however, without conditions. As must ever be kept in mind, God does His part perfectly, but nothing can be effected unless man co-operates. To understand the terms of the promise of life in union with Him, we must go back to the preceding verse in St. John's narrative, in chapter xii—" He that loveth his life shall lose it." [1] This is the translation in our Authorized Version; but there is a question about the verb which we translate *lose*. Scholars tell us that perhaps a better rendering is, " He that loveth his life shall destroy it," and this corresponds quite exactly with the truth regarding sin. Our first parents loved self and their own selfish inclinations more than they loved God and His service, and thus by their own evil wills they wrought their own destruction. Our Lord, therefore, tells us plainly that in order to gain the promise, we must love not self, but Him; we must serve not our own purposes, but we must consecrate ourselves to the fulfilment of His divine purpose, and this fulfilment lies in loving God and our neighbour, and in the consequent work of serving our neighbour and God in love.

We can better understand the implications of our Lord's words by a paraphrase, as is so often necessary in order to secure the shades of meaning which are involved : " If any man serve me let him follow me, and, not as the result of an arbitrary action on the part of God alone, but as a consequence of his co-operation with me in faithful discipleship, it shall come to pass that where I am there shall also my servant be." This is the indispensable procedure if we would find our place in the bosom of the Holy and Ever-Blessed Trinity, in union with the Eternal Son-made-Man. There is an emphasis on the first personal pronoun in the Greek original of this passage, indicated by its position in the sentence, which is lost in the translation. Taken in the order of the words as the Evangelist wrote them, the passage is as follows : " If me any man serve, me let him follow." Our translators have sacrificed the emphasis for the smoothness of the English. [2]

v

Referring back to St. Paul's statement that God " will have all men to be saved, and to come unto the knowledge of the truth," [3]

---

[1] St. John xii. 25.
[2] Whatever the inadequacies of the A.V., this is not meant as a criticism. The translation was made not for the use of students, but " to be read in churches." A smooth rendering was therefore desirable.
[3] 1 St. Tim. ii. 4.

we are to note that this knowledge is no mere knowledge of the truth, communicated, as it were, from a distance in an intellectual manner, but we participate in the knowing and loving of His blissful Godhead. In short, we, in a manner we cannot understand, share in the processes of knowledge and love which are going on unceasingly in the bosom of the Holy Trinity. St. Peter's assurance that we are " partakers of the divine nature " must mean this or it can mean nothing, for the divine nature cannot be separated from the divine knowledge and love. God and His attributes are one. " What God has, that He is." [1]

We have said that the Incarnation was a definite happening in human history; but it is more than this. It is not a mere event which occurred many centuries since, and was recorded, and took its place in history, and then was done with, save as a memory. It is a tremendous and present living factor, not only for the human soul of Incarnate God, but in its practical application to every one of us to-day. It is the greatest and most transcending factor and force in the universe. It stands utterly unique. From its very nature, nothing can enter into comparison with it.

His Humanity is one with the Godhead, and we are one with His Humanity. Therefore, so long as we are one with Him, we are united to the Godhead. He partook of our human nature in order that we might partake of His divine nature. The Fathers of the Church are very bold in their language as they discuss this great truth. In the second century St. Irenæus teaches that the Son of God became the Son of Man that man, having been taken into the Word, and receiving the adoption, might become the Son of God.[2] St. Cyprian says, " What man is, Christ willed to be, in order that man may be what Christ is." [3] St. Athanasius, a very exact theologian, who never used words carelessly, says, " He was made Man in order that we might be made God." [4] In a sermon attributed to St. Augustine we find the identical saying.[5] The union between God and man is a sure expectation for every soul.

In the solemn mingling of the water and wine in the chalice in the Eucharist, immediately before the consecration of the bread and

---

[1] St. Augustine, *De Civ. Dei*, xi. 10; Migne, P. L., Tom. 41, Col. 327.

[2] St. Irenæus, *Advers. Hæreses*, III. xix. 1; Migne, P. G., Tom. 7, Col. 939. Again he says: " Through the measureless love He has for us, He became what we are that He might fit us to be what He is." *Ibid.*, Col. 1120.

[3] St. Cyprian, *De Idolorum Vanitate*, Pt. II, xi.; Migne, P. L., Tom. 4, Col. 599.

[4] St. Athanasius, *De Incarn. Verbi*, liv. 5; Migne, P. G., Tom. 25, Col. 192.

[5] St. Augustine, *Serm.* cxxviii.; Migne, P. L., Tom. 39, Col. 1997. " Factus est Deus homo, ut homo fieret Deus." Migne lists this among St. Augustine's " supposed sermons," but the teaching is undoubtedly his.

wine to be the Body and Blood of Incarnate God, the priest prays, " O God, who didst wonderfully create, and yet more wonderfully regenerate the nature of man, grant that by the mystery of this water and wine, we may become partakers of His Divinity who did vouchsafe to become partaker of our Humanity."

All this applies to us in no general way, no running in under the terms of some general amnesty, but each one of us is dealt with by the love of God as though he were the only soul in existence. Realizing this great uplifting truth, St. Augustine cries out in an excess of joyous gratitude, " O Thou good Omnipotent, who so carest for each one of us as if Thou didst care for him alone; and who carest for all as if they were but one: " [1] God proceeds not from the general to the particular, but from the particular to the general—if indeed there is anything in God's view which can at all be thought of as general. He loves the whole human race because He first loves every individual soul in it. Our vocation is being fulfilled when we receive that love into our hearts, when we give Him the fulness of our love in return.

VI

The question has been debated whether it was the purpose of God that the Eternal Son should have become incarnate had man not sinned. Theologians have brought their learning and intellectual skill to bear upon both sides of this question. While there may be much devotional edification in discussing such issues, we must remember that the answer is known to God alone, and He has not seen fit to reveal it. We must therefore proceed with caution and with great reverence in discussing this problem. No one can dare to dogmatize about it. We may have our opinions, but God alone has the answer.

It is a principle generally recognized, however, that in the case of every enterprise, whether it be human or divine, the means employed should in some degree be proportionate to the end in view. We do not use a steam hammer to crack a walnut. Of course, since there can be no real comparison between the finite and the infinite, there can be no real proportion between the action of God in the Incarnation, and the fruits of the Incarnation as seen in the finite life of man. But we can look at these subjects only from the human standpoint, and since God has given the revelation, it is allowed to us to inquire whether it is proportionate to the mighty and

[1] St. Augustine, *Confessions*, iii. 11; Migne, P. L., Tom. 32, Col. 692.

mysterious work of God in the Incarnation that the only object in the divine view was to repair a breach, to do no more than to restore something which had been lost.

St. Thomas Aquinas is generally thought to take the position that there would have been no Incarnation had not man needed redemption from sin. St. Thomas was perhaps the greatest teacher the Church has had since St. Augustine, and whatever he says must be given the most reverent consideration. It has been pointed out, however, that while he might seem to take this position, there are to be found in his works the mention of many motives for the Incarnation which are independent of the sin and the fall of man—motives which relate solely to the establishment of the super- natural order amongst men, to the foundation and realization of the order of grace, the end of which is the glorification of God through the exaltation of man. To take any other position would seem to say that God was, in some sense, forced to the Incarnation by the needs of man. But even supposing that the Incarnation was the only means God could have used for man's restoration, would this not bring up the question, " Does God exist for man, or man for God? " This question is directed against the spirit which makes man the centre of God's activities, rather than everything, as must be the case, centring in God Himself.

Would we not under-estimate the supernatural dignity of the God-Man if we should make the object of His mission nothing more than the repairing of a deficiency? It is quite conceivable that there might be a restoration of the original righteousness with which man was endowed in the beginning without Christ becoming Incarnate, or man being made " partaker of the divine nature " and being set in the way of finding his destiny in the bosom of the Trinity with Christ the Eternal Son.

We cannot conceive, however, of the manhood being taken up into God had God not humbled Himself to take our nature in the Incarnation. God condescended to man. Man had no power to rise to God. The essential character of His work was not merely to reconcile and acquit. It is to elevate and exalt humanity to the divine plane, making it to participate, by an ineffable and mysterious resemblance, in the very nature of God. As the Head of the race, the God-Man raises the souls who are one with Him to an incom- prehensible and immeasurable height of glory and dignity.

It is inevitable that this operation of the Eternal Son in His human nature should repair all defect and deficiency in the soul which is thus elevated to the heavenly plane. If the primary purpose in the divine will is the raising of man to a state of union with God, then all fault and deficiency must of necessity be obliterated in order that this exaltation be possible. We are not, however, to think of it as a chronological sequence. It is not that the soul, having been freed from guilt and sin, is then raised to a state of union with God. The bringing of the soul into union with God and the elimination of moral and spiritual deficiency are one and the same divine action. They are only different aspects of the same divine process. One cannot occur without the other.

The ancient teachers of the Church rejoiced in describing the fall of man as the *felix culpa*, the happy and blessed fault which made possible the raising of man to a height of holiness such as he had not possessed before the fall. They could not have used this expression had they believed that the purpose of the Incarnation was confined to the taking away of sin, and to man's restoration to the place he had held before he sinned, with nothing beyond this embraced in the divine intention.

St. Leo, in his first sermon on the Ascension, speaks of the exaltation of Man in the Mystical Body of Christ to the highest plane by means of the Incarnation, and says, " There was great and unspeakable reason for joy, when in the sight of the holy multitude of the disciples the nature of mankind ascended above the dignity of all heavenly creatures, rising higher than the ranks of the angels, to be elevated above the height of the archangels, and to find no limit to its progress until, received to the seat of the Everlasting Father, it should be associated on the throne with His glory, to whose nature it was united in man. Since, therefore, Christ's Ascension is our exaltation, and the hope of the Body is raised whither the glory of the Head has gone before, let us be glad with worthy joy, and rejoice with devout thanksgiving; for to-day not only are we confirmed in the possession of Paradise, but we have also with Christ penetrated the heights of heaven, and have gained greater things by the unspeakable grace of Christ than we lost through the malice of the devil."

VII

There exists in the Godhead a principle of infinite communication of Himself. God the Father, by an infinite and eternal generation, communicates the fulness of His Deity to the Eternal Son. In the Incarnation God, the Eternal Son, takes to Himself a created Humanity. He, then, through the operation of the same principle, communicates His Divinity to this Humanity. Further, to all those who are made one with Him He communicates the same divine nature, through this same principle of communication which God is continually exercising.

When we speak of the continual exercise of this principle of communication, we mean that the divine communications are not made once for all, but are, in their infinite fulness, continuous. As God the Father is eternally communicating the totality of His life to the Son in the bosom of the Blessed Trinity, so is God the Son continually communicating the fulness of His divine life to His Sacred Humanity, and, again, through this Sacred Manhood, He is unceasingly communicating this same divine life to the souls of those who are one with Him, whom He has drawn into the infinite current of His divine Being. So long as we are " in Christ " the stream of His life and power is being poured into our souls, not only without a moment's cessation, but in ever-increasing force and volume, to the utmost of our capacity to receive it.

Further, the divine life of which we are made partakers is exercising its infinite energy within us, and is, through us, seeking to communicate itself to others. We cannot keep this life to ourselves, " for none of us liveth to himself." [1] If we sought to avoid sharing with others this divine nature and life, we ourselves would instantly forfeit it. Not to share it is to lose it.

In union with Christ we are taken up into the Godhead, and as we participate in His mysterious life, there is bestowed upon us a capacity for glorifying God in an infinite manner, because as we share in the life of the Incarnate Son, we must, of necessity, have an integral part in His work of giving glory to the Blessed Trinity. This is the objective of our incorporation " with Christ in God," and as long as the continuous and ever-increasing stream of the divine Nature infloods our souls, we are able to give a correspondingly continuous and increasing glory to the triune God, to whom be ascribed all honour, might, majesty, glory and dominion, through the eternal ages. This high and heavenly privilege belongs to us not individually, but to us as members of Christ's Body, and so as members one of another.

The Eternal Son alone is able to honour the Father in the manner which is due to Him. This honour and glory the Son renders to the Father not only in His divine nature, but also in His Humanity, and He further gives this honour to His Father in His Mystical Body, the Church, of which He is the Head, and of which each one

[1] Rom. xiv. 7.

of us is a member, and, as such, each one in the Communion of Saints is made capable, " in Christ," of giving to the Father a glory like that which He receives from the Son. The works of Incarnate God belong to us, since He is our Head. His worship in Heaven, His intercession, His obedience, His sufferings, all are ours. Whatever He does for the glory of the Father we can claim as our own because of our solidarity with Him. As Scheeben says, " Not only are we brethren in the Lord Christ, but we form with Him, so to speak, one single Son in the Father's eyes." This is what the apostle meant when he said we are " accepted in the beloved." [1]

This is the teaching of Scheeben, who was perhaps the most profound mystical theologian of recent centuries. His style is not easy, but it is worth careful attention, for it expresses the truth, magnificent beyond our knowing, beyond the grasp of any save the infinite mind of God Himself—the truth that the Christ-possessed soul, its understanding and power of intelligent appreciation brought to the highest degree possible in the creature, is a dweller amid the secrecies of the Godhead, plunged in the unfathomable depths of Divinity, " into the ocean where all streams find their resting-place." [2] Scheeben goes on to say, " Do we not see to what extraordinary grandeur the Incarnation exalts man? It appears at once as the foundation and crown of a communion of the super-natural life of man with the Holy Trinity. Participation in the eternal life of the Godhead could not be established on any other foundation. Grace alone could bring man only a trickle of that life. But a real and entire communication, a communication by which man is drawn into the current of the divine life to imbibe it in the Son, and by the Son in the Father, to receive in himself, in the Son and by the Son, the personal Spirit of the Son as his Spirit—such a communication is established only by the Incarnation. In Christ it places man upon the throne of God, makes him participate in the dignity of the divine Persons, and introduces him into the Trinitarian relations. It transports him into the bosom of God to make him enjoy the essential life of the divine Persons in the most real and intimate union with them."

Scheeben concludes his argument with a fine passage : " How much more glorious the Incarnation appears," he says, " when considered from this point of view than when considered as simply a means of lifting up the race from its fall, or as the means of

---

[1] Eph. i. 6.
[2] Tyciak, *Life in Christ*, Chap. vi.

merely restoring the union with God that was broken off by sin." [1]

Such is the glorious, loving purpose which God has for His people. It only remains for them to yield themselves to be one with Him that they may reign with Him in order to lay hold of this all-transcending honour which He has prepared for them.

VIII

No sin of man, however serious or long continued, can quench the love of God for His creatures, or cause Him to swerve from His purpose of bringing us into a union of eternal love with Himself. It is a great and comforting truth that God does not need to be reconciled to man. Nowhere in the New Testament is there to be found a word that implies that God is a reluctant Deity, angry because of the sins of men, needing, like some heathen divinity, to be appeased. As we have seen, when man sinned it was not God who withdrew Himself, but it was man who fled from the face of God. God's reaction to sin was only to pursue man all the more with the offers of His forgiving love. We find the idea of propitiation used in the Scriptures, but in no case does it mean that God needs to be propitiated. The word appears only twice in the New Testament, in both instances in the first epistle of St. John, where the same expression is repeated: "He is the propitiation for our sins." [2] The scriptural conception of this and kindred words is never that of appeasing one who is angry with an offender, but rather of altering the character of that which, from its own nature, is alienating in its effect, and interposes an obstacle to fellowship. Such expressions as "propitiating God," or God "being reconciled," are wholly foreign to the teaching of the New Testament. It is man who needs to be reconciled to God. The propitiation is directed to the sinner and to his sin, and has the effect of neutralizing the sin so that fellowship with God can be restored. The idea of the efficacy of the propitiation made by Christ corresponds with St. Paul's simple but tremendous expression, "in Christ." He who is grafted into Christ is the object of the life-giving, purifying action of His Precious Blood, and partakes of the virtues of His life and death. This grafting into Him does away with the sinful character of man, which is what alienates him

---

[1] I am indebted for much of the foregoing argument to a series of articles on the teaching of Joseph Scheeben, by Dom Augustine Kerkvoorde, O.S.B., published in *La Vie Spirituelle*, in October, November, December 1939, and January 1940.

[2] 1 St. John ii. 2; iv. 10.

from God. This elimination of the sinful character and endowing man with the Christ-character is the work of propitiation which our Lord wrought. God's love never varies, but remains the same through all the vicissitudes of man's sin, although He cannot violate His own nature by receiving the impenitent or treating sin as though it were not sin. The object of the propitiation is not God, but man who has estranged and alienated himself from God.[1]

In the divine urgency to fulfil His loving purpose of restoring man, God calls us continually, " My son, give me thine heart." [2] Let us rise up, and make as continual a response: " Lord, take my heart, for I cannot give it Thee; and when Thou hast it, keep it, for I cannot keep it for Thee; and save me in spite of my sins." [3]

O Blessed Lord Christ, our Refuge and our Strength, Thou Hope of mankind : whose light shineth from afar upon earth's darkling clouds : Behold Thy redeemed ones cry unto Thee : Thy banished ones, whom Thou bringest home through the power of Thy Precious Blood, call to Thee. Fulfil in them Thy loving purpose. We are tossed upon the waves of this world. Thou standest on the shore beholding our sore peril : Save us and help us.

[1] Westcott, *Comment.*, I St. John ii.   Brooke, *Crit. Comment.*, I St. John ii.
[2] Prov. xxiii. 26.   [3] Prayer ascribed to Fénelon.

Christ lives in the memory, stirring it up lest it should forget Him. He lives in the intellect, and enlightens it that it may penetrate celestial secrets and hidden mysteries. He lives in the will, enkindling it that it may become wholly like to fire, mount upward and be immersed in God. He lives in the imagination, directing it, and adorning it with wondrous images symbolizing the divine secrets.

LUIS DE LA PUENTE.

God is Spirit, Intelligence, and Love; so the soul of man is spiritual, intelligent, and loving. The intellect and the will are the two great capacities of our spiritual nature; and they each want filling, the intellect with knowledge, and the will with love. Thus they tend to their perfection, to the fulness of knowledge, and the fulness of love; which tells us that they are made for God: for certain it is that no creature can supply such fulness, since creatures are but limited recipients themselves, and like us seeking to be filled. Hence the Angelic Doctor tells us that " man's desires can be satisfied by none but God alone. . . . Nor is that desire satisfied till he come to the First Cause which is God."

H. REGINALD BUCKLER.

CHAPTER IV

THE HEART'S THIRST FOR GOD

I

WE have considered the primary factor in the redemption and exaltation of man—namely, that in spite of man's sin, God never gave up His loving purpose of uniting His creature to Himself. The other great factor, equally necessary, as God has willed to decree it, is man's longing after God. In hardly anything has God's love to man been more graciously manifested than in His refusal to allow sin to quench the desire of the human heart for the Creator. In this every human soul, whatever its evil heritage or its actual sins, shows that it retains something of the dignity which must attach to the creature made in the image of the Creator. St. Bernard comments on this with his usual penetration. " The soul," he says, " is a noble creature whose greatness is revealed in the fact that she possesses in herself such a capacity for participating in the perfections of the Divine Word, and in her yearning for the same, she gives proof of her righteousness." [1]

This longing is found in sinners as well as in saints. It expresses itself in every aspiration of the human heart after higher things, even if the particular aspiration itself be not wholly good or desirable. Man's heart is full of a divine discontent which, if he will but follow his ideal of goodness, poor, inadequate, and wrongly conceived as that ideal may be, will bring him nearer to God. It was one who called himself an atheist who wrote of

> " The desire of the moth for the star,
>   The night for the morrow;
>   The devotion to something afar
>   From the sphere of our sorrow."

Shelley was unconsciously expressing the dumb hunger of ignorant, fallen man for God. St. Augustine phrased it very beautifully when he said, " Thou hast made us for Thyself, and our heart shall find no rest until it rest in Thee." [2] Even the foulest orgies of paganism are but the reaching out of poor, blinded man after " the unknown God."

[1] St. Bernard, *Serm. in Cant.* lxxx; Migne, P. L., Tom. 183, Col. 1167.
[2] St. Augustine, *Confessions*, i. 1; Migne, P. L., Tom. 32, Col. 661.

Our Christian vocation is God's correspondence with this longing on the part of man. All Christian revelation is a pointing the way back to God. And it is not only a showing of the way, but it is the actual bestowal of the means and powers which, if faithfully used, will enable us to walk in the way that leads to Him, and to attain to Him perfectly in the end. Grace is the power which makes sure and certain our ability to come back to Him, and to maintain our union with Him in this world; and it stands as a pledge of the complete union we shall have with Him in the world to come.

II

We must not, however, think of this desire for God as a natural endowment of man. It is a survival of the supernatural endowment of man. It is a survival of the supernatural gift which was made to man in the beginning, and which was sadly obscured, but not wholly lost, when man sinned and fell from his high estate. One of the most blessed truths of our holy faith, the consideration of which must ever fill us with gratitude and gladness, is that man is not wholly depraved. If man were totally depraved, as some have taught, he would not know that he was depraved at all, for he would be able to have no conception of good and would be incapable of making any comparison between good and evil. He is indeed far gone from righteousness. As St. Paul expresses it, " All have sinned, and come short of the glory of God," [1] but the divine spark still glows, though dimly, in every human heart. It needs only to be fanned into a flame, and fed with the fuel of grace, and it will increase until it fills the whole man with the fire of divine love, which will burn away all sin and dross, all that is not pleasing to our loving God.

God furnishes the fuel in superabundant supplies. We are to take care that it is used to keep the fires of love burning. Every desire for prayer, be it ever so slight, every interior suggestion to kindly thought or action, is not only a personal call from God who loves us, but it is an opportunity to feed more generously the flame which is the life of God Himself dwelling within us; and each opportunity, faithfully employed, leads us swiftly and directly to the fulfilment of our desire, into a life of closer and more loving union with Him.

Since this desire is a gift from God, in order that it may be rightly directed and continuously increased we must be assiduous

[1] Rom. iii. 23.

in our work of prayer. Again and again in the voice of the Church's Liturgy is found the assurance that in Him, and in Him only, shall we find the grace of desire. In the Easter collect we declare not only that He doth " put into our minds good desires," but that he does this by a " special grace." In the collect for peace we address Him as the one " from whom all holy desires do proceed "; and in another collect, one of the most beautiful in the Church's Liturgy, we ask, " Grant unto thy people that they may desire that which thou dost promise." [1] The Church is ever praying for this grace of desire, and God is ever responding to this prayer by giving to His people an ever deeper longing after Him, that they may seek and find Him.

The gift of holy desire is not an endowment for this life only. To him who seeks to cultivate it through prayer, and through an earnest effort to do the thing which it is given to him to desire, the gift will persist beyond the bounds of time into eternity. As in this life, so in the life to come, will it stimulate the soul to reach out ever more earnestly after God. " Desire and love for Christ will remain when the ages are no more, and will be as great and as wide as the greatness and wideness of eternity." [2]

Every response which God makes to our prayer for the increase of holy desire is a stage in the continuous and progressive call to us to love and serve Him, and also a stage in the growth in our desire, and therefore in our expanding capacity to respond. This involves a very comforting truth : the fact that any duty is proposed to us in our conscience is the proof that we have the power to perform it, and to perform it well. There is never a time when such an one can say, " My burden is greater than I can bear." The presence of the burden, whatever it may be, is the proof of our ability to sustain it in a manner which will be pleasing to God.

It is possible, however, that a soul through scrupulosity may have a mistaken idea of the requirements of conscience. There are fearful souls who, while eagerly desiring to love and serve God, are harrowing themselves continually, wondering if they are fulfilling the divine will, and ever afraid lest they are falling short of God's purpose for them. This is not the place to discuss the subject of scruples, that bane of the spiritual life of many. Suffice it to say that those who yield to such scruples are taking from God the character of a loving and kind Father. They are assuming that God is a hard master, and they are making it impossible to look upon Him with the humble, loving trust of a child. We need say

[1] Collect IV after Easter.   [2] Luis de Leon, *Nombres de Cristo*, III.

E

here no more than this, that where anyone finds the temptation to scruples of this kind intruding itself, he is to give himself the benefit of the doubt, if doubt there be. The persistent and strongly willed diversion of the mind from such scrupulous thoughts, whenever they occur, combined with frequent acts of love to God, will work a cure.

III

While men are to be humble, and to this end are to practise the virtue of humility, it is not to the glory of God for us to underestimate what His love has done for us in response to the desire of our hearts. We are children of God and heirs of heaven, and we should recall continually the exalted station to which He has raised us, in order that we may be incited always to live in a manner worthy of the children of God, impelled ever to thirst for Him more and more, and to employ the means that will bring us into ever deeper union with Him.

We must remember gratefully and humbly, recalling our own unworthiness, that every opportunity that God gives to serve Him, every duty and consequent blessing that He makes known to us, has been prepared for us by His loving omnipotence from all eternity. What possible reason have we, then, for shrinking from desiring with poignant desire that which His love has prepared for us from the eternal ages? No presumption lies in this. Rather is there ingratitude if our desire does not flame high.

He who prepared for us the heavenly destiny, prepared also the way in which that destiny was to be achieved. No detail of this method escapes Him. God has devised innumerable occasions and conditions which, if rightly used by us, will not only produce a continual deepening of our desire, but will bring a complete fulfilment of this desire for God and for the things of God. His divine solicitude has ordained it that there shall be at set times, and as the result of the employment of the appointed means and occasions He has prepared, a special increment of love and joy accruing to us. Each Communion we make, each period we devote to prayer, each good work done for love of God and our neighbour, however unimportant men may count it, brings this divine increase. This hour is made ready in the determinate counsel and foreknowledge of God, in which He is to crown our unworthy souls with some great and loving blessing that in and through us His own glory may be enhanced amongst men. However commonplace the external action may appear, the moment in which this purpose of God is to be fulfilled in me is a tremendous moment, one of transcending and eternal importance, because, if I am true to the divine leading, it will be one in which there will be achieved in me that which He has prepared, and for which my soul has longed and desired.

If there were but one such moment in a life, with what joy and quivering anticipation should we approach it. Is it not infinitely more thrilling that the great love of God, and His longing for my love, supplies me with a score of such opportunities every day? If the soul were capable of understanding, even for a little moment, the meaning of all this, it would be plunged into an ecstasy of desire and longing for the things which God has prepared for those who love Him.

IV

We are not, however, to think of this increase of love and desire as taking place only at the particular moment of Holy Communion, or prayer, or when we have actually done some good work for God's honour. True, these occasions, if sedulously improved, bring to the soul renewed infloodings of grace. But for those who are " in Christ " the process of increase is unceasing. This blessed increment is not dependent for its continuance upon repeated and separate acts of the will. Having once for all consecrated ourselves to God, and by His Spirit maintaining ourselves in union with Him, there is one unbroken flow of love and power from the Heart of God into our hearts. It is not one gift here and another there, according as we do one thing or another in response to His grace, for as by our union with Him we are engulfed in the very lifestream of the indivisible Trinity, so we receive unceasingly, sleeping or waking, the riches of the divine nature. With this steady increase, the soul, tasting the sweetness of indwelling Divinity, is overwhelmed with an ever-deepening desire for the living, loving God. Desire engenders desire, as love begets love. It is well expressed in the ancient hymn on the Holy Name of Jesus:

> " For they who eat Thee hunger sore,
> And they who drink Thee thirst the more;
> Desiring nought below, above,
> Save Jesus whom their spirits love."

It is an overwhelming thought that God should desire my love, and that He should have wrought so mighty a work of redemption in order to win it, to that end infusing into my soul an inexpressible and irrepressible yearning for Him. It is no wonderful thing that I, knowing what God is, knowing how gracious He has ever been

to me, and conscious of the blessings that He is continually preparing for me, should love Him, and thirst for Him, as for the One in
whom alone I can find ultimate satisfaction and joy. But it is a
wonder beyond our knowing that He, knowing us, and how we
have wounded Him and offended Him, and how we shall again
and again do Him the same despite, should love us; and more
than this, that He should desire that we love Him; and that He
should find His joy in our love, and His grief in our neglect of Him.
Christ weeping over Jerusalem is the picture of the divine Love
yearning for the love of His people who have rejected Him. The
prayer attributed to St. Francis of Assisi sets forth this glowing
truth:

"O Lord Jesus Christ, may the sweet and burning power of
Thy love so absorb my soul that I may die for love of Thy love who
didst die upon the cross for love of my love."

We have here a reflection of St. Augustine's " *Moriar ne moriar,*
Let me die lest I die: " [1] let me die to self and to the world lest I
die unto God. Not only did He love us unto death, even the
death of the cross, but, amazing to relate, He died in order to win
our love, so mightily did He long for the love and devotion of our
sin-stained hearts. No wonder the apostle cried out in glad
astonishment: "Behold what manner of love the Father hath
bestowed upon us! " [2]

The Christian soul should meditate continually upon the wonder
of the divine love for sinners, for nothing can so stimulate our love
and desire for Him as the thought of His love for us; and nothing
will so enlighten our blind longing after Him as the consideration
of this love for us, wholly unworthy as we are.

v

Since desire and love walk ever hand in hand, it were well for
us to consider at this point their relation to each other, even at the
risk of anticipating our later consideration of the virtue of love. We
are to keep ever in mind that whenever we speak concerning the
love of God, we are not thinking of our love for Him, but of His
love for us. When He commanded His disciples, " Continue ye in
my love," [3] He did not mean " Continue to love me." This, of
course, He expects of us, but it was not of this that He was speaking
at that time. In the first place, when He spoke of " my love," He

---

[1] St. Augustine, *Confessions*, i. 5; Migne, P. L., Tom. 32, Col. 663.
[2] 1 St. John iii. 1.   [3] St. John xv. 9.

did not use a word corresponding to the possessive pronoun *my*. The Greek equivalent is very exact. St. John tells us that He said, " Continue ye in the love which is mine." A paraphrase will bring out the meaning. It was as though He had said, " Continue to live and to labour in the power of the love which is mine, and which I will give unto you, the love which corresponds to my nature and character, the nature and character of the God-Man in which you are made to share."

The word we translate " continue " is the same word which in the fourth verse of this fifteenth chapter we translate " abide "— " abide in me and I in you." In the seven verses which begin with verse four of this chapter this word is used no fewer than ten times by our Lord, and every time it is used in an emphatic sense. The word has two implications: first, it signifies a permanent state, and second, a growth in that state, certain prepared and ordained means being used in order to secure this permanence and increase.[1]

It has ever been a common error amongst men to think that the love of God means our love for Him. Man is ever thus inclined to make himself the centre and source of all things. Our Lord had occasion to correct this in His discourse in the upper room. Though His disciples had been under His instruction for three years, they still thought that it had been their desire and love for Him that led to their choice of Him as their Master. He corrects this error. " Ye have not chosen me, but I have chosen you." [2] It was as though He were saying, " Ye did not desire Me; I desired you, and you were able to acquiesce in My choice of you only because I infused into your souls a desire for Me." His saying is made all the more emphatic by His placing the negative first. He clears their minds of error before He reveals to them the truth that it was His loving initiative and choice which made them His disciples and sons of God. St. John, many years afterwards, had occasion to correct this same false notion. " Herein is love," he wrote, " not that we loved God but that he loved us." [3] And, again, in the same epistle he said, " We love him because he first loved us." [4]

The consciousness of the great love wherewith He has loved us arouses in us a desire for Him which impels us to seek after Him.

---

[1] This μένω is a noble word which has been claimed by many languages. It was used universally in the Greek. St. John uses it, in one form or another, thirty-six times in his Gospel, and twenty-six times in his epistles. The genius of the Latin tongue seized upon it, translating it into such words as *maneo, mansio,* et al. English gathered it to itself as *manor, mansion, permanent,* etc. All the romance languages retain it.

[2] St. John xv. 16.   [3] 1 St. John iv. 10.   [4] 1 St. John iv. 19.

Our love does not originate within ourselves. It has its beginnings, and finds its impulse, nowhere else than in the infinitely loving Heart of God. His love for us stimulates us to a desire and a love which is as wide as heaven and earth, and the more we love, the deeper will be our desire for Him who is the fount and source of all love.

VI

Let us consider what we mean by desire. Desire has been defined as a movement of the will towards some spiritual excellence which we do not yet possess, but which is fitting for us, and which we are capable, by the help of God, of attaining. This involves, first, a sense of our need, and second, the conviction that God will indeed give us that good thing which is the object of our desire, provided we do our part to lay hold of what He had promised. If that which we desire were unattainable, the thought of it would engender despair, not desire. The Fathers and teachers of the Church are never weary of insisting on the necessity of desire, and they make it the basis of all Christian living. St. Augustine sums it up in one of his brief, pregnant sentences: " The life of the Christian is one continuous desire for holiness." [1]

We have seen that the desire of the soul for God may even be a dumb desire, a blind reaching out after God and the things of God, even without full realization of who and what God is. It is not unlikely that such a desire may be the best, because it realizes only its own need, and has no selfish ideas, rooted in proud self-sufficiency, of how that need is to be filled. " For very many, indeed, the whole of prayer consists in the expression of that desire and longing:—' My God, I want.' ' What do you want? ' ' I know not what I want, but I want.' In how many is this the prayer of their whole lives: beautiful and powerful prayer, truly contemplative prayer, though such souls, because they seem to get no farther, think they do not pray at all." [2]

Desire must be characterized by a *humble, strong, steadfast, energizing* disposition of the will.

Our desire must be humble, but this does not mean refusing the call of God because of a sense of unworthiness. That would be a

---

[1] St. Augustine, *on* 1 *St. John*, Tract. iv. 6; Migne, P. L., Tom. 35, Col. 2008.

[2] Goodier, *St. Ignatius Loyola and Prayer*, p. 165. A soul, earnestly seeking after God, said not long since with grief and tears, " I don't know how to pray. I can only go before our Lord and kneel down, and say, ' Dear Lord, I don't know how to pray; I don't know what to say to You. I only know that I love You with all my heart.' " And the dear soul did not realize that this was the best and highest prayer of all.

false humility, and false humility is always pride. St. Paul never said a more humble thing than when he cried, " I can do all things through Christ which strengtheneth me." [1] It was a boast, but not a boast of self. It was a magnifying of God. We find the same principle in the Magnificat, which is a supreme expression of humility; and yet the Blessed Mother did not dishonour God by minimizing the mighty work He had wrought in her. She knew, as we must know, that, as a matter of fact, we are totally unworthy of doing the least thing for God, or to serve Him in any particular. But she also realized, as we must realize, that " He that is mighty hath magnified me," or, as the Authorized Version very well translates it, " Hath done to me great things."

Our desire must be strong—that is, no mere weak wishing as a child may wish for some impossible thing, but a powerful movement of the will to lay hold upon the thing desired. It must be steadfast, no sudden flaming up of emotion only to die down, but it must be an enduring attitude of will. It must also be energizing, giving birth to a real purpose and plan, and producing a courageous spirit of initiative.

Such desire after God constitutes an actual laying hold upon God, for if such desire be present, He Himself does all the rest. The psalmist had a clear knowledge of this through his own experience. He cries with unfaltering faith, out of the darkness, " O God, thou art my God, early will I seek thee; my soul thirsteth for thee, my flesh also longeth after thee, in a barren and dry land where no water is." Thus crying in the darkness, swiftly is he able to say, with perfect confidence, " My soul shall be satisfied even as it were with marrow and fatness, when my mouth praiseth thee with joyful lips." [2] He who clings to God as his God will soon rejoice in the consoling realization of the satisfaction which nothing in time or in eternity can take from him.

VII

We must consider the principle that in the use of the will we are not required to make conscious acts of the will continuously. A virtual intention suffices. We determine in our wills to do a certain thing, and then proceed faithfully to use the means which will bring the thing to pass. It is not required for the integrity of our resolution that we be continually repeating the act of the will consciously. The like principle holds with desire. We do not have to be pro-

---

[1] Phil. iv. 13.   [2] Ps. lxiii.

jecting Godward a continual conscious stream of desire. From its nature, the desire will emerge into the conscious plane from time to time, but it is enough for its integrity, and for its consequent acceptance with God, that we make a direct renewal of our desire and longing for Him occasionally only, provided we persist in the pursuit of the object of our desire. Indeed, it might easily distract us from the work necessary for obtaining the end so earnestly desired, if we too frequently gave our time to indulging the conscious longing.

It has ever been a principle upon which God has dealt with men that the thing which a man earnestly desires to do, if he does what lies in him to realize his desire, is accredited to him as though he had already accomplished it. This applies to desires both good and evil. Our Lord declares that if a man lusts to do evil, it is accounted to him as though he had actually achieved it.[1] Likewise, he who wills to do the Father's will does not lose his reward if, through no fault of his own, he is unable to carry out to the full his desire and purpose in outward action.[2]

The teachers of the Church have again and again set forth this principle as one that is not open to question. St. Bernard tells us that "an unwearied desire for progress, and a ceaseless striving for perfection is to be reckoned to be perfection."[3] St. Augustine was especially devoted to this doctrine, and, particularly in his teaching concerning prayer, he repeats it again and again. "Loving desire prayeth always," he says. Again, "If thou art ever longing, thou art ever praying. When sleepeth prayer? When desire grows cold." And again he says, "If thy desire continue uninterrupted, so does thy prayer also."[4]

One can therefore readily see how necessary it is to guard and direct one's desires, for according to a man's desire so is his life and character. And with every desire, character is the more permanently conformed, either to Christ, or to the world.

O gracious Jesus : In the power of Thy love, lift me up above the darkness of this world, that I with undimmed vision may in humble love contemplate Thee, O dear Desire of my heart.

---

[1] St. Matt. v. 28.   [2] St. John vii. 17.
[3] St. Bernard, *Epist.* ccliv. 3; Migne, P. L., Tom. 182, Col. 460.
[4] St. Augustine, *En. in Ps.* xxxvii. 14; Migne, P. L., Tom. 36, Col. 404.

The passing of the lover into that which is beloved is neither violent, nor painful, nor laborious, nor enforced, but free and voluntary, sweet and of great delight. And hence the will, which is in this way united with the thing it loves, can by no act of violence be withdrawn from it, save by its free will alone. Would, O my God, that my will were deprived of such freedom, and of all desire to be free, that when I had once loved Thee, I might never turn back, nor change either love or will, but might love for ever that highest Goodness and infinite Wealth wherein my heart perpetually burns in living flames of love. But love itself is free, though the will pass into the thing that is loved; and thus the will remains ever will, and has its freedom of power and desire, although by love it be transformed into the Beloved. A marvellous thing it is that in this transformation of the lover into the Beloved, the love becomes as the object of its love, and as is the love, so is the will whence it is born.

DIEGO DE ESTELLA.

CHAPTER V

THE SOUL'S UNION WITH GOD

I

WE have seen something of the purpose and philosophy of the Incarnation. We have seen that it offers the divinely ordained plan and means in the following of which, under the guidance of the Holy Ghost, man may become partaker of the divine nature, and thus fulfil the purpose of his being, and attain to his destiny, which lies within the infinite cycle of the Triune Godhead.

As we have thought before, while we are to be humble in all things, and set no great store by ourselves because God has promoted us to so great honour, yet it would be nigh to blasphemy if we did not appreciate at its fullest value the transcendent thing that He has done for us. Maintaining this sense of our own nothingness and unworthiness, it were impossible for us to exalt too highly what the loving Father has wrought on our behalf.

The ancient Fathers of the Church were very bold when they spoke of the work of God in the Incarnation. St. Irenæus taught " that because of His immeasurable love He became what we are that He might fit us to be what He is." [1] We have already quoted St. Athanasius as saying that " Christ was made man, in order that we might be made God," [2] and St. Augustine adopts St. Athanasius's language as his own. Later writers are no less bold with a boldness born of an understanding of the wonderful work which God has done for His people. They were never involved in the false humility which would minimize what God had done for man. St. John of the Cross reflects the teaching of the Fathers when he says that God became Incarnate that man might become *endiosado*. This word is one that challenges our attention. There is no English word which exactly corresponds to it. To render it literally into English, we might use the word which Dr. Pusey coined, " engodded." " Our nature, in Jesus, was engodded, deified," he said.[3] It is commonly translated—for it is a word found in the

---

[1] St. Irenæus, *Adv. Hær.*, V Praef.; Migne, P. G., Tom. 7, Col. 1120.
[2] St. Athanasius, *Orat. de Incarn.*, liv. 5; Migne, P. G., Tom. 25, Col. 192.
[3] Pusey, *University Sermons*, 1859–1872, p. 338.

ordinary Spanish lexicons—*deified*, but one cannot feel satisfied with this conventional rendering. St. John's meaning must have gone deeper than that conveyed by this ordinary Latin derivative. The idea of deification was a common one amongst the ancients. Great heroes were commonly deified, and in later ages all the Roman emperors were raised to Olympus. Amongst the ancients deity was a cheap thing.

None of the great teachers of the Church whom we have quoted could have meant that we are actually changed into God, for there can be but one Eternal and Infinite. Did they not have in mind what St. Peter meant when he said that we are made " partakers of the divine nature," [1] and also what is taught in the creed, that " the Manhood was taken up into God," which was what happened to the Sacred Humanity of Christ in the moment of its creation? St. John of the Cross would have said *endiosado*. So, if where He is there are we to be also, we, too, in a real sense must be *endiosado*, " engodded."

The hypostatic union between Christ's Humanity and the Second Person of the ever-Blessed Trinity is a mysterious thing peculiar to Himself. No one can share it. Through it, the Humanity of Christ possesses a grace wholly unique, in the literal sense of that adjective. For anyone to share the grace of the union which Christ has with God, he would have to be himself Incarnate God. But we can and must share that which effects our union with God—namely, the gift, and consequent state, of sanctifying grace. Christ was endowed with this sanctifying grace in His Sacred Humanity, as well as with the grace of His hypostatic union, and that which comes to us through the Incarnation is nothing less than His own sanctifying grace, participation in which He bestows upon us. Our grace is essentially the same as that with which His Humanity is endowed. This is the life which God has prepared for us from eternity.

II

Repeatedly our Lord promises to His people the gift of eternal life. This must mean nothing less than a participation in the life of God Himself, for, as St. Peter says, we are " partakers of the divine nature." [2] Now, there can be but one eternal life, and that is the life of God. His is the only life that can have the quality of eternity, and we can have life eternal only through union with Him. The expression, to " have eternal life," is a favourite one

[1] 2 St. Peter i. 4.   [2] 2 St. Peter i. 4.

with St. John. It occurs no fewer than seventeen times in his Gospel, and six times in his first epistle. In nearly all of these instances in his Gospel they are given as direct quotations from our Lord Himself. In His conversation with Nicodemus He uses the expression twice: "As Moses lifted up the serpent in the wilderness, even so must the Son of man be lifted up: that whosoever believeth in him should not perish, but have eternal life." "For God so loved the world, that he gave his only begotten Son, that whosoever believeth in him should not perish, but have everlasting life." [1] In the same chapter St. John, testifying to our Lord's mission, says, "He that believeth on the Son hath eternal life." [2]

Amongst the typical declarations by our Lord of the gift of life, He says, "He that believeth on him that sent me, hath everlasting life." [3] In His discourse in the synagogue at Capernaum He uses the expression several times. [4] In St. John's first epistle the expression occurs six times, one of the representative instances being his saying, "This is the record, that God hath given to us eternal life, and this life is in his Son." [5]

In nearly all the cases where "eternal" or "everlasting life" is spoken of, the verb form indicates that this life is not promised for the future, but is ours here and now. The tense is the present. The gift of eternal life was made to us once for all in our baptism, but it is a gift which must be kept continually in action. Life means unbroken continuity. Where life ceases to function, even for a moment, it ceases to be. God wills His eternal life to function in and through us, and the power of this gift of eternal life is ever on the increase. It is a continual giving on God's part, and a continual appropriating of the gift on our part. We do not receive this increase passively. "Lay hold on eternal life," is the injunction St. Paul gives to St. Timothy, his son in the faith. [6] We sometimes see an epitaph which states that the one commemorated "entered into life eternal" on such-and-such a day, the day being that of his death. Such a statement is unfortunate. The soul does not wait until the end before receiving eternal life. Unless he receives it in this life, and lives it here by the power of the Holy Spirit, there is no hope of receiving it at all. [7]

---

[1] St. John iii. 15, 16.   [2] St. John iii. 36.   [3] St. John v. 24.
[4] St. John vi. 40, 47, 54.   [5] 1 St. John v. 11.   [6] 1 St. Tim. vi. 12.
[7] Such expressions in the New Testament, A.V. and R.V., as "eternal," "everlasting," "for ever," "without end," etc., are variant translations of the Greek word αἰώνιος, which implies *eternal*. The original of the word implies an age. Note the English derivitative, *æon*. Those who seek to escape our Lord's teaching of eternal punishment, by stressing the idea of an age which will come to an end, must also dismiss His promise of eternal life, for He uses this same word to

III

Eternal life does not mean life without end. The quality, not the extension, of the life, is what the Scriptures have in mind. There can be nothing quantitative about it. Eternal life is the life of the Eternal One, and in Him is neither beginning, nor duration, nor end, for this would contradict any conception or idea of infinity. He simply *is*. His life is an everlasting present; it has neither past nor future. It is a created participation in this eternal life which is promised to those who believe the revelation of Jesus Christ, and serve Him faithfully. The promise of life eternal is not a promise of mere immortality. Immortality belongs to man by nature, whether he be lost in hell, or glorified with Christ in heaven. We do not have to be in Christ in order to be immortal. We do have to be in Him in order to have a participation in the eternal quality of the life of the Godhead.

Eternal life is not something we are striving to win. It is the gift of God in baptism. We have it now in possession. The Christian warfare is not waged in order to secure eternal life, but to maintain and develop it. When St. Paul adjured St. Timothy to " lay hold on eternal life," he meant that he was to work for its deepening, for it depends on each soul what degree of participation in the divine nature and holiness it possesses.

There is a significance in St. John's repeated use of the expression to " have eternal life." This is no passive partaking, as when a child has its father's nature whether it is aware of it or not. The emphasis is on the word *have*. This Greek word is to be taken much in the sense of the old legal term, " to have and to hold." To possess life is more than merely living. Possession means having power over the thing we possess, power to use it, power to direct and develop it—alas, power to cast it away and lose it.

Let us have no fear lest we go too far in our conception of this relation to God. In the first place, we are to remember that it is not a relationship of our imagining, or of our making. It is the objective creation by the infinite personal love of our God for us. We should have no hesitation, no shrinking, in asserting our claim to possess eternal life, short of actually making ourselves to be God. Christ is in the bosom of the Father. If we are indeed " in Him," we are, of necessity, where He is. The utmost, ultimate reach of

---

describe the eternal reward as He does to describe the eternal punishment. See St. Matt. xxv. 46. In Rom. xvi. 26, St. Paul uses the same adjective by which to describe God Himself.

human conception of what this means would be a poor thing compared to the reality. Really to grasp this meaning would be the finite compassing the Infinite. We cannot take God wholly into ourselves, but God can take us wholly into Himself. The finite cannot comprehend the Infinite, but the Infinite can comprehend the finite. The realization which is given to the loftiest saint of our relation to God is but a faint, symbolic gesture compared with that relation as it really is—that is, as God sees it. No wonder St. Paul cried, as it were in an ecstasy, " Eye hath not seen, nor ear heard, neither have entered into the heart of man, the things which God hath prepared for them that love him. But God hath revealed them unto us by his Spirit: for the Spirit searcheth all things, yea, the deep things of God." [1]

And all this is the product of the divine love for us poor sinners. Sursum corda! Let us lift up our hearts, crying, " Behold what manner of love the Father hath bestowed upon us, that we should be called the sons of God, and we are." [2]

IV

Let us consider what is this life of union with God which He has prepared for us. In baptism we were made members of Christ, who is very God, organically one with Him as the branch is one with the vine to which it belongs. It was on the occasion of His institution of the Holy Eucharist, the great and continuing Sacrament of union between God and man, and therefore between man and man, that He said, " I am the vine, ye are the branches." [3]

St. Paul carries on the same teaching with a like simile in his epistle to the Romans. He says, " Thou being a wild olive tree wert grafted in among them "—that is, among the true branches—" and with them partakest of the root and fatness of the olive tree." [4] The life of the tree flows into the engrafted branch, and their life becomes one. The root is the origin and source of the tree as the Godhead is the root and origin of Christ, the true Vine. When we are grafted into Him, we then become partakers of the divine Nature as the branch becomes partaker of the nature of the vine. But partaking of the nature of the root must issue in bearing fruit, and so we become partakers also of the fatness of the tree, and this is the participation in the life and work and merits of Christ. Through the operation of His life in us we, like the engrafted branch, " partake of the root and fatness thereof."

[1] 1 Cor. ii. 9.   [2] 1 St. John iii. 1.
[3] St. John xv. 5.   [4] Rom. xi. 17.

St. John gives us the same truth in the simple, unargued statement, " He that hath the Son hath the life; and he that hath not the Son of God hath not the life." [1] The original of this passage places the definite article *the* before the word life, implying that the gift is not just life in general, but " the life " which is the life of Christ Himself, of Him who said, " I am the Life." [2] In another place St. John says, " God is love; and he that abideth in love abideth in God, and God in him." [3]

No question of similarity arises here. The life we live is not *like unto* that of the divine Son; it is the *identical* life of the Son, just as the life of the branch is the identical life of the vine.

If we will be careful always to think of this discourse in the Upper Room as a sermon, as we might call it to-day, delivered at the first Eucharist, perhaps light will be thrown upon many of its passages. This should be kept in mind especially when we read such passages as St. John xv. 1 to 17, inclusive, and Chapter xvii, in which we find the great proclamation, the supreme revelation, of the fundamental and eternal relationship established by the New Covenant between God and man, which relationship we can possess only through union with Christ's Sacred Humanity, as He Himself said, " No man cometh unto the Father, but by me." [4]

The Beloved Disciple's narrative of the happenings of that night omits any notice of the Institution of the Eucharist, because his Gospel was, as we know from its history, written only to supplement the narrative of the three other Evangelists. He rarely included in his Gospel anything that appears in the others, as his explicit intention in writing was to supplement, not to duplicate, their accounts. But the whole of our Lord's instruction on that night to His disciples fits into the context of the Eucharist.

This is notably the case in those passages in which He insists again and again upon the principle of unity between the soul and God, and upon that love which must exist between Christians as the inescapable consequence of their union with God, and therefore with each other. After instituting the Eucharist and giving them their First Communion, He prays that they may be one in Him even as He, the Eternal Son, is one with the Eternal Father: " As thou, Father, art in me and I in thee, that they may also be one in us . . . I in them, and thou in me, that they may be made perfect in one." [5]

Our Lord, in the great high-priestly prayer in St. John xvii,

---

[1] 1 St. John v. 12. [2] St. John xiv. 6. [3] 1 St. John iv. 16.
[4] St. John xiv. 6. [5] St. John xvii. 21–23.

speaks of the unity between the Father, Himself, and His people, as that which will enable the world to know " that thou hast sent me, and hast loved them even as thou hast loved me." This last sentence is the supreme revelation of the love of God to man. Nothing in the New Testament goes, or can go, beyond this assurance. If we are one with Christ, the Father will love us with the same love with which He, the Father, in the bosom of the Holy Trinity, loves God the only begotten Son. We are caught up into the cycle of the infinite love which constitutes the life and the oneness of the Trinity. We are in the Son, and He is in us. Therefore, the Father sees the Son and those who are in union with Him in a single glance. He cannot see the Son without at the same time seeing those who are one with this divine Son; nor can He see them other than in the Son as one with Him. He cannot accept His own Incarnate Son without by the same act accepting those whom He sees to be one with the Son. Here we see the manner " wherein he hath made us accepted in the beloved." [1]

But we are not to think that the Father stands apart, as it were, and sees us in the Son as though that were something outside of Himself. Our Lord made this clear when, speaking of certain mysterious aspects of His work for those who believe on Him, He said it was done " in order that they all may be one, even as thou, O Father, art in me and I in thee, in order that they may be one in us." From the essential nature of the Godhead, he who is one with the Son must also, of necessity, be one with the Father and the Holy Ghost—that is, with the whole Godhead; and since there is but one love in the Godhead, if we are one with Christ, the Father must love us with the same love with which He loves His Son and the Holy Ghost. This, as we have said, is the supreme revelation of the fact and mode of the love of God for man.

This union is achieved, first of all, in the sacrament of baptism, as we have already said, but it can be maintained only through the habitual receiving of the Body and Blood of Christ in the Eucharist— that is, the continual receiving of the Humanity of Christ as indissolubly united to His Divinity. This our Lord declared when He said, " Except ye eat the flesh of the Son of man, and drink his blood, ye have no life in you." [2] The form of the verbs " eat " and " drink " in this passage implies a habitual course. That which they were to receive was not to be His suffering Humanity, or Humanity girt about with infirmity, as in the days of His earthly pilgrimage, but Himself, in His human and divine fulness, risen,

---

[1] Eph. i. 6.   [2] St. John vi. 53.

F

ascended, and glorified at His Father's right hand. These words reflect the same teaching which our Lord gave when He said, "Whoso eateth my flesh and drinketh my blood hath eternal life. . . . He that eateth my flesh and drinketh my blood abideth in me and I in him. As the living Father hath sent me, and I live by the Father: so he that eateth me, even he shall live by me." [1] As the soul, present in the body, gives life to the body, and without the soul the body is dead, so is Christ the life of our souls, and without Christ the soul is dead. The Spanish mystics were fond of the thought, and they repeatedly use the expression, "Christ, a soul unto my soul."

v

Thus far we have spoken chiefly of the part that God plays in the work of our redemption and sanctification, but God does not work alone. We have our part to perform continually after the divine life has entered into our souls. What part, then, have we in securing the continuance of this life of union? St. Thomas Aquinas gives us four points, which he has called "The Mode of Perfect Love," [2] by conforming to which we enter more and more perfectly into union with God.

First, refer every purpose and action to God. Before acting, ask yourself the question, Is it pleasing to Him? Pray for guidance, lifting the heart to Him at the moment the question arises. Having done this, use the best judgment you have, and go boldly forward if it be necessary to act immediately. If there is doubt, give God, not self, the benefit of the doubt. Remember there are always three answers to our prayers which are possible. God may say, Yes; He may say, No; He may say, Wait. It is not always ours "to know the times or the seasons, which the Father hath put in his own power." [3] When the converted Saul, ready to consecrate himself to the utmost to our Lord, asked the question, "What wilt thou have me to do?" [4] the reply was quite different from that which he expected. His impetuous spirit was eager to do something immediately. He had never brooked delay. Trained as he was in the belief in the necessity of the works of the law, he wished now to work somewhat for God. There was much of self in this demand to be told what to do. But our Lord was to teach him better things. The divine reply was a denial of his petition. He was to be taught the lesson of patient waiting upon God. Many a

[1] St. John vi. 54–57.   [2] St. Thomas, *De Perf. Vit. Sp.*, Ch. 5.
[3] Acts i. 7.   [4] Acts ix. 6.

soul, unwilling to tarry the Lord's leisure, has been led into sin by an unbridled eagerness to do something for God. So the answer was given him: " Arise, and go into the city, and it shall be told thee what thou must do." [1] He knew not how long the delay would be, but with instant obedience he complied, and his obedience was the earnest of the great work he was to do for the glory of God and the building up of His Church, of the great things he was to suffer for His Name's sake. The Spanish mystic, Juan Falconi, sums it up when he says, " Let us walk in total resignation, never desiring more than God desires for us." [2] This was the divine testing of the great apostle of the Gentiles. His whole future career hung on how he would react to this divine command. Had he implied that here and now he must do some great thing, his vocation would have been at an end. We cannot lay down conditions and terms on which we will work for God. But just because he was ready humbly to obey, having no regard for consequences, for even his own yearning for the divine service, God was able three days later to say to Ananias, " He is a chosen vessel unto me, to bear my name before the Gentiles, and kings, and the children of Israel: for I will show him how great things he must suffer for my name's sake." [3]

Having referred every question to God, and having acted as He guided us, we must then offer our action to Him. Such sincere offering will fill out all our inadequacies, and though we may often find later that our judgment was not wholly wise so far as the action itself was concerned, we need have no fear. God asks only humility, and a pure intention of heart, not perfection of judgment. We can trust Him to overrule and correct as He sees it to be necessary.

VI

The second rule for the perfect life of union with God is to subject the intellect to Him, which is only another way of saying that we must obey the divine command to love the Lord our God " with all our mind." [4] This means that every thought is to be brought into captivity to the Holy Spirit, and this, in the last analysis, is to govern our life by reason. Love is the only reasonable basis of life. In whatever sphere, life without love is contrary to reason, and all human experience shows that it can lead only to chaos and destruction. St. Bernard says, " God is supreme wisdom,

[1] Acts ix. 6. [2] Juan Falconi, In Peers, *op. cit.*, Vol. II, p. 364.
[3] Acts ix. 15-16. [4] St. Matt. xxii. 37.

and He is therefore to be loved wisely, as well as tenderly." Our exercise of love embraces in its action all the rules and lessons and practices of perfect wisdom. By cultivating in our daily thoughts, words, and deeds the spirit of love, we make it possible for the wisdom of God to operate within us, and every such operation makes us more and more wise with the wisdom of God, and insures an ever-developing rightness of judgment in all things. Many of us have observed by experience that our natural judgment is not good. We have learned to distrust it. But there is a profound sense of comfort in the assurance that if we go forward, submitting our judgment to the best of our ability to the guidance of the Holy Spirit, it is inevitable that, as time passes, our judgment will be more and more perfected; and, in the meantime, imperfect and blundering as it may be, God will never allow it to lead us into sin, however we may fall into mistakes. We shall be able to depend on it, not because it, in itself, is reliable, but because we have yielded ourselves wholly to a Guide, who cannot, and will not, allow us to go astray. We shall find an ever clearer answer to the prayer which is so constantly on our lips, that we might " have a right judgment in all things." [1]

VII

Thirdly, in order to deepen our union with God, we are to consecrate all of our affections to Him. That is " Thou shalt love the Lord thy God with all thy heart." [2] Love lies not in the emotions, but in the will, and our Lord has promised that those who will to do His will shall be shown the way of love and service, and shall be given the wisdom to walk in it with steadfast faithfulness.[3]

Love is cultivated by acts of love—that is to say, by definitely and deliberately thinking loving thoughts, speaking loving and kindly words, and performing deeds of love and kindliness. As St. Francis de Sales teaches, we learn to love by loving, as we learn to speak by speaking, to walk by walking, to study by studying.[4] There can be no question that if we compel ourselves to think, and say, and do, loving things, and divert the attention persistently from those which are unloving, love will increase within us until it possesses us wholly. If we thus love God and our fellow-man, the continuance and growth within us of the life and power of Christ, who is God, will be assured. The will to love produces love. The cynical, jaded spirit of Byron flung out the rhetorical question,

---

[1] Collect for Pentecost.   [2] St. Matt. xxii. 37.   [3] St. John vii. 17.
[4] Camus, *Spirit of St. Francis de Sales*, I, § ii (Lear Ed.).

" Is human love the growth of human will? " assuming, of course, a negative answer.   What the poet meant was not love, but passion, indulged without check or restraint, a mere impulse to which free rein is given to run its course on the lowest, and often most debased, emotional levels.   But if by love we mean the holy gift of power which has its source in God, and can function only through the Holy Spirit, we can readily see that its growth does indeed depend upon the human will, co-operating with God.   He who persistently wills to love God and his fellow-men will be given the actual ability to love in ever-expanding capacity, and this love will lead on to a deeper and more effective union with God.   He who has not this will to love will not be able to receive the gift of love which God offers to all men as a free and precious endowment, but which He forces upon none.

VIII

Every other rule and principle of the perfect life in God grows naturally out of the life of love.   If we can consecrate all our affections to God, loving Him and all others in Him, for Him, and according to Him, there will be no relation in life which will not be under the unifying and governing power of love.   The divine love will take everything into its infinite embrace.   In a great passage, St. Augustine describes for us this divine process by which God, loving us with an everlasting love, claims all our love for Himself.   He says, " When our Lord commands us to love Him with all our heart and soul and mind, He leaves no part of our life unclaimed.   He does not allow place for the enjoyment of anything apart from Himself.   Whatsoever offers itself to be loved, is carried on in the full-flowing tide of love to God alone. . . . The soul refers all the love of itself and of others to the love of God which suffers not the smallest ripple to turn aside that would diminish the fulness of its flow onwards to God." [1]

This will bring the crown of perfect union with God without possibility of failure.   In the beginning of our life of love this depends upon the conscious direction of the will, but repeated acts of love speedily produce the interior habit of love, so that we shall be able always to respond swiftly on every occasion with aspirations of love, Godward and manward.   Life will then become one steady current of love, and this is the perfect life, the life of union with God, His very life of love being lived within us, and our life lived wholly within Him, we one with Him, and He one with us.

[1] St. Augustine, *De Doctrina Christiana*, I. 22 ;   Migne, P. L., Tom. 34, Col. 27.

This longing for union with God seems to be a consequence of the primitive revelation given to men by God in the beginning of the life of the race. Everywhere we find it. However men may have debased themselves through sin, however they may, in their ignorance, have built up for themselves degrading systems of religion, God has not permitted them to lose the longing and desire for Himself. Where men have been faithful in following the light that has been left to them, though they know little of the true revelation of His love, He gives the vision of what their union with Himself means, and also the grace to rejoice in this vision. Jalal-ed-din-Rumi, a Persian mystic, who had no revelation given him in his faith beyond the dark Allah of Islam, gives us a parable of the working of the unitive power of the divine love:

" A lover once came by night before the door of his beloved, and knocked. Then she cried, ' Who knocks there? ' And he answered, ' It is I.' She did not open the door, but said harshly, ' Away with you.' Then the young man went abroad, and wandered through the world, until love, with its irresistible strength, drove him back to the abode of his beloved. And he knocked again, gently and softly, with shy hope. And again the question of his beloved rang out, ' Who knocks there? ' And he answered, ' It is thou who standest once again before the door.' Then the one whom he adored opened to him, with the words, ' Enter, beloved, my little chamber is not large enough for two, but since thou art nought but I, there is room in the chamber, and at the board.' " [1]

The passionate longing for God does not arise out of the natural heart of man; it is the everlasting love of God which allures the soul, and draws it into the innermost Holy of Holies of the divine Being. He is " the Hound of Heaven " who pursues man, and will not let him go. His cry is ever, " I have loved thee with an everlasting love "; [2] and the Holy Spirit Himself prepares for us the only answer the soul, smitten with love, can give—" O knit my heart unto thee that I may fear thy name." [3]

O Lord of love ; draw me into the deeps of the ocean of Thy love. In that deep calm, unbroken and profound, may neither sound nor motion of the world assail my heart to draw my love from Thee. O that I might be stilled in Thee alone : no knowledge, no desire, nought to ask, nought to seek— only to love.

[1] Quoted in *Prayer: A Study in the History and Psychology of Religion*, by Friedrich Heiler, pp. 190–191 (trans. by McComb).
[2] Jer. xxxi. 3.   [3] Ps. lxxxvi. 11.

Grace alone can make us participate really and formally in the Deity, in the intimate life of Him whose children we are by grace . . . because grace in us is the radical principle of essentially divine operations, that will ultimately consist in seeing God immediately, as He sees Himself, and in loving Him as He loves Himself. Grace is the seed of glory.

REGINALD GARRIGOU-LAGRANGE.

Grace perfects nature. It does not destroy it.

ST. THOMAS AQUINAS.

CHAPTER VI

THE WORK OF DIVINE GRACE

I

In considering the Christian vocation, we are to keep ever in mind that without God man can do nothing. We have nothing that we have not received. " When He crowns our merits, He does nothing more than crown His own gifts to us." [1] Even our co-operation with Him cannot be regarded as an independent and co-ordinate factor in the prosecution of our vocation. Throughout the entire process of salvation, in its beginning, in its progress, in its final consummation, the initiative lies wholly with God. Even our desire to work along with Him has its initial impulse, as well as its continuance, not primarily in any human will, but in the loving will of God alone. We could not respond if He did not give us the call. Nor could we, however deeply conscious of His call, make even the first movement towards responding, unless God gave us the power to do so. Our freedom of will to respond to God, or to reject His call, is in itself a gift from Him. Man's liberty to serve, or to refuse to serve, is never to be thought of as a primary and independent liberty, inherent in our nature. It is a freedom with which we are endowed by Him, and we could neither possess it, nor have the power to use it after it came into our possession, save by the free and gracious act of God. Every act of the human will has its source in the eternal decree by which He created man in His own image, and by an act of His own will, endowed him with the power of freedom, and also with the capacity to use that freedom, man to be free even as God is free. Therefore, that which sets the will moving, and keeps it on its steadfast way to God, is nothing less than God and His grace working in us. But for Him we would have no power either to respond to Him or to turn away from Him.

In this discussion it is a wholesome thing to keep in mind that, just because it is a great mystery, it is difficult to express the exact meaning of grace. We have no English word which covers its meaning, nor, for that matter, have either the Greek or Latin tongues. Accommodated words are used in this connection in all

[1] " Cum Deus coronat merita nostra nihil aliud coronet quam munera sua." St. Augustine, *Epist.* cxciv. 19; Migne, P. L., Tom. 33, Col. 880.

three languages. But the difficulty here is no greater than what we find in attempting a terminology of the Trinity or the Incarnation. It is, however, fundamental to our understanding of our relationship to God for us to keep in mind that what we call grace is a gift of spiritual power of which we, of ourselves, are totally helpless to lay hold.

The English word *grace* is derived from the Latin *gratia*. Every form of this word, and every shade of its meaning, support the fundamental idea of this mystery, since they imply that which is given without any sort of deserving in the recipient. This is witnessed to by the fact that such English words as gratuitous, gratuity, and several others, which imply a gift which is not owed to the recipient, and which he has no right to claim or demand, are derived from the Latin *gratia*. It is true that God requires us to co-operate with Him if we are to receive grace; but our co-operation, however complete it may be, does not, in any sense or degree whatever, make us deserving of the gift. By co-operation we only, by the direct help of God, create the condition which makes it possible for us to receive His gifts of grace. To use the comparison which has been common for centuries amongst spiritual teachers, the dryness of the wood does not cause it to burn, but is the condition which enables the fire when it is applied to the wood to perform its function. The corresponding Greek word χάρις, which is used everywhere in the New Testament, carries with it the same meaning. Whether it conveys the idea of gifts of grace and beauty of mind or body, or spiritual gifts, it implies always a gift which cannot possibly be merited.

St. Bernard, in common with all the Church's great teachers, shows us that " grace is necessary to salvation, but free will is equally so; grace in order to give salvation, free will in order to receive it. . . . Therefore, we should not attribute part of the good work to grace, and part to free will. It is performed in its entirety by the common and inseparable action of both, entirely by grace and entirely by free will, but everything has its source in God and in the free gift of His grace." [1]

Let us add one saying more from the masters, and this from the gentle and always gracious saint of Annecy. St. Francis de Sales writes, " The chains of grace are so powerful, and yet so sweet, they they allure the heart, but never shackle our liberty." [2]

[1] St. Bernard, *De Gratia et Libero Arbitrio*, Chapters i and xiv; Migne, P. L., Tom. 182, Col. 1002 and 1027.
[2] St. Francis de Sales, *Treatise on the Love of God*, Bk. ii, Ch. 12.

II

Here, as always, man must co-operate. God honours man by giving him a share in the work of his own salvation and redemption, although his participation in it depends on the divine activity within his soul. Man's part is not necessarily a conscious co-operation in every detailed instance. His intention to co-operate may be virtual—that is, it may have all the validity, all the essential qualities, of the will-to-co-operate, without the conscious, formulated act of the will in each case. The continued, unbroken attention and advertence of the intellect is not required at every moment in order to maintain the effective intention and attention. It is as though a man on a journey had his mind engaged with other thoughts en route, absorbed, it may be, in reading or conversation, although his intention to arrive at the destination by the use of the right means persists. Such virtual intention is sufficient for the living of the Christian life adequately, provided one uses faithfully and intelligently the appointed means, as the traveller uses the right means of transportation.

The grace necessary to the soul is a free gift of spiritual power from God. Not to use it is to lose it. This is the law which governs every gift of strength or power, whether it be physical, intellectual or spiritual. Neglect its use and it will soon become atrophied. It must be exercised in order either to be maintained or developed.

III

All the work of grace looks to the achieving of the atonement, of complete reconciliation of man with God. In short, the work of grace is the work of applying the atoning merits of Christ to the individual soul. It will be well at this point to consider the mystery of the atoning work of Christ, and how it is to be applied to His people.

Most of our theological terms are derived from Latin or Greek, as these were the languages commonly in use during the ages when the great truths of revelation were being clarified. But the English tongue in recent centuries has supplied one of the most essential of these terms—namely, the word Atonement; that is, the at-one-ment, the reconciliation of sinners with God. The word seems to have been coined by Tyndale, and was first used in his translation of the Bible in 1526.[1] In rendering 2 Corinthians v. 18, he used

---

[1] Consult *Oxford English Dictionary*.

the expression, " to preach the atonement." The Authorized
Version translates it, " the ministry of reconciliation." There is
no difference of meaning between the two. Atonement and reconciliation mean the same thing. In the Authorized Version of
the New Testament the word atonement occurs but once. This is
is in Romans v. 11, where it is said that we " joy in God through our
Lord Jesus Christ by whom we have now received the atonement ";
but in the margin the word *reconciliation* is given as an alternate
reading. The corresponding Greek word is used frequently
(καταλλαγή), but in every other place it is translated by the word
reconciliation.

The work of atonement, or reconciliation, was not only the
satisfaction which Christ made for man's sin on the cross, but it
includes the entire work of the God-Man: His Incarnation and all
that belongs to His Incarnate life, His thirty-three years of teaching,
His suffering and rejection through His whole ministry, His Cross
and Passion, His death and resurrection, His ascension, without
which as man He could not have opened the Kingdom of Heaven to
all believers; His sending the Holy Ghost to dwell in His people
individually in their souls, and corporately in the Church. It
involves all the work of the Holy Spirit through the ages in stimulating souls to the use of the Sacraments, and to prayer and good
works, and in every aid given in times of temptation and trial.
Everything that Christ does through the Spirit for souls is a part of
His work of reconciling man to His Father, but it is all given force
and efficacy by the Passion and death of Christ.

All that Christ has done, and all that He is doing in heaven at
this present time, is a part of His work of reconciliation. There are
those, not a few of them people of earnest faith and devout life, who,
having a zeal not according to knowledge, think of the Incarnation,
and our Lord's subsequent life on earth, including the Passion on
Calvary, as historical events, tremendous in their meaning, but
which are, nevertheless, happenings of the past, having no connection with us save as an example and a glorious historical memory of
what the goodness and mercy of a forgiving God wrought for our
salvation. But what have these events to do with us to-day? How
are the benefits of them to be applied to us ? How do we appropriate
this salvation to ourselves?

IV

These questions bring us to the Sacraments, which were ordained
by Christ to be the means and instruments through the use of which

He was to transmit to His people His grace, the power and strength of His life as the God-Man. We have thought that the human powers of Christ are transmitted to us. In the exercise of these powers we learn the method, and develop the capacity for living the Christian life. Through the Sacraments all the powers of His Sacred Humanity are at our disposal. His Incarnate Life is made our life through these sacramental means, and all that He did, or does now, in that Incarnate Life, is for our salvation and sanctification. The Fathers were accustomed to speak of the Sacraments as the extension of the Incarnation—that is, the extension across the ages of the life of Christ, the God-Man, to the souls of His people.

Baptism is the initial sacrament. In it we are grafted into Christ so that His life comes into us as the life of the vine enters into the branch when it is engrafted into it. The necessity of this sacrament is set forth by Christ in His saying, " Except a man be born of water and of the Spirit, he cannot enter into the kingdom of God." [1]

The other Sacrament required for salvation is the Holy Eucharist, which is the perpetuation across the ages of the virtue and power of His Cross and Passion, and is the Food of Life which if any man eat he will live for ever. Again it was our Lord who said, " Except ye eat the flesh of the Son of man and drink his blood, ye have no life in you." [2] The Apostle St. Paul tells us that " as often as ye eat this bread and drink this cup, ye do show the Lord's death till he come." [3] The Eucharist provides not only for the feeding upon the sacrificed Lamb of God, but it is the perpetuation of the Sacrifice of Calvary, the continual presentation, the pleading of it, before the Father. The active, living virtue of this Sacrifice did not come to an end when our Lord died at three o'clock on the first Good Friday. The Scripture teaches us that He rose from the dead, and ascended into heaven, and there, in His great Intercession, He pleads that Sacrifice before God for the souls of men. We on earth, in the service which He instituted and commanded to be offered, also plead the same Sacrifice before the Father. The language of the Liturgy makes this clear. The priest at the altar consecrates the bread and wine in accordance with our Lord's command, to be His Body and Blood, the living, glorified Body which is at the Father's right hand. Our Lord is then really and objectively present under the veils of bread and wine. This presence is objective in the sense that the fact of it is not, and cannot be, conditioned, or affected at all, by man's belief or unbelief in it. He being thus

[1] St. John iii. 5.   [2] St. John vi. 53.   [3] 1 Cor. xi. 26.

present, we offer Him to the Father, not merely lest we should forget His merciful work of love, but as a Sacrifice, not presented before the people, but before the Father. The priest, speaking for himself and for the people, recites the solemn prayer of oblation immediately on the completion of the consecration:

" According to the institution of Thy dearly beloved Son, our Saviour Jesus Christ, we, Thy humble servants, do celebrate and make here, before Thy Divine Majesty, with these Thy holy gifts, which we now offer unto Thee, the memorial Thy Son hath commanded us to make." [1]

In one of the great liturgical hymns there is set forth in three brief lines perhaps as complete a statement of the truth of the Eucharistic Sacrifice as has ever been produced:

> " We here present, we here spread forth to Thee,
> That only Offering perfect in Thine eyes,
> The One True, Pure, Immortal Sacrifice." [2]

It would not be possible to describe any sacrifice save the actual Sacrifice of our Lord on Calvary in these words. The Sacrifice of the Cross is not a mere event in history which occurred some nineteen hundred years ago. Not only in that ancient day and time, but " here " and " now," as we use our time-terminology, we present to the Father this offering of the Lamb of God, slain on the cross for the salvation and sanctification of His people. This is what we do as often as we eat this Bread and drink this Cup in obedience to the command, " Do this as a Memorial of Me." The Sacrifice of the Eucharist is a real, not a symbolic, sacrifice because it is an actual perpetuation of the Sacrifice of the Son of God on Calvary, and is identical with it. It is not a repetition, for that Sacrifice was offered once for all. This " One, True, Pure, Immortal Sacrifice " which was made on Calvary, Christ pleads continually before the Father in heaven on our behalf, and we plead the same Sacrifice at the altar on earth for the glory of God, and on behalf of our needs. The heavenly pleading and the earthly pleading meet and become one in Calvary. Time and space are eliminated in these Mysteries of God's ordaining, for there is no time or space with God. As He does nothing in the future, likewise

---

[1] This prayer of Oblation is not in the English Prayer Book, but it appears in many other Anglican Liturgies. It was adopted by the Church of England in the Prayer Book of 1928, but its use was forbidden by the civil authority. Therefore, although not in actual use, it is the authorized teaching of the Church of England.

[2] William Bright.

He does nothing in the past, His whole life and work constitutes an eternal IS. "Thy years are one To-day; thy To-day is Eternity."[1]

Not only in baptism, not only in the Holy Sacrifice of the altar, and in Holy Communion, the feeding on the sacrificed Lamb, but in every other Sacrament there is extended to the souls of men the virtue and efficacy of the Incarnation and the Atonement; indeed, of all else that Christ does and has, according to their need, and to the requirements of the life and labour to which God calls them. He is, in His Sacred Humanity, "full of grace," and we of this fulness receive with every reception of a Sacrament, according to our measure and need. The revealed way of receiving the grace of our Lord Jesus Christ is primarily through Sacraments.[2] The Sacraments are the means through which the grace of the reconciliation to God, which is necessary, is applied to us. Once received, grace grows through prayer and good works; but as the first reception of it was a sacramental gift, so the continuance of grace is the sacramental life, which is tantamount to saying that the whole life of the Christian, his every thought, word and action, is essentially sacramental in its character, and if this sacramental character were to fail for a moment, all these things would instantly cease to be of any value or avail.

This idea of the continuance of the sacramental life is not left by the Church to be implied, but she has ordained that it be expressed explicitly again and again, and with emphasis, in every act of administering the Sacraments. Immediately after the act of baptizing a child, the priest prays " that he may continue Christ's faithful soldier and servant unto his life's end." In the laying on of hands in confirmation, the Bishop prays for the candidate that " he may continue Thine for ever," and after receiving Holy Communion the prayer is made that " we may continue in that holy fellowship."

In this reconciliation to God through these sacramental means

---

[1] St. Augustine, *Confessions*, i. 7; Migne, P. L., Tom. 32, Col. 665.

[2] While not undertaking to discuss the subject here, we must keep in mind that sacramental grace comes to the soul through accepting the Covenant of Christ and living in accordance with its terms, as they are set forth in the teaching of the Church and of the Scriptures. He who knows the terms of the Covenant and refuses to comply with them cannot expect God to make an exception for him and bestow upon him the grace which he would have had had he been obedient to the revelation. But while God binds us to the use of the sacraments, He does not bind Himself. He may, and, without doubt does, bestow, in ways not revealed to us, grace sufficient for their sanctification on those who, through no fault of their own, do not know His revelation, provided they are faithful to what they have. These are the " uncovenanted graces " which the loving justice of God gives to those who faithfully live up to the light given to them by Him who " lighteth every man that cometh into the world."

it is not contemplated that there will ever again be a breach between God and the soul. In the administration of these sacraments no reference is made to such a possibility. St. Paul, therefore, must be construed as speaking sacramentally when he says, " God hath reconciled us to himself by Jesus Christ," and again when he says, " God was in Christ, reconciling the world unto himself." [1] In these passages, and in many others, it must be noted well that we are told that it was God who did the work of reconciling. He it was who procured the at-one-ment of man with Himself, a re-creation, as it were, of the soul. Our part is that of co-operating with Him in the continual application to ourselves of the results and merits of that Atonement. He it is who gives the sacramental reconciliation; it is we who receive it. In no passage in Scripture is there any intimation that God needed to be reconciled to man. Man needed to be reconciled to God, God never withdrew Himself from man. It was man who broke the bond of unity with God, and the Eternal Son took our nature just in order that through Him as the God-Man this unity might be restored. The initiative lay always with God, and it was ever a glad, a loving initiative, grudging nothing, not even His own life.

v

It might not in the nature of things have been absolutely necessary for Christ to have wrought the Atonement and recon-ciliation through suffering. But He suffered because God willed to use this method of suffering to crown the work of Atonement. The basis of the Atonement lies in the Incarnation, in the act of God becoming man. Whether He would have willed to become Incarnate had man never broken the bond, had there never been any sin for which to atone, is a matter of speculation which does not concern us here. But it was the will of God that the Eternal Son made Man should by suffering redeem the world. " It pleased the Father that in him (that is, in Christ) should all fulness dwell; and, having made peace through the Blood of the Cross (that is, through the sufferings of the Incarnate Son), by him to reconcile all things unto himself." [2] In the Messianic prophecy of the Passion we find the same note: " It pleased the Lord to bruise him." [3]

In the act of the Incarnation, Man, in the Sacred Humanity of Christ, did actually become one with God, the Second Person of the Indivisible Trinity, and, therefore, became one with the

---

[1] 2 Cor. v. 18–19.   [2] Col. i. 19–20.   [3] Isa. liii. 10.

Godhead. The Man, Christ Jesus, the second Adam, perfect and complete Man in all respects, was wholly united to God; and the purpose of His entire life-work, both in His suffering life on earth and in His glorified life now in heaven, is to bring all other human souls into such perfect union with Himself that they may enjoy a complete reconciliation with God; for he who is at one with Christ is one with God, for Christ is God. That there was only one human soul who at the moment of the Incarnation was made one with God, does not change the fact that man was in reality reconciled to God. To question this would be like questioning the fact of the Atonement on the ground that while millions have rejoiced in its fruits, others have chosen to reject these fruits.

However man may speculate on the subject, there is no question that this work of atonement is the reversal of the fall of man; it is the washing away of every sin, the deliverance from the bondage of Satan, the reconciliation of the human race to God, if men will but accept that reconciliation.

Our Lord Christ completed this reconciliation once for all, and offers it to us, but we have to lay hold of it, and this work on our part by the help of the Spirit is not done once for all. It is progressive and continuous as long as we live in this world. By baptism we enter into a *state* of reconciliation with God, but there are degrees of perfection of reconciliation within that state, somewhat as one may be in the state of being a scholar, though there are varying degrees of scholarship. So it is with the saints, by which we mean all those who have entered into and are progressing in the state of reconciliation with God. Speaking of them, St. Paul compares them with the stars, and says that " one star differeth from another star in glory," [1] but none the less they are all stars of God.

VI

Grace is always to be thought of as an objective moral and spiritual force infused into the soul by God. It alone enables us to become " partakers of the divine nature." [2] It is the principle within us of all the divine operations, which operations, if we do not offset them by sin, will issue for us in the glorious vision of God, enabling us to see God in some such manner as He sees Himself, to know Him as He knows Himself, to love Him as He loves Himself, and to rejoice in Him for eternity. Grace is not given for any mere adornment of the spiritual man, but for purely utilitarian purposes.

---

[1] 1 Cor. xv. 41.　　　　[2] 2 St. Peter i. 4.

G

The soul in grace is indeed full of a God-given beauty, of His own beauty which He imparts to us; in imparting grace to us, the Holy Spirit seals us with the very seal of the Holy Trinity. But in this life all the grace that is given is actually needed in order to fulfil the purposes of God. There is no grace which can be said to be superfluous if our vocation as Christians is to be fulfilled as God intends it to be. Says St. Francis de Sales, warning us against frittering away the love and grace which are bestowed upon us: " We have not nearly so much love as we stand in need of. We fall infinitely short of having enough wherewith to love God," [1] although God in His great compassion overlooks this lack, and assures us that it will be supplied if we are faithful in using the gifts He gives. Its faithful use will generate further grace.

This is the case because the divine purpose and vocation for every soul is high and glorious beyond the power of the human mind to conceive. When the apostle said, " Eye hath not seen, nor ear heard, neither have entered into the heart of man, the things which God hath prepared for them that love him," [2] he was not speaking of the special gifts which the love of God might prepare for one or another, but of the total vocation which He has bestowed upon every Christian soul. This vocation can find its ultimate fulfilment only in the bosom of the Holy Trinity, amid the infinite activities of the innermost mysteries of the divine Being. In a sense and degree which we cannot comprehend, we are to be, indeed are now, partakers of these mysteries. When we realize that we must progressively and continuously for eternity participate in the Being of the Infinite God, we can see that every grace possible in this life, and every possible glory in the life to come, are essentially necessary to the carrying on of the vocation to which we are called. Neither in time nor in eternity does God cease to give, or we cease to receive; therefore there can be nothing superfluous in the gifts which God makes to us. We have absolute need of every gift bestowed in order to carry out the purpose of God, and to fill the void in our souls, the void which is continually recurring with the ceaseless expansion of our capacity thus to participate in God, and which is being continually filled, as more and more we partake of the divine Nature.

VII

What we call divine grace is the life of God in the soul, the life which is nothing less than that of Father, Son, Spirit. " Grace is

---

[1] St. Francis de Sales, *Devout Life*, Pt. III, Ch. 18.   [2] 1 Cor. ii. 9.

really and formally a participation in the divine nature precisely in so far as it is divine, a participation in the Deity, in that which makes God God, in His intimate life. As rationality is what makes man a man, the Deity is the constituent essence of God, such as He is Himself. Grace is a mysterious participation in this essence. . . . But no created or creatable nature can resemble God exactly in so far as He is God. Grace alone can make us participate really and formally in the Deity, in the intimate life of Him whose children we are by grace . . . because grace is in us the radical principle of essentially divine operations, that will ultimately consist in seeing God immediately, as he sees Himself, and in loving Him as He loves Himself." [1]

It is this presence of the divine life which sanctifies the Christian. The soul is holy because God, who, through His infinite love, desires ever to abide in His people, is holy. It is as though when He comes to dwell in us, to each soul He says, as to His servant of old, " Be ye holy: for I am the Lord your God." [2] By this indwelling, the Holy Spirit transmits to the souls of men the same glowing dispositions of love, towards both God and man, as animate and govern the human soul of Christ, He according to His perfect nature, we according to the measure of our finite possibilities. The true disciple lives in Christ, for Christ, and according to Christ. And this indwelling is mutual, for Christ dwells also in the disciple in the plenitude of His sanctity and power, in the perfection of His ways, and in the holiness of His Spirit.

Herein lies a double gift: first, the gift to us of Himself, the very Triune Divinity Itself, which is the uncreated Gift; and second, the created gift of grace which is the effect of the presence of the Ever-Blessed Trinity within us, which Presence is possible only when we become one with Christ, who is one with this glorious and indivisible Trinity.

By this indwelling we are made sons of God by adoption; but it is more than adoption as we are accustomed to use that expression. The man who adopts a child goes through the legal forms which give that child the rights and privileges of sonship. But he cannot impart his own nature to such a son. Not so is it with the divine adoption. The apostles do not hesitate to claim for the Christian soul something more than adoption, even generation. " According to his abundant mercy he hath begotten us again unto a lively hope." [3] St. John assures us again and again that we are " born

---

[1] Garrigou-Lagrange, *Christian Perfection and Contemplation*, pp. 55–56.
[2] Lev. xx. 7.   [3] 1 St. Peter i. 3.

of God," [1] and when St. James says that " of his own will begat
he us with the word of truth," he does the startling thing of using
a Greek verb which means not the action of the father in begetting,
but that of the mother in bringing forth the child.[2]

VIII

Formal definitions of such principles must always be inadequate,
for the poverty of human language cannot measure up to the
richness of God's goodness, and of His loving revelation of Himself.
Keeping these overwhelming truths in mind, we may attempt the
following as a working definition of the created grace—that is, of
the sanctifying grace which dwells in the Sacred Humanity of
our Lord :

*Grace is the vital, divine principle of purification, illumination and
sanctification, which resides in the Sacred Humanity of Christ, and which is,
by the Holy Ghost, transmitted from Him to us, increased, and, if lost,
restored, by making us one with Him in love, through a worthy participation
in the Sacraments.*

Wherever God enters and dwells, there must dwell divine
purity, light, and holiness, for God is purity, He is light, He is
holiness, and these so-called attributes are one with His essential
Being.

Before going further, let us note the significance of the word
vital in this definition. In our ordinary speech we are accustomed
to use this word loosely to convey the idea that the thing in question
is of importance. It is used in no such loose sense here, but in its
original, strict, etymological sense. It signifies that which is
essential to life, as when we say that the heart is a vital organ of
the body. As the body quickly perishes when the heart within it
ceases to function, so without grace the soul is spiritually dead.

Let us not make the mistake, however, of thinking that this
vital principle upon which we depend can exist apart from Christ
Himself. It is transmitted to us in the same act by which we are
made one with Him who said, " I am the Life." [3] We cannot
receive anything that belongs to His being save in receiving Him,
all that He is and all that He has, so far as our capacity permits.
It is not possible that Christ should be divided, and if we receive
Him at all, we receive *totus Christus*, the total Christ.

We must also consider the word *divine* if we would grasp the full

---

[1] 1 St. John ii. 29; iii. 9; iv. 7; v. 1; v. 18.
[2] St. James i. 18.　　　　　　　　[3] St. John xiv. 6.

significance of what we mean by grace, its origin, its gift, and its operation. This vital principle dwelling in the Humanity of Christ, and transmitted from Him to all who are one with Him, has its origin in God. In the first place, it was infused into the Humanity of Christ at the moment of the Incarnation, by an act of God. It was transmitted to us from His Humanity by an act of God. Its maintenance in us, and the unbroken continuity of its work within us, depend wholly on God. Without the action of God within us it is not even possible for us to desire grace, much less to receive it, or in any sense or degree to make use of it after it has been received. As we have seen, the receiving of God, and the participation in the grace of God, are the same action. In the moment of baptism we were grafted into Christ, the God-Man. He was united to us and we to Him. In that instant His life became our life, just as the life of the vine becomes the life of the branch when it is engrafted into the vine. We were then made partakers of the divine Nature, and in that partaking we became sharers in this grace which resides in the Sacred Humanity of Incarnate God.

To use grace, we must at every moment do the thing which the Holy Ghost in our conscience urges us to do. This is not to be done, however, with strain and stress, as though we were working with our own weak power alone. It is God in all His power who comes to our help in the least of our labours. Luis de Ponte, with the boldness of the true mystic, tells us that man " becomes omnipotent through participation in all the virtues of God." [1] His power is not divided so that in helping us He uses much here and little there. In whatever God does, the totality of His omnipotence acts, for the Infinite cannot be divided. It is our part to yield ourselves to the Spirit. The energy of our whole being is to be concentrated upon keeping ourselves " in the Spirit," rather than driving ourselves to do, of ourselves, what we conceive, often wrongly and foolishly, to be the will of God. " As many as are led by the Spirit of God, they are the sons of God." [2] We are too prone to chart out a way for ourselves and then, having decided what we wish to do, call upon the Spirit to help us to achieve our own will. It is to be feared that not a few souls, through lack of knowledge, seek to live their lives on this principle, and for this reason their efforts are a painful struggle, and bear little or no fruit. Better far to throw our sails to the wind of the Holy Ghost, and let Him blow us whither He will. It will take all the application and power of

[1] Quoted by Professor Peers, in *Studies of the Spanish Mystics*, Vol. II, 339.
[2] Rom. viii. 14.

our wills to give the required co-operation with God by looking to the sails. We can and must leave the responsibility for wind and weather to the Holy Spirit, who bloweth where He listeth. The force and direction of the wind belong to Him. We have enough to do to make sure of our humble co-operation with God, without troubling ourselves with that for which we shall not be asked to render an account.

IX

Let us consider how this grace works. We receive this vital spiritual principle which dwells in the Sacred Humanity of our Lord, first, in baptism, and its power is deepened with the worthy reception of every other Sacrament. What, then, is the effect of this grace which God, in His love, so generously bestows upon the soul? The fullest answer to this question which we could possibly give would be only a partial and inadequate one. We know certain effects of grace, but its work is as hidden and mysterious as grace itself. God works secretly in our souls, and perhaps one of the great surprises which will be ours when we come to see Him face to face will lie in the revelation to us of His extraordinary love and goodness in that He has " translated us into the kingdom of his dear Son," [1] by which we have passed from our original state of sinfulness into His very Self, for if we are one with Christ we are, of necessity, where He is, and He is in the bosom of Godhead.

But, although we are incapable of knowing the fulness of the working of grace, God has, for our encouragement and edification, revealed to us much that goes on within us as the result of the gift of grace. First of all, there is the operation of the principle of purification. In the Sacrament of Baptism we receive, through being grafted into Him, the infusion of sanctifying grace, and the primary action of grace is to eliminate all that is within us which is contrary to the love of God. When grace comes in, instantly all mortal sin, and everything which belongs to it, vanish, as the darkness in a closely shuttered room when the windows are thrown wide open.

This principle of purification is not one which acts once for all. Its work is continuous. Once having been admitted to the soul, it begins the process of purification, which will last as long as life lasts. It cleanses more and more. In the great psalm of penitence, the fifty-first, the prayer of the royal penitent was that God would wash him more and more. Our translation, " wash me throughly,"

[1] Col. i. 13.

gives a suggestion of the meaning, but the Hebrew original implies repeated washings. There is never a time in this life when we cannot profit by the cleansing work of grace, but if its work is to be continuous, so must our penitence be continuous and abiding. The psalmist prayed for the continuous washing of his soul from guilt, and pleaded, as the ground of forgiveness, not only that he acknowledged his transgressions, but that " my sin is ever before me." Not that he brooded over sins which had already been for-given, but that he could never cease to be conscious of the fact that he had wilfully and grievously wounded the loving heart of God. This was ever before him, goading him on to the loving work of reparation, of filling up the measure of the past.

If we, in a spirit of abiding penitence, have our sins ever before us, God has promised by His prophet that He will cast all our sins behind His back.[1] Our penitent remembrance of our sins will cause Him to forget them. Nor, as we have thought, is there to be any morbid brooding over past sins. Rather do we keep them in mind with deep and loving joy, and ever-flowing gladness. This finds its source in the consciousness that the goodness and love of God have forgiven us, however black our sins may have been. He has restored to us the hope and assurance of the eternal destiny of glory that awaits us in union with Him in the innermost cycle of His Trinitarian mysteries, the mysteries which we cannot under-stand, but into which we can, and must, enter, and which we are to enjoy forever.

x

Further, the grace which comes by Jesus Christ is a principle of illumination. The darkness of sin done away, the effulgence of Him who said, " I am the light of the world," [2] shines more and more into our hearts.

Let us consider, first, that the light of grace illuminates the understanding, enabling us to " have a right judgment in all things,"[3] giving us power to know, to perceive, and to appreciate at its true value the divine purpose as it is revealed to us.

This enlightenment of the understanding does not mean, how-ever, that all perplexity will be cleared up. It is often God's will that we remain in doubt. Our understanding is none the less enlightened if it gives us perfect realization that God intends us to tarry His leisure, to wait patiently on Him. There is a difference between knowledge and understanding. I may know a fact which

---

[1] Isa. xxxviii. 17.   [2] St. John viii. 12.   [3] Collect for Pentecost.

I do not comprehend intellectually. Our Lord laid down this principle when He said to His disciples, " It is not for you to know the times or the seasons, which the Father hath put in His own power." [1] They were to wait at Jerusalem until they received the promise of the Father, even the Holy Spirit, although they knew not when or how the Spirit was to come, or even what the Holy Spirit was. Yet they had clear knowledge that God willed them to wait, and they acted upon this knowledge.

For all this we have to importune God in prayer. The Holy Ghost alone can do this work for us and within us. Even His omnipotence can effect this only if we respond to His leading and are faithful in our life of prayer and Sacrament, seeing to it that the grace thus given, the vital spiritual principle of the Humanity of our Lord, is actually used, so far as in us lies, for the accomplishment of good works.

But a second consideration awaits us. This principle of our Lord's humanity which is imparted to us works not only upon the understanding, but upon the will, which is the governing faculty of man. Unless it is aroused and inflamed to do something, to act definitely upon the knowledge and understanding we have, then this knowledge and understanding will be for our spiritual condemnation rather than for our help. So grace, acting upon the will, really enables us to do something definite in the service of God. If this vital principle of the spiritual life be in us, then Christ is in us, He in us and we in Him, and we are therefore able to bring the active quality of His goodness and power into all that we are, and into all that we do.

When we speak of actions, we do not mean external service only. It is the working of this same principle which enables us to develop our interior life, without which the external action will be of no avail. This grace gives us the capacity for prayer and for all that interior aspiration Godwards which is the spring and fountain out of which arise the exterior works for God's glory. But without the co-operation of the will, grace must fail. Grace is the indispensable element which makes the service of God possible. But mere possibilities count for nothing unless they are translated into actualities. A man is not accounted to be good because he *can* be good, but only when he *is* good in actual practice. This is a dual activity, that of God and man, working together in the activities of the divine life which is infused through the Sacraments.

[1] Acts i. 7.

XI

The third principle which is transmitted to us through union with the Sacred Humanity of our Lord is that of sanctification. The Holy Spirit is not given to Him by measure,[1] and when we are grafted into Him, and receive His life, we receive also the Spirit of God which dwells in Him in Its fulness. The Spirit is the Sanctifier, and the work of making us holy, which is nothing less than giving us a continually increasing participation in the holiness of God, goes on without ever ceasing, unless we erect a barrier to it by sin. Like everything else in the spiritual life, it must be ever progressing, or it will be on the decline.

This growth in holiness is not to be understood as a progress in ethical perfection, but as a mystical assimilation to the Godhead. It is not the consequence of anything that we do; it arises wholly from what God does. It is He, working within us, who produces holiness. We cannot plan holiness, nor can we, strictly speaking, seek after it. It lies in the loving work of God within us. We remove the obstacles, and He does the rest. It is ours to cleanse the vessel; it is His to fill it. "The more thou dost empty thy heart of that which is thine own, the more abundantly will I fill it with that which is Mine," [2] said our Lord to St. Catherine of Siena. "When we for love of God empty our souls of all affection for creatures, then does the great God immediately fill them with Himself." [3] But when we have learned to love God as we ought, we can then, animated by a new life and principle of love, return again to creatures, and see and love and serve God in them, giving them the fulness of our love for His sake.

If we are the faithful children of God, then there can be no question that we are holy. If we have complied with the conditions of sonship, if we have received the grace that comes in the Sacrament of baptism, and are using the ordained means to maintain ourselves in grace, then the power of God is working within us, and we are growing in the life of sanctification. It may be slow, it may be swift; but that has nothing to do with the main issue. He who is by virtue of His essential being the Holy One, has given His holiness to us. We are by grace what He is by nature and essence, for grace is a participation in His divine nature. St. Augustine, having in mind all the wonderful work which our Lord has done, and is doing for us, wisely says, "If you do not call

---

[1] St. John iii. 34.
[2] St. Catherine of Siena, *Dialogue on Consummate Perfection.*
[3] St. Teresa, *Interior Castle,* Man. VII, ii. 9.

yourself holy, you are ungrateful to the Lord." Unless we are guilty of mortal sin, and have not repented of it, to say we are not holy is to repudiate our divine sonship.

XII

Encompassed in the work of these three divine principles, purification, illumination, and sanctification, which reside in the humanity of Christ, and which are transmitted to us in the Sacraments, there are certain effects of grace which it is edifying to study. Grace is the supernatural power infused into the soul, by the use of which the Holy Spirit produces definite results in the lives of those who submit to His guidance. It is grace which changes the potential into the actual, which makes practical that which might otherwise remain naught but a beautiful theory of life and conduct. " By grace we not only discover what ought to be done, but also we do that which we have discovered; by grace not only do we believe what ought to be loved, but we also love that which we have believed." [1]

Another of the chief of these effects is the strengthening and harmonizing of the powers of the soul. The philosophers have ever been seeking after goodness. Aristotle thought it could be secured by the avoidance of extremes, keeping to what is called the golden mean. Socrates believed it could be found by acquiring wisdom, although his constant question, What is wisdom? has never found an answer save in the contemplation of Him who is essentially the divine Wisdom. Plato's idea of goodness was that it lay in harmony. Plato was right, but his harmony was unattainable by man, for his system involved no conception of supernatural and divine aid, without which moral and spiritual harmony is but a beautiful dream. The Christian philosopher, Boethius, came much nearer the truth when he identified love with the principle of cosmic harmony; and by " cosmic " is meant the material, the intellectual, the moral, the spiritual—nothing being excepted from subjection to this reign of love, under the personal direction of the Holy Spirit which is given unto us.

Where grace reigns, there reigns the Spirit of God, who ordereth all things sweetly, and therefore harmony reigns. Under the rule of grace, when raised to its highest power, there are no interior

---

[1] " Non solum ut facienda noverimus, verum etiam ut cognita faciamus; non solum ut diligenda credemus, verum etiam ut credita diligamus."—St. Augustine, *De Gratia Christi et de Peccato Originali*, Lib. I, cap xii; Migne, P. L., Tom. 44, Col. 367.

conflicts, no weak hesitations; decisions are quick and ready and right; new and greater facility of action is imparted; hidden and unsuspected powers are released, and brought into effective action. Man is able to strike the key-note of the Incarnation, and of the covenant of the Incarnation. When the angel made the transcending annunciation to Blessed Mary, he declared that " with God nothing shall be impossible." [1] St. Paul interpreted this, and applied it to himself, as we can and must apply it to ourselves, when he said, " I live; yet not I, but Christ liveth in me," [2] and therefore, " I can do all things through Christ which strengtheneth me." [3]

Another effect of grace is that the soul, filled with the indwelling God, finds that everything which is done by it is raised to a supernatural dignity. The smallest action, seemingly the most casual detail, is given an eternal quality, for it is God within us who is the real worker, and there can be nothing small or great in the work of the Deity. Because He is infinite, everything He does possesses an infinite quality. Thus is finite man, through grace by which he is made partaker of the divine nature, enabled to perform works of infinite worth. As the Humanity of Incarnate God was " full of grace and truth "; " as in Him, with the increase of His stature, that wisdom which, proceeding from the Beatific Vision in which His soul ever saw all things clearly, admitted of no increase, was outwardly to man's eyes more and more unfolded—so, in His servants, the life of God's grace unites itself with each opening power, sanctifies the will, informs the understanding, kindles the affections, masters whatever would oppose itself to the mind of God, possesses the soul according to its capacity, with the full flood of divine holiness." [4]

Grace, if it is present at all, works like leaven, not waiting for any conscious direction on our part. God indwells the soul who is in grace. Where God dwells there His unceasing and infinite operations go on. God is essentially unceasing activity, and He could not cease to work without ceasing to be. I lie down to-night to take my rest. For many hours my consciousness is submerged in sleep; but God does not suspend His activity. Unless there be some evil in my soul to raise a barrier, the operation of indwelling grace, of divine love and power, is uninterrupted, and I rise on the morrow stronger in the Lord and in the power of His might, than when I went to rest. Whether sleeping or waking, grace works

---

[1] St. Luke i. 37. [2] Gal. ii. 20. [3] Phil. iv. 13.
[4] E. B. Pusey, *University Sermons*, 1859–1872, p. 281.

to make the co-operating soul more holy, more like unto the indwelling God; and therefore in all things strong and beautiful, morally and spiritually.

Thus does grace carry us on without a moment's cessation of its activity to the inevitable, inescapable, and glorious destiny of perfect oneness with God, and therefore of perfect holiness, which is the holiness of the Godhead Itself.

This is the Christian vocation. To nothing less than this does He call us, and He endows us with His own love and holiness and power that we may not fail of His purpose.

O loving and compassionate Lord : Give me to drink, as far as mortal man may ask, of the rivers of grace which flow from Thee, Father, Son, Spirit—the grace of Thy consubstantial love, the grace of Thy co-eternal love. May Thy love enfold me as a heavenly vesture that I may come into Thy presence clad only in the beauty of Thy grace.

What can be said of the Christian virtues, especially when they live by the grace and inspiration of Christian charity, but that they emanate in their principle from the sanctity of God, are given to the soul upon the measure of her condition, and are distributed through all her powers, and worked into our life, by the labours of the will? They make the soul luminous with the light of justice, harmonious with the beautiful order of their action, noble through obedience to the Eternal Love. When God sets charity in order within us, all the virtues receive the fire of her life, and God reigns through her gentle power as the queen of the soul. By reason of her origin this divine virtue is most pure; minds defiled cannot defile her, but she removes the stains of error whithersoever she comes. She is of such potency that anger and discontent disappear in her presence; of such fortitude that she grows stronger in adversities; of such liberty that oppression only increases her freedom; of such altitude that no human power can reach her; but she graciously descends to the humble.

WILLIAM BERNARD ULLATHORNE.

CHAPTER VII

" YE SHALL RECEIVE POWER "

I

THE central promise which our Lord made to His disciples in the course of the instructions which He gave them during the Great Forty Days after His Resurrection was that " Ye shall receive power, after that the Holy Ghost is come upon you." [1]

This is one of the many instances where God condescends to take the natural, and often perverted, longing of the human heart, and to transform and refine it into something which can be used to carry out the highest and holiest purposes of His will. The desire for power is universal. We see it developing in the earliest years of the growing child. Much of the misbehaviour of young children arises out of the desire to exercise their newly discovered powers; and in this, as in most other things, the child is father to the man. Many of the moral delinquencies of men are the expression of their desire to use their abilities according to their ignorant or perverted ideas and wishes. Handicapped by the failure to recognize real values, we do the wrong thing to the dishonour of God, and to our own, and to others' hurt.

God, in His loving condescension, has taken this universal human instinct, and seeks to satisfy it by giving us power to use it with a right judgment, and really to accomplish through its use that which will be of ultimate and enduring value.

Let us examine and see what we mean by power. According to one authority, power consists in " such an absence of external restriction and limitation that it depends only upon the inward determination of the subject whether or not it will act." [2] This definition suffices if we are looking only for the negative quality involved in the idea of power. We fallen creatures are indeed restricted by the conditions of our nature, but much more is involved in our power to act than the determination of our own wills, which of themselves can do nothing in the spiritual world. Our Lord, in making the promise of power to His followers, surely meant something more than the removal of moral restrictions. The

[1] Acts i. 8.   [2] Century Dictionary.

restrictions may be removed, but this removal would not in itself produce power, either of apostleship or Christian living, unless this power were an endowment of human nature, which it is not.

" Ye shall receive power " indicates the creation of positive gifts. The word which is used—δύναμις—is not negative in its force. From it are derived such words in English as *dynamic*, *dynamo*, *dynamite*. These words do not suggest the mere removal of limitations. When we speak of a man as being a dynamic character, we mean that he has force, initiative, readiness and courage, the qualities of strong leadership amongst his fellows.

We may venture the following definition, which, while far from being adequate, may give us a working basis. Power may be defined as the possession of the right, ability and freedom to act with efficiency in some given sphere in relation to a definite objective. Power in itself is neither good nor evil. Its character depends upon how it is used. There are many kinds of power. We may enumerate physical power, political or social power, intellectual power, and moral and spiritual power. Real, objective, and enduring value lies only in spiritual power. By spiritual power we mean the power which is bestowed upon us by God, who is Himself the only original power, and the only source of real power. One may possess great physical powers, but in a brief time they decay. The same is true of intellectual power, which is constantly confused with the possession of mere knowledge or information;[1] and political or social power, which are practically the same thing, lasts as long as men allow themselves to be influenced, and no longer. Moral power lies in a higher sphere, but unless rightly used, and by this use and exercise rightly developed, it may become a menace to society and to souls, to one's own soul more than to any other; and therefore be doomed to complete frustration in the end, for, save where it has a spiritual basis, morality becomes mere natural ethics.

Not so with spiritual power—that power which God infuses into the soul of man through union with the God-Man, Christ Jesus. He pours His love into our hearts, for all truly spiritual power is one with the power of love. The love of God, and of our fellow-men, cannot be perverted. It is impossible to use the love of God for an evil purpose. I cannot do an evil thing save in so far as the love of God is first driven out of my heart. Every sin has a double aspect. First, the love of God is rejected; then, and not until then, is sin, which is the work of Satan, accepted and enthroned

---

[1] " Knowledge comes, but wisdom lingers." Tennyson, *Lockesley Hall.*

in its place.   Of course, not every sin expels the love of God utterly.
There is venial sin, the " sin not unto death," [1] as St. John calls it;
but even in this case we forbid the love of God to function within
us in its full measure, and he who persists in denying the power of
God to work within him will sooner or later find himself entrapped
by the tempter into mortal sin which involves the deliberate casting
out of the power and love of God from our hearts.

Spiritual power has to do with eternity, not with time only.   It
is the greater means to the final end which is the Beatific Vision of
the Holy Trinity.   But it is more than a means.   When the end
is attained, the means which led to it will not be cast aside and
forgotten.   Through all eternity we shall be called upon to exercise this power which God bestows upon us through uniting us
with the Sacred Humanity of Incarnate God.   It is the Christian
endowment which is given not merely for the purposes of our life
in this world, but as that which we are to share with our Glorified
Lord in the heavenly kingdom.   He who gave the assurance that
" ye shall receive power, after that the Holy Ghost is come upon
you," also said, " All power is given unto me in heaven and in
earth.   Go ye therefore and teach all nations, baptizing them in
the name of the Father and of the Son and of the Holy Ghost:
teaching them to observe all things whatsoever I have commanded
you: and, lo, I am with you alway even unto the end of the world." [2]
The Great Commission which every soul " in Christ " is given in
one manner or another to discharge, can be carried out only by
our participating in the power which is given unto Him in heaven
and in earth.

II

What, then, is this power?   There are many references to it in
Holy Scripture, and it will be well for us to consider some of the
more important of them.   One of the most illuminating is found
in the sixth and seventh chapters of the Epistle to the Hebrews.
Here the writer is speaking of the heavenly High Priesthood, of
which the earthly priesthood exercised by men is an extension.
He is setting forth the truth that there can be but one priest, who
is the risen and ascended and glorified Christ Jesus.   He is the
eternal priest.   There are not in the Christian dispensation successive generations of priests, as under the old Covenant, for He
is a Priest forever after the order of Melchisedek, and as such He
will continue forever.   Those who are one with Him in His

[1] I St. John v. 16.   [2] St. Matt. xxviii. 18-20.

H

Mystical Body, the Church, partake of the power of this priesthood; and it is a priesthood " not after the law of a carnal commandment, but after the power of an endless life." [1] The individuals who share His priesthood on earth come and go, as did the levitical priests, but the priesthood itself is everlasting. It never ceases.

Being priests unto God, participants in Christ's eternal priesthood, our whole life, from the necessity of what it essentially is, becomes sacrificial, even as His life is sacrificial. Not only at the Eucharist do we offer ourselves to God to be " a reasonable, holy and living Sacrifice," for our priesthood does not express itself only from time to time in isolated sacrificial acts, but rather is the whole life sacrificial. If we are indeed consecrate to God, then God leaves nothing unclaimed in our life. Everything that we are, and everything that we do, every relationship which we form, is to be made an oblation to Him, offered in union with the great and all-sufficient Sacrifice which Incarnate God made on Calvary to the Father.

In this passage in Hebrews where we speak of the power of an *endless* life, the adjective properly means *indissoluble*. Our life is merged with His glorified Life, and it is not contemplated that this union will ever be dissolved. It is not only endless in point of duration, but unless the whole principle of His kingdom is utterly and completely violated, it is not possible that this union which ensures us a participation in His Priesthood, and therefore in His sacrificial work and power, can ever be dissolved. The " power of an indissoluble life " is a power which can never cease to function, so long as that life is ours.

This power is His own power transmitted to us, not as a gift apart from Himself, but we have it only because we have Him, and we have Him only through being one with Him in the bosom of Godhead. In the final issue there can be but one power—the power of God. As each adorable Person of the Blessed and Indivisible Trinity possesses that power in its totality, so each member of the Body of Christ, being made partaker of the divine Nature, is made partaker of the divine Power.

St. Paul declares to the Philippians that he has nothing of his own, but he hopes to be found to have " the righteousness which is of God by faith in order that I may know him and the power of his resurrection." [2] The apostle here puts his finger on the one point which it is necessary for us ever to remember. We are to keep in mind, and allow ourselves in all things to be governed by, the transcending truth that we are living members of Christ's risen

---

[1] Heb. vii. 16.   [2] Phil. iii. 10.

Body. We have been taken integrally and organically into that Body which is the shrine of Godhead, and have been made one with that Humanity which at the Incarnation was taken up into the Godhead. We are members of the Body of Him of whom St. Peter said, " It was not possible that He should be holden of death." [1] Only through realizing this truth shall we, like St. Paul, be able to rejoice in the " power of his resurrection." This means that all that we are, and all that we do, shall find its efficient cause, its motive force, and its pledge of eternal permanence before God, in our participation in the life of the risen, ascended, and glorified God-Man, Christ Jesus. This is " the power of his resurrection." If we are in Him, and He is risen from the dead, then we, too, are risen. As with Him, death hath no more dominion over us. Our life is being lived in the same power in which His is being lived.

In the dawn of Easter morning the Church cries aloud to us in the first Scripture read at the altar for that great feast, " If ye then be risen with Christ, seek those things which are above where Christ sitteth on the right hand of God. Set your affections on things above, not on things on the earth. For ye are dead, and your life is hid with Christ in God." [2] Note the two pregnant expressions—" hid *with Christ*," and " *in God*." Here we find the reference to the mystical union of the soul with God through Christ, which is so often repeated in St. Paul's inspired writings. We have been raised " together with him," and as a consequence we are " hid with Christ " and therefore we are " in God." The Father cannot but respond to the prayer of the Son, " Father, I will that they also, whom thou hast given me, be with me where I am." [3] Indeed, long before He prayed this prayer in the Upper Room, He prophesied its fulfilment when He said, " If any man serve me, let him follow me, and where I am, there shall also my servant be." [4]

III

For the supreme manifestation of this gift of power to His people we must go back to St. John's proclamation of the Incarnation in the beginning of his Gospel. " As many as received Him," the evangelist says, " to them gave he power to become the sons o God." [5] The word here used is not the same as that which appears in our Lord's Ascension Day promise to the disciples that they should receive power after that the Holy Ghost was come upon them. St. John's expression is a nobler one than that which St.

[1] Acts ii. 24. [2] Col. iii. 1–3. [3] St. John xvii. 24.
[4] St. John xii.26. [5] St. John i. 12.

Luke chose by which to report Christ's Aramaic saying. It has the force of our English words, *privilege, right, prerogative*. But it must come to the same thing, for if the right carries not with it the power to exercise it, the promise is a mockery.[1] This prerogative is not inherent in man. It is a free gift, a wholly unmerited gift, from God—" to them *gave* he power." [2] It is not something which is added to what God's people already possessed even in germ. St. John clearly indicates that it was a wholly new state of being—the raising up of the soul to a new plane of relationship with God which man had never known before. It was a new thing in the world, a new overflowing of the divine love upon the creature, that man should be made partaker of the divine Nature, and of the divine Power, and thereby become a co-heir with God the Eternal and Only-begotten Son.

And what is this so transcendent blessing, this Sonship in God which we are given the power to attain? Again, in order to grasp its real significance—we can never grasp it fully, so far is it beyond the reach of the finite mind—we must look more closely at the meaning of the language used by St. John. In the New Testament there are two words which in our English version are translated by the word *son*. These are υἱός and τέκνον. The first of these words implies the dignity of heirship, while the second refers to the community of nature which the son has with the father, that which calls out all the intimate tenderness of the relation between child and parent. The first involves the suggestion of the official and legal status as a son, as we speak of a " son and heir," or, " the son of the house." The word τέκνον has in it nothing of this legalism. It implies first of all a community of nature, resulting in an intimate relationship of reciprocal tender love and trust, such as exists in the ideal relation between parent and child. St. John's use of the word includes the idea of the presence of the divine principle, which presence makes them the children of God, and it includes also the notion of growth, resulting from the divine life within, which increases from the vital germ until it reaches its full maturity of our God-endowed humanity in the Beatific Vision of God.

Perhaps an illustration from real life will make the thought clearer. I know an old lady in her nineties who has two sons, both priests, both advanced in years, both of whom have made worthy records in their service of God in the Church. They come to see her from time to time, but she never says to her friends, " My sons are coming." She is proud of these sons, and rightly so; but such

---

[1] Vide Alford, *Comment. N. T., in loc.*   [2] St. John i. 12.

an expression might easily suggest a mother's pride in the position they have made for themselves. It is something deeper and sweeter than this which fills the mother's heart. She always says, " The children are coming." Here is a note of tenderness which the word son rarely sounds. If she spoke the language of St. John, she would say, " Ta tekna, the children "; and could we read the unconscious thought of her mind behind the expression, we would find such thoughts as these: " The children, those to whom I gave life; whose nature is my nature; over whom my heart ever broods with the yearning of a mother's love."

St. John, himself, always tender and loving-hearted, set as he is in the apostolic band to interpret the Heart of God to His people, never uses any other but the word τέκνα to indicate the children of God. The other word, υἱός, fine, even noble as it is, is not in his vocabulary when he comes to speak of the relation of the Father to the children of the kingdom. Moreover, he never uses τέκνον in the singular, but always in the plural. Always has he before his mind the vision of the family of God, the Mystical Body, knit together as it is in one communion and fellowship by the bond of a love which God Himself pours into our hearts; or, rather, we should say, by a love which is very God Himself indwelling the souls of His children, for since " God is Love," [1] we cannot differentiate between the love of God and the Being of God. As this same apostle of love has said, " He that abideth in love abideth in God, and God in him." [2] He made no attempt to distinguish between God and the love of God, for He and His attributes are one. " What God has, that He is," said St. Augustine; [3] and St. Bernard gives us the glowing assurance that " Love is both God and the Gift of God." [4]

IV

Our " childship " in God, to which we are given power to attain, involves Him as our Father, but we must not forget the maternal element which inheres in the Being of God. As we have already noted when St. James tells us that, " of his own will begat he us that we should be a kind of firstfruits of his creatures," [5] he uses a verb which describes not the act of begetting by the father,

[1] 1 St. John iv. 8 and 16.
[2] 1 St. John iv. 16. In this passage the word *abideth* (μένω) implies the permanence of the indwelling.
[3] " Quod habet, hoc est." St. Augustine, *De Civitate Dei*, xi. 10; Migne, P. L., Tom. 41, Col. 325.
[4] St. Bernard, *Epistle*, xi. 4; Migne, P. L., Tom. 182, Col. 111.
[5] St. James i. 18.

but that of bringing forth by the mother. We have suggestions of this mysterious and most comforting truth of the divine maternity in not a few places in Scripture. More than once in the Old Testament do we find the Spirit of God comparing Jehovah to the mother bringing forth and nourishing her children. This is reflected in a singularly beautiful manner in that rich and gracious word, loving-kindness, which is used so frequently of God's attitude towards His people. Lexicographers tell us that the corresponding Hebrew word is untranslatable, and its meaning can only be appreciated dimly by comparing it with the ecstatic thrill of love which the mother-bird experiences as she hovers over the nest where lies her young.[1] It would seem impossible for the ideal of the tender mystery of maternal love to be carried farther. God is to us both Father and Mother. " As a father pitieth his own children, so is the Lord merciful unto them that fear him." [2] " As one whom his mother comforteth, so will I comfort you." [3]

In such wondrous wise does the love of God work. Far beyond the dreams of prophets and seers has been the fulfilment of the promise to be a Father to His people. But when He gives us the prerogative and the power to become the children of God, partakers of His own nature, He entrusts us with a privilege and a responsibility which no man can carry if left to his own resources. But God leaves no soul in dependence upon its own power only. He Himself has said, " Without me ye can do nothing," [4] and the terms of the promise demand unceasing labour on our part. All men are given " the right to become the sons of God," [5] but it is ours to claim and exercise this right and power; and the zeal with which we claim and exercise it is the index of our standard of spiritual values.

The Holy Spirit does not leave us without manifold helps that we may bring this heavenly business to its eternal issue. The Christian endowment is a thing so rich and full that no man can grasp and appreciate the height and depth, the length and breadth of it. In the very act of making us members of Christ in baptism, by which Sacrament we are made partakers of the divine Nature and, in union with His Sacred Humanity, are taken up into the Godhead, the Holy Spirit of God fills us with the power of gifts and graces beyond all human comprehension. We do not attempt to solve their mystery; we bow down in grateful adoration. We experience these heavenly things, and are content.

Let us now be definite and concrete. The basic endowments

---

[1] Vide Gesenius, *Hebrew Lexicon.*   [2] Ps. ciii. 13.   [3] Isa. lxvi. 13.
[4] St. John xv. 5.   [5] St. John i. 12.

of the Christian soul are the virtues, or spiritual powers, of faith, hope, and love. These are the divine forces which work in and upon the soul, conforming it to the pattern of the Blessed Trinity. The exercise of these virtues is necessary to salvation and to sanctification. It will be of no benefit to us, but rather to our certain condemnation, if God endows us with these powers and we do not use them. The old principle applies here: we have already considered that a man is not counted good because he *can* be good, but because he actually *is* good. For this reason we are taught that perfection, which as members of Christ we are seeking, is not to be found in the possession of good habits in themselves, but in the acts which are the expression of these habits.

Faith, hope and charity are called the theological virtues, or powers. As we have seen, the word " theological," used in this connection, has no reference to a knowledge of religious science, as we commonly employ it. It has nothing to do with learning. It simply means that they come from God as a gift; that they are to be exercised in the grace and power of God, and in relation to Him; and that where faithfully used, they lead the soul into an ever-deepening union with God. They are wholly unmerited gifts which God makes to the humble soul. We cannot possess them in the natural man, for they are in all respects supernatural. There is, of course, a certain natural faith, hope and love, but these are not the powers of which St. Paul writes so glowingly in the thirteenth chapter of his first Epistle to the Corinthians. By God's gracious and loving help, we shall proceed to consider these theological virtues with the hope and prayer that we may all be given through this consideration a firmer grasp on the verities of the Faith which have been revealed in His Church; that we may enjoy that sense of imperturbable security which comes from the exercise of the good hope which God has infused into our hearts; and that love, the supreme power with which the Spirit endows us, may burn out all that is evil, and rule and govern our hearts in the grace of the indwelling Lord, and exercise to the utmost, both in time and in eternity, that unitive power which will make us one with Him in the Holy and Indivisible Trinity.

O Gracious Lord of Love, give me constancy in loving Thee ; unfaltering perseverance in serving Thee ; Pour into me Thine invincible power against every spiritual enemy, that in the secret sanctuary of Thy love I may possess and enjoy Thee through endless ages of ages.

I beheld with the eye of my soul the Light Unchangeable He who knows the Truth knows what that Light is, and he who knows it knows Eternity. Love knoweth it. O Truth who art Eternity, and Love who art Truth; and Eternity who art Love!

ST. AUGUSTINE.

The present moment is ever filled with infinite treasures; it contains more than you have capacity to hold. Faith is the measure. Believe, and it will be done unto you accordingly. Love also is the measure. The more the heart loves, the more it desires; and the more it desires so much the more will it receive. The will of God presents itself to us at each moment as an immense ocean which no human heart can fathom; but what the heart can receive from this ocean is equal to the measure of our faith, confidence and love. The divine will is an abyss of which the present moment is the entrance. Plunge into this abyss, and you will always find it infinitely more vast than your desires.

PÈRE DE CAUSSADE.

CHAPTER VIII

THE VIRTUE OF FAITH

WE have considered that the theological virtues or powers (for the word *virtue* has in its original significance the same meaning as *power*) are so called because they come from God, being infused into the soul by Him. They can only be exercised in the grace and power of God, and under the direction of the Holy Ghost; and, rightly used, they lead the soul steadily and inevitably to God. Their origin is not in us, or in anything natural. It lies in God Himself. These powers or virtues enable us to act in a manner and degree wholly beyond our ordinary natural ability. In their exercise we transcend any capacity which we have in ourselves, or are able to acquire by any human effort, and by their use we are able to aspire rightly and wisely to those things which are impossible to man without the direct and continuous help of the Holy Spirit. Faith, hope and charity are free gifts from God. We cannot deserve them, nor can we receive them, much less can we use and develop them, unless God gives them to us, and continually answers the prayer which the Church places on our lips and in our hearts, that He would " give unto us the increase of faith, hope and charity." [1] It is His only to bestow; it is His only to give the increase.

I

The word *faith* has been used in various senses, and as we consider the theological virtue of Faith, we shall have to exercise care in order not to fall into confusion as to its significance. The importance of Faith is showed by the fact that the word appears, in one form and significance or another, on an average of more than twice in every one of the two hundred and sixty chapters of the New Testament. In every instance, whatever its significance, the word is derived from a Greek verb which means to persuade ($\pi\epsilon i\theta\omega$), indicating that God, in His tenderness, leads us persuasively to belief in Him. He respects the freedom of the human will. There is no compulsion, no rush of overpowering revelation,

---

[1] Collect for XIV Sunday after Trinity.

sweeping away the reason and all power of doubt. His attitude is ever that which He took towards faithless Judah when, by the prophet, He cried to them, "Come now, and let us reason together."[1] St. Francis de Sales tells us that the Almighty, to impart to us the gift of Faith, "penetrates the soul, and proposes to the understanding the objects of its belief in so gentle and persuasive a manner that the will is powerfully inclined to assert its freedom and authority over the understanding, and thereby reduce it to an acquiescence, unhesitatingly and fully, in the truths revealed."[2] He further says that "grace is so gracious, and so graciously does it seize on our hearts to draw them, that it in no way offends the liberty of our will. It touches powerfully, but yet so delicately, the springs of our spirit that our free will suffers no violence from it."[3]

The virtue of faith is defined as a supernatural, intellectual quality infused by the act of God into man, by the use of which the Holy Ghost enables us to apprehend truth solely on the authority of God, without any evidence of experience, or any argumentative proof. By the use of Faith we believe in God even as a little child believes in its father; and believing in Him, we believe so firmly and unquestioningly all the truth that He has revealed concerning Himself, as to be able readily to base our whole life and activity upon it.

The natural faith which is a part of the endowment of every soul has many analogies to, if not characteristics in common with, the supernatural gift and virtue of faith. The little child begins its life in total ignorance, and its mind is first opened by the faith which by natural instinct it places in those about it. Without this natural faith it could make no beginning whatever towards acquiring knowledge of any sort. Within a few years that which the child has accepted on faith develops into a well-organized body of knowledge through thought, observation, and its own experience. Nor does this instinct of faith cease to work as the years pass. Our human tendency is always to believe what is told us unless we have some positive reason to doubt. Without this faith, human society could not exist. Take it away, and the whole social fabric would immediately crumble. Nor without it could the race make any advance in knowledge. However we may have developed it for ourselves later on, the foundation of all knowledge, in whatever sphere, rests upon the authority of someone else. Those who, as is so common to-day, in the mad pride of man's intellectuality, inveigh

[1] Isa. i. 18.　　[2] St. Francis de Sales, *The Love of God*, Bk. ii, Chap. 14.
[3] St. Francis de Sales, *The Love of God*, Bk. ii, Chap. 12.

against what they call authoritarianism, are vainly seeking to ignore one of the most powerful and constant factors in human nature, and one so universal that no human being in his right mind, or group of human beings, has ever yet been discovered who did not govern all life by it. Both in human and divine knowledge faith teaches us those things which, without the use of this faculty, it would be an impossibility for us ever to know.

II

There is so much loose thinking and loose teaching in our time concerning Faith that it would be well for us to clear the field somewhat by considering first what the supernatural virtue of Faith is not.

(*a*) It is not superstition. Superstition concerns itself with, and puts in the place of God and His truth, vain, crude, and often base and degrading figments of the diseased human imagination. Superstition may change its form, but it never progresses; it is never positive or constructive. It leads to nothing save to ever grosser superstition. Faith, on the other hand, is perpetually engaged with truth, infinite and divine, and, therefore, it must, of necessity, be ever progressing to higher things; it must be ever exploring vaster ranges of the eternal verities.

(*b*) Faith is not credulity, which is that " indolent abdication of the responsibility of judgment in favour of every pretender, that superficial assent, lightly given and lightly withdrawn," which, " is utterly at variance with the intense clear vision, and with the resolute grasp of Faith." [1]

(*c*) Faith is not intellectual conviction. If I am convinced of the truth of a proposition by some irrefragable logical argument, or through indisputable external evidence, this is not Faith. In such case reason is compelled to believe, but the only compulsion that lies in Faith is that which rests upon the authority of God, who reveals the truth which we accept in Faith. The Christian is not especially concerned with harmonizing Faith and reason. Indeed, Faith demands an unqualified and implicit acceptance of many truths which seem to the limited human intelligence to be clean contrary to reason. Doubtless our present mode and range of reason is but a faint reflection of the power of reason which will be ours when, in the presence of the Beatific Vision in heaven, we shall know even as we are known.

[1] Westcott, *The Historic Faith*, pp. 5–6.

And yet we must not forget that reason, incompetent as it may be in this present life to deal with the higher things, is the noblest natural gift which God has bestowed upon man, and without the use of reason we could neither learn nor comprehend anything. Richard of St. Victor, one of the great masters, who did not trouble himself about squaring Faith with human reason, nevertheless said, " We must try as far as possible to understand by reason what we believe by Faith." But faith must do its work before the power of reason can be invoked.

Further, of those truths which are discoverable by reason, by meditation, or by other natural exercises, we gain a deeper and surer knowledge and insight through the application of the virtue of Faith. To one soul who lacks, or who has neglected, the gift of Faith, truths which he may hear are meaningless, while to another who has diligently cultivated this virtue they bring a flood of illumination and joy.

Faith is not to be subordinated to reason, any more than the divine is to be subject to the human; but we must ever remember that reason is a gift of God in the natural sphere, as Faith is in the supernatural, and that right reason is not without the guidance of the Spirit of God. Therefore, the truth which we discover by the right use of reason is just as truly a revelation from God as that which in the supernatural life is given to us through Faith. In one case the mode of revelation is indirect, in the other it is direct but the source and origin of all truth is the same. It comes from God.

(d) Faith is not opinion, it is not any man's way of looking at supernatural things. Our opinions are often just the result of the working of our prejudices. Faith has nothing to do with what I may think, it has no connection with certain views I may have. It is based upon a profound recognition of truth, as that truth is revealed to us by the Holy Spirit. It may, and often does, run contrary to all my ways of thinking. These ways of thinking, these opinions, change continually, but faith, if it is real, endures. " It was not ' opinion ' for which martyrs died, or confessors underwent the loss of all things, or the poor endured their privations triumphantly, or men, like ourselves, forsook all for the love of Christ to gain Christ. ' Opinion ' sheds no patience over racking sufferings, nor light from above upon the bed of death. And whence had they their conviction? Perhaps they knew not. It crowns all human grounds of belief, but itself lies deeper than all." [1]

[1] E. B. Pusey, *University Sermons*, 1859-1872, p. 346.

It may surprise some to be told that this virtue of Faith which God infuses into the soul at baptism, is not that which we have in mind when we speak of trust and confidence in God. This would be to confound the virtue of Faith with that of Hope.

It is therefore imperative, in considering what faith is not, that we keep in mind the distinction between faith and hope. There is a widespread confusion as to the meaning of the two words which has led to serious errors in religion; and these errors do not lie in the realm of a speculative theology which might be remote from the actual practice of the Christian life. They affect disastrously the daily living of the life in Christ.

It was certain of the 16th-century continental reformers who introduced a new thing into religion when they declared that the faith by which men are justified before God is nothing more than confidence in the divine mercy. They obscured the distinction between faith and hope, and this obscuration has affected fundamentally the belief and thinking of most of those who have been influenced by the Reformation theology. The ancient belief, set forth, as we have seen, in the Scriptures, and held by practically all Christians for 1600 years, was that faith implied the exercise of a moral and spiritual power infused into the soul by God, the use of which enabled men to give an unquestioning intellectual and moral assent to the divine revelation, and to maintain a firm belief in the necessary truths which cannot be rejected without grave peril to our eternal salvation. The power which enables us to give this assent is the infused theological virtue of faith. Hope does not enter into this field.

This confusion is the greater because we find the idea of trust attached to the word faith as one of its meanings, and it is commonly, and quite properly, employed in this sense, but when it is so used it does not imply the theological virtue of faith. The virtue of faith is an infused power by the use of which we are able to accept without question all that God has revealed of Himself, of His nature and of His work, as well as the truth concerning the nature of man. Trust and confidence in God are the exercise of the virtue of hope which we shall consider later. Hope is dependent upon, but it is not one with, the virtue of faith. As a result of this confusion there are souls who are seeking after God, but who are gravely handicapped by an ignorance of the existence of such a gift as the theological virtue of faith; and whose exercise of hope is wanting in that vigour and liveliness which must characterize it if it is to be an effective power, for hope is the daughter of faith. Those who have not by faith known and accepted God as He is, cannot have a steadfast consciousness of security in Him, which is the very essence of hope.

Faith is not, then, in itself, hope and trust. It is the foundation, the necessary and indispensable foundation, of all the trust and confidence which we have in God, and of the hope which we repose in Him. The Epistle to the Hebrews teaches us that " without faith it is impossible to please God." It is clear that the inspired author does not mean in this passage to speak of faith in the sense of trust, for he goes on directly, without any break in the sentence, to say, " for he that cometh to God must believe that he is." [1] Faith accepts God, His existence and His revealed nature, and, having done this, it is impossible for it not to accept with like implicitness all the revelation of His love and goodness. Our trust and confidence, our hope, rest upon the divine assurances which have been given to Faith, and which Faith has accepted. Faith is not confidence and trust, but Faith is the mother of confidence and trust. We can hope in God only when we are able to say, " I believe in God."

III

Faith is, as we have said, an intellectual quality infused into man, and man himself, through the operation of both his mind and will, is the subject who in union with the Holy Spirit must act in every exercise of, and consequent advance in, Faith.

In the discourse which our Lord gave in the synagogue at Capernaum, which St. John reports in the sixth chapter of his Gospel, He leads up to the proclamation, " He that believeth on me hath everlasting life," by declaring that " no man can come to me except the Father which hath sent me, draw him "; and the purpose of this drawing is that they may " all be taught of God Every man, therefore, that hath heard and hath learned of the Father, cometh unto me." In coming to Him, it is only by the exercise of this supernatural Faith that we can lay hold of the bless ing. St. Paul presents this truth again and again, so importan did he regard it. Repeatedly he declares that it is only tha " righteousness which is of Faith " which makes it possible for u to be pleasing to God.[2] " Justified by Faith " is an expressior which occurs again and again in the apostolic writings.[3] In non of these passages is the reference to a trust in God, but to the virtu

---

[1] Heb. xi. 6.   [2] Rom. iii. 22; ix. 30; Phil. iii. 9.
[3] Rom. iii. 22, 28; v. 1; Gal. ii. 16; iii. 8; St. James ii. 21, 24.

of Faith by which we live, which is infused into the soul, the supernatural power that enables us not merely with an intellectual
assent, but "with all thine heart," [1] as St. Philip required of the
Ethiopian eunuch, to believe in God and in all that He has revealed,
and to live according to that belief.

The Epistle to the Hebrews speaks of our Lord as "the author
and finisher of our faith." [2] He who at the beginning of our
Christian career infused into us this divine gift, will also finish His
work in us, bringing it to that fulness of perfection where faith will
be lost in the glorious sight of the Beatific Vision, which is the final
destiny of us all. The life of faith here is the beginning of the life
of glory in heaven. It is of the same essence, and if we would know
what the life of grace is, we must study it in its supremest development—namely, in the life of heaven which is its consummation.[3]
"Eternal life *begun*," says Bossuet, "consists in knowing by faith—
a tender and affectionate knowledge which inclines the soul to love.
Eternal life *consummated* consists in seeing God openly, face to face." [4]

Faith is the power which enables us not only to see the things
of God, but also to interpret them. Without this divine gift of
Faith we would be like a man who heard the sounds of music, but
who could neither recognize their beauty and sweetness, nor understand what the composer meant to convey. For, as St. Paul says,
"The natural man receiveth not the things of the Spirit of God:
for they are foolishness unto him: neither can he know them,
because they are spiritually discerned." [5]

IV

This faith by which we live is of no avail unless it is a faith in a
Person. It is not a confidence that a certain desired event is bound
to come to pass because I pray. God does answer prayer. His-
torically there can be no question about this, and that He does
answer prayer is a fundamental part of the revelation which is the
object of our faith. But faith is not a sense of assurance that I am
going to get that for which I ask; rather, it is faith in God, Father,
Son, Spirit, to whom I pray. This faith involves six points:

(*a*) I believe that God is,[6] that He really exists as He has
revealed Himself—Father, Son, Spirit, three divine Persons in
the one God, and that these Three Persons are in all things
equal.

[1] Acts viii. 37.   [2] Heb. xii. 2.
[3] See Garrigou-Lagrange, *Christian Perfection and Contemplation*, p. 121.
[4] Bossuet, *Meditations on the Gospels*, Pt. II, 37th day.
[5] 1 Cor. ii. 14.   [6] Heb. xi. 6.

(*b*) I believe that He has a personal relation to, and interest in, His creation. Our God is no remote Being, like the God of the deists.

(*c*) I believe that His relation to men is that of a loving, tender Father; of a Saviour who died that we might live with Him forever; and of a Sanctifier, the Holy Ghost, who makes us holy by infusing into us the essential holiness of God.

(*d*) I believe that He is infinitely powerful, infinitely wise, infinitely loving, and that these attributes, with all His other attributes, constitute His essential, infinite Being. I believe that " What God has, that He is." [1]

(*e*) I believe that He can do everything that He wills to do.

(*f*) I believe that He wills to do for me everything which, in His perfect love and wisdom, He knows to be good for me.

This brief summary does not, of course, cover every detail of our Faith, but the implications included in these statements are sufficient to show us its foundation, and what the total object of Faith must be. " I believe in God "—it is all bound up in this one brief, pregnant sentence. Study this one compact statement, and you will find contained within it everything that is necessary to make our Faith a rounded whole.

The primary object of our Faith, therefore, is God Himself, and, as a necessary consequence, it is also the sum total of the truth which He reveals concerning Himself, His Being and His operations, both within the inner cycle of His infinite Trinitarian life, and in His relation to His creation. To repeat the words of the apostle, " He that cometh to God must believe that he is." [2] What God is in the fulness of His infinite Being, no finite mind can comprehend. When He revealed Himself to Moses in the desert, the most He could say which the mind of His servant could at all grasp, was, " I am that which I am." [3] Someone has based an act of faith on these words, and it is possibly the best act of faith that could be made. It asks not what, or why, or how, but it takes God at His word— " O God I know not what Thou art, but I believe with all my heart that Thou art what Thou art." God is what He sees and knows Himself to be. We cannot see or understand this in its fulness, but through the exercise of the supernatural gift of Faith we are able to accept it without doubt or question, whatever it is.

V

Faith unites us to God, and makes us, as St. Peter assures us we are, " partakers of the divine nature." [4] In this partaking we

---

[1] St. Augustine, *De Civ. Dei*, xi. 10; Migne, P. L., Tom. 41, Col. 325.
[2] Heb. xi. 6.   [3] Exod. iii. 14.   [4] 2 St. Peter i. 4.

become sharers, so far as such an ineffable thing is possible, in God's own divine knowing. If we see God at all, we can only see Him with the eyes of God, seeing Him as He sees Himself. "God is light," [1] and only by sharing His light can our spiritual vision function. St. Paul's summons to the lukewarm Ephesians, "Awake thou that sleepest, and arise from the dead, and Christ shall give thee light," [2] applies to all. Only by a participation in the light of Him who is the divine Light is there any possibility of seeing God; but this possibility is made a glorious actuality through Faith. "In thy light shall we see Light." [3] By entering into His essential light shall we be able to see Him, the true, eternal, and living Light. This seeing Him by faith is a faint but assured anticipation of the glory of the Vision which is to be, which will be ours when we enter into the fulness of the heavenly destiny which will be the fulfilling of all knowledge. St. Augustine points out that the light of the sun first shows itself, and then makes manifest those things which we would see.

Faith accomplishes for us all these things, and many other spiritual marvels and human impossibilities, of which we shall have no realization until we see God face to face. "By faith," says a devout and learned teacher, "the light of God becomes our light; His wisdom our wisdom; His knowledge our knowledge; His Spirit our spirit; His life our life." [4] Thus do we become "partakers of the divine nature," [5] sharers in these attributes which constitute the very Being of the Deity, for "what God has that He is." [6]

God Himself is declared very exactly in the creeds of the Church to be the primary object of the work of faith. Both the Nicene and the Apostles' Creeds fall into three distinct sections, according to the number of the Divine Persons in the Holy Trinity. We say, "I believe in God the Father Almighty"; then, "I believe in Jesus Christ, His only Son our Lord"; and third, "I believe in the Holy Ghost." Everything else in the Creeds—all that tells us of the nature and relationships of this Triune God, or His work— is supplementary to these three great fundamentals upon which everything else rests. Having thus expressed our simple faith in the one Triune God, in the Three Adorable Persons of this Ever-Blessed and Indivisible Trinity, we go on to declare further our full

---

[1] 1 St. John i. 5.   [2] Eph. v. 14.   [3] Ps. xxxvi. 9.
[4] Gay, *Christian Life and Virtues*, Vol. I, p. 156.
[5] 2 St. Peter i. 4.
[6] St. Augustine, *De Civ. Dei*, xi. 10; Migne, P. L., Tom. 41, Col. 325.

I

faith in, and adherence to, all that has been revealed to us concerning the Being and operations of the Godhead.

VI

After accepting the revelation of the Nature and Being of God, the essential absolute in Christian faith is the divinity of Jesus Christ. By divinity we mean that He is " very God of very God . . . being of one substance with the Father," and equal to the Father and to the Holy Spirit in all things. Without a firm and unshaken faith in His Godhead, the fabric of Christianity tumbles to pieces. Our Lord made this very clear in a passage the real point of which is often overlooked. When the Jews asked Him the question, " What shall we do, that we might work the works of God? " He gave them a very unexpected answer. He said nothing of the works of the law, or of charity even, but declared, " This is the work of God that ye believe on him who he hath sent." [1]   No work can count of any value before God unless it is based upon a belief in Jesus Christ as He has revealed Himself as very God.

If He is only human, to pray to Him, to worship Him, is idolatry; and to trust Him is only to take my chance on a man like myself whom, in my fallible judgment, I consider to be good. But it would be folly even to take this chance, for He died nearly two thousand years ago, and if only human, can do nothing for me now.

Love for Him, if He is but human, would likewise be foolish, for it would be on the same footing as loving Plato or Confucius, or any other man who lived some thousands of years ago, and who has no longer any part in the affairs of this world. No sane person would apply the power of love in such a manner. Indeed, the philosophical idea of love forbids us to love a person who has long since been dead and whom we never knew, and cannot know. Love does not work in this way. Love is a unitive virtue, and binds together hearts that love each other. This involves intimate personal relationships which it is impossible to have with a mere man who has been dead for two thousand years.

If Christ is but human, then His teaching could not be the object of Faith, for the essentials of it involve claims which are preposterous were He but man. He demanded that all men should accept His personal dictum on every possible subject without reservation, and this under penalty of eternal expulsion from the presence of God. He asserted His claim to forgive sins, and also

[1] St. John vi. 28–29.

to transmit that same power to His followers. He set Himself up as the infallible Judge of the world, proclaiming His right and power to mete out eternal rewards and punishments. In His own teaching, and that which He required His apostles to give, the assertion is repeatedly made that He is the Jehovah of the Old Testament, the God who made heaven and earth, and who rules the universe. These claims show that if He was not God, He was far from being a great moral teacher.

It has been said that He was either God or a bad man. More truly might it be said that He was either the Infinite God or that He was a madman. No sane human being, however bad, could make the claims which He made basic for His disciples, and for His Church for all time. Nor could any sane man take such an one as his infallible master. Christ is the eternal God, or He is nothing to us. Next to our belief in the actual existence of the Triune God Himself, that this God-Man, our Lord Jesus Christ, is very God of very God, is the first and most necessary article of our faith. Our belief in the truths concerning these divine Persons is subsidiary to our faith in the Persons themselves. We believe that which they have revealed because we first believe in them. This is the essential principle of discipleship. We accept *in toto* the teaching of the Master because we first accept the Master. We do not believe in Him because of anything which He in His goodness has done, or is doing, or anything which we think or believe He may do. We believe in Him regardless of anything He may do. We love Him and serve Him for what He is, not for what He does, unspeakable as must be the love and gratitude that we owe Him for the goodness and mercy and loving-kindness which have followed us all the days of our life. St. Francis Xavier in his noble hymn, *O Deus, ego amo Te*, expresses the thought of every true disciple:

> " E'en so I love Thee, and will love,
> And in Thy praise will sing,
> Solely because Thou art my God,
> And my eternal King."

VII

This Faith, this living body of revealed truth which we are able to make our own through the exercise of the virtue of faith, is never to be thought of as the mere sum of the supernatural truths which God has made known to us. This would be a grave error, somewhat analogous to saying that God is the sum total of His attributes. The Faith is a living organic structure growing out of a living basic principle, which principle is God Himself, and working according to the law of its own nature. Just as a scientist can make a special study of one or another aspect of nature, but cannot divorce the thing he is studying from the rest of nature, so I can think separately of each truth which God has made known to me, but I cannot separate it from the whole body of supernatural truth. A physician may make a special study of the heart, but in doing so he does not leave out of consideration the fact that the heart is one of the mutually interdependent members of the body. So each truth might be compared to an organ of the body which, without the other organs, would be a dead thing. Likewise, every revealed truth fits into, and is dependent upon, every other truth. As the heart without the other organs would be a mere mass of dead tissue, so a truth without being organically related to every other revealed truth would have no life in it. It is precisely this which makes a selective religion, one which picks and chooses what it will accept of divine revelation, no religion at all. It can have no organic unity, and therefore no life.

St. Thomas teaches us that he who rejects certain revealed truths and accepts certain other articles of the Faith, however firmly and implicitly he may adhere to them, does not hold that which he believes through the operation of the supernatural gift of Faith, but only by his own will and judgment.[1] The supernatural power of Faith does not work piecemeal. If it works at all, it enables the soul to receive the whole revelation of God. For example, a man may study the revelation of Christ's Divinity, and say, " This seems entirely reasonable, and I will accept it." He may then go on to consider the revelation concerning the Person and the work of the Holy Spirit, and the Sacraments; and so through the whole range of the Catholic Faith, reaching the same conclusions in the same manner. Thus he may find himself in agreement, point by point, with all that God has revealed, but he has not come to the fulness of truth through the supernatural gift of Faith within. He has arrived at his belief only through human considerations and reasonings, which are essentially opposed to the nature of Faith. One cannot take the Faith to pieces in any such manner as this.

However, we cannot from this conclude that God may not, in His love and wisdom, use this piecemeal acceptance of truth as one of the means by which to bring the soul to a right, full, and integrated belief. On the contrary, we know that He often deals

[1] St. Thomas, *Summa*, 2.2 Q. 5, Art. 3.

with humble, sincere seekers after truth in this way, the Holy Ghost leading them on to the point where they become susceptible to the influences of grace, and when they yield themselves to it, the infused virtue of Faith consolidates and unifies in a manner wholly supernatural all that they have received. But they come to that point when, no longer depending on their own judgment and will, they humbly submit to the Spirit, and are willing to receive the fulness of the Faith, not because it now seems right and reasonable to them, but solely because God has spoken it. Nor dare we say that the Holy Spirit may not Himself have been the Guide and Teacher in the piecemeal process which has brought such a soul to see and love the truth. In this fashion does His prevenient grace constantly work. God is always willing to take the soul where He finds it, and lead it on to better things.

When the New Testament speaks, as it so frequently does, of the Faith by which we are saved, it means a belief in God, and in the whole body of truth which He has revealed to us concerning His nature and work. In short, the facts of the divine revelation constitute " the Faith "; it is that to which St. Jude referred when he commanded the faithful " earnestly to contend for the Faith once delivered unto the saints," and to build themselves up " on your most holy Faith." [1]

Little is said of trust and confidence in any of these passages, wholly necessary as that is, and stressed as it is in all Scripture. One who has a wrong idea of God may still have confidence in Him. The heathen put their trust in their false and imaginary deities. This is, therefore, not what the apostles mean when they speak of " the Faith."

VIII

Since, then, there is, so far as we know, no salvation for those who knowingly refuse the Faith as Christ has revealed it in the Holy Scriptures and in His Church, it will be well for us to review a few of these passages.

St. John makes it clear that his primary purpose in writing his Gospel was not that men might trust in God to get them out of their troubles and to answer their prayers, but that " ye might believe that Jesus is the Christ, the Son of God; and that believing, ye might have life through his name." [2] Belief in Jesus of Nazareth as God and Lord of heaven was the one fundamental requirement necessary in order to " have life."

---

[1] St. Jude 3 and 20.   [2] St. John xx. 31.

The most poignant occasion in all of the New Testament history on which this truth is taught, is found in the account of the raising of Lazarus, and the accompanying record of how our Lord called out the faith of his sister Martha.[1] When she complained "Lord, if thou hadst been here, my brother had not died," He replied in those words which through all subsequent ages have been of unspeakable comfort to millions of souls: "I am the resurrection and the life; he that believeth in me, though he were dead, yet shall he live, and whosoever liveth and believeth in me, shall never die." This tremendous revelation He made to a simple village woman in her grief; and then He added the peremptory challenge, "Believest thou this?" He was not suggesting that she put her confidence in Him. It was something greater than this. In the presence of death, under the most solemn conditions, He demanded of her a declaration of faith in Himself as the life, as life from the dead. It was impossible that she could at that time have understood the meaning of His words, but she did not ask for understanding. Because she first believed in Him, she experienced no difficulty in accepting anything He might present to her as His teaching. She therefore gave her answer instantly and without qualification, indeed even going beyond what He had required of her: "Yea, Lord, I believe that thou art the Christ, the Son of God, that should come into the world."

In St. John's account of "the night in which he was betrayed" we find our Lord following the same principle in the last discourse He gave His disciples. In response to their eager questioning, He draws out their faith, and seeks to have them commit themselves by declaring it explicitly. St. Philip asks, "Lord, shew us the Father." He replies, "Believest thou not that I am in the Father, and the Father in me? . . . Believe me, that I am in the Father, and the Father in me . . . He that believeth on me, the works that I do shall he do also, and greater works than these shall he do."[2] Around the table where the great Sacrament of His Body and Blood has just been instituted, He gives them the profoundest instruction of all His ministry. It is punctuated with questions and answers, until finally all their questions are set at rest, and the disciples declare, "We believe that thou camest forth from God."[3] He has obtained from them this credo, the declaration of their faith; His purpose is accomplished, and He now speedily draws the discourse to a conclusion, and ends that long and momentous evening—the most momentous, perhaps, in all human history—

[1] St. John xi.   [2] St. John xiv. 10, 11, 12.   [3] St. John xvi. 30.

with the great prayer which the Beloved Disciple records in chapter seventeen. In this prayer, in their awed presence, He renders, as it were, His account to His Father, and testifies to Him of their declared faith : " I have given unto them the words which thou gavest me, and they have received them, and have known surely that I came out from thee, and they have believed that thou didst send me."

In this same prayer our Lord sets forth the truth that faith must go before any adequate knowledge. He prays for the unity of His followers in order that, seeing their oneness in love, " the world may *believe* that thou hast sent me " (verse 21), and then, as a consequence of this belief, that " the world may *know* that thou hast sent me " (verse 23). In these words our Lord provides the basis of the later maxim which the great masters of the Faith have made the ground of their teaching, " *Credo ut intelligam*, I believe in order that I may know."

Nearly the whole of the fifth chapter of St. John's first epistle, beginning with the words, " Whosoever believeth that Jesus is the Christ is born of God " inculcates the same truth concerning the Faith. Many passages might be drawn from St. Paul's epistles, but one will suffice to illustrate his invariable teaching. In Romans ix. 10 he writes, " If thou confess with thy mouth the Lord Jesus, and shalt believe in thine heart that God hath raised him from the dead, thou shalt be saved." Here was required a definite, objective belief in certain historical facts, not mere intellectual assent, but belief from the heart. Nothing was said about trusting in God. Trust was altogether necessary, but to believe in the God-Man, as St. Paul requires, would in any normal mind produce a complete trust, whereas a trust without the belief would be without foundation and therefore could not endure.

The actual practice of all the apostles and their companions, in their missionary work, coincides always with what they taught in their writings for the edification of their children in the Faith. St. Philip the Deacon, when he baptized the Ethiopian eunuch, required such a belief of him. The Ethiopian's reply to the demand was, " I believe that Jesus Christ is the Son of God." [1] The implications of this declaration covered the whole range of the Christian revelation, and it was sufficient. No other demands were made upon him, and he was forthwith baptized. Explicit acceptance of the truth of the objective facts which God has taught His people concerning Himself and His work for men and for their salvation is fundamental in the strictest sense. Faith is the virtue,

[1] Acts viii. 37.

the power, delivered to the soul by the Holy Spirit, the use of which enables men actually to accept these facts as they are embodied in Holy Scripture and in the teaching of the Church, and not only to believe them, but to govern their lives according to them.

IX

The steadfast exercise of this virtue of Faith is necessary to the Christian life, for only by exercise can it be developed, and a power which is not developed and increased will soon perish. The chief exercise by which faith is developed is that of prayer, which we define as any loving communication between the soul and God; but, on the other hand, we must have some degree of faith before we can pray. By the persistent use of prayer we enter more and more intimately into the life of God, and so participate the more in His nature. In prayer we find close, personal association with Him; we keep ourselves in His presence, uniting ourselves to Him in acts of devotion, in affections and aspirations. In short, we are walking with God. All this is our act of union with God, and His acceptance of our devotion is His act of union with us. By repeated, or rather continuous, acts, we more and more dwell in Him, and He in us. This is the most direct and complete fulfilment of our Lord's promise, " If any man love me, he will keep my words; and my Father will love him, and we will come unto him, and make our abode with him." [1] The Holy Spirit is unceasingly seeking to draw us ever more deeply into the orbit of His own infinite life, to give us ever richer participation in His Triune Divinity, and Faith is the means by which we enter into this mysterious relationship. As we, believing, co-operate with Him and yield ourselves to His leading, we shall be cementing with Him a union which is never to be violated. Every Communion we make, every lifting of the heart to God in faith, every good action, is an entering more fully into Him, and He into us. We partake more and more of the divine Nature, we share ever more fully in His essential love and power, in His wisdom, in His holiness.

This sharing ever more fully by faith in the life of God will induce an ever-increasing love and trust and confidence. In other words, we will live by our Faith. There is no surer truth in human life than that a man lives as he believes. If I have faith in my friend, I will trust him. If I have faith in the integrity of my business associates, I will give them my full confidence. If I believe the roads are safe, I will walk abroad. Test it in whatever depart-

[1] St. John xiv. 23.

ment of life you will, and you will find that the law of belief is the law of living—*lex credendi, lex vivendi*. St. James, who teaches us so much about Faith, begins and concludes his epistle with strong statements as to the necessity of the prayer of Faith, which prayer must be based on a full and profound belief in God.

To accept God as He has revealed Himself brings, as does nothing else, peace and tranquillity. If I believe that He is my loving Father, if I have a profound, unswerving conviction that He is infinitely wise and strong, and that all His strength and wisdom are engaged in my behalf, then, regardless of whatever terrifying perils may seem to impend, all anxiety vanishes, and with faith, and a resulting confidence, I am able to "serve Him with a quiet mind." [1] Anxiety always comes from fear, and fear means a want of faith. If I really believe God to be what He is; if I, nothing wavering, believe His relation to me to be what He has declared it to be, every fear will be cast out by His perfect love dwelling in me. In times of stress there is always temptation against faith; but there is likewise ever the power to trample the temptation under our feet, and to rise on the wings of faith to the calm of a perfect assurance in Him who tells us that always and in every contingency, "underneath are the everlasting arms." [2]

Service "with a quiet mind" is always good service. Calm and control produce conditions under which all our powers, natural and supernatural, are at their best. No good work has ever been done in anxiety and agitation, for they paralyze our abilities. To know that "I can do all things through Christ" [3] scatters unnerving fear to the winds, releases reservoirs of power hitherto undreamed of, and enables us easily to compass that which to the natural spirit were wholly impossible achievements. Through faith we are able to employ the divine omnipotence in our work for Him, and nothing is stronger than the strength of God. "This is the victory that overcometh the world, even our faith." [4]

Lord, I believe that Thou art the Way, the Truth, and the Life. Make me so to walk with Thee that by Thee I may come to the Father ; make my faith strong to believe all that Thou hast revealed, for Thou art the very Truth. Give me Thy life that I may say, " I live, yet not I, but Christ liveth in me." By Thy divine omnipotence direct and strengthen my faith ; by Thy divine wisdom instruct and enlighten it ; by Thy divine goodness sustain and perfect it, that I may abide in Thee, unchanging to the end.

[1] Collect, XXI Sunday after Trinity.   [2] Deut. xxxiii. 27.
[3] Phil. iv. 13.   [4] 1 St. John v. 4.

Our consciousness of Sonship expands into a consciousness that we are of God. The sense of solidarity with God is the virtue of Christian hope. It is a *virtus divina;* that is, a breaking forth of divine power. In hope the soul shares the Father's infinite consciousness of Himself and of His power. . . . How His consciousness must be penetrated with sublime light, unfathomed depth, imperturbable security! . . . Our own poor tremulous experience of ourselves is immersed in God's calm security, is enlarged in God. Our hope, although not yet fulfilled in the absoluteness of everlasting possession, but walking still in the twilight of faith, is nevertheless already an echo of that unbroken, glad, secure sense of triumph with which the Father possesses Himself in the fulness of His divine essence.

Julius Tyciak.

CHAPTER IX

THE VIRTUE OF HOPE

I

In our study of Faith we have seen that there is a natural as well as a supernatural faith. What we call natural faith is that instinct which causes normal human beings to have the confidence in each other which is necessary for the existence of human society. We find a like exercise of natural hope in every human mind. It is taken cognizance of by the philosophers, who number it amongst the passions, or appetites. They define it as a longing for something which is lacking to us, and which is fitting for us, and possible to gain, but with effort. In actual operation, however, this natural hope is often the diametrical opposite of the Christian virtue of Hope. I am asked if I am going to be able to carry out some plan or work which is very near to my heart. I reply, " I hope so "; and often the very tone of my voice has in it a quality of doubt, sometimes almost of despair, which is the philosophical opposite of Hope as the Christian exercises it. I hope to attain my aim, but I should be rather surprised if it came out as I desire.

Quite contrary to this, the Christian's hope is a supernatural virtue or power, which God infuses into the soul at the moment of its being made one with Christ in baptism; and we may define it as that steadfast expectation of the supernatural and heavenly things which are sure to come to pass, if we do our part, because God has promised them.

Faith, as we have learned, imparts to the *reason* a supernatural gift which enables it to accept, without doubt or question, the revelation of divine truth as God has given it, and solely on His authority. In like manner, hope communicates to the *will* an invincible supernatural confidence and trust in God, and in His promises, and out of this confidence grows the power courageously to pursue and to lay hold upon the highest good, which is God Himself, and upon everything which leads to Him. Hope gives the soul the consciousness of its power to attain to God. The stronger this power, the greater is the soul's certainty and assurance; and this assurance of power fills it with that sense of security and consequent satisfaction which invariably mark the truly hopeful soul. Hopefulness and a settled cheerfulness always go together, and this virtue has the force to overcome anything that might militate against the ability to be "joyful through hope." Joy is the inevitable fruit of hope, even in the merely natural sphere, and by the degree of joy which the soul possesses and exercises is to be judged its hold upon the virtue of hope.

II

As we have thought again and again, God always does His work perfectly. Supernatural hope allows for no doubt or contingency so far as He is concerned. The only doubt possible arises from the question as to whether we will to do our part, whether we will carry out the conditions which God, in His desire to make us co-workers with Himself, has laid down for us to fulfil.

At this point enters once more the consideration of our co-operation with God, which, as we have seen repeatedly, is necessary in every relationship which we have with Him. It is of supreme importance, however, to remember that no co-operation with God is possible unless God Himself takes the initiative. His prevenient grace—that is, the grace which goes before and produces our desire for Him in the first instance, and our ability to respond—is absolutely necessary. Any movement of the soul towards God, however slight, is the direct result of the action of God in the soul. Of ourselves we can do nothing. If this should tend to discourage anyone, let him remember that God stands always ready and eager to bestow upon us the rich and everlasting blessings of His kingdom, and that He gave His own life on the cross in order to gain for us the practical power to lay hold of the things for which we hope.

Faith assures us that we are the children of God, and if children, then of necessity we are, as St. Peter tells us, "partakers of the divine nature," [1] because a child must always partake of the nature of its father. This assurance of our divine sonship passes into an ever-growing realization that we are of the family of God; that, in being grafted into Christ, we have been, along with Him, taken up into the Godhead. Being thus made partakers of God Himself, we share not only His knowledge, His wisdom, His love, His holiness but, as the result of that sharing, we possess also the triumphant consciousness of the imperturbable security which He possesses in the essence of His divine Being. This sense of deep oneness with

[1] 2 St. Peter i. 4.

Him, of " solidarity with God," *is* the exercise of the virtue of hope.[1]

III

Hope is exercised in the life of probation here on earth, and it is the beginning of the divine possession, which possession grows and increases until hope is lost in the full fruition of the Beatific Vision of God in heaven. In that blessed state this divine vision will no longer be the object of our hope, for that which we possess in its fulness we no longer hope for. " What a man seeth, why doth he yet hope for ? "[2]

If our faith is right, then our hope gives a security which nothing can shake. It is " an anchor of the soul, both sure and steadfast, and which entereth into that within the veil, whither the forerunner is for us entered, even Jesus ";[3] and because He has, in His Sacred Manhood, entered there, we too, being one with Him, have made our entrance into that blessed state where He is in the bosom of the Trinity; for He has promised, " Where I am there shall also my servant be."[4] This life in God is ours now in a definite manner and degree. It continually deepens until it attains its perfection in the final vision of God.

Our hope is not based upon anything that we do, or on anything that we are. Nor is it based only upon what God does, or has done. If the latter were the case, our hope could not reach beyond our own conscious experience of God, or our knowledge of the experience which others have had of Him. Hope is based upon what God *is :* He is love, goodness, power, wisdom, holiness. Our hope—that is, our assurance of security—lies in these. A child runs to its mother in some moment of new peril. It has never seen the mother under these circumstances before, and it is impossible for it to know what she can or will do. But it trusts what the mother is, and feels secure. So we trust what God is, and therein lies our imperturbable calm of hope.

IV

The primary object of hope is no ephemeral thing. If we made the things of the world the object of our hope, experience would soon disillusion us, and we would see that they lacked two essential elements—that of permanence and that of perfection. Earthly things quickly pass away, and even when they seem to persist, they lose the quality which can satisfy, for we are made for God, and

---

[1] See Tyciak, *Life in Christ*, pp. 36–37.   [2] Rom. viii. 24.
[3] Heb. vi. 19.   [4] St. John xii. 26.

nought but God can supply the interior peace and satisfaction which the heart of man requires. Because man is made for God, he is made for perfection, and the ineradicable principle of perfectibility which operates in every soul will not allow us to rest save in Him.

St. Thomas points out that the object of man's will and desire is the universal good which is God Himself, just as the object of the intellect is truth, which also is God, though man may not realize that what he is reaching after in his continual discontent is really God. Since neither the will, nor the intellect, is ever willing to stop half-way, but must be pressing on—no will or intellect which is not in a state of decay is ever being satisfied, but is always desiring more—therefore, nothing can satisfy the human spirit save God Himself. Hence, He, and He alone, the Infinite One, is the ultimate object of man's hope.

The final object of hope can lie only in the ultimate things, and God Himself is the only real Ultimate. Our hope, therefore, looks unto Him, for " He has made us for Himself, and our heart can find no rest until it rest in Him." [1] " I am thy exceeding great reward," [2] God declared to His servant of old, and it is on this that we base our hope. Repeatedly in Holy Scripture we are assured that He alone is the object of our supernatural expectation; not His gifts or rewards, but Himself. " And now, Lord, what is my hope? My hope is even in thee," [3] cries the psalmist as he contemplates the perils of the spiritual life, and the imminence of sin. He reasons with His soul again and again, sternly urging and exhorting it to trust in God: " Why art thou so heavy, O my soul, and why art thou so disquieted within me? put thy trust in God; for I will yet give him thanks, which is the help of my countenance and my God." [4]

The Scriptures, more than once, give us a stronger expression than this which we have just considered. " God is our hope and strength," [5] the psalmist says in another place, as he meditates with calm joy upon the security which he has in God, come what may in the way of earthly disaster; and again he says, " Thou art my hope." [6] St. Bernard, commenting on this last passage,[7] says that the psalmist means, perhaps, something fuller and more sublime: that my hope is not only " in Him," but it is God Himself; for more properly is that called our hope which we actually hope

[1] St. Augustine, *Confessions*, i. 1; Migne, P. L., Tom. 32, Col. 661.
[2] Gen. xv. 1.   [3] Ps. xxxix. 7.   [4] Ps. xlii. 11; xliii. 5.
[5] Ps. xlvi. 1.   [6] Ps. lxxi. 5.
[7] St. Bernard, *Serm*. ix. n. 8; Migne, P. L., Tom. 183, Col. 220.

for than that wherein our hope lies. There are indeed, perchance, some who hope to obtain from the Lord certain gifts, temporal or spiritual; but perfect love hopeth only for the Highest, crying aloud in the vehemence of its longing, " Whom have I in heaven but thee? " [1] The great prophet of Judah's captivity gives a like assurance, and comforts his stricken people with the beatitude, " Blessed is the man that trusteth in the Lord, and whose hope the Lord is." [2]

V

With the richer revelation of hope given by our Lord, the apostles of the New Covenant are tireless in their teaching concerning this divine virtue. St. Paul's epistles are filled with passages in which he triumphantly announces the virtue of hope as one of the sure bases of the life of those who are in Christ. " For we are saved by hope," he cried to his spiritual children in Rome.[3] The apostle means to say that he who does not hope in God can find no salvation, because he has no incentive or stimulus to spiritual effort to drive him on in a loving service of the Master, and possesses no ground of trust and confidence amidst the trials which are inevitable in the course of the soul's warfare. In the twelfth chapter of the same epistle he sets forth his magnificent catalogue of the marks of the true Christian, and central amongst them is that of " rejoicing in hope." He who hopes in God can find no room for melancholy in his soul, but only the joy of the anticipation of those blessed things which have been promised by Him whose promise cannot fail.

To the Colossians St. Paul proclaims that " the mystery which hath been hid from ages and from generations, but now is made manifest to his saints," is nothing less than, " Christ in you the hope of glory." [4] This same Lord Jesus Christ, he writes to St. Timothy, " is our hope." [5] The limits of the New Testament itself are the only limit we can find to the constant teaching of the joy and comfort of hope.

God is the primary object in the exercise of hope, but in His wisdom and love He has ordained that we are to attain to Him only through the use of certain means and instruments which He has prepared for us. Without the help of the grace of God we can do nothing, and grace comes to us only through the use of the Christ-ordained Sacraments. Once hope is received, it is to be developed through prayer and good works, which are also the

[1] Ps. lxxiii. 25.   [2] Jer. xvii. 7.   [3] Rom. viii. 24.
[4] Col. i. 27.   [5] 1 Tim. i. 1.

objects of hope, although they are what St. Thomas Aquinas calls the secondary objects. Christian hope is, therefore, directed also towards all the supernatural helps God offers us. It looks to the overcoming of evil, to the resistance of temptation, to the opportunity and capacity for good works, both interior and external; it looks to the joy which results from the flooding into the soul of ever more abundant streams of grace, to the ever-deepening participation in the merits of Christ, to the acquisition of all virtuous and Christ-like habits. Indeed, hope leaves nothing unclaimed as its object that will bring us nearer to God and develop in us more fully the divine character and likeness. The gift of hope is the divine pledge of the destiny God has ordained for us.

God is the ultimate objective, and the final fruition, of hope. This fruition, which is the possession of the Beatific Vision, belongs not to this life, but to the life in Paradise. The secondary objectives of our hope, however, often find their realization here; and in many cases must find it, for they are the means the use of which carries us on to the final goal. We hope for opportunities of grace and service, and this hope is, in a measure, fulfilled with every Communion we make, with every prayer we offer, with every good deed we are able to perform. These occasions of fulfilment are the progressive steps which lead on to the great and final fruition of our hope. The psalmist's words, which we must make our own, are a great act of hope: " As for me I will behold thy presence in righteousness, and when I wake up after thy likeness I shall be satisfied with it." [1] Living and serving and loving God under the incomplete revelation of the Old Covenant, the psalmist did not realize that in this cry of hope he was reaching out after the Beatific Vision. Only in Paradise can be found that satisfaction which he here assures himself will be his.

VI

Even natural and temporal blessings and advantages, as men count them, can be the object of supernatural hope, provided we are resolute to use all such, not as ends in themselves, but as means whereby we glorify God. Indeed, in the Lord's Prayer we are commanded to pray for temporal gifts, and whatever we can make the subject of our prayers we may also make the object of hope, provided, as we have said, that we are firm in our purpose to employ such gifts to His honour. We sometimes hear it said that the Lord's Prayer gives, first of all, certain prayers looking to the

[1] Ps. xvii. 15.

glorifying of His Name and the building of His kingdom; and that these petitions being faithfully used, we are then, and not until then, to pray for the supplying of our own needs. But this is not the way to look at the Prayer. Every petition in it is directed solely to God's honour and glory. We pray that certain of our needs may be supplied, but the object of these prayers is that we may be the better equipped in every way, physically, temporally, as well as spiritually, to exalt Him through our service. So, the prayers for our daily bread, for forgiveness of our sins, and for deliverance from the power of the evil one, are all humble acts of hope. We pray in hope, and in the fulfilling of our prayer is the fulfilling of our hope. The final deliverance for which we pray, the deliverance from all that is not God, will be the final fruition of the hope we have in Him.

VII

Hope is an intermediate virtue, standing midway between faith and love. Faith makes evident our sonship in God, and sonship is, by its nature, a relationship of dependence and trust—that is, a relationship which, in our earthly life and service, is to be sustained and strengthened by hope. As a consequence of this, love is inevitable. Faith passes through hope into love. When we are dependent on some one, and find that one to be in the highest degree kind and generous, loving and tender, strong and swift to help, we cannot but give him the full love of our hearts.

Hope is also the safe midway between two great and common perils of the soul, presumption and despair. There are those who dare to hope to receive the blessings of God's mercy and everlasting bounty while they themselves do nothing to lay hold upon so great a salvation. They are guilty of the sin of presumption, expecting of God the reward when they have failed, of their own fault, to do aught that would render them worthy of it. Presumption is a sin of dishonesty, for it seeks to claim that which is not its due.

On the other hand, there are unhappy souls who are not willing to take God at His word, who refuse to believe in the revelation of His love and mercy, and who, in spite of His assurances, count " the prize of the high calling of God in Christ Jesus " [1] as something beyond their grasp. These fall into the sin of Judas, which was the sin of despair. He would not believe that had he in loving sorrow confessed his sin, our Lord would have forgiven him freely, as He forgave St. Peter. He refused to believe our Lord's word when

---

[1] Phil. iii. 14.

K

He said, " Him that cometh to me I will in no wise cast out." [1]
He knew nothing of the virtue of hope.

Presumption is a denial of the divine justice; despair, a denial
of the divine love. Both are the results of spiritual pride. The
presumptous soul thinks God is to be taken lightly. He sets small
store by the Passion which our Lord endured, and in the enduring
of which He gave testimony to the awful malice of our sin. On the
other hand, the despairing soul is too proud to humble himself
to learn what the Holy Spirit would teach him of the love of God
for sinners. He cannot abide the thought of God's condescending
to him. He resents being treated with condescension, even though
it be the condescension of love. Such despair is peculiarly dreadful,
since it is the worst form of pride, and pride is the worst form of sin.

VIII

Perhaps we can do nothing more profitable than to consider the
act of hope which is used widely by Christian folk everywhere. It
is a prayer which should be in daily use by every soul who is reaching out earnestly after God. By thus continually testifying to our
hope, we strengthen our hold on this divine virtue.

" *O God, I hope in Thee for the pardon of my sins, for the help of Thy
grace, and for everlasting life, because of Thy love, Thy promises, and Thy
power.*"

Our hope is in God—" O God, I hope in Thee." But in order
to attain to God, we must first find pardon for our sins. This is
required by the natural law as well as by the supernatural. He
who dishonours another, and hopes for the favour of the one he has
wronged, without first giving some expression of sorrow for his evil
course, is going contrary to all human instincts. The necessary
pardon can come only through penitence, through that godly
sorrow which has its root in love for God whom we have wounded
by our sins. Penitence is a supernatural gift from God, and our
hope is that He will make us continually penitent, in order that we
may receive more and more the continual pardon which is required
because of our continual sins. Even after He has taken away our
sins through the Precious Blood of our Lord Christ, and all guilt
is removed, His pardoning grace continues to cleanse us more and
more. In our translation of David's great psalm of repentance [2]
we use the expression, " Wash me throughly from my wickedness."
The fine old archaic word " throughly " conveys little of the

[1] St. John vi. 37.　　　　　[2] Ps. li.

psalmist's meaning to many minds. The Hebrew original implies a continual washing, the divine grace working upon us to make us ever more and more clean, not only from sin, but from all its debilitating effects and consequences. The Latin rendering in St. Jerome's Vulgate version, " *Amplius lava me*, Wash me more and more," presents the thought of the psalmist, and this every sinner must make his own.

But the pardon of sin is not enough. If God should forgive us and then leave us to our own devices, speedily would we again be in the toils of Satan. But God does not leave us to ourselves. " He knows whereof we are made; he remembers that we are but dust," [1] and the action of His pardoning grace is only the beginning of the gracious work which He would make in our souls. Therefore, we hope not for pardon only, but for the help of His grace. True, " He died that we might be forgiven," but this did not satisfy the conditions, or the demands of God's infinite love. We need to remind ourselves again and again that the absence of sin is not holiness. Our call is far greater than merely to stand guiltless in the sight of God. He must see Christ in us, and see us in Christ. He has ever greater gifts for us. He died that we might be forgiven, but He also " died to make us good," that we might share His goodness and holiness, that we might become " partakers of the divine Nature." [2] The negative work of cleansing the penitent soul is only the preparation for the great positive work which God does in the souls of His people, the work of building them up, and making them more and more like unto Himself.

Penitence is not merely an act; it is the state of being of those who are conscious of having sinned against a loving Father. Nor is His pardon an act, done once for all and completed. He makes clean our hearts which had been the habitation of Satan, but not content with this, He draws the penitent soul more and more deeply into the very depth of His own divine Being, making us continually more and more sharers in all that He is and in all that He has, so far as we have the capacity to receive these ineffable gifts. So through the exercise of hope we have the certain and joyful expectation, the sense of unfailing security, because the unceasing streams of His love and grace are poured into our hearts through our oneness with Him through Christ Jesus, who is Himself the fulness of all grace and truth. " His compassions fail not; they are new every morning." [3] So, while we do not brood over our sins which have been forgiven, nevertheless the true penitent

---

[1] Ps. ciii. 14.   [2] 2 St. Peter i. 4.   [3] Lam. iii. 22–23.

can never forget that he has sinned against so dear a God and Father. This memory is a stimulus to the work of reparation which is due to Him whom we have wronged, and penitence is the spring and fount of reparation.

Lastly, we hope for everlasting life. When we recall our definition of hope it seems almost paradoxical that we should hope for a share in the eternal life of the Godhead as though it were something in the future, for we have seen that the possession of eternal life is not a promise for the future, but a pledge of present possession, here and now. " He that believeth on me hath "—not will have at some indefinite future time—" eternal life." [1] But this seeming paradox is disposed of when we remember that this life does not consist either of one complete gift made to us once and for all; or of a series of gifts. It is one continuous, unbroken flow from the heart of God into our hearts, because we are immersed in the very life-stream of His own Being. Our hope is for the continuance, for the ever-deepening increase, of that flow, for the always richer entrance into the " glad, secure sense of triumph with which the Father possesses Himself in the fulness of His divine Essence." [2]

IX

In our act of hope we declare further the grounds upon which we base our hope: " Because of Thy love, Thy promises, and Thy power."

When we speak of the love of God we are, of course, speaking of His essential nature, for, as St. John twice declares, " God is love," [3] that is, He does not possess love as we might be said to possess it, for, as St. Augustine says, " Whatever He has that He is." [4] Since He is very love, then every action of His is, of necessity, an act of love, and there can be nothing in the operation of the divine life which is not the working of love. We know that He loves us, and out of this knowledge there arise that complete trust and confidence which we repose in Him.

Out of His love proceed the " great and precious promises " [5] which God makes to His people, and we are assured that " He is faithful that promised," [6] that " the Lord is not slack concerning his promise as some men count slackness." [7] However, it is a common occurrence in our relations with our fellow-men that, in

---

[1] St. John vi. 47.   [2] Tyciak, *op. cit.*, p. 37.   [3] 1 St. John iv. 8 and 16.
[4] St. Augustine, *De Civ. Dei*, xi. 10; Migne, P. L., Tom. 41, Col. 325.
[5] 2 St. Peter i. 4.   [6] Heb. x. 23.   [7] 2 St. Peter iii. 9.

all good faith, we make promises which, when the time comes, we are not able to fulfil. Circumstances over which we have no control bar the way, and the promise fails. Our acceptance, therefore, of human promises, however sincerely they may be made, however we may put a dependence on them, must be always with reservation. We trust the intention and good faith of him who promises, but we throw an anchor, as it were, to windward, in order to protect ourselves against possible failure. Not so is it with the promises of God. He can do all that He wills to do, and He wills to do everything that His perfect wisdom knows to be good for us. His power is infinite, and no condition can arise which can successfully work against the omnipotent love which is ever active in our behalf.

We trust in Him implicitly. To the best of our ability we do our part, and nothing then can be wanting to us. So, we hope in Him because of His love, His promises, His power. None of these can fail.

x

Like every power and virtue we may possess, hope once infused into the soul must be developed. St. Paul, in his great epistle of hope which he wrote for the instruction of the Christians in Rome, tells us that we are " to abound in hope through the power of the Holy Ghost." [1] Systematic exercise is necessary to the healthy development of any power which we have. The principal method we have to employ here is that of prayer. Every prayer, of whatever kind, is an act of hope, the expression of the trust and confidence we have in God. To express it strengthens it. By prayer we build up an ever stronger hope. Prayer and hope continually react on each other. Each builds up the other. Without some degree of hope, prayer would be impossible, and without prayer no increase of hope, no abounding in hope, could be achieved. Prayer is the atmosphere and breath of the soul. Every prayer, of whatever kind, is the exercise of the virtue of hope. When the apostle says that we are to abound in hope, the word he chooses with which to convey his meaning is one of the strongest in the language of the New Testament. It implies an increase of hope without measure, and to be able thus to " abound in hope in the power of the Holy Ghost," we need to exercise ourselves in prayer ceaselessly. St. Paul in another place puts it in a powerfully epigrammatic and emphatic form when he commands the Thessalonians, " Unceasingly pray." [2]

[1] Rom. xv. 13.   [2] 1 Thess. v. 17.

As every prayer is an exercise of hope, so every sin of every kind arises from a failure in hope. Sin is alluring to us because of some fancied good which we suppose the act of sin will produce. Our hope is not sufficiently strong to sustain us in patiently waiting until God, in His own appointed time, bestows upon us the promised blessing. Our first parents were not content to tarry God's leisure and wait for the richer revelation that He had for them, but they anticipated God's will in revealing to them the knowledge they naturally desired. The first sin, whence came all our woe, was a sin against the virtue of hope, and every violation of God's will in the history of mankind has been of like character. Sin sacrifices the promised beatitude of heaven for which we hope, for the evanescent pleasure of the present moment.

XI

What are the effects of the exercise of this virtue? Of the gracious gifts which follow upon hope we may name three out of many. In the first place, as with the possession of all other real power, it brings a sense of peace. The apostle prays, " The God of hope "—that is, He who bestows upon us the virtue of hope, and with it gives continual opportunity for its growth and increase— " fill you with all joy and peace in believing." [1] The verb which the apostle uses here is the same one (πληρόω) that is found constantly in the New Testament, and which always implies being filled full; " that ye may be perfect and entire, wanting nothing," [2] as St. James describes the ideal state of the Christian soul. He who hopes in God is troubled at nothing, for he has placed his confidence, once for all, in Him who cannot fail. " The eternal God is thy refuge and underneath are the everlasting arms." [3]

Wherever hope is mentioned in Holy Scripture, the very language used witnesses to the strong calm which is the possession of him who hopes in God. Serene, he faces every exigency of life. He knows no agitation or anxiety. However disaster may seem to shatter every plan or purpose, because he knows God, he knows also with certainty that in the end all will be well. This knowledge and experience of God is the basis of our hope. St. Bernard testifies that just as it is impossible to know God in any real measure and not to love Him, so it is equally impossible to know Him and not to find Him that hope and strength which will calm the unrest within. Note the quiet spirit of the psalmist as he says, " God is our hope and strength, a very present help in trouble," [4] and again,

[1] Rom. xv. 13.   [2] St. James i. 4.   [3] Deut. xxxiii. 27.   [4] Ps. xlvi. 1.

" I have a good hope because of thy word." [1]   Here is no vehemence of speech.   He does not have to bolster up his courage with strong language.   He knows whom He has believed, and, like the apostle, he is " persuaded that he is able to keep that which he has committed unto him." [2]

Of two further fruits of hope we are told by the apostles.   St. John assures us that when Christ " shall appear we shall be like unto him, for we shall see him as he is."   He then adds, " and every man that hath this hope in him purifieth himself even as he is pure." [3] St. Paul writes to the Romans, " If we hope for that we see not, then do we with patience wait for it." [4]

Such are the fruits of this virtue.   Hope leads to patience, and patience to purity.   Patience, St. James tells us, leads to a perfect work,[5] and purity of heart leads to the vision of God in love.   Can the soul desire more?

Blessed be the God and Father of our Lord Jesus Christ, who, according to His abundant mercy, hath begotten us again unto a lively hope by the Resurrection of Jesus Christ from the dead : Strengthen this hope in us, O Lord, that its blessed fruition may bring us peace at the last.

[1] Ps. cxix. 81.
[4] Rom. viii. 25.
[2] 2 St. Timothy i. 12.
[5] St. James i. 4.
[3] 1 St. John iii. 2–3.

By love alone we are turned to God, united with God, transformed in God, made one spirit with Him, beautified here by grace, hereafter by glory. For love rests only in the Beloved; Love, I say, which is charity, is the way of God to men, and the way of men to God. God has no dwelling where there is no charity. But if we have love, we have God, for " God is love." Hence love admits no medium between itself and its object, which is God. Therefore, it never rests until it passes all things and attains to Him, transforming the lover in the Beloved, so that one lives in the other. This love is the life of the soul, and its perfection; in which are the whole law and the prophets. Hence, the apostle says, " Love is the fulfilling of the law," and " the end of the commandment is charity."

ALBERTUS MAGNUS.

Love is the confounder of all antitheses. It breaks the line between here and the hereafter; between change and the changeless; time and eternity. It is peace in conflict; contemplation in the midst of action; sight piercing through faith. For in love the divine meets the human; heaven comes to earth when Christ is born, and man rejoices in the Truth.

JOHN BURNABY.

CHAPTER X

THE VIRTUE OF LOVE

I

IF we found perplexity and ambiguity in the use of our ordinary English words *faith* and *hope*, much more shall we find these difficulties when we come to consider the nature of love. This single word may indicate the basest of human passions, or it may express what is the essential life of God Himself. Such is the poverty of our English tongue that we cannot use this word at all without in every instance accompanying its use by an explanation of what we mean by it. Like hope, it is numbered by the philosophers amongst the eleven natural passions, or appetites. We place it first, for all the other passions are subsidiary to it, and dependent on it.

St. Augustine, following certain ancient philosophers, reduces these passions to four: love, joy, fear, grief; but he gives love the mastery of them all. Speaking of the good will which is the motive power in our love for both God and man, he says, " He who resolves to love God, and to love his neighbour as himself, not according to man, but according to God, is, on account of this love, said to be of a good will. . . . The right will evidences, therefore, a well-directed love and the wrong will gives evidence of an ill-directed love. Love, yearning to possess its object, is what we think of as desire; securing it, and taking satisfaction in it, is joy; fleeing that which is opposed to it, is fear; and experiencing that which is contrary to it, when it has befallen us, is grief. These motions are evil if the love be evil; they are good if the love be good." [1]

Whether in his interior life, or in his external life, man is, therefore, guided by love, and St. Augustine tells us that " good or bad loves make good or bad lives." [2] In other words, a man lives as he loves. This is true in every sphere of human life.

The Christian virtues are needed for our perfection; no one of them can be omitted. But just as love dominates all the passions,

---

[1] St. Augustine, *De Civ. Dei*, xiv. 7; Migne, P. L., Tom. 41, Col. 410.
[2] " Ex amore suo quisque vivit, vel bene, vel male."—St. Augustine, *Contra Faust.*, Lib. v. 11; Migne, P. L., Tom. 42, Col. 228.

it is likewise the virtue which is necessary for the perfection of all other virtues. It "inspires them, rules them, animates them, or informs them, and assures their perseverance, by making their acts converge toward the last end, toward God, loved above all. . . . Not only does charity assemble all our powers, inspire our patience and perseverance, but it also unites souls, and leads them to unity in truth." [1]

St. Paul exhorts the Colossians: "Put on, therefore, as the elect of God, holy and beloved, bowels of mercy, kindness, humbleness of mind, meekness, longsuffering, forbearing one another, and forgiving one another, if any man have a quarrel against any: even as Christ forgave you, so also do ye." This is a formidable list of required virtues, but the apostle adds one more which is supreme over all others: "And over and above all," he says, "put on charity, which is the bond of perfection," [2] that is, this charity is "the power which unites and holds together all those graces and virtues which together make up perfection," [3] the perfection to which every soul is called, and to which in the end every soul can, and must, attain, unless he is to fail of his God-appointed destiny. Even if it were possible for one to practise the form of certain virtues, they would stand in isolation, without relation to the others, with no plan, no organic unity, no common objective, unless they were united by the motivating virtue of love, which is "the bond of perfection." St. Paul makes this clear in his treatise on love in 1 Corinthians xiii. No matter what spiritual powers one may possess, even to the working of great miracles, without charity it is nothing. Love is the soul of all the virtues, giving them life, even as our souls give life to our bodies.

Without love, no virtue can exist at all. We possess life only as we are in union with God, and love is the essence of the life of God. Without it there can be no life. As St. Augustine says, "Our life is love; and if life is love, hate, which is the absence of love, is death" [4]—that is to say, we live to the things we love, and we die to the things we hate. If we love God, we live to God. We are to hate sin and the world, and by the world we mean human society organized without any reference to God. We are to die to all that pertains to worldliness and sin; and love, which is God, is to reign sovereign over all. Virtue is an organic whole. We can no more separate the virtues from each other than we can

---

[1] Garrigou-Lagrange, *Christian Perfection and Contemplation*, p. 139.
[2] Col. iii. 12–14.   [3] J. B. Lightfoot, Commentary, *in loc.*
[4] St. Augustine, *Ennar. In Ps.* liv. 7; Migne, P. L., Tom. 36, Col. 633.

separate the organs of the body and still maintain life. Love binds the virtues together and gives life and unity and force to the whole. In the physical body the mysterious thing we call life ensures co-ordination and action of the organs which without life would be but an assemblage of dead parts. What life is to the body, love is to the soul.

II

Love, whether it be good or evil, has four concomitants. It is always accompanied by sympathy between the souls that love each other; there is the desire for the companionship of the beloved; certain tastes are found to be held in common; and there is always a tendency to do that which will please the one we love. We can see at a glance that the working out of these four elements produces good or bad lives, according as the love is good or evil. If I sympathize with that which is good, if I desire and seek association with those who are high and noble in character, if I cultivate tastes in common with them, and seek in all things to please them, my life can scarcely escape being a good life.

In our present study we are not thinking of love in any merely natural or human sense, but of the love which is " of God," or rather, should we say, the love that " is God "—St. John uses both these expressions [1]—and which no soul can possess unless it comes as a gift from Him. St. Bernard tells us that " love is both God and at the same time the gift of God." [2] There is one fundamental difference between love and the other theological virtues. Faith and hope are exercised only in this life; love endures forever— " love never faileth "; [3]—and it will find its perfect exercise only in the life to come. Faith and hope are exercised in time *towards* God; love is exercised both in time and in eternity *in* God.

We may define this supernatural love for convenience of study, but from its very nature love is difficult of definition. We are able to say with some degree of clarity what faith and hope are, but love, being a projection into His creation of the very nature and quality of God Himself, eludes exact description. But definition is not necessary. We can do better than define it. We can experience it, and exercise it. The humble, devout soul feels towards it as Thomas à Kempis felt towards sorrow for sin when he said, " I would rather feel compunction than to know the definition thereof." When we come to the final evaluation of our lives, God is not going

---

[1] 1 St. John iv. 7 and 8.
[2] St. Bernard *Epist.*, xi. 4; Migne, P. L., Tom. 182, Col. 111.
[3] 1 Cor. xiii. 8.

to ask us to give a definition of love. He is going to ask if we have lived loving lives.

But, be this as it may, definitions are intellectually economical. If we are able to put as clearly as possible in a brief formula of words what we mean, it saves the trouble of having continually to explain. Spiritual writers have therefore always ventured, inadequate as it may be, a definition of love. It is the virtue, the power, which God infuses into the soul as a free and unmerited gift, by use of which we are in reality able to love God above all else for His own sake, and in the way in which He loves Himself; and, as a consequence of this, to love our neighbour for God's sake.

This theological virtue of love can and must find practical place and exercise in the lives of all men, even of those who are unlearned and ignorant. Whatever a soul's limitation, it can always love. A mystic has expressed this well: " All can love Thee: rich and poor, simple and unlearned, small and great—all can give their hearts to Thee; for all can love. None too weak, none too poor, none too old, none too young. Perchance thou canst not fast; thou canst not bear the biting discipline, or labour much, or go on distant pilgrimage—but thou canst love." [1]

If the love we have is what St. Augustine means by a good love, even if it is being exercised only in the natural sphere, and without conscious reference to God, the theological virtue of love, when infused into our souls, embraces this natural love, supernaturalizes it, and raises it to another plane. It gives it a higher principle; it affords it a new and more powerful motive; and it presents it with a nobler object upon which to exercise itself. Nowhere do we find more fully exemplified the teaching of St. Thomas Aquinas that grace does not destroy nature, but perfects it.[2] It transforms it into the supernatural, and thus gives it a divine principle upon which to operate. This transformation of our natural love proposes to us this new motive by revealing God to us as the supreme Good, the supreme Beauty, and as the One in whom alone our aspirations can find their fulfilment. In respect to the object of our love, by this supernaturalization we come to know God no longer merely by reason, or through the study of His creation, but He is revealed to us as the Holy Trinity, Father, Son, Spirit, whom to know is to love. The lack of love for God is the proof of our lack of knowledge of Him, and the degree of our love is the degree of our knowledge.

[1] Diego de Estella, *Meditations*, lix.
[2] St. Thomas, *Summa*, 1. Q. 1, Art. 8.

Also, our fellow-men are revealed to us by this supernatural love as the objects of our love because they are fellow-sons of God with us through Him who is the first born among many brethren.[1]

III

Love is assumed always to be based on knowledge. This knowledge, however, is not that which is gained by intellectual study or by natural observation. It is rather the spiritual knowledge which is acquired by faith and prayer. It is based on knowing God rather than knowing about God. If from our experience of Him we know God to be all lovable, we cannot fail to love Him, if we ourselves are in any degree what we ought to be. Man first knows God by faith. We accept what He reveals of Himself on His authority, and, having thus accepted Him, we are prepared to experience God, to company with Him in prayer, and thus to gain ever greater knowledge of His perfection of goodness and beauty, and of His infinite lovableness. The knowledge of His love for us, of which we are given an ever-growing consciousness by faith and by experience of Him, naturally inflames our love more and more, for love begets love, and nothing so challenges love as the realization that we are loved by one whom we recognize as superior to ourselves. In so far as we realize who and what God is, and who and what we are, and know what His love for us is, shall we be able to love Him.

But whatever our love may be, and however it may grow and develop, we must ever recall the thought, to which we return again and again, that nothing of this depends upon any natural capacity or process. We have no capacity for supernatural love save through the operation of the virtue of love which God bestows upon us, along with the other theological virtues, in our baptism. " The love of God is shed abroad in our hearts by the Holy Ghost which is given unto us." [2] By no other means or agency is it possible for love to find its way into our hearts; and the same Holy Ghost is the agent who, if we co-operate with Him, is ever engaged in increasing this love in us more and more.

The Christian's love for God is far higher than that which was possible under the Old Testament dispensation, because the revelation of Himself under the New Covenant is fuller and deeper. The love we bear to God is a love which we have for the Holy Trinity. When we use the word God we use it in a far different

---

[1] Rom. viii. 29.   [2] Rom. v. 5.

sense from that which was understood by the patriarchs and prophets. We give our love to God the Father, we give it to God the Son, we give it to God the Holy Ghost. The revelation of the work of each Person of the Trinity, and of the relations which exist between them, the infinite and all-loving activities of the interior life of the Godhead, present to us a rich store of knowledge never dreamed of by prophet or seer of the Old Covenant. Each divine activity revealed to us gives us opportunity and occasion for a love based on a knowledge of God for which the holy men of old longed, but which was not vouchsafed them.

To the Christian soul, even if it does not always think of it directly, there is a consciousness, when it prays, of the office and work of the adorable Three-in-One, the Persons of the Blessed and Indivisible Trinity. Likewise, when we think of God's love for us we have always in mind that there is but one love in the Trinity. This one love is the infinite love of Father, Son, and Spirit. When the love of God is shed abroad in our hearts, though the Holy Ghost is the agent in the work, it is the action of the three Divine Persons, pouring out upon us all the infinite fulness of the triune love. As love is of the essence of God, and the divine essence cannot be divided, so the divine love must be given in its fulness to each soul, according to the measure of each. All the love that dwells in the Godhead is given to each one of us, so far as we are able to receive it. The overwhelming consciousness of this truth gives us, as nothing else can, a realization of the lofty dignity of the human individual, made as he is in the image and likeness of God.

While love is based on knowledge, this knowledge is only instrumental to the producing of love. Knowledge cannot unite us to God. Love alone is the unitive virtue. Knowledge is the continually deepening foundation upon which love is based, but having performed its office, it will cease. "Whether there be knowledge, it shall vanish away," but "love never faileth."[1] "Knowledge leads to the gate, but love alone can enter in, while knowledge stands without."[2]

The presence of love in the soul is not only linked to knowledge, it not only imparts the power to see the mysteries which God would reveal to us, but it also bestows the gift of interpretation which is not vouchsafed to the intellect. St. Augustine in a beautiful passage sets this forth. In one of his sermons on St. John's Gospel

[1] 1 Cor. xiii.
[2] "Amor intrat, ubi scientia foris stat."—Luis de la Puente, *Expositio moralis in Canticum in Canticorum,*" Bk. viii, cap. vii.

he is explaining to the congregation the meaning of our Lord's saying, " No man can come to me, except the Father which hath sent me draw him." [1] In the midst of his discussion he seems to have been suddenly overwhelmed by the realization that no man, of himself, can grasp the profound meaning of these words. He abandons the effort to explain them with the moving cry, " Give me a lover: he will feel that of which I speak; give me one who longs, who hungers, who is a thirsty pilgrim in this wilderness, sighing for the springs of his eternal homeland. Give me such a man: he will know what I mean." [2]

This saying of St. Augustine's brings us to one of the many paradoxes which we find in the divine revelation of the relations that exist between God and man. We do not recede from the proposition that knowledge is a necessary basis of love. If we did not know of the existence of God we could not possibly love Him. If it had not been revealed that God is good, there would have been nothing in our knowledge of Him which would have appealed to our love. But there is the counter-truth that knowledge is dependent on love. Pascal draws a distinction between the natural love for our fellows and the infused love of God. " To love man," he says, " we must know him; to know God we must love Him." [3] The sage and saintly Frenchman knew that without understanding, knowledge was of no avail, and that to understand another there must be a corresponding degree of love. It would be quite impossible in any reality and fulness to understand one for whom we had no love. Love brings understanding as does nothing else. We can see this truth more clearly, perhaps, if we look at it from the opposite point of view. We would not be willing to trust a man's judgment of another if we knew that he hated that other. We would trust only love to give a right understanding and appreciation of a man's character. Is it for this reason that before we are capable of acquiring any knowledge of God, He pours into our hearts, through the Sacrament of baptism, the great gift of His love? Love stands waiting and alert, to guide the soul in the very first awakening of the knowledge of Him, and it proves the only efficient guide through all life.

IV

The object of love is both God and man. This is set forth in the fundamental law of the Old Testament Covenant, which our

[1] St. John vi. 44.
[2] St. Augustine, On St. John, xxvi. 4; Migne, P. L., Tom. 35, Col. 1608.
[3] Quoted in Pusey, University Sermons, 1859–1872, p. 222.

Lord re-promulgated: "Thou shalt love the Lord thy God with all thy heart, with all thy soul, and with all thy mind. This is the first and great commandment; and the second is like unto it, thou shalt love thy neighbour as thyself." [1] In His re-promulgation of it our Lord added these words, "On these two commandments hang all the law and the prophets." That is to say, the whole obligation laid upon man by the law and revelation of God, in both the Old and New Covenants, is fulfilled by him who conforms himself to this precept of love for God and for his fellow-man. As St. Paul says, "Love is the fulfilling of the law." [2] "Love and do what you like" [3]—that is to say, he in whose life love is a consistently operating force in every relationship will, as an inevitable consequence, find himself fulfilling the law of God, and he will have no liking for anything that is contrary to God's will.

While we are bound to love both God and man, the primary object of man's love is God. This is set forth in what our Lord calls "the first and great commandment." But it is not an arbitrary command, for not to love God is the most calamitous deprivation to which a soul can subject itself. This involves not only a loss of the joy of so blessed a love in this life, but the loss of an infinite objective gain in the life to come. St. Augustine's question is an understatement which is pathetic in its force: "Is it a slight woe if I love Thee not?" [4]

St. Francis bases this love on an affinity between God and man. By affinity we mean that there is something inherent both in the nature of God and in the nature of man which draws them together in love. In other words, it lies in the very essence of things that an all-predominating love should exist between them. This affinity exists fundamentally in the fact that in creating us in His own image and likeness, He used Himself as the pattern and model upon which man was formed, so far as the finite creature could be conformed to the Infinite Creator. Man is a spiritual being because God is Spirit; man possesses freedom of will even as God is free; our God is a personal God, and man is a person; he is endowed with reason which enables him to be like unto God in the possession of knowledge, although human and divine knowledge are totally different from each other both in kind and in degree, as well as in their manner of operation. Where love fails, it fails

---

[1] St. Matt. xxii. 37–39.   [2] Rom. xiii. 10.

[3] "Dilige et quod vis fac."—St. Augustine, *On 1 St. John*, Tr. vii; Migne, P. L., Tom. 35, Col. 2033.

[4] "Parvane ipsa est, si non amem Te?"—St. Augustine, *Confessions*, i. 5; Migne, P. L., Tom. 32, Col. 663.

solely because man has through sin broken away from God, and by this sin has introduced into his nature that which nullifies the love that normally should bind them together. We have the evidence of this affinity in the fact that, when separated from God as he may be by sin, man never ceases to long after Him; nor does God ever cease to seek the love of man.

We must understand, however, that God does not need anything that we can give Him. He seeks our love, and inspires us to love Him. He seeks our love, and inspires us to love Him, because we cannot fulfil the purpose of our being save through loving Him. We love God, we serve Him, we worship Him, we glorify Him, because to do these things is necessary to our spiritual growth and maturity, not that God in any sense profits by what we can give Him.

The human understanding has an insatiable longing and desire to know more of God, even though it may be ignorant of who God is; and the will possesses a like insatiable appetite to love, and to find the perfection which lies in God only; while God Himself possesses infinite stores of blessings, and an infinite inclination to pour out these blessings upon men. Therefore, says St. Francis, the soul has reason to exclaim, " I cannot have been made for this world! There is some sovereign Good on which I depend, and some infinite Workman who has imprinted on me this interminable desire to know, and this longing which cannot be gratified; for this reason I must strain and reach up towards Him, to be united and joined to His goodness, whose I am, and to whom I belong. This," concludes the saint, " is the affinity between God and man's soul." [1] When, therefore, God commands love He is only asking that man follow out the instincts of his own nature, for in the hearts of all men, though they know God not, and though they may never have heard the words of the great Bishop of Hippo, there is the thought, " Thou hast made us for Thyself, and our heart shall find no rest until it rest in Thee." [2]

But God Himself, not any gift of His, is the reward for which we must look. " He who seeks from God any other reward but God, and for it would serve God, esteems the gift more highly than he does the Giver. What then? Hath God no reward? None save Himself. The reward of God is God Himself. This reward the soul loveth. If it love aught beside, it is no pure love." [3] Even

---

[1] St. Francis de Sales, *The Love of God*, Bk. I. xv.
[2] St. Augustine, *Confessions*, i. 1 ; Migne, P. L., Tom. 32, Col. 661.
[3] St. Augustine, *Ennar. in Ps.* lxxii. 32 ; Migne, P. L., Tom. 36, Col. 928.

L

though God had given us no revelation concerning the destiny of man, the observation of the natural man, and of his aspirations, would have told us something of this great predestination. Père Saint-Jure puts it well when he says: "Our great avidity, our unquiet eagerness, our insatiable curiosity to see, to hear, to know, and possess something new, are evident marks that created things are not our end, since it is the property of the end to calm the heart and appease the desires of the soul." [1]

v

St. Bernard develops the philosophy of love which St. Augustine had shown to be so attractive, and demonstrates that love is its own reward, although he is reluctant to introduce any idea of reward whatever in his discussion of love. "I look with suspicion," he says, "on that love which appears to be supported by the hope of any other reward than a return of love. Such love is weak, and expires if its hope of reward is withdrawn from it. Pure love derives none of its strength from hope. Love itself is the sole dowry, and the sole hope, of the spouse of God. This is all-sufficing for her, and with this alone the bridegroom is content. He requires nothing else, and she possesses nothing else." [2]

The love of God in itself brings indeed the richest reward that it is possible to find in any relationship into which the soul of man can enter, but "love is no hireling; she seeketh not her own." [3] Love never bargains, love gives, and her joy lies solely in giving. The love which had in it any thought or hope of gain would cease to be love. The test of love lies in the fulness and freedom of its giving. That we love God in any measure at all is the comforting evidence that we have given ourselves up to Him at least in some degree. "The price of love is yourself, *prætium caritatis tu*," [4] said St. Augustine, and the freer and fuller the surrender we make of ourselves, the greater the gift of love we are able to appropriate to ourselves, and to enjoy.

In this spiritual process there is continual action and reaction. First, God gives His love, and then by exercising it towards Him we gain still richer gifts, which in their turn produce in us ever greater powers of loving; and so on, indefinitely does the interflow of love, in an ever-increasing flood, pass between the Heart of God

[1] Saint-Jure, *L'Homme Spirituel*, Pt. II. c. 3, § 3.
[2] St. Bernard, *Sermo in Cant.* lxxxiii. 5; Migne, P. L., Tom. 183, Col. 1183.
[3] St. Bernard, *De Diligendo Deo*, ch. vii; Migne, P. L., Tom. 182, Col. 984.
[4] St. Augustine, *Sermo* xxxiv; Migne, P. L., Tom. 38, Col. 212.

and the heart of man. He gives His love to us with no other purpose than that it be returned to Him so that He may give it again in ever more copious and abounding streams. He gives us His love just in order that we may have the power of loving Him. Indeed, love stands distinguished in this respect, that in the case of it alone can men make a return to the Creator which is like unto His gift to them. We cannot return goodness for goodness, or mercy for mercy. We can give back love for love in never-ceasing flow. God knows that those who love Him are blessed, beyond all measure, by this very love which they receive from Him, and give back again to Him. It is a divine flood, issuing from the heart of God, catching up the soul, and the soul's love, in its irresistible tide, and bearing it up into the very cycle of love which constitutes the life of the Ever-Blessed and Adorable Trinity Itself.

VI

St. Bernard in his analysis of love [1] shows that it proceeds by four degrees. First, man, being in a state of nature, loves himself for his own sake, which is self-love. But if he knows his own true interests, even in the least measure, he soon comes to realize that he is not sufficient unto himself, and that some higher power, outside of himself, is indispensable to him and to his development. This raises him to the second degree of love, in which he loves God, not yet wholly for God's own sake, but because of the benefits he can obtain from Him. "Thus," says the saint, "man, by nature animal and carnal, with no love but for himself, is brought through self-love to love God, realizing that all his powers, at any rate for good, are derived from God, and without Him he is capable of doing nothing." The enjoyment of the divine gifts and blessings, God's goodness to him in his weakness and trials, will, however, soon give him that experience which will show God to be all-lovable and infinitely good, and the earnest soul will pass into the third stage of love, in which he will love God for God's sake only. "It will be impossible," says the saint again, "when we begin to know Him, that knowing Him, we will not come to discern His sweetness. It follows then that we are brought to love Him rightly far more for the sweetness and beauty that we find in Him than for any benefits that our self-interest desires." [2]

This third degree of love, if persisted in, will lead on to St.

[1] St. Bernard, *De Diligendo Deo*, ch. viii–xi; Migne, P. L., Tom. 183, Col. 987–995.

[2] St. Bernard, *De Diligendo Deo*, ch. vii; Migne, P. L., Tom. 182, Col. 987.

Bernard's fourth and final degree, in which the soul can no longer find any satisfaction in self, but gives the full love of the heart to God for no other reason than that He is God, the infinitely good and therefore the infinitely lovable One.   It is rare that in this life one can attain to this final degree of love, save, perhaps, for some brief and occasional interval when the heart is, in deep contemplation, rapt wholly out of self into God.   To quote St. Bernard again, " This is no mere human happiness, it is life eternal so to lose one-self, as if one were wholly emptied of self, as though indeed, one existed not. . . . O pure and holy love: most sweet and blessed affection: O complete submission of the disinterested soul! most perfect in that there is no thought of self! most sweet and tender because the soul's whole consciousness is divine! To attain this is for the soul to be deified. It becomes as a drop of water which appears lost if mingled with wine, taking its colour and taste; or, as the atmosphere, glowing with the effulgence of the sun, seems itself to be transformed into light rather than itself to be illuminated. . . . In this, our human nature is not destroyed, but it acquires a new beauty, a higher power, a more radiant glory." [1]   The fulness and permanence of this degree of love will be attained when the soul sees God face to face in the joy of the Beatific Vision, for this is the goal, the only goal, of all our loving. " Then shall we be altogether immersed in the fathomless depths of eternal light and of a luminous eternity." [2]

St. Bernard sums up the whole matter in a series of glowing sentences: " Love is a going forth of the soul, not a contract. . . . It is its own satisfaction. Its recompense lies in the object of its love. . . . True love seeks no reward. . . . He who loves God needs to be urged by the promise of no other recompense than God Himself. . . . Once attain unto Him and there is peace; it is not possible to go beyond this. . . . He kindles desire in thy heart, and He is the object of all desire. Love is complete in itself, and in the soul into which it has once entered it overcomes and transforms all other feelings. The soul that loves, loves and knows naught besides. Love alone suffices of itself, pleases of itself, and because of itself love is its own merit, its own reward. Apart from itself, love requires no motive, and seeks no fruit. Its fruit lies wholly in its exercise, in its enjoyment of itself. I love because I love; I love in order that I may love." [3]

[1] St. Bernard, *De Diligendo Deo*, ch. x; Migne, P. L., Tom. 182, Col. 991.
[2] St. Bernard, *De Diligendo Deo*, ch. xi. 30; Migne, P. L., Tom. 182, Col. 993.
[3] St. Bernard, *Sermo in Cant.*, lxxxiii, 3, 4; Migne, P. L., Tom. 183, Col. 1182.

St. Bernard goes on to show that love is not a hireling, and seeks not her own, because she already, in the simple fact of her existence, possesses to the full the fruition of all that can be hers, for the fruition of God cannot be distinguished from the love of God.[1] " No one can seek the Lord who hath not already found Him, for it is His will that He be found in order that He may be the more earnestly sought, and sought that He may be the more entirely found. But though He may be sought and found, He can never be forestalled: He is always first. If we think to be beforehand with Him, and say ' Early in the morning will I cry unto Thee ', it is nevertheless certain that our prayer would be cold if, O God, Thy inspiration did not precede it." [2]

In order not to misinterpret the whole subject, it is necessary for us to keep clear in our minds that this love of which St. Bernard speaks so eloquently is not what is sometimes popularly, and too often meaninglessly, called mystical love. It is not the love of the ecstatic. It is the love which in every soul must be possessed and developed, unless that soul is to fail utterly to attain to the only destiny which God intended for it in its creation.

VII

St. Francis de Sales calls the beginnings of the exercise of this divine virtue the love of *complaisance*. This French word has a different connotation from the smug English word *complacency*, by which it is usually unhappily translated. It means the profound satisfaction, and fulness of loving content, that the soul enjoys in its realization that God is great and good and loving, and that He pours out His love upon us, and desires above all things the love of our hearts. In short, with the love of *complaisance* we love Him just because He is God, just because He is what He is—infinite love, infinitely loving, infinitely lovable.

The satisfaction which we experience in the consciousness of His love is not dear to us merely because it makes us happy. This might easily be a form of selfishness, and no real love is ever in any degree selfish. Just in the measure that selfishness enters, love must depart. Our deep, calm sense of satisfaction comes from dwelling upon His love, His goodness, His wisdom, indeed upon all His perfections, so far as they have been made known to us, to all of which we ourselves aspire. St. Francis tells us that through love

[1] St. Bernard, *Sermo in Cant.*, xviii. 3; Migne, P. L., Tom. 183, Col. 861.
[2] St. Bernard, *De Diligendo Deo*, ch. vii; Migne, P. L., Tom. 182, Col. 987.

we enter into God's perfections as though they were our own; and in this love we become " partakers of the divine nature." [1] The saint goes on to say that " the love of *complaisance* is therefore a reciprocal donation, in virtue of which we can truly say that we belong to God, and that God belongs to us." [2] We find our joy in Him, but this is not all: the great and infinitely loving God, although He needs nothing from us, finds also His joy in us. " The Lord hath pleasure in his people," [3] and they seek ever to heed the apostolic injunction, " Rejoice in the Lord alway, and again I say rejoice." [4]

The exercise of this particular phase of love consists in rejoicing in God on account of what He is. St. Francis gives us a gracious act of love which expresses what we would here seek to convey: " How beautiful art Thou, my Beloved, how beautiful art Thou! Thou art all desirable, yea, Thou art desire itself. Blessed be my God for ever because He is so good! Whether I die or whether I live, too happy am I in knowing that my God is so rich in all goodness, His goodness so infinite, His infinity so good!" [5]

Describing how we lay hold of, and enter into the very sanctuary of the divine perfection, the Saint goes on to declare how this wonder is achieved: " Such is the sweet and noble robbery of love, which, without taking away from the beauty of the Well-Beloved, adorns itself with His radiance: without disrobing Him, clothes itself with His vesture; without taking anything from Him, yet appropriates to itself all that He has; and without impoverishing Him, is enriched with all His treasure." [6]

" Thereby," says Adolphe Tanquerey, " we draw unto ourselves the perfections of the Godhead. God becomes our God: we live on the thought of His perfection, His goodness, His sweetness, His divine life; for the heart feeds upon such things as it delights in. Thus are we enriched by the divine perfections, which we make our own by a loving complacency." [7]

---

[1] 2 St. Peter i. 4. We commonly speak of God's attributes and His perfection as though they were manifold; but we must keep in mind that " in Him there is one only most simple infinite perfection, and in that perfection one only most sole and pure act. Yea, to speak more holily and wisely, God *is* one unique and most uniquely sovereign perfection, and this perfection is one sole most purely simple and most simply pure act, which, being no other than the very divine Essence itself, is, as a necessary consequence, ever permanent and eternal."—St. Francis de Sales, *Treatise on the Love of God*, Bk. ii, ch. ii.

[2] St. Francis de Sales, *Treatise on the Love of God*, Bk. v, ch. iii.

[3] Ps. cxlix. 4.   [4] Phil. iv. 4.

[5] St. Francis de Sales, *Treatise on the Love of God*, Bk. v, ch. i.

[6] St. Francis de Sales, *Treatise on the Love of God*, Bk. v, ch. i.

[7] Adolph Tanquerey, *The Spiritual Life*, No. 1227.

VIII

Love is never content with finding joy and satisfaction in its exercise. Love must act as fire must burn and light must shine. The love that receives all, and is not eager to give all to the Beloved, is a love which has upon it the mark of death. "Love asks all; love gives all. Thou askest all from me; Thou gavest all for me. Teach me to give myself to Thee." [1] So, the mere joy and satisfaction of love passes quickly, yea, in the very moment of its taking form, into the self-forgetting love of *benevolence*. The word *benevolence* is derived from two Latin words which mean *good-will*. Where true love dwells in the heart there is, of necessity, a strong, resolute good-will, a will that no labour can daunt, to do the good pleasure of the Beloved, to honour and glorify Him to the utmost, sparing self in nothing, but rather counting it all joy if we have the opportunity of sacrificing self to the utmost for His good. This is the law of love, and there can be no exception to it.

It is this love of benevolence that goes out continually, not only towards God, but, because towards Him, it also goes out to our fellow-men. It is this which moves us to acts of charity, to feed the hungry, to visit the sick and those in distress, and all because the infinite good-will which dwells in the Sacred Heart of our Lord dwells also in us because we are one with Him, and longs to express that love in relation to Him, and to our fellow-men wherever our love can, in any way, supply their needs and longings.

Of course, since God is infinitely perfect, it is impossible for us to contribute anything to Him, but none the less is the heart which is full of the love of God eager and alert to work for His honour, and to bring others to see the joy of His service. Indeed, herein is the great missionary motive that lies behind all the work which the Church has ever done for the evangelization of the world. The primary purpose has been to exalt Him by bringing the nations to lay the tribute of their love and service at His feet. This has not been the result of a merely formal obedience to Christ's command to carry the good news of the Gospel everywhere, but the true altruist, he who loves his fellow-men, into whose heart God has infused His love, is consumed with a burning desire, a desire so poignant that it inflicts a pain, keen beyond the power of words to express, that all men should share in the joy and blessing of loving and honouring Him.

---

[1] "*A Talkynge of the Love of God*" (14th Century). Edited by Gilbert Shaw.

O good Jesu, Thou knowest the longing of my heart, that I desire above all things to love Thee : Make me to love Thee who hath so loved me. Thine I would be for Thou hast bought me for Thine own. The price of Thy Precious Blood hast Thou paid for me, sinful, unworthy, ungrateful. Thou who didst give Thyself for me, give Thyself to me. Knit my heart to Thy Heart ; hold me fast till I am lost in Thee ; hold me fast till I am found in Thee.

By love I mean not any natural tenderness, which is more or less in people, according to their constitutions; but I mean a larger principle of the soul, founded in reason and piety, which makes us tender, kind, and benevolent to all our fellow-creatures, as creatures of God, and for His sake. . . . The love, therefore, of our neighbour is only a branch of our love to God. For when we love God with all our hearts, and with all our souls, and with all our strength, we shall necessarily love those beings that are so nearly related to God, that have everything from Him, and are created by Him to be the objects of His own eternal love. If I hate or despise any one man in the world, I hate something that God cannot hate, and despise that which He loves.

WILLIAM LAW.

CHAPTER XI

"AS I HAVE LOVED YOU"

I

THE requirement of the divine precept of love is not yet exhausted, for we are not only to love God with all our heart and soul and mind, but our neighbour as ourselves. There is a difference between "the first and great commandment" and the second, which "is like unto it." We are to love God with all our heart and soul and mind; but we are to love our neighbour as ourselves. We are, as St. Augustine says, "to love God as God." [1] There is to be no limit to this love, nor are we given any pattern for it, because since there is no other love which can be compared to the love which we should have for God, there is no standard by which we can measure it. Since the love of God is the highest thing possible, it cannot be thought of as conforming to a standard. St. Bernard therefore tells us that we are to love God, not according to any measure, but freely and without measure. [2] He Himself is the infinite measure of love, and all must be conformed to Him.

But we are given a standard by which we are to love our neighbour—"thou shalt love thy neighbour *as thyself*." Our Lord here teaches that there is a right self-love which is to be the pattern of our love for our fellows. St. Augustine discusses the subject at length, and we draw from his argument the conclusion that self-love can be good, or it can be evil.

The wrong self-love is that which moves us to put self and the pleasing of self into the place of God and the pleasing of God. To quote his well-known saying, this is "the love of self, extending to the contempt of God, *Amor sui usque ad contemptum Dei.*" [3] In whatsoever degree we allow self to thrust God out, in that same degree we bring Him into contempt. Such love tends "not so much to egoism as to atheism," [4] for it drives God out of our life; it makes Him, so far as our moral relation to Him is concerned, as

---

[1] St. Augustine, *De Disciplina Christiana*, 3; Migne, P. L., Tom. 40, Col. 670.
[2] St. Bernard, *De Diligendo Deo*, ch. i; Migne, P. L., Tom. 182, Col. 974.
[3] St. Augustine, *De Civ. Dei*, xiv. 28; Migne, P. L., Tom. 41, Col. 436.
[4] Burnaby, *Amor Dei*, p. 255.

though He were not. This is the consequence of a false self-love, the fear of which we should have ever before us as a deterrent.

In order, then, to understand the manner in which we are to love our neighbour, we must first inquire concerning the right love of self. He who loves himself desires the best and most lasting blessings for himself. Now, the richest blessings we can have in this life and in the life to come arise out of loving God. St. Augustine says, " That man is the truest lover of himself who devotes his whole life to gaining a hold on the unchangeable life, and cleaves to God with every affection of his soul." Therefore, he who would love himself well and rightly must base this love of self upon his love for God, for if he love not God, he is failing to do that which will bring to himself the benefits which man naturally seeks to gain for the one whom he loves. If I love myself I will strive with all my power to secure for myself the highest good, and the highest good lies in God and in the Love of God. St. Augustine tells us that " the more we love God, the more we love ourselves. Therefore, we love God and our neighbour with one and the same love. We love God for the sake of God, and we love ourselves and our neighbour also for the sake of God." [1] We love God with all our heart and mind and soul. We give Him our total love, but it must ever be kept in mind that our love for God is never exclusive. In includes and gathers up all other right loves into the one current of love for God.

When we love God wholly, we ourselves are the gainer, and the more we love Him, the greater our gain. St. Augustine in another place shows that if we keep to ourselves the good things which God gives us, the joy we might find in them will quickly be blighted. The spiritual masters compare this to what we are told in the history of the wanderings of Israel in the wilderness. Those who hoarded the manna which God sent to them, on the morrow found it corrupted when they sought to use it. " The possession of goodness," says the saint, " is by no means diminished by being shared; on the contrary, the possession of goodness is increased in proportion to the concord and charity of each of those who share it. He who is unwilling to share this possession will be incapable of holding it, and he who is most generous in giving it out to others, will have the greater abundance for himself." [2] We do not lose what we give to others. On the contrary, to employ the love which God bestows upon us in loving our neighbour will, by the law of divine

---

[1] St. Augustine, *De Trinitate*, viii. 12; Migne, P. L., Tom. 42, Col. 959.
[2] St. Augustine, *De Civ. Dei*, xv. 5; Migne, P. L., Tom. 41, Col. 441.

usury, increase without ceasing, and indefinitely, the treasure which God has given to us.

St. Bernard has made a comparison of the soul which is in God with the air which on a brilliant day is so saturated with the light of the sun that it seems to be light itself rather than being illuminated by light.[1] We can carry this simile further. The light of the sun passes through space at a speed which the mind cannot conceive; but while all space is flooded with light, it is visible only when an object offers itself upon which the light may strike, and from which, as from a secondary source, the rays can be reflected and further distributed. Thus does God, the true and eternal Light, show Himself through the souls that will receive Him. Thus does the divine love, which is God Himself, flow out from the depths of His divinity into our souls, and thence passes into the souls of others. The divine life and love and light flow out from God to us, and their overflow from us into the souls of our brethren constitutes the love of our neighbour.

II

It is evident, then, that we are called to love our neighbour, not because we happen to like him. It must be more than a love of natural congeniality. We must love him because we see him as a brother, as a child of the same Father in heaven, as a member of the same divine family and household as ourselves, as a partaker of the same divine nature which is our heritage. It may be that this neighbour is a sinner, it may be that he is an alien from God, who has not yet partaken of the nature of our Father; but we recognize him as one whom God is insistently calling to that divine union, as one whom He loves to the uttermost, and for whom He gave His life.

We have seen that our love for our neighbour lies in our love for God, for we find the ground of that love in the fact that God dwells in him either potentially or actually. We love God in our neighbour, and, as a necessary consequence, we love our neighbour in God. We see in him the image of God, marred, it may be, and obscured by sin, but we realize that this image can be, and is to be—if God's purpose and will be not frustrated—renewed and restored. We realize that God not only created this image, but that all the outgoing of the divine love for fallen man is for the purpose of effecting this re-creation. If we love God, we cannot but love him towards whom God maintains such an attitude, for

[1] St. Bernard, *De Diligendo Dei*, x; Migne, P. L., Tom. 182, Col. 991.

we see in him a capacity for knowing, loving, and serving God, which capacity can never be lost in this life. Even the soul most debased and depraved by sin still has within itself the materials out of which the Holy Spirit, if allowed, can reconstruct a worthy temple for the indwelling of the Holy and ever-Blessed Trinity. Further, when we think of the glorious potentialities that reside in such a soul, both for the divine honour and for its own everlasting good, the thought of the grave possibility of the eternal loss of all this must fill us with an overwhelming, pitying love like unto that which overflowed from the Sacred Heart of the Lord Christ when He wept over Jerusalem. To contemplate the possibility of such a tragedy cannot leave us unmoved. If the love of God be in us, we shall long to do all we can to bring this life-giving love to the souls of all our fellows, that they too may rejoice in the same love which we have received from God, the gift of which is the supremest blessing that can be given us, or which our fraternal love can desire for others.

The love of our neighbour is not mere altruism; it is totally different from that which men call philanthropy. It is not to be thought of as the extension of any natural love such as we bear towards those to whom we are bound by ties of natural affection, even if that extension be as wide as the whole human race. The source and origin of our love for our neighbour lie in God Himself. It is totally different in its nature from any earthly love, however noble and unselfish such love may be. The love we are commanded to give to our neighbour must be a supernatural love, and when we say supernatural, we mean a love which has its origin in God, which is a free gift from God, a gift which cannot be had in any other way, and which is exercised not according to any human standard, or from any earthly incentive, but only according to God, for God, and in God.

If we are made one with God, we are caught up into the full tide of the love which constitutes the very life of the Holy Trinity, and unless we resist the force of this divine current, our love must take the same direction as His. We know that this stream of the divine love flows ever in the infinite fulness of its measure upon His creatures, and will flood their being with all its transforming power, unless they close their hearts against Him. It follows inevitably that if we have been made one with God, we must love whom He loves, and love our neighbour with the same love with which God loves him.

" A new commandment give I unto you, that ye love one another as I have loved you." The last clause in this command is the emphatic one—" as I have loved you." We have no love of our own which we can give to our fellow men. With the same love with which Christ has loved each soul for whom He died, and which He mysteriously transmits to us, must we love every soul of our fellow-men. This is the test. If we love not our neighbour, then it is certain that we have not been made one with God. In our work of loving we are not being carried along on the current of His love.

At this point, for our consolation we are to remember that God's love is ever manifested in His patience with our infirmities and our slowness. He does not demand perfection of love from us all at once, or even perfection of effort. We are to strive, by the help of the Holy Ghost, to enter into the spirit of His love. Undismayed by our many difficulties and our frequent lapses, we are to seek to practise love by doing the things which make for love, loving God and our neighbour even a little in order that we may learn to love more. If in the main we are making some degree of progress, He is content, and will give us His continual divine assistance, and in the end will make our love perfect.

III

Love is a unitive virtue, whether it be the power that operates within the Being of God, or that which man is permitted to exercise. It binds together into one those who love one another. It binds man to man. It binds man to God. It binds God to God. It is the essential indwelling love in the Godhead which effects and maintains the unity of the Three Persons in the one divine nature. " For what," asks St. Bernard, " in that Supreme and Blessed Trinity is it that maintaineth that supreme and ineffable Unity, save love? Love, then, is a law which in a manner holdeth the Trinity in Unity, and bindeth it together in the bond of peace." [1] St. Augustine gave St. Bernard the basis of his teaching when he said, " If, then, my soul and thy soul, when we mind the same thing, and love one another, become as one soul, how much more must the Father who is God, and the Son who is God, be one God in the fountain of love." [2]

" The aim of love is nothing else than the union of the lover with the one loved," [3] and this power works not only to bind the

---

[1] St. Bernard, *Epist.* xi. 4; Migne P. L., Tom. 182, Col. 111.
[2] St. Augustine, *On St. John* xviii. 4; Migne, P. L., Tom. 35, Col. 1538.
[3] St. Francis de Sales, *Treatise on the Love of God*, Bk. I, ch. ix.

Eternal Trinity into an infinite Unity, but, since it is God's own divine power that works in us, it is this love also that knits the souls of men together in the unity of the Mystical Body of Christ. It is the unifying force of love that makes us members one of another, as it is love that makes us one with Him. " The glory which thou gavest me, I have given them in order that they may be one even as we are one: I in them, and thou in me, that they may be made perfect in one." [1]

There are two stages in this unity: the true believer, being " in Christ," is, through the working of the divine gift of love, made one with God, the Holy and Indivisible Trinity; and because the faithful believers are all at one with God, they are one with each other, and, with our Lord, the Head, they constitute one Body. St. Augustine is very bold and says, " Let us give thanks that we are made not merely Christians, but that we are made Christ. . . . *Plenitudo Christi, caput et membra* . . . the head and the members make the fulness of the one Christ." [2] Thus does the operation of love bring into being the Mystical Body of Christ, in which we, partaking more and more of the divine nature, will gradually come to that unity, both with God and with one another, which will be the attainment of the final fulness and completeness of love in the perfected Body of Christ amid the glory of the Beatific Vision.

IV

Love is, however, not only a unitive virtue; it is, of its own character, also a communicative virtue. The divine nature, of which we are made partakers in our baptism, is the essential life of love, because " God is love." [3] As St. Bernard shows us that the love of God not only flows but overflows,[4] so His life, which is His love, reaches out beyond Himself to His creation. Since this outflowing of the divine life is an essential characteristic of the Godhead, therefore the divine life which is within us must follow the same operation, and must, of necessity, flow out from us into the lives of others. If the love of God flows into us at all, it must, from its very nature, overflow our hearts into the hearts of others. It is impossible for it to be held within the bounds of our own being. Since God is love, He must communicate Himself; and if He dwells in us and we in Him, this communicative character acts in and

---

[1] St. John xvii. 22, 23.
[2] St. Augustine, *On St. John*, xxi. 8; Migne, P. L., Tom. 35, Col. 1568, 1569.
[3] 1 St. John iv. 8, 16.
[4] St. Bernard, *Serm. in Cant.* xviii, 3, 4; Migne, P. L., Tom. 183, Col. 860, 861.

through us as inevitably and as necessarily as it does when He gives Himself directly to us.

In the beginning of our life in God we were caught up into the life-current of the Blessed Trinity, and that current, as we have seen, must ever return to the bosom of God, even as water must find its level. St. Bernard, in the midst of his panegyric on the virtue of love, abruptly makes a qualification which must be taken into account. "Love is a great reality, and very precious," he says; but he lays down one absolute condition—"provided it returns to the Principle on which it rests, provided it is kept in continual relation with Him who is its origin, and draws from that divine source waters that flow unceasingly in ever greater abundance." [1]

We cannot repeat too often the principle that the love which God pours into us is not something apart from His life. It is the very life of God Himself, which is ever flowing out to all who will receive it. It makes no difference whether this flowing is directly from God, or through us, He using our hearts as a channel for the current of His love. If we love not our neighbour, then we are deceiving ourselves in thinking we possess His life at all. As we have just been considering, to love God without loving our neighbour is an impossibility. Let us not lose sight of the truth that wherever God is, there all the operations of His being are carried on, and if He dwells within a soul, all the love that He has for the world finds the arena of its activity in that soul. How can we do other than regard with profound and venerating love every soul whom God so honours?

In teaching that the love of God in our hearts must overflow into the lives of others, St. Bernard is not content to think of the lives of the faithful as channels through which the love of God flows. Rather does he desire our hearts to be reservoirs which are so filled to the brim that love gushes over on every side in generous floods into the parched souls of men. A channel may carry but a trickle of water, and it may irrigate in some measure the areas upon which it empties itself; but the reservoir filled to the full gushes over instantly with every increase of its own supply. It is not possible for there to be further inpouring of the gifts of God without there being immediately a proportionate outpouring of love to others; and the fulness of the reservoir is the guarantee that it will give of love to its neighbour even as it receives from God. The full vessel easily, without effort, gives. So long as the reservoir of the heart

[1] St. Bernard, *Serm. in Cant.* lxxxiii, 4; Migne, P. L., Tom. 183, Col. 1183.

M

is full, it cannot choose but give, and since the streams of divine love flow into the heart that will receive it without ever ceasing, so does the heart give without ceasing of its love to others. St. Bernard's simile is an illuminating commentary on St. Augustine's teaching: " Every man, provided he loves God, loves his neighbour as himself, and if he loves not God he does not love himself." [1]

The basis for these truths as taught by these great saints is found in St. John's first epistle:

" Beloved, let us love one another: for love is of God; and everyone that loveth is born of God, and knoweth God. He that loveth not, knoweth not God, for God is love. In this was manifested the love of God toward us, because that God sent his only begotten Son into the world that we might live through him. Herein is love, not that we loved God, but that he loved us, and sent his Son to be the propitiation for our sins. Beloved, if God so loved us we ought also to love one another. No man hath seen God at any time. If we love one another, God abideth in us, and his love is perfected in us. . . . If a man say, I love God, and hateth his brother, he is a liar: for he that loveth not his brother whom he hath seen, how can he love God whom he hath not seen? And this commandment have we from him, That he who loveth God love his brother also." [2]

v

We have already considered the new commandment that " ye love one another as I have loved you." But how has He loved us? He tells us plainly: " As the Father hath loved me, so have I loved you." [3] The word " as " in these passages does not mean " like unto," but " in the same manner as." The adverb does not imply likeness, but identity. In order to love, we make use of His own essential love which He pours into our hearts. Indeed, we have the gift of His love only because we have the gift of Himself, for we cannot discriminate between God and the gifts of God. When the apostle says that " God is love," he is saying that God and love are one and the same. As St. Augustine says, " What God has, that He is," [4] and St. Bernard tells us that " Love is both God and the gift of God." [5]

Thus is it given to us to participate in, and exercise, the very

---

[1] St. Augustine, *On St. John*, lxxxvii. 1; Migne, P. L., Tom. 35, Col. 1852.
[2] 1 St. John iv. 7–12, 20–21.   [3] St. John xv. 9.
[4] St. Augustine, *De Civ. Dei*, xi. 10; Migne, P. L., Tom. 41, Col. 325.
[5] " Recte dicitur caritas et Deus, et Dei donum."—St. Bernard, *De Diligende Deo*, xii; Migne, P. L., Tom. 182, Col. 996.

love which operates between the Persons of the Adorable Trinity. In this essential way we become partakers of, and are able to keep in action in our human, earthly relationships, the divine nature which is Love. It is with His own love that we love our neighbour. Indeed, we can go further, and say that it is God Himself abiding in us, who seizes upon our faculty for loving, and employs it with which to love our neighbour. The love-indwelt soul can say, " I love, yet not I, but Christ loveth in me." In the measure in which I yield myself to Him, shall I be able to love my neighbour. So the effectiveness of His love in this ministry of love, which He entrusts to us, depends upon the fulness with which we consecrate ourselves to Him as instruments for His using. God is within us: He is the life of the soul, even as the soul is the life of the body. If God dwelling within us did not function, it would mean that He ceased to exist in us.

We must ever be clear in our minds what the Christian life is. Love is the essential soul of it. It must be a life of love; that is, it must be the constant operation of the life of God, which is love, within us. Love is the essential working of the divine life. As this was set forth in the life of the Eternal Son in the days of His earthly pilgrimage, so must it be set forth in our life in all its relationships. Everywhere in His life was this note sounded. His earliest proclamation of the purpose of His coming to earth and taking our nature was that " God "—that is, the Blessed Trinity, Father, Son, Spirit—" so loved the world that he gave his only begotten Son that whosoever believeth in him should not perish, but have everlasting life." [1] Time would fail us to list the numberless passages in the Scriptures which set forth love as the ever dominant note in God's dealing with His people. This same note must be present in our lives in our dealing with our fellows.

VI

We are not asked to give to everyone the same kind of love that we give to a parent, to a blood-brother, or to an intimate friend. It is not the love of congeniality that we can give to everyone; but the love of benevolence, which we saw was to be exercised towards God, must be, in its proper manner, exercised also towards our neighbour. It is the love which arises from an attitude of good will to all. It is the warm, kindly, sympathetic spirit which excepts no one from its embrace, and which impels us on every occasion to go out promptly, easily, sweetly, and unselfishly to all our fellow-

[1] St. John iii. 16.

men. It is the spirit which makes it impossible for us to think, or speak, or act, in an unkindly fashion.

It was the exercise of this love which our Lord said was to be the sign that we were His disciples: " By this shall all men know that ye are my disciples, if ye have love one to another." [1]   Let us not misinterpret these words, however, as meaning that this brotherly love should reign only amongst His professed disciples. Our love must be as broad and as deep as the divine love itself. Every soul that God loves, every soul for which Incarnate God died, must be equally the object of our love. Are we giving this supreme sign of discipleship? It requires much vigilance and labour. We cannot conceive of anything finding place in human life but has its beginning, whether it be good or evil, in thought. If we promptly repel the evil thought, resolutely divert the mind from it by a strong impulse of the will; if we deliberately bring in kindly, loving thoughts, we shall soon acquire the mental habit of thinking the thing that is right, so that nothing contrary to love will be able to enter. St. Paul gives us the charter by which we are to work: " Whatsoever things are true, whatsoever things are honest, whatsoever things are just, whatsoever things are pure, whatsoever things are lovely, whatsoever things are of good report; if there be any virtue, and if there be any praise, think on these things." [2] This is not an exhortation; it is a command from the Holy Spirit—" think on these things." If we are to cultivate the life of love, it is imperatively necessary that we obey the apostolic command. Herein lies the practical technique of love. By enforced acts of the will, constantly repeated, we are to acquire the habit of thinking loving things, expelling from the mind by these acts those thoughts which are, in any degree, unkind, untrue, or unlovely.

But the love of God and man is not an interior thing only. It must be expressed continually in our external life. Nor is the Christian life a negative thing, a mere refraining from that which is unkind, uncharitable. There is nothing negative about St. Paul's injunction to the Philippians. We must be watchful for every opportunity to speak the loving, kindly word, to do the kindly act to all with whom we come in contact.

VII

Finally, let us not make the mistake of thinking that this work of love is only in imitation of Christ. He is indeed our example, as

[1] St. John xiii. 35.   [2] Phil. iv. 8.

St. Peter says,[1] but if that were all, we should have little hope of reaching the goal. Without Him, we would have no power to follow Him. " God is love, and he that abideth in love abideth in God and God in him." [2] The life of the faithful is not a mere likeness to that of our Lord. It is this, but it is far more than this. It is His actual life being lived in us. He is the motive power in all that is good in me. He claims my mind with which to think and plan; my will with which to work; my heart with which to love. " In him we live and move and have our being," [3] and if the abiding is mutual, as St. John declares it to be, He also in us lives and moves and has His being. In all things spiritual we must find the truth of St. Paul's holy boast, " I live, yet not I but Christ " —who is God—" liveth in me." [4] He calls us to the most sublime of all adventures, the search after love. The richer the treasure we unearth, the fuller the pledge of riches yet to be revealed.

O Saviour and Lover of men, who dost love us with an everlasting love : Fill my heart with Thy love, that making it Thy very own, it may become the willing instrument of Thy love to all the sons of men. As Thou hast loved me, teach me to love them, so that, knit together in Thy one Heart of Love, we may be Thine through ages of ages.

[1] 1 St. Peter ii. 21.
[2] 1 St. John iv. 16.
[3] Acts xvii. 28.
[4] Gal. ii. 20.

Love is strength, love is beauty, love is delight, love is pasture, food, and drink. Therefore, pursue love, the sweet and salutary bond of souls; for without it the rich man is poor, and with it the poor man is rich. Love is patient in misfortune, moderate in good fortune, strong in suffering, glad in toil, secure in temptation, large-hearted in hospitality; among true brethren most happy, among false brethren most patient; composed in the face of insults, kindly towards hatred, calm towards anger. What has strength like that of love? strength not to avenge, but to forget! O Love that ever burnest, Love that art never quenched. O God, my Love, inflame me.

ST. AUGUSTINE.

CHAPTER XII

THE MOTIVE POWER IN THE SPIRITUAL LIFE

I

WHAT is the motive power that lies behind the Christian life? It is the working of the love of God in us, manifesting itself in our life; that is, in what we think and say and do and, therefore, in what we are.

Let us note carefully what we have considered before: that when we speak of the love of God we do not mean our love for Him, but His love for us. It is the operation of His omnipotent love which opens in our hearts fountains of love, which have long since been sealed by sin, or which, perhaps, have never yet been allowed to flow. Therefore, we are taught to pray, " Pour thy love into our hearts," and why? In order " that we, loving thee above all things, may obtain thy promises." If we cannot love God, we cannot love our neighbour; love can have no place in us at all, unless it come from Him as a gift. The working of His love in us is " the fulfilling of the law," [1] and by no other means is it possible for us to fulfil His law and thus achieve our destiny. Love ever longs to do to the utmost the will of the beloved. This is a law of human friendship, and also a law of the divine friendship. Unless this law operates, there is no friendship, no love.

This fulfilling is not to be thought of as a mere compliance with the details of what the law of God demands, however full that compliance may be. The Greek word St. Paul uses ($\pi\lambda\acute{\eta}\rho\omega\mu\alpha$) has a qualitative rather than a quantitative significance, implying the character of being full. It is a word which is used constantly in the New Testament, and it always implies fulfilment in the supreme degree, the leaving of no lacks, no voids, but the highest climax of achievement—in short, that perfection to which, as we have seen, every soul is called by God. It is employed in its completest sense by our Lord; when speaking of Himself, He said, " Thus it becometh us to fulfil all righteousness." [2] The same principle applies to us, but His fulfilment of righteousness is complete, nothing is wanting.

---

[1] Rom. xiii. 10.   [2] St. Matt. iii. 15

Our degree of fulfilment at its highest is according to the measure of the gift of God.

II

The love of God which works in us for our perfection is not only the love of the Father; it is not only the love of the Son; it is not only the love of the Holy Ghost, although it is the Holy Ghost who sheds abroad this love of God in our hearts;[1] it is the one love which is exercised by the Holy Trinity, by the Three Persons in the One God.

To understand this, we must consider the Holy Trinity and the nature of His Being, so far as it has been revealed to us, and so far as our finite minds can grasp it. First, we look at St. John's simple statement, "God is love."[2] God does not possess love in the sense in which man possesses it. I may or may not have love in my heart, and it would make no difference in the fact of my existence. Loving or unloving, I still am I. Not so with God, because love is His essence. Since God is pure and ceaseless activity, if love ceased to work in God, His essence would cease, and we would have the unthinkable thing of God ceasing to be. God is love, and there is no supernatural love save that which arises from a communication of God Himself to the soul. As St. Peter says, we are made " partakers of the divine nature,"[3] and that nature is in its essence pure love. When we partake of the divine nature, by a " created participation " we enter into the eternal and uncreated Love. All the attributes of God are but the varied manifestations of His love which is Himself. He sheds abroad His love into our hearts by the Holy Ghost. Love is of God; that is, not only a gift of God, not only something which flows out from Him, but it is very God Himself. As Walter Hilton says, " There is no gift of God that is both the Giver and the Gift but this gift of love."[4] Hilton is here repeating the teaching of St. Bernard, who, as we have noted, declares that " love is rightly said to be both God and the gift of God."[5] Therefore, the love of God cannot be measured quantitatively. So far as it operates at all it operates universally; it is applied to everything, and whatever God loves He loves with the infinite totality of the divine love.

Love confined to a limited sphere, or with a term set for it, is not love at all. To confine love is like confining fire in an airtight vessel. The flame quickly perishes under such conditions.

---

[1] Rom. v. 5.   [2] 1 St. John iv. 8, 16.   [3] 2 St. Peter i. 4.
[4] Walter Hilton, *Scale of Perfection*, ii. 36.
[5] St. Bernard, *De Diligendo Dei*, xii; Migne, P. L., Tom. 182, Col. 996.

So does the love of God perish when we seek to limit it.   This may seem a contradiction, since we have to work in a limited sphere, being finite and limited as we are.   It may seem that our responding love to God would be cramped and confined, but with its every impulse, love must overflow the bounds of its confinement.   From the necessity of its nature, as St. Bernard says, love, wherever it flows at all, must overflow.[1]   The Sacred Heart of our Lord goes out in perfect love to everything and to everyone, because His Sacred Humanity is filled to the uttermost with the divine love, which is a fire which feeds upon all that it touches.   If our hearts are one with His Heart, they must, of necessity, follow all the outgoings of His love.   Since God is love, it is impossible for us to find God without finding love; nor can there be any exercise of the divine life in us which is not an exercise of love.

All this follows upon the truth which St. Augustine expresses in his epigrammatic saying, " Whatever God has, that God is," [2] and it must be remembered that this is said not of any one Person of the Trinity, but of the Godhead, of the three Persons in the oneness of their nature.   What one Person in the Godhead has, all have.   Each Person possesses and exercises all the infinite love that constitutes the Godhead.   In the Holy Trinity there is but one will, one power, one wisdom, one knowledge, one love; and just as we say, " God is love," we say also that God is power, God is wisdom, God is knowledge.   Each Person of the Trinity possesses the infinite fulness of all these.   To paraphrase the words of the Athanasian Creed, " The Father is love, the Son is love, and the Holy Ghost is love: and yet they are not three loves but one love "; and the same paraphrase may be made in respect to any attribute of God.

We are to understand this to be the truth, and we are to accept it as such.   Not that we understand this truth itself, for that would be to understand the Infinite Mystery of the Godhead, which is beyond the grasp of any finite mind.   But without being able to fathom the mystery through our understanding, we humbly accept what God has revealed about Himself, just as the little child accepts what its father tells it, though it cannot yet understand the things it is told.

If through faith we accept these truths implicitly and humbly, and solely on the authority of God, we shall save ourselves from

[1] St. Bernard, *Serm. in Cant.*, xviii. 3, 4; Migne, P. L., Tom. 183, Col. 860, 861.
[2] " Quod Deus habet, hoc est."—St. Augustine, *De Civ. Dei*, xi. 10; Migne, P. L., Tom. 41, Col. 325.

errors into which many have fallen, such as that which places
merciful Son over against a wrathful Father as though the Godhead
could be divided against Itself. Thus, when our Lord said, " God
so loved the world that he gave his only begotten Son to the end
that all that believe in him should not perish but have everlasting
life," He meant that God the Father, God the Son, and God the
Holy Ghost, so loved the world. This love was a single act on the
part of the divine Three-in-One. The operation of this uncreated
divine love in us produces a created love in us wherewith we love
Him.

III

Considering His love for us, thus poured forth in infinite streams,
how can we withhold our love from Him? Do we withhold it?
There are many tests by which we can discover the answer to this
profoundly important question. Let us take five of them, and by
applying them to ourselves, try to see whether we love God or not,
whether love is the motive power in our life. These are general
tests, and are equally applicable, as we shall easily see, to the love
we have towards God, and to that which we have towards our
neighbour.

Let us enumerate these tests before we consider them in detail.

(a) Love longs for, and seeks to know the beloved;
(b) Love desires and seeks the presence of the one loved;
(c) Love hates the smallest offence against the one loved;
(d) Love is ever thoughtful of the beloved one;
(e) Love is never content with what it does for a loved one.

(a) The natural action of love is to seek to know the object of
love. If I meet a man and am drawn to him in love, I shall inevitably desire to know him intimately, and I will leave no means
unemployed by which to know him better. It is a principle of all
human action that if I will a certain end, by the same act of the
will I also will to use the means by which that end can be attained.
If I will to go to a certain place, I also will to use the means of
transportation which is necessary in order to get there. The means
by which we gain an intimate knowledge of men is by intercourse
with them, by conversing with them, and so learning their character
and modes of thought. If I love God, I shall desire to company
with Him, and to company with God means to pray, to speak with
Him constantly and lovingly. St. Teresa's definition of prayer is

value here: " Prayer is an intimate friendship, a frequent converse, heart to heart, with One whom we know to be our Lover." [1]

Another means of knowing a man is to do his will. One who has for many years been employed by another, and who has faithfully conformed his will daily to the will of that other, learns to know the mind of the master. After a time, he is able under almost any circumstances to know what the master would think and wish. He does not have to be told on every occasion. Intuitively he will divine what is wanted. He knows how the master's mind works.

This continual longing for, and consequent effort to know God will not only be the evidence of our love for Him, but it will also act to deepen our love; for we shall be gaining more and more knowledge of how all-lovable God is, and " to know Him is to love Him."

(b) Love desires and seeks the presence of the one who is loved. We have, already, in a former chapter, dealt with the meaning of desire. All that was said there applies to the desire for the presence of God. It is not a weak wishing, but a strong, steadfast, energizing movement of the will which is enduring, and which gives birth to strong purpose, and to an organized plan, and produces a courageous spirit of initiative, all working towards the inner and all-satisfying consciousness of the objective companionship of God the Holy Trinity, our Father, our Saviour, our Sanctifier.

The desire leads to a seeking after Him, and the idea here is of a persistent seeking. When our Lord said, " Ask, and it shall be given unto you; seek, and ye shall find; knock, and it shall be opened unto you," [2] the form of the verbs, as well as the context, shows that He meant continued action, and this action is to have no end as long as we live in this world. He had just spoken the parable of the man whose friend came to him at midnight to beg three loaves of bread, who would not rise to give to him for friendship's sake, but because of his importunity. The command to ask, to seek, to knock, really means " Keep on asking, keep on seeking, keep on knocking." All the commentators on this passage call attention to the ascending note of intensity in the three verbs. Not only ask, but go out and seek diligently; and not only that, but knock importunately at the door where the desired treasure awaits you. The work of prayer, through which we find the companionship of God, is not to be foregone lightly because, perhaps, we find prayer difficult. The value of prayer is to be estimated not in terms of pleasure, but rather in terms of struggle.

[1] St. Teresa, Life, vii. 7.   [2] St. Luke xi. 9.

If prayer were always easy, all the world would be praying. If we are to find God at the end of the way, then surely must we be willing to pay the cost. In the Garden the night before His Passion, our Lord, "being in an agony," did not abate the force of His prayer, but "prayed more earnestly." [1] His manner of praying is our model.

(c) Love hates even the smallest offence against the beloved. We are often tempted to do what conscience knows is wrong, but the matter is not grave, and although we know that it will wound our Lord, we have our own way, instead of giving Him His way in our hearts. We trade on His love, as though we said, "He loves me; He will forgive me; I will risk wounding Him." How long would an earthly friendship last under these conditions? Not so does love work, if it be a true love. Real love is fiercely intolerant of anything, however small, that offends the loved one.

(d) The fourth test is akin to this third one. Love is always thoughtful of the loved one. How often do we wound the feelings of a friend, and excuse ourselves by saying, "I did not stop to think." But love is always thoughtful, always alert. A laggard love is no love at all.

(e) The last test we shall consider is far-reaching and all-embracing. Love is never content with what it does for the beloved. Only a dead love can say, "I have done much for my friend, and he should be content; I will do no more." This is what St. Augustine meant when he said, "Say enough, and you are lost. Always increase, always make progress, always go forward, stop not in the way, turn not back, turn not aside." [2] If I love God, it is impossible for me to cease to give Him my love and service. This motive power will drive me on with ever-increasing love, for it is of the essence of love to give. There are always still greater things which I can consecrate to Him. In the ancient palace at Bruges the visitor sees everywhere the old motto of Louis of Flanders—*Plus est en vous*, There is more in you. No matter how far love has driven us to serve, there is always something further we can do to manifest our love, and in the loving heart there is always the urge to do more. When the urge ceases, love has died.

IV

Not only can we never be satisfied with what we do for God, but He is never satisfied with the measure of our service. Hi

---

[1] St. Luke xxii. 44.
[2] St. Augustine, *Serm.*, clxix; Migne, P. L., Tom. 38, Col. 926.

love, infinitely eager to raise us to the highest place possible for us in His kingdom, longs for us to give ourselves to Him to the utmost, for only by giving can we gain. So, while never content with what we give God, we should never be content with what we receive from Him, but with an ever-increasing love we should long for Him to give Himself to us more and more, for on the measure of what we receive from Him depends our capacity to love and serve Him. As He gives, He expands our capacity to receive. That we might receive these continually augmented gifts, we should be doing those things which will enable Him to impart Himself to us in ever more abundant streams of love, for the measure of His gifts depends not only on His love for us, but on the measure of our response. He cannot give aught to the indifferent or unwilling soul, because such a soul is incapable of receiving.

God gives always more than His promise seems to offer. This is inevitable, because the promise can be conveyed to our intelligence only through the weak and limited medium of language which is incapable of expressing even the deeper desires and movements of the human spirit, much less the infinite purposes of God. Not that God could not express the promise in terms commensurate with the gift promised, but we would be utterly incapable of understanding it.

Speaking of the love that He gives to us His people, our Lord says: " As the Father hath loved me, so have I loved you." [1] All the infinity of love which dwells in the Holy Trinity the Father gives to the Son, and it is with this same love that He, the Son, loves us. He loves us with the absolute totality of this infinite love, and He asks us to love Him in like manner, so far as such a thing is possible: " Thou shalt love the Lord thy God with *all* thy heart, and with *all* thy soul, and with *all* thy strength, and with *all* thy mind." [2] Let us note the insistent repetition of the word *all*. In the original Greek the word denoting *whole* (ὅλος) is used, which is an even stronger expression than is indicated by our English word *all*. He asks us to give Him the totality of our love, but He does not ask us to give to Him more than He has given to us. And yet, how poor and mean a thing it is that we give Him when compared with the unspeakable gift which He, in His mighty love, is continually bestowing upon us of His own infinitely loving and lovable Self. " I have given thee all, and I will to have all again," [3] He says.

He is ever waiting to open wider the floodgates of love, if only

[1] St. John xv. 9.   [2] St. Luke x. 27.
[3] Thomas à Kempis, *De Imitatione Christi*, iv. 4.

we co-operate with Him to remove the obstacles. He is continually crying, "My son, give me thine heart," and we must continually be giving our hearts to Him, that He may more and more fill them with Himself, making us always in fuller and deeper measure partakers of the divine nature. So must we ever pray that He, not just once for all—however generously—but continually may pour His love, which is Himself, into our hearts.

But we are to remember that we would have no power whatever to love God, or to receive His love, if He did not take the initiative and shed abroad His love in our hearts. He endows us with the ever-expanding capacity for loving Him not only that in this exercise of His loving-kindness we might find our reward in loving Him, but in order that He might rejoice in the love which we give Him. We have said that it is the essence of love to give. This quality governed our Lord's work for us when He was on earth, and it governs Him now as He dispenses His gifts from heaven; and He asks us to allow the same law to govern our loving.

Therefore, God is never content either with what He does for us or with what we do for Him. He is never satisfied with us, for He sees limitless possibilities in us of still greater growth in the heavenly life. Further, while we are not satisfied with what we do for Him, neither can we be satisfied with what He does for us, for every increase of His love for us produces in us a greater capacity for receiving Him. Every increase of grace and love so expands our capacity for love as to create a throbbing void within, which aches to be filled more and more with the fulness of God. The moment we cease to yearn after Him, in that moment would our capacity to receive Him cease to expand. It would be the beginning of spiritual stagnation and death. Behind His giving lie the infinite stores of His love, all of which is ours so far as we can receive it, and our capacity is without limit either in time or in eternity. Under the action of the Holy Spirit it will grow and increase forever, and keeping step with this increase, there will be the increase of the joy which must always accompany love.

v

It is not only the nature and office of love to give, but the giving is also according to the nature of the lover. God gives to the soul, and the soul gives to God, each according to his own nature. I am finite and limited. Therefore, at best, I can give to Him of my love and service only in a finite and limited way. But

God is infinite, and He pours out upon me His infinite love, which is His very Self, the length and breadth and depth and height of which no man can measure. But again let us remind ourselves that we are never to think of God or of His attributes—(which are the same as Himself: " What God has that He is " [1])—after a quantitative manner. When we speak of immensity as one of His attributes, we do not mean that He is so vast that it is impossible to measure Him, but that measurableness is something which cannot be thought of at all in connection with the Infinite. We, therefore, pray Him, not once or twice, but continually, " Pour into our hearts such love toward thee, that we loving thee above all things, may obtain thy promises which exceed all that we can desire." [2]

Thus it is seen that the motive of the spiritual life, that which gives it force and driving power, is love; and when we speak of the spiritual life we are speaking not only of what we do, but rather of what God does within us, for He is the author of all spiritual life; upon Him all things depend. Love is the motive in the Godhead which led Him to create us in His own image out of nothing. Love is the motive in the Godhead which impels Him to bring us into our Father's house again; love is the motive which brought Him down from heaven to become Man in order that as Man He might redeem His people; love is the motive which impelled Him to pour His love into our hearts in order that we might have the power of loving Him, for without Him there is no such power.

The motive in the spiritual life is therefore seen to be of a two-fold operation: it works in the heart of God and it works in the heart of man, but in both at every step it is God who works " to will and to do of His good pleasure." [3] We can do nothing without Him, and in thinking of what we call the spiritual life, again we are to remember that we are thinking not merely of the life of our human spirit, which may be bad—Satan has a life which is wholly spiritual, but wholly evil—but of the life and action of the Holy Spirit, the Third Person of the Blessed Trinity, within us.

Our part is to make our response. This done, He is able to sanctify us unto eternal life. Little by little His work goes on within us, and every step that is motivated by love is a step forward in our participation in the essential holiness of God, and a closer oneness with Him in the unifying power of love. We grow in holiness as we more and more partake of the divine nature. Dwelling through all eternity in the bosom of Godhead, amid the ineffable

---

[1] St. Augustine, *De Civ. Dei*, xi. 10; Migne, P. L., Tom. 41, Col. 325.
[2] Collect VI Trinity.   [3] Phil. ii. 13.

mysteries of His life, our capacity for union with Him will be ever expanding and ever filled, until we are " filled with all the fulness of God." [1]

Lord, Thou knowest all the longings of my heart; and well Thou knowest that I have no power to do the thing I would unless Thy love come swiftly to my help. Bind fast my will that, consecrated to Thee, it may have no power to free itself from Thee.

[1] Eph. iii. 19.

N

This our Beauty is eternal: He will never fail; love thou Him with all thy heart, for He hath loved thee dearly, and hath granted thee such manifold delights. Rest thou in His arms. What sweetness, and what joy shalt thou know, when once thou art reposing in those arms of His. Then shalt thou forget the world; then shalt thou taste the sweetness of the Lord. And there at last, joined in union of spirit with the Omnipotent, shalt thou become so strong as in no wise to fear thine enemies.

ALONSO DE OROZCO.

Since love draws the will after it, and she, being mistress of the other faculties, draws them with her likewise, it follows that the Beloved becomes lord over the lover, and the lover is transformed into the Beloved. Let us love the Lord our God with all our hearts, and with all our strength, both of soul and body, with all our powers, both outward and inward, and with all that we are, so that we may be changed into Him wholly, and that there may be no part in us that is not thus ennobled.

PEDRO MALON DE CHAIDE.

CHAPTER XIII

THE EXERCISE OF LOVE

I

PROGRESS is a law of life. Whether it be in the physical, the intellectual, or the spiritual sphere, where progress ceases, decay and death begin. Whatever power may be given to us, it is necessary, therefore, to exercise it, or we shall speedily lose it. Strength and skill of bodily faculties soon fail if they are not exercised. Cease for some years to employ certain intellectual gifts and they become atrophied. Neglect the spiritual endowments, the graces which God bestows upon us, and we lose them.

Progress lies in a ceaseless effort to reach out after the object we desire to attain, and in spiritual things to reach out after these things humbly and persistently is to attain, for the desire for perfection is accredited to us as perfection.[1] It is not possible for any man to fail in this endeavour if he be faithful and persevering. The great Carthusian master, Dionysius, tells us that " Continual striving for the growth of divine love obtains its increase within us. And as we renew our endeavours, God gives fresh succours; as our Lord said, ' To everyone that hath shall be given, and he shall abound.' [2] Grace, therefore, secures further grace; a greater grace follows a lesser; progress serves to further progress; gain follows gain; and merit increases merit; the soul striving for more as it obtains more; and new acquisitions spurring us on to fresh endeavours." [3]

We have already considered that in the spiritual sphere progress in the use of the gifts and endowments which God bestows means nothing short of the development of the life of God within us. The cessation of progress means the cessation of His activity within our hearts. We are partakers, by virtue of the Sacraments, of the divine nature. God is pure activity, and it is unthinkable, if He dwells in us at all, that He should not continually act within us. Therefore, if we find that the divine life is no longer operative in us, we know that it no longer dwells within us. As we remarked in the

---

[1] St. Bernard, *Epist.* ccliv. 3; Migne, P. L., Tom. 182, Col. 460.
[2] St. Matt. xxv. 29. [3] Dionysius, *De Laude Vitæ Solit.* A. 35.

preceding chapter, this is the ground of St. Augustine's saying about spiritual progress, " Say, Enough, and you are lost." [1] To say, " Enough, I will strive no more for the increase of grace within me," is to forbid God's action in us, and so expel Him from our lives.

Therefore, the primary obligation of the Christian is to exercise continually the divine life which is given to us, and this is to exercise love, since " God is love." [2] To speak of exercising love is only to speak of the activities of the divine love within us. If we love God and long for the rule of His love in our hearts, the Holy Spirit will arrange this co-operation speedily, and whatsoever we do, we shall be able to say with St. Augustine, " For the love of Thy love I do it." [3] All supernatural love is a sheer gift from God, and it is the contemplation of His love for men that stimulates men to love Him. " O Thou good Omnipotent, who carest for everyone of us as if Thou didst care for him only, and carest for all as if they were but one." [4] Remember that we can bind and stay the divine activities by refusing to submit ourselves to God, by resisting the leading of His Holy Spirit in walking the way of love. On the other hand, every loving thought, word, or deed is a fuller surrender of ourselves to Him, which enables Him to make us more fully His own. With every such act of co-operation with Him, He claims ever deeper areas of our life for Himself, and all the more richly does He make us partakers of His own divine nature.

The technique of exercising love is a simple thing, even if it be not always easy. Modern psychology has a maxim to the effect that we learn by doing, and there are naïve psychologists who imagine that this is a discovery of their science in our own time. But when they talk of learning by doing, they are but repeating the teaching of holy men of old who many centuries since laid down this principle. St. Augustine, fourteen centuries ago, was teaching those who sat at his feet that we love in order that we may love. St. Francis de Sales, three centuries ago, dealt with the same subject. " There are many," he said, " who want me to tell them of methods and systems, and secret ways of becoming perfect; and I can only tell them that the sole secret is a hearty love of God, and the only

[1] St. Augustine, *Serm.* clxix; Migne, P. L., Tom. 38, Col. 926.
[2] 1 St. John iv. 8, 16.
[3] " Amore amoris tui facio istud."—St. Augustine, *Confessions*, ii. 1; Migne, P. L., Tom. 32, Col. 675.
[4] " O Tu bone omnipotens, qui sic curas unumquemque nostrum, tanquam solum cures; et sic omnes tanquam singulos."—St. Augustine, *Confession* , iii. 11; Migne, P. L., Tom. 32, Col. 692.

way of attaining that love is by loving. You learn to speak by speaking, to study by studying, to run by running, to work by working; and, just so, you learn to love God and man by loving." [1]

Four hundred years ago Francisco de Osuna, the Spanish mystic, struck an even deeper note when he covered the whole ground by his teaching that " the problem of how to begin is solved by beginning; the problem of how to continue by continuing." [2] Modern psychology, valuable as it has been in many spheres, has never been able to go beyond the wisdom of these masters. They never heard of the science of psychology, but because they knew both God and man, they were profound psychologists.

II

Since man's life is to be a continual preparation for what lies ahead, and this preparation must begin with the casting out of the things which are in any way contrary to the good we would cultivate, it would be well for us to glance at the ways along which every soul has to advance in its journey Godward.

We are familiar with the divisions of the spiritual life commonly spoken of ever since the days of the Fathers of the Church as the purgative, the illuminative, and the unitive ways. By the help of the Holy Spirit we must cleanse the vessel before He can fill it with Himself, and therefore the purgative way has to be followed before we can enter upon the illuminative, or the unitive way. Not only are there certain bad habits to be purged out, but we have to be ever on guard lest something enter into our way of thinking and acting which will renew the evil habit we had succeeded in conquering in a certain degree. Every purgation produces, as its result, an increment of spiritual light, and an increase of union with God.

Since the early ages of the Church, those who are seeking to walk in these ways have been distinguished as beginners, proficients, and the perfect. The beginners are those whose energies have to be devoted largely to breaking off old habits of sin and resisting the assaults of the evil one. The proficients, walking in the way of the divine light, are those who are able to direct their major efforts along positive lines, rather than negative, and who are advancing in the exercise of love and of the other Christian virtues. These are they who are not only free from mortal sin, but who have effectively renounced all love for venial sin, although from time

---

[1] Camus, *The Spirit of St. Francis de Sales*, I, § ii (Lear translation).
[2] Francisco de Osuna, *First Spiritual Alphabet*, xiv. 2.

to time they may fall through weakness or surprise, but neve
deliberately, and they have the grace quickly to recover themselve
through penitence in every case of failure.

The perfect, those treading the way of union with God, ar
they who have attained to such a degree of unity with Him, wh
have so deeply partaken of the divine nature, that they are abl
to enjoy Him with far less of distraction of will than was possibl
in the purgative and illuminative ways. They avoid any deliberat
commission of even the slightest sin or imperfection, and are alway
alert to respond to the inspiration and leading of the Holy Spirit.
Those who have advanced in any marked degree in this way, whil
far from finding prayer easy—indeed, they are the ones whom th
devil most fears, and therefore he attacks them more persistently—
have their wills so devoted to God that they are able, whether i
be in darkness or in light, to maintain at least a sub-conscious sens
of the loving and strong presence of God, and an attitude of almos
continuous recollection and prayer.

It must be remembered, however, that these three ways are no
separate and distinct. Rather should they be thought of as th
threefold way, for no one in this life ever comes to the time whe
there is not need of cleansing; and such progressive cleansin
admits greater light into the soul, and makes it possible to be unite
more completely to God the Ever-Blessed Trinity.

III

To come down to the study of practical methods, if we woul
cultivate the gift of love which has been bestowed upon us, w
should, first, resolutely repel every thought which we realize o
suspect to be in any degree contrary to the loving spirit of our Lore
Such thoughts will constantly project themselves into our mind
We should feel no alarm or distress at their presence, or at thei
continual recurrence. They are the temptations of the adversary
They are not sins in themselves. On the contrary, if we deal wit
them wisely, as the Holy Spirit will always teach us how to do, s
far from being a hurt to our souls, they will prove to be opportuniti
of victory, of victory over Satan in the power of the divine love.

In considering these temptations, we must keep in mind th
distinction between temptation and sin. In matters of though
any suggestion must take complete form in our consciousness befo
we can judge of its character whether it be good or evil, wheth

[1] St. Thomas, *Summa*, 2.2, Q. 24, Art. 9.

it should be entertained or rejected. Sin is impossible without consent of the will, and the will cannot act intelligently until the judgment is able to decide concerning the character of the suggestion, and this decision cannot be reached until the suggestion has been faced squarely and fully.

Where the thought appears to be unloving, the better way of resisting it is to divert the attention from it by an act of the will, rather than to fight it. No one cares to be ignored, and Satan, who is the personification of pride, will not persist in his solicitations to sin when he finds that he is treated with contempt. By force of will, make yourself think of something loving, and the evil thought will not have opportunity to inflict any hurt.

In the second place, he who would cultivate the gift of love must remember our Lord's strong words about those who presume to sit in judgment on their fellows. The easy, glib habit of condemning things and persons is not only an unlovely one, and wholly anti-social, but it is clean contrary to the spirit of Christ, and can never be exercised without peril of grave sin. He who indulges such a practice is not living the life of love.

Thirdly, flee as from the face of a serpent the almost universal habit of repeating unkind and critical things which we have heard or thought, about others. This is one of the prime tests of love, even in the merely natural and human sphere. If we love a person, we do not make his faults a theme of common conversation, but, on the contrary, we are sensitive to any such criticism being made in our presence, and we are eager to defend him; or, if we realize that the situation cannot be defended, we are alert to change the subject of the conversation because it wounds our love.

IV

But even if we succeeded in repelling all unloving suggestions, this would not constitute the life of love. The absence of sin, as we have already observed, is not holiness; and the mere absence of that which is unloving in actual thought or word is not love. Love is the most powerful positive factor in human life.

If we are to live the life of love, if we are to cultivate the divine gift within, it must be accomplished by the performance of definite acts of love. To go back again to the psychological principle set forth by all spiritual teachers, ancient and modern, we learn to be loving by doing, thinking, and saying loving things. There is no other way by which we can learn the holy science of love. By strong and persistent use of the will we are to force ourselves to practise love, to turn the heart ever lovingly towards God, to think loving thoughts about others, to say loving things concerning them, to do loving acts to all who may cross our path, as often as the opportunity can be found or forced. We must go out of our way to be kind and loving, not waiting until by some fortuity an opportunity arises.

One of the best methods of cultivating a loving spirit is to acquire the habit of making acts of love and praise to God frequently during the day. Begin the day with a resolution to speak lovingly to our Lord often. The simpler such prayers are, the better. Such as the following have been used by many souls with great profit:

"Jesus, I love Thee, and I want to love Thee more."
"Lord, Thou knowest all things: Thou knowest that I love Thee."
"I will love Thee, O Lord my strength."
"O send out Thy Light and Thy truth that they may lead me."
"O God, Thou art my God: early will I seek Thee."
"Praise the Lord, O my soul, and all that is within me praise His Holy Name."
"I will magnify Thee, O God my King, and I will praise Thy Name for ever and ever."

Most of the above devotions are taken from the psalter, the most ancient prayer-book the world knows. A cursory glance through its pages will reveal many others which one can select for himself. Sometimes it is profitable to use a line or more from some familiar hymn, such as:

> "Come to my heart, Lord Jesus,
> There is room in my heart for Thee."

or again:

> "Jesus, my Lord, I Thee adore,
> O make me love Thee more and more."

Those who have sought to gain a habit of loving God in this simple but effective way often have the same complaint to make. They say, "I begin the day with a resolution to make such acts of devotion frequently, and when the day is half over I suddenly realize that I have not thought of it once." This should cause no distress of mind. No fault has been committed. We have only been the victim of our natural infirmity of forgetfulness, which is often strongest in respect to things of God, just because the things of God are so intangible in any natural sense.

There is an exact and efficacious thing we can do when the

thought of our resolution comes to mind. The moment it is recalled, even though the day be nearly over, immediately repeat some of the acts of devotion you had purposed to use. And not only repeat them, but if it be possible, take a minute or two, and very slowly and deliberately, with strong concentration, make over and over again some protestation of love to God. If you give a full minute to this exercise in your heart, you will almost invariably find that it will make such an impression on your mind that in a very few minutes you will think of it again. Then once more repeat it over and over. Such exercises will soon produce a spirit of recollection, which will mean that many times during the day your resolution will easily be recalled, and in a short time you will secure the mental habit of turning to our Lord with constant acts and aspirations of love.

If we have earnestly formed them in the mind, and made a definite offering of them to God, such purposes and resolutions will remain just below the surface in the sub-conscious mind, alert and swift to emerge on the least provocation; and the Holy Spirit, who presides over all these operations, will most surely furnish the provocation again and again if we pay any sort of serious attention to His promptings. But the process has to be practical. Not only should the mind be in actual communication with God, but, even though silently, it is well that the lips should form the words expressive of our desire and love for Him. Where it can be done without intruding our devotions upon others, there is a real spiritual, as well as psychological, value in repeating such acts aloud. There are not a few souls who have deceived themselves with the notion that if they think about loving God they are loving Him, or if they think about prayer they are praying. Nothing could be more tragically untrue. One might as well expect to gain bodily nourishment from thinking about a beefsteak instead of actually eating it. Love can be cultivated only by thinking thoughts that are loving, by speaking words of love, and performing acts motivated by love.

There are, thanks be to God, many souls whose days are filled full of such devotion, who, whenever there is a pause in the day's work, find the mind swiftly and readily turning to our Lord with loving thoughts and ejaculations. Such souls are learning more and more to walk with God daily; they are learning the science of the saints; and no one save those who have had this experience can know the joy that comes from such a life.

Another method, employed by many through the Christian

ages, is to connect some common act which is frequently performed, with prayer. St. Teresa used always to make some ejaculation of devotion to our Lord when she went up the stairs. It soon came to pass that she could not go upstairs without the thought of these prayers coming to her mind immediately. Blessed John Keble every morning, when washing, used to repeat his baptismal vows as a pledge of renewed service to God for that day. Very soon it was almost impossible for him so much as to wash his hands without the thought of that pledge coming to his mind again, and the renewal of it being again offered.

There are scores of little daily happenings which can be associated in the mind with prayer and aspiration Godwards. When I turn on a light, when I open a door, when I sit down to read, when I am handed my mail, when I answer the telephone, or hear a bell ring, when I go out or come in—these, and a score of other acts which will easily occur to the mind, can be associated with prayer. If we really persevere for a brief time in the effort, the physical act itself will remind us of the prayer.

v

The prayer of love must, however, be translated into action. We are commanded to love our neighbour as well as to love God; and if we really love Him, and express our love for Him in such acts and aspirations as we have considered, there will inevitably be an outward exercise of love—a loving of our neighbour in and through Him. If our heart is one with His Heart, it cannot possibly fail that we should love as He loves. Our love will be caught up into the current of His love, and as His love is ever directed in its infinite power towards His creatures, our love will, as we have seen, be driven in the same direction.

This exercise must in some definite way be organized. Just as we train ourselves by repeated acts of the will into the habit of loving God, so by like acts of the will are we to discipline ourselves with a discipline which will develop a permanent state of interior love towards all those who are about us. Nothing will so create this spirit of brotherly love as the practice of interior acts of love towards all men. We are to make an act of love in our hearts towards everyone we meet, be he stranger, chance acquaintance, or friend. Send out a loving, kindly thought to the man or woman, or the little child, whom you meet in the street. In a public conveyance say to yourself repeatedly, "These people are my brothers in Christ; He gave His life for them in love; and I must love them too." The late Father Huntington, the founder of the Order of the Holy Cross, a man of profound recollection, and of a rugged, practical saintliness, once, on returning from a long missionary journey, said to one of his brethren, " I tried to remember to pray down God's blessing silently upon everyone whom I had occasion to greet. It created everywhere a loving atmosphere which I cannot describe."

Let it be that we never make any personal contact unless it be a contact full of the warmth of a sympathetic love and kindliness, which, as we have already seen, constitutes the love of our neighbour, and ere long we shall need no reminder. The habit once formed, the heart will of itself radiate love without having to wait on the spur of the will to impel it along this blessed course.

This condition once effected, the course of love will run in an even current, ever deepening and widening as the strength of love develops. Let there be a definite form and plan for the creation of a life of love; and this will not be difficult. It will be accomplished if we go forth daily with the resolve that we will perform a certain number of kindly acts. These acts may not be such as men would count as important. Indeed, it were better that they should be little actions or thoughts, for life is made up of little things, and the life of love is no exception. Further, if they were important acts which the world might take account of and praise, there would be an almost inevitable temptation to pride, which, if yielded to, ever so slightly, might spoil all. There is not much room for pride in the performance of simple little deeds of goodness which, if looked at from the human point of view, are so slight and inconsequential that they would never be remarked on. So, let us devote ourselves to little acts of kindness, of courtesy, of helpfulness, so small that the one for whom they are done might not recall them five minutes later, and yet on our part they are deliberate acts of love, the deliberate surrendering ourselves to the guidance of the Holy Spirit, that His love may work in and through us; the deliberate effort by His grace to cultivate the Christ-life within us. Just as the good craftsman devotes as much care and skill to the minor and hidden details of his work as to that which will be more in evidence, so are we to give all that lies in us to perfecting in every detail the offering we are making to God.

Our Lord Himself illustrated all this in a very vivid way in response to the cynical question of " a certain lawyer " who, to test Him, instead of asking, " What is love? " asked, " Who is my neighbour? " His answer was to give the parable of the Good Samaritan.[1] It will be worth while to read this parable over carefully, and to note how exceedingly detailed is the account of the particular external actions by which the Samaritan gave expression to the love he bore to the stranger in trouble, whom he neither knew, nor had ever seen before. The account of no parable spoken by our Lord is so rich in the narrative of detailed and separate actions. When the Samaritan saw the man " he had compassion on him," which was the moving of the interior spirit of love that dwelt within him. But this was not enough. Without delay, " he went to him "; he " bound up his wounds "; he " poured in oil and wine "; he " set him on his own beast "; he " brought him to an inn "; he himself " took care of him "; and on the morrow, before departing, he contracted with the innkeeper to look after him, agreeing to pay when he came again whatever he might spend. Here are eight separate actions which our Lord recounted by which the Good Samaritan gave expression to the love which ruled his life.

If we were watchful of our course of thought and action we would soon acquire the ingrained habit of reacting in a kindly, loving spirit to every situation that arose. Life would be shot through and through with love, and the reign of Christ within and without would be complete.

By such persistent acts, acts of which we do not grow weary, and which we pursue with courage, we form the habit of love. The habit will then reproduce its acts, and character depends on the habits which govern us. Show me what a man's habits are, and I will tell you what his character is; and destiny depends on character.

VI

God's pre-ordained destiny for every soul is a heaven of union with Himself in perfect love. This heavenly union must have its beginning, and its partial development here. This beginning was made when we were made one with our Lord, the God-Man, in baptism. The life we live in the grace of love here on earth is essentially the same life as that of the blessed in heaven. In substance, the life we live in Christ is the supernatural life which shall be ours in the presence of the Beatific Vision. The only difference is in the stage of development. Death does not mark the cessation of one life and the beginning of another. It is the passing from a phase of life in God which is incomplete, and subject

[1] St. Luke x. 30.

to many vicissitudes, to another phase of the same life which is full, and which can have neither interruption nor ending. Grace and love are the seed of glory in the soul which will germinate and expand into the eternal harvest. With the proper cultivation, these gifts to the soul on earth develop normally into the life of heavenly glory, as the life of the child, given the right care and nourishment, develops into the mature life of the man. The work of developing the life of the soul lies in the unceasing exercise of love to God and to our neighbour.

We must emphasize the unbroken continuity of the life of love. No form of life can persist unless it moves in unceasing flow. If the life of the soul met with a break, or cessation, it would perish, and only the merciful action of God Himself would be able to restore that life. If love continue in action, the soul will pass swiftly and surely on towards the heavenly consummation. If love fail, the life of the soul will languish and perish. We have already quoted Bossuet's saying, that " eternal life *begun* consists in knowing God by faith with a tender and affectionate knowledge. Eternal life *consummated* is the open vision of God face to face; " [1] but the life is the same life. " Our interior life must, already here on earth, become the normal prelude to the Beatific Vision." [2]

As we have thought again and again, this work is one of partner-ship between God and the soul. He does His part perfectly. Our part, at best, is an imperfect work; but if we do what we can, and do not grow weary of this well-doing, our practice of love will enable the infinitely loving activity of God to work effectively; that is, to work so as really to effect things, to achieve results in us which He has fore-ordained, and which will endure forever.

This is the Christian vocation. There is none other. Nor is there any other method of fulfilling it save this method of love. If we can make even small progress in this pursuit of love, our vocation will be fulfilled. God does not ask us to do great things. He does ask that we move forward by the ever-present help of His Spirit. If, when He comes at the last to receive the account of our stewardship, we are found making progress, all will be well with us for eternity.

O Jesu, gracious and tender, pour into my heart Thy grace and Thy wisdom, Thy charity and Thy chastity, Thy humility and Thy love : and grant that where sin had reigned, the peace of Thy Heart, the joy of Thy mind, and the sweetness of Thy Spirit, might find an everlasting abode.

[1] Bossuet, *Meditations on the Gospels*, Pt. II, 37th Day.
[2] Garrigou-Lagrange, *The Three Ways of the Spiritual Life*, p. 30.

Build for yourself no other road for the attainment and possession of the Truth, than that which has been built by Him who, as God, saw the weakness of our walking. And that is, first, Humility; second, Humility, and third, Humility. Not that there are no other commandments to be named; but unless Humility precedes, accompanies, and follows all our good actions; unless Humility be set before us for our beholding; beside us for our adherence; over us for our restraint, then all the good of our joy in any right action is wrested from us by pride.

ST. AUGUSTINE.

CHAPTER XIV

THE LIFE OF HUMILITY

BEFORE we enter upon any consideration of humility, let us understand that this virtue cannot exist save as a gift of grace from God, who loves us, and in His love desires to make us like unto His dear Son. The knowledge of it must be experiental. No one can have any real idea of what humility is unless, in some measure, God is enabled to bestow on the soul which is responsive to Him, the gift of being humble. Let us, therefore, pray Him earnestly that as we study the conditions of this virtue, we may be able to make it a controlling factor in our nature by the help of His Holy Spirit.

The attitude of the world in respect to humility is a strange one. Pride, at least in theory, is universally condemned. No one regards it as a lovely quality. Tell a man that he is consumed with pride, and he will feel aggrieved. But, on the other hand, few men want to be humble. Many admire humility at a distance, but few wish to come to close quarters with it. The Gospel accounts of the life and words of Christ excite admiration. Thoughtful people, regardless of their religious beliefs or opinions, agree that He was one of the most beautiful and lovable characters in history, but the majority have no intention of emulating Him. For the most part, they would feel disgraced if they had to endure even a small part of the humiliation which our Lord and His apostles bore with great joy for love of God. " They scorn to learn of Him because He is meek and lowly in heart." [1] The very reason that our Lord gave for learning of Him, they make the grounds of their rejection of Him. In our study of humility we must keep before us the fact that we are considering this virtue with one end in view only; namely, in order that we may learn how to be actually humble in the common experiences and relationships of every-day life.

I

The main thesis we are seeking to establish is that the Christian life consists in holiness, and we have learned that there is but one

[1] " Dedignantur ab eo discere quoniam mitis est et humilis corde."—St. Augustine, *Confessions*, vii. 21 ; Migne, P. L., Tom. 32, Col. 748.

holiness, and this the holiness of God Himself: "Thou only ar[t] holy," declares the divine revelation.[1] The holiness which i[s] essential to man is a participation in the holiness of God, a partak[-] ing, as St. Peter teaches us, "of the Divine Nature," which i[s] intrinsically holy.[2] But the nature of life is such that it canno[t] exist in a vacuum. It must function under certain conditions an[d] in certain relationships. God alone is absolute, existing withou[t] necessary relativity to anything; although even within the Godhea[d] itself there are relationships between the three Divine Persons.

Humility was the primary condition governing the human lif[e] of Christ on earth, and it is the condition prerequisite to the posses[-] sion and development of the spiritual life by men. Our Lord said "Learn of me, because I am meek and lowly in heart."[3] Meek[-] ness, lowliness, humility, are essential in the strict sense of the word to the Christian life. Without these there is no Christian life. Th[e] proud Christian is a contradiction in terms.

Because of our failures and infirmities, not to speak of our sin[s] we need to be constantly recovering lost ground, as well as goin[g] forward. In our spiritual growth we shall always in this life b[e] like the child who needs both the material with which to build u[p] the increase of the growing body, and also that which is necessar[y] to supply the waste of tissue caused by its daily activities. Bot[h] with the body of the child and with our souls the increase must kee[p] well ahead of the waste, else there will be arrested developmen[t] and stunted growth. Our participation in the divine holiness, an[d] our exercise of it, must follow a like rule and principle. We mus[t] continually be increasing in spiritual stature, and, at the same tim[e] we have to be repairing the losses caused by our failures an[d] infirmities. All this is dependent upon definite conditions, and th[e] primary condition of the Christian life and growth is that of humilit[y] The soul which is not humble, which is motivated by pride, canno[t] partake of the divine holiness, or of any virtue which God woul[d] bestow upon it.

These two qualities, humility and holiness, react continuall[y] upon each other. Humility makes the soul ready for sharing th[e] divine holiness, and guarantees its continual increase. Holines[s] once bestowed, operates to develop and deepen the virtue [of] humility, which again in its turn draws upon the divine holiness fo[r] the soul's further sanctification. This process is endless so long a[s] we are in the grace of God. The loftier the aim in holiness, th[e]

[1] Rev. xv. 4.   [2] 2 St. Peter i. 4.
[3] St. Matt. xi. 29.

reater must be the degree of humility. The higher the structure,
he deeper must the foundation be laid.

II

In all ages, from apostolic days to the present, the teachers of
he Faith have written at great length of the virtue of humility, but
one of them has attempted to give a definition of it. They have
old us much of the grounds of humility, in what it consists, of the
ffects of its operation in the soul, and of the indispensable necessity
of cultivating it. But so extensive is its embrace, so deep and wide
he range of its activity, and so universally and essentially does it
overn all other virtues, that those who have spent all their life
nd energy, under the guidance of the Holy Ghost, in its cultiva-
ion, have agreed that it is indefinable. There is no human ex-
ression which can set forth in any fulness what is meant by humility.
t. John Climacus, after a profound discussion of the nature and
peration of this virtue, declares that " humility is a grace of the
oul which cannot be expressed in human language, for it can be
nown only by experience. It is an indescribable treasure, and
an be thought of only as a gift from God." To define it, he says,
would be like trying to explain the flavour of honey to one who
ad never tasted it.[1]

A thousand years after St. John Climacus taught, St. Francis
e Sales told us that there were two virtues which, while they must
e continually exercised, must be rarely if ever spoken of. " These
re the virtues of chastity and humility. This is because it is
ifficult to touch them without leaving some tarnish on them. No
ongue can express their value, and to speak of them at all without
aying all that their worth demands, is to lower their excellency.
ven if we praise humility in itself we are apt to awaken the desire
f it through self-love, which is the enemy of all virtue. The more
 man realizes that he has a reputation for humility, the more he
vill think himself to be humble, and the more he thinks he is
umble, the less humility he will possess." [2]

Although humility is a virtue which suffers if it be exposed to
he view of men, this does not mean that it gives no indication of
ts presence. There is a habit of exterior humility which is main-
ained in the outward appearance of those who seek, like our Lord,
o be meek and lowly. " There is, exteriorly, a self-restraint, a

[1] St. John Climacus, *Scala Paradisi*. Grad. xxv; Migne, P. G., Tom. 88, Col.
89.

[2] Camus, *Spirit of St. Francis de Sales*, p. 121. (Ed. 1899.)

O

reserve, a calm which gives to the whole physiognomy that ineffabl
beauty, that harmony, that charm which we express by the word
modesty. The look is modest; the voice is modest; the laugh i
modest, and every movement is modest." [1] Modesty, one of the
most beautiful qualities of character that man can possess, is the
outward and visible sign of the interior grace of humility. There
is never any difficulty in recognizing the modest and humble spirit
but the humble soul is unaware that it is giving any evidence of the
presence of this Christ-like disposition.

Our spiritual teachers, though they do not venture to define
humility for us, have sought to describe it, and they agree that i
consists in the subjection of all our powers to the will of God
Repeatedly does our Lord set forth this principle as the foundation
of His own mission: " My meat is to do the will of him that sen
me "; [2] " I seek not mine own will, but the will of the Father ";
" I came down from heaven, not to do mine own will, but the wil
of him that sent me "; [4] " Not my will but thine be done." [5] I
was this complete submission to, and oneness with, the will of the
Father that enabled Him to offer Himself as the one from whom
alone full meekness and lowliness of heart could be learned. [6]

St. Bernard carries on this truth in one of the best statement
on the nature of humility: " The fulness of humility consists in
subjecting our wills in all things to the will of God." [7]   In another
place he says, " Humility is the virtue by which one, through a
true knowledge of what he really is, becomes of no account in his
own eyes." [8]   In short, the call to humility which our Lord give
us is the call to truth, to reality, the call to rise above self-deception
Knowledge of self is the basis of humility as humility is the basi
of all the other virtues. The mere natural realization of what we
are may, however, lead to despair, as in the case of Judas when he
realized his sin. It must be a supernatural knowledge of self
leading the soul, with profound and loving trust, to flee to God
who alone can give succour. This knowledge can be acquired, no
by comparing ourselves with others, as we are so prone to do, bu
by comparing ourselves with God, for the ground of our humility
must always be the vision of Him. The more we can see God and
realize His transcending purity and goodness, the more we realize
our own lack of all that makes us worthy of Him.

---

[1] Gay, *Christian Life and Virtues*, Vol. I, p. 370.
[2] St. John iv. 34.   [3] St. John. v. 30.   [4] St. John vi. 38.
[5] St. Luke xxii. 42.   [6] St. Matt. xi. 29.
[7] St. Bernard, *Serm. de Diversis*, xxvi. 2 ; Migne, P. L., Tom. 183, Col. 610.
[8] St. Bernard, *de Gradibus Humilitatis*, I ; Migne, P. L., Tom. 182, Col. 942.

III

The word *humility* is derived from the Latin word *humus*. It means the soil under our feet, out of which grow all things necessary for man's sustenance. It is the lowest of all, but, like the virtue to which it gives its name, it is the primary and most important of all. We have to be careful, however, not to misunderstand what is meant when it is said that humility is the primary and most important virtue. It is primary, but this is not to say that it is the highest of the virtues. Faith, hope and love are the crown of the divine gifts.[1] " Without faith it is impossible to please God ";[2] " We are saved by hope ";[3] if I " have not charity, I am nothing." [4] The soil out of which all things grow is the primary and indispensable factor, but without the harvest which it actually produces, it will be of no help or avail. Likewise, while humility is primarily indispensable, it is of no avail unless out of it grow the virtues on which depends man's spiritual development. St. Basil, using another metaphor, teaches the same truth when he says that humility is not only a grace and virtue, but that it is the casket and treasure-house which contains all other graces and virtues.[5]

Humility enables us to see ourselves as God sees us; for we are exactly what He sees us to be, nothing more, nothing less. As with every other power, in order to maintain and develop it, we must use it. What, then, constitutes the practice of this virtue? Again we go to St. Bernard for an answer. " Humiliation," he says, " is the path to humility, as patience is to peace, as study is to knowledge." [6] As the teaching of our Lord, and also of His apostles, shows, we are in the strength of the Holy Spirit to humble ourselves. But this work of humiliating self is one that has to be done discreetly. There are certain simple practices, and certain cautions, which we must keep before us if we would do this most necessary work wisely and well.

First, it is never well to seek deliberately any outward humiliation, lest we become guilty of the sin of presumption. We are ignorant of our own powers, and to seek humiliation is to assume that we know what is good for us in our spiritual education, whereas we are blind and ignorant, and know not our own needs, or how to supply them if we knew them. If we take up our cross daily, with patience and perseverance, we shall find humiliation enough

---

[1] St. Thomas, *Summa*, 2.2, Q. 161, Art. 4.   [2] Heb. xi. 6.
[3] Rom. viii. 24.   [4] 1 Cor. xiii. 2.
[5] St. Basil, *Constitut. Monasticæ*, cap. 16; Migne, P. G., Tom. 31, Col. 1378.
[6] St. Bernard, *Epist.* lxxxvii; Migne, P. L., Tom. 182, Col. 217.

of God's own making. To identify ourselves with our Lord, to walk in His footsteps, will lead us in the way which will show us the lesson, and give us the grace to learn it—the lesson of meekness and lowliness of heart.

The second consideration is that, although we are not to seek humiliations, neither are we to endeavour to avoid them. Our Lord spoke of the daily cross, but in many instances He does not compel us to carry the cross He has prepared for us. We can refuse it, and our failure to make progress in the Christian life is often because we avoid the cross. We do not want to be identified with Him. We stand in terror of being misjudged, of being criticized, of being misrepresented, or treated with injustice. In short, we stand in fear of being made like unto our Lord, who suffered all these things. Even the crosses which we are compelled to bear become to us a curse rather than a blessing unless we accept them in a humble spirit, believing that whatever God sends or permits must be for our good in the divine purpose, provided we co-operate with Him by accepting that which He gives.

Thirdly, we must learn by hard practice how to be joyful and full of thanksgiving for the humiliations which we meet. This may not be a natural or an emotional joy, but rather like the gratitude and joy with which one submits to a painful and dangerous operation because one knows that it is necessary for the restoration and maintenance of health.

Fourth, we must, as far as we can, shun praise. We too often gladly accept commendation and praise when in our hearts we know full well that we do not deserve them. In accepting them we are acting a lie to ourselves, which is a serious sin. Praise in most cases is but the expression of the ignorance of the one who commends what he happens to like in us.

Lastly, while keeping in mind what we have already considered —namely, that it is often dangerous to seek humiliations—there are certain courses we may follow in which we can humble ourselves without the peril of presumption. Our spiritual life suffers from the tendency to express our opinions freely, and as though they were worth the consideration of all men. It is a wholesome act of humility to withhold the expression of our opinions, at least until others have spoken, or until we are asked to give our judgment. Often when we have accurate knowledge of a subject which is being discussed, it is a real act of mortification to refrain from speaking; and this constitutes the exercise of humility. One of the most frequent and hurtful occasions of pride is the readiness with which most of us give our opinion, or instruct others, on any subject that might be introduced into a conversation. A wholesome exercise of humility is to yield our opinion without hesitation unless we are sure that in such yielding some fundamental truth will suffer. We are not called upon to correct all the inaccuracies of others. To do so leads inevitably to pride and vanity, and to argue merely to discomfit an opponent is one of the most despicable forms of pride, and is utterly destructive of all humility. In most instances it constitutes the fullest essence of pride, it involves a great lack of charity, and is often clean contrary to ordinary truth and honesty. We are, under these circumstances, not even sincere with ourselves.

Many other ways of humbling oneself might be suggested, but the soul that is eager to become like the Lord Christ, " meek and lowly," will have no difficulty in discovering them. As often as he goes amongst his fellow-men constant opportunities will present themselves where he can put himself in the lowest place, preferring others to himself in honour.

This humbling of ourselves is not to be thought of as an end in itself. In God's purpose the aim and end is that we may be exalted into heavenly places. The practice of humility is the means by which we are made capable of the divine exaltation. Our Lord teaches us that " he that humbleth himself shall be exalted," [1] and St. Peter adds to this revelation by declaring : " Humble yourselves, therefore, under the mighty hand of God that in due time he may exalt you." [2] We are to note that God's action here awaits our response to His prevenient grace. He cannot exalt us until we have, always by the help of the Holy Ghost, created the condition of humility which is prerequisite to this exaltation. He would promote us to great honour, but it depends on us. " Descendite ut ascendatis," says St. Augustine—" Descend in order that you may ascend." [3]

The Rule of St. Benedict, which above all other monastic rules has been regarded as " the Holy Rule," and which deals at great length with the virtue and practice of humility, speaks not of the depth of humility, but of the *culmen humilitatis*, the height, the climax, of humility. St. Bernard gives us the same thought. Humility is in its own nature a high, not a low, thing.

God is described by the prophet as the One who " dwells in the high and holy place," and also as dwelling " with him that is of a

---

[1] St. Luke xviii. 14. [2] 1 St. Peter v. 6.
[3] St. Augustine, *Confessions*, iv. 12; Migne, P. L., Tom. 32, Col. 701.

contrite and humble spirit." [1] Not two places are spoken of, for
the humble dwell in the high and holy place with God who exalts
them, and He is able, according to His laws of dealing with the
souls of men, to exalt them because, and only because, they are
humble of heart. Exaltation is the only purpose of God for the
soul. Humility is the only means by which it can be reached. Not
to attain to humility is failure; to attain to it is the final triumph.

Every sin has its root in pride, and as humility is the destruction
of pride, where it dwells in the heart pride and its fruit of sin can
have no place. The humble heart is the pure heart, and the pure
heart is the heart that can see God, and the vision of God is the
ultimate destiny which He has prepared for every soul.

The sum and substance of the Christian life is set forth by St.
Paul in the thirteenth chapter of his first Epistle to the Corinthians,
where he shows that love and humility walk ever hand in hand.
" Charity suffereth long, and is kind; charity envieth not; charity
vaunteth not itself, is not puffed up, doth not behave itself unseemly,
seeketh not her own, is not easily provoked, thinketh no evil,
rejoiceth not in iniquity, but rejoiceth in the truth; beareth all
things, believeth all things, hopeth all things, endureth all things." [2]
He here presents for us the ladder of love and humility by which
souls mount up to God. He gives the perfect description of the
humble soul. Love cannot grow save out of the rich soil of humility.
Picture a heart full of humility, and we shall have a picture corresponding to just what the apostle describes in this great dis-
quisition on love.

IV

St. Benedict gives twelve degrees of humility, and under these
he sets forth the principles and practice of this fundamental virtue.
Time would fail us to explicate all that the saint says or implies
concerning this essential quality in the Christian. We need to
consider only the more important points. He tells us that he who
would hold himself in the right attitude towards God must " consider that he is always beheld from heaven by the eye of God."
This reminds us of what we have already thought—namely, that
we are exactly what the omniscient eye of God sees us to be, no
more and no less. No judgment we may form concerning ourselves counts; no opinion that man may have of us is to be considered. All these are worthless. We are what God sees us and
knows us to be, and to dwell upon the thought that there is one

[1] Isa. lvii. 15.   [2] 1 Cor. xiii. 4–7.

who sees us as we really are, one whose every judgment is perfect and infallible, will tend powerfully to keep us humble in our own eyes.

The saint goes on to say that one is " not to love his own will, or to delight in gratifying his own desires." He would have us here place the emphasis on the words *love* and *delight*. In this he anticipates the teaching of many later saints that there is no wrong in having a will of our own, or in forming an opinion. The evil enters in when we set our hearts upon them, and hold fast to our will or opinions, and are impatient of having them baulked. He further says that in order to carry this out one must " for the love of God submit himself in all obedience," and " if this obedience be hard, and contrary things be done, he should embrace them patiently."

St. Benedict was writing for Religious who were bound under the vow of obedience, but the principle holds good for every man. The Religious takes his vow in order more surely to secure the mortification of the inevitable self-will which is the root of every sin that ever entered the world. While we are not all bound by monastic vows, we are all bound by our baptismal vows, which are immeasurably more important and all-embracing than any other possible vow. In baptism everyone vowed himself to renounce the devil and all his works, which means the mortification of self-will, for if self-will be not, with steadfast purpose, kept in abeyance, a flood of sin will enter in to the dishonour of God and the undoing of the soul.

What credit, what merit is there in being patient if everything is always done according to our wills, and if nothing is ever contrary to us? How can we endure hardness as good soldiers of Jesus Christ if nothing is ever made hard for us? We must not forget St. Bernard's saying that " humiliation is the path to humility as patience is to peace, as study is to knowledge." [1] It is often humiliating to have our wishes and our will set aside, but without humiliation there is no gaining of humility, and without humility there is no Christ-character, and without the character of Christ stamped on the soul, there can be no salvation.

The last-quoted saying of St. Benedict is worthy of careful consideration. The word which we translate by *embrace* is *amplectatur*, and it implies that the motive of this embracing lies in a love for that which is embraced. The word here is not used to indicate that we love the mortification of self-will, and those things which are contrary to us, because we have a natural liking for them. Few

[1] St. Bernard, *Epist.* lxxxvii; Migne, P. L., Tom. 182, Col. 217.

outside the ranks of the great saints can be expected to rise up to so high a level. But we can love the things that are contrary to us for far nobler reasons.

First, we love them because, bringing us, as they do, into humiliation, they are definite means by which we lay hold upon the grace and power of God. To reject them would be to reject the grace of God, for it is a truth which must always be recognized that to reject the means necessary to gaining a desired end, is to reject the end itself. Second, we must, if we are faithful at all to Him, love that which will stamp us with the likeness of Christ. He said, " I am meek and lowly in heart," [1] and only by attaining to a like meekness and lowliness can we be worthy to be His disciples. And, thirdly, it would be wholly unreasonable for us not to love that which will exalt us to the kingdom of heaven, and bring us peace at the last, even if there be, for the time being, suffering and sacrifice involved in our embracing these things.

These considerations, and many more like them which could easily be presented, show the truth of St. Paul's declaration that thus to yield ourselves to God is a " reasonable service." [2] Indeed, it is the only reasonable service. All else is unreasonable, destructive of our own best interests, even if we did not consider at all the debt of service we owe to God as to the one who has prepared for us so great and blessed things.

v

One more thought given us in St. Benedict's counsel concerning humility is suggested by the word *patience*. It implies a state of contentment, of being full, satisfied that God in His love has given us such gracious opportunities to suffer somewhat for Him. When with insult and contumely the Jewish council sought to disgrace and humiliate the apostles in the eyes of the people, they " departed from the presence of the council, rejoicing that they were counted worthy to suffer shame for his name." [3]

They had learned of Jesus the lessons of meekness and lowliness, and they took these happenings as the special mark of God's favour. They understood and rejoiced in the truth that " whom the Lord loveth he chasteneth, and scourgeth every son whom he receiveth." [4] In their heart all the while was the thought of the psalmist: " Thou of very faithfulness hast caused me to be troubled." [5] So often we cannot bring ourselves to accept this essential principle of the

[1] St. Matt. xi. 29.   [2] Rom. xii. 1.   [3] Acts v. 41.
[4] Heb. xii. 6.   [5] Ps. cxix. 75.

spiritual life—namely, that in order to reach the perfection which our Lord commanded, and which He has pledged Himself to give us if we will meet the conditions He lays down, we must receive correction. Realizing gratefully what the divine discipline had wrought in him, the psalmist cries, " Thy loving correction shall make me great." [1] To be reluctant to receive it, means either that we think we are already perfect and need no correction, or that we really do not desire the perfection which consists in being like Him in His Sacred Manhood. We are content with our low level of spirituality. Our soul's ambition does not soar high. We are ready to cry " Enough," forgetting the teaching of St. Augustine that he who cries " Enough " is lost.[2]

Our Lord promised to His disciples that in the world they should have tribulation,[3] and this promise was made because of the need of every soul to be purified and strengthened. If it became Him who knew no sin, and in His own nature possessed absolute perfection, still to be made " perfect through sufferings " [4]—that is, to learn experientially through pain and humiliation in His Human Nature what He already knew in His infinitely perfect knowledge as God—how much more do we sinners in our weakness require to be purged and perfected through like suffering. If we are to be His disciples we must share His cross, and where in all the world's history can be found a more complete and searching humiliation than that which He of His own will chose to endure on Calvary when He hung naked and despised, rejected of men?

He calls us to take up the cross daily and follow Him. He seeks in His great love to humble us along with Himself in order that with Himself He might exalt us to the kingdom of His glory. " Hard and contrary things " come to us in the course of our life, but He endured them first. In sending us humiliation He calls us into fellowship with Himself, into a oneness with Him, for if we accept our vocation to be meek and lowly with Him, then will come to pass the saying, " Both he that sanctifieth and they who are sanctified are all of one, for which cause he is not ashamed to call them brethren." [5] He offers us the grace of humility that in the power of that grace we may rejoice in being made like unto Him who " for the joy that was set before him endured the cross, despising the shame." [6]

---

[1] Ps. xviii. 35.
[2] " Si autem dixeris sufficit, et peristi: semper adde, semper ambula, semper proface; noli in via remanere, noli retro redire, noli deviari."—St. Augustine, *Sermo* clxix; Migne, P. L., Tom. 38, Col. 926.
[3] St. John xvi. 33.   [4] Heb. ii. 10.   [5] Heb. ii. 11.   [6] Heb. xii. 2.

In the history of St. Francis of Assisi we are told that the saint in the beginning of his vocation suffered much scorn and contempt from men, but when his sweetness and goodness won them, and they recognized Christ who was in him, they then had nought but honour and veneration for him. But it was not honour from men that he was seeking; and instead of finding satisfaction and pleasure in it, he grieved that God did not seem to count him as any longer worthy to suffer humiliation and shame for His Name's sake. He wondered wherein he had failed in His service, that God should withdraw from him the opportunity of being one with his Saviour in being despised and rejected.

Let us, then, look to the example of our Lord Christ, and to the interpretation of that example as it is given to us by His saints. Let us heed the words of the Apostle of Humility: ." Consider him that endured such contradiction of sinners against himself, lest ye be wearied and faint in your minds." [1]

One serious warning is needed when we strive to make progress in this most essential virtue of humility. The nearer we draw to God the more clearly we see ourselves, and therefore the more sinful we seem in our own sight. Indeed, as we go on in this course of the spiritual life, our sins appear to us to be more and more grievous and frequent. But we must not permit the tempter to deceive us at this point. He will seek to persuade us that the effort after God is only increasing our sins continually. The more we try, the worse we are, we think. Under these conditions many a soul has grown discouraged and has given up the struggle.

But they forget a natural principle. If I go into a long-unused room the windows of which are tightly closed, I cannot see the dust and grime which lie over everything. But let in the light, and immediately I see the true condition, and then shall I be able to do what will be necessary in order to cleanse and purify it. Likewise, when I let the light of God's presence into my heart, as I draw nearer to Him, in the ever-increasing light which shines upon my soul, I can see myself as never before. Every flaw and fault stands out in glaring contrast to the purity of God to whom I have drawn so near. It is not that I am more full of sin, but only that I am able in that light to see my sins clearly, as was not possible before His light shone into my heart.

So it has ever been with the saints. Job in ancient days cried, " I have heard of thee by the hearing of the ear, but now mine eye seeth thee. Wherefore, I abhor myself, and repent in dust and

[1] Heb. xii. 3.

ashes." [1] St. Peter, witnessing the great miracle of the draught of fishes, fell on his knees before our Lord, and said, "Depart from me, Lord, for I am a sinful man." [2] St. Paul, speaking of sinners, said, " of whom I am the chief." [3] We know that these were not great sinners. Indeed, they were especially honoured of God because of their sanctity, but companying with Him continually, they saw and realized their sins, and thought themselves to be the most evil of men.

St. Gregory the Great, one of the great teachers of the Church through the ages, explains this phenomenon. In his commentary on the book of Job, he says, " Holy men, the more they advance in virtue, the more unworthy do they seem to themselves to be; for when they are near to the Light they discover in themselves all that was hidden, and the more beautiful does that appear upon which they gaze. Everyone who is illuminated by the True Light, by learning what righteousness is, learns also what sin is." [4] We cannot learn the first without learning the second. This is the law of the life in God; and when we here use the word law, we use it in its scientific sense, not in reference to any mere regulation imposed by authority, either divine or human, but of the operation of the relations which of necessity arise from the very nature of things, as when we speak in astronomy of Kepler's law. God being what He is, and man being what he is, it is not possible for us to draw near to Him without realizing our unlikeness to Him, and at the same time being filled with a longing to become as He is. By approach to Him we learn what righteousness is, and in the light of that knowledge we learn also of the nature of sin, and of its presence in us.

Thus humility marks those who have opened their hearts to God, and have in consequence received great light from Him. Persevered in, this will lead on to the final and highest stage, the *culmen humilitatis*, as St. Benedict calls it, the highest point of the virtue, where, " having ascended all these degrees of humility, the soul will presently arrive at that love of God which, being perfect, casteth out fear; whereby he shall begin to keep without labour, and, as it were, naturally and by custom, all those precepts which he had hitherto observed through fear; no longer through the dread of hell, but for the love of Christ, and out of a good habit and a delight in virtue." [5]

[1] Job. xlii. 5–6. [2] St. Luke v. 8. [3] 1 St. Tim. i. 15.
[4] St. Gregory, *Moralia*, xxiii. 3; Migne, P. L., Tom. 76, Col. 251.
[5] St. Benedict, *Regula*, cap. vii; Migne, P. L., Tom. 66, Col. 371 *sqq.*

This operation does not take place all at once. Little by little shall we go forward until we reach the blessed life which God has prepared for His people in the world to come. Then we shall be wholly governed by the divine will. We shall, as Dante puts it, be " inwilled with His will," [1] but until that time, by faithful diligence and vigilance we have to keep our wills alert. We have not only to attain to His meekness and lowliness, but it will require all our powers, guided by the Spirit, to maintain ourselves in this blessed condition, and to grow and develop in it.

By the application of the will we must repeat the acts of humility again and again; that is, give ourselves to the humiliating course which alone can lead to the state of humility. Thus will the habit of humility be formed, and, once formed, it will produce its own acts. As St. Benedict says, we shall " as it were naturally and by custom " be able to imitate Christ; or rather, it will be more than an imitation, for Christ will dwell within us, and in and through us and our faculties, will He exercise His own holiness and humility. Then shall we be able *promptly*, *easily*, and *sweetly*, to live Christ's life of humility.

(a) Promptly, because love will be the driving motive. Love is not calculating. It does not count the cost. It asks for no reward save the joy of acting according to its nature. This means that love is always swift. A laggard love is a contradiction in terms.

(b) Easily, because none of these things will it undertake in its own strength, but in the strength of God. Acts of humiliation will often be against our nature, and we, if left to ourselves, would shrink from them, but they conform us to the Human Nature of our Lord, and if we are one with Him, it will be the omnipotence of God which will work in us " both to will and to do of his good pleasure." [2] We are to remember again that as God Himself is the indivisible God, so are His attributes indivisible. He does not employ a greater or less part of His omnipotence when He comes to the aid of our weakness, but the whole omnipotence of God operates within us, enabling us with ease to follow Him. There will be no strain or stress. When we are under a strain it means that we are undertaking something beyond our strength; but nothing can be beyond the strength of God with which we are working. Von Hugel has a passage in one of his letters, expressive of this truth. He says:

" Our ideal must be, in and for the long run, a genial, gentle leisurely expansion, no shaking of the nerves, no strain, no semi

---

[1] Dante, *Il Paradiso*, III, 70–85.   [2] Phil. ii. 13.

physical vehemence, no impatient concentration. Suffering and strain may come to us; but all this will, where good, be upborne and expanded into peace and humble power, if we keep little in our own eyes, gently watchful, and united to God in love." [1]

(c) If what we have been considering can be carried out in any reasonable degree at all, the habit of humility will, of necessity, also operate *sweetly*. This means that even the things which are most contrary to our nature will be met with a gentle, loving, restful, but strong and steadfast interior joy which will speak of peace within—peace which is " the tranquillity of order," [2] all things being ordered according to God.

Thus the Christ-character which has been formed within us will operate and control, and we shall live according to the character of Him who said, " Learn of me, for I am meek and lowly in heart." [3] He will rule and direct us in all our ways, not that we may always be kept in the lowest place, but that in the end we may be promoted to great honour. It was said of Him that He " humbled himself, and became obedient unto death, even the death of the cross; wherefore God also hath highly exalted him." [4] As with Him, so shall it be with us. " He that humbleth himself shall be exalted." [5]

VI

Many and great and precious are the promises He has given us. It will be well for us, in conclusion, to recall once more what these promises are. Thus shall we be the more stimulated to accept the humiliations which His love sends, in order that, having suffered with Him, we may be counted worthy to reign with Him.

The revelation concerning the divine purpose in the humbling of His people began far back in the earliest days of the Old Testament Covenant. Recounting the trials to which God subjected His people in the " great and terrible wilderness," Moses declares that it was all that " He might humble thee, and that he might prove thee, to do thee good at thy latter end." [6] The books of the Old Testament during every period continually repeat the declaration of this purpose of God. He aimed to do great things for them, this was the ultimate objective; but, first of all, they must be humbled. God, who knew what was in man, knew that to exalt him without first humbling him would be to his hurt rather than

---

[1] Von Hugel, *Letters to a Niece*, p. 46.
[2] St. Augustine, *De Civ. Dei*, xix. 13; Migne, P. L., Tom. 41, Col. 640.
[3] St. Matt. xi. 29.   [4] Phil. ii. 8.
[5] St. Luke xviii. 14.   [6] Deut. viii. 16.

to his advantage. We find this especially set forth in the proverbs of Solomon. " When pride cometh, there cometh shame, but with the lowly is wisdom." [1] Twice does he give us the inspired epigram, " Before honour is humility." [2] There is scarcely a book of the Old Testament which does not contain the like teaching often repeated.

Repeatedly in the Gospels is the lesson inculcated with dramatic vividness. Our Lord places a little child in the midst of the multitude, calls their attention to the child abashed and covered with confusion at being set in so conspicuous a place, and declares that " whosoever shall humble himself as this little child, the same is greatest in the kingdom of heaven." [3] Three times, using almost the same words, He declared the solemn warning that " whosoever shall exalt himself shall be abased," but He adds the assurance, " He that shall humble himself shall be exalted." [4]

Whatever else the apostles taught, this also was their constant theme. Scores of times they repeat it. St. Paul gives as one of the marks of the " elect of God " " humbleness of mind, meekness, long-suffering." [5] St. James repeats the words of our Lord as recorded in the Gospels, and commands, " Humble yourselves in the sight of God, and he shall lift you up." [6] And St. Peter commands the faithful to " be clothed with humility, for God resisteth the proud, and giveth grace to the humble. Humble yourselves therefore," he says, " under the mighty hand of God that he may exalt you in due time." [7]

As we thought in the beginning of our study, the call to humility is a call to truth, a call to reality, a call away from that self-deception which is a temptation common to all men, and one to which we all too frequently yield. The human mind is made for truth as the eye is made for seeing, and the ear for hearing. " Ye shall know the truth and the truth shall make you free," [8] said the Master. So, humiliation leads to humility, humility leads on to the truth, and the truth shall make us free with the glorious liberty of the sons of God.

O Thou Lord and God : Of Thee I would learn how to please Thee, how to praise Thee, how to love Thee. Of Thee I would learn how to be humble, how to die to self, how to live to Thee, my All, my only Good.

---

[1] Prov. xi. 2.   [2] Prov. xv. 33; xviii. 12.
[3] St. Matt. xviii. 4.   [4] St. Matt. xxiii. 12. St. Luke xiv. 11; xviii. 14.
[5] Col. iii. 12.   [6] St. James iv. 10.
[7] 1 St. Peter v. 5–6.   [8] St. John viii. 32.

In sin man casts out grace, deadens his own ear until God's voice sounds fainter and fainter, and comes seldomer, and at last there follows the stillness of death. It is heard no more. God leaves the soul, and it is dead. Every wilful sin is a part of this deadening of the soul. Ye cannot wilfully refuse to hear in one way or at one time, and hear at another. Ye cannot stop your ears to part of God's message, hear and not hear at will. The soul is a beautiful instrument, attuned by the hand of God, and breathed in by His Holy Spirit. It cannot be attuned and untuned at once. It cannot yield at once the harmony of heaven and the jarring discords of the world.

EDWARD B. PUSEY.

Mortal sin is a sort of deicide. That this thought make an impression upon us, we must think of the personal share we have had in Christ's bitter Passion. It is I who betrayed my Master with a kiss, and at times for even less than thirty pieces of silver. I was with the rabble that cried out, " Not this man but Barabbas; crucify Him." I was with the soldiers, lashing Him through my self-indulgence, crowning Him with thorns through my interior sins of pride and sensuality, laying the heavy beam upon His shoulders, and nailing Him to the cross.

ADOLPH TANQUEREY.

CHAPTER XV

THE LOSS OF HOLINESS

I

WE have considered the call which God gives all men to the life of holiness. We have seen that this vocation coincides with a universal instinct in man to reach out after God. It is not only that God has made it clear that we are made for Him, and that the spirit of man can find no rest save in Him, but in all human history there is no mention of a tribe or people who have not practised a religion which they believed would bring them into some kind of harmony with the god they worshipped. The universal instinct, which would seem to take precedence of all others, is the religious instinct; and for their religion, as for nothing else in human life, men have always been willing to die, while religious apostasy has ever been regarded as the basest of all apostasies.

In consideration of this, one would think that the natural outcome would be that men would in reality conform themselves to the ideals which they find in their religion; but this is precisely what we do not observe in human life. It is the common experience to find men willing to die for their faith, but not willing to make the necessary sacrifice of their wills and passions in order to live for it. Any high degree of holiness has always been rare; and such is the downward tendency of our nature, that the most difficult achievement in the whole moral sphere is to acquire and maintain the holiness which all Christians agree is the greatest desideratum in life.

One of the chief inquiries which must find place in any study of religion is concerning the cause of this discrepancy between the ideal and the reality in the lives of men. What causes this signal failure to attain to the holiness to which we aspire? The inquiry will lead us into the darkest and most sorrowful ways of human life. The answer is not difficult to find. Men have in every age descanted upon the evils of life. We talk of the evils of sickness, of poverty, of bereavement, and of death, which most men regard as the supremest of evils. But if we analyse these, we shall find that none of them are essential evils; indeed, none of them are any-

P
209

thing more than temporary in their effect, and, painful as the effects might be, they pass away. There is but one ultimate and essential evil in the world, only one thing that can keep the soul of man from entering into, and making his own, the holiness of God, and thus achieving his ordained destiny. Indeed, all other so-called evils, if used in the right manner, work for man's highest good, in that they can be made to be the unfailing ways and means of bringing him nearer to God and more into union with Him. This one thing is sin. Sin has rightly been said to be the worst thing in the world because it is the only thing which can stand between God and the souls He has created for Himself. Sin, and sin only, can frustrate His all-holy will.

Holiness lies in conformity to the divine will. The root of all sin lies in the dominance of man's self-will. There has never been a sin, great or small, from the day of the first transgression until now, that was not conceived in man's self-will. St. Bernard says " Let self-will cease, and there will be no hell, for upon what does that fire fasten its rage but upon self-will?"[1]

If sin is the only thing that can stand between us and the eternal purpose which the love of God has purposed for us, then surely it is a subject we must study well, that we may know how to avoid it, lest it make wreck of the soul which God has purchased for Himself at no less a price than that of the life of His only begotten Son upon the cross. We need to know something of its nature, we need to know the methods and signs of its approach, and to know what is necessary in order to conquer in this warfare which God has set us to wage for His honour.

II

It is significant that it was the apostle of love who was inspired by the Holy Ghost to give us the fullest teaching concerning sin. It is in his first epistle, which is the deepest treatise on the love of God ever written, that St. John reveals to us the awfulness of sin. Through all this epistle the apostle weaves threads of warning against sin, parallel with assurances of the divine love. He speaks as the apostle of justice as well as the apostle of love; but when he speaks as the apostle of justice, he does not cease to be the exponent of love, for the justice of God is one aspect, and a very necessary aspect, of the divine love. God is the God of justice because, first of all, He is the God of love. In so far as love ceases to be just, it ceases to be love in any real sense. Justice is not to be thought of

[1] St. Bernard, *Serm.* iii; Migne, P. L., Tom. 183, Col. 290.

only as that which accords to everyone his rights and privileges. Justice under certain conditions withholds privileges, and cancels rights ; it metes out penalties, according to that which is due.

Justice allows for no confusion between error and truth. It will have none of the tolerance which claims the same privilege and freedom for error and falsehood as for divine truth as revealed by God Himself. Such tolerance is a denial of the real existence of truth, and of the fact that the mind of man is made for truth. It denies that the destiny of humanity can be achieved only by following truth. " Ye shall know the truth, and the truth shall make you free." [1] He who loves God and his fellow-man can never consent to the toleration of what is false, in either belief or action, for error enslaves the souls of men under the power of Satan, and brings these souls into the everlasting bondage of evil. The operating principle of justice is love; love cannot tolerate that which will work injury to the object of love, and error is always hurtful. There are those who are rigidly intolerant of conditions which work harm to the body, but who refuse even to recognize the existence of moral and spiritual error which work degradation to the whole character of man, whether he is viewed from the standpoint of the individual or of the race. Such an attitude is, and of necessity must be, utterly remote from one who is governed by justice and love. We must, however, make a sharp distinction between the toleration of sin and the toleration of the sinner. God sets for us the example : He abhors the sin, but He loves the sinner—yea, He gave His life for him on the cross if by any means He might bring him back to Himself who is the Truth and the Life.

There is an old Arab legend of how one evening the patriarch Abraham was sitting at the door of his tent when he saw a wayfarer approaching. Bowing himself before him, he asked the stranger to accept his hospitality. When he had washed his feet, and they had eaten, the guest knelt on the ground facing the setting sun, and, with many prostrations, made his devotions. The patriarch watched him curiously, and with dark suspicion, and when he had fulfilled his worship, he inquired what it meant. The man told him that the sun was his god, and that he had made his evening prayers to him. Angry, and jealous for the honour of God, Abraham drove him out into the night. And God came to him in a vision upon his bed, and said, " Where is the stranger whom I sent unto thee ? " The patriarch replied, " Lord, he would not honour and worship Thee, and I drove him from me." And God

[1] St. John viii. 32.

answered him, saying, " If I have borne with him these forty years, couldest thou not have borne with him for one night? "

The just one, whether human or divine, is he who never winks at sin, not only because of the principle involved, but because of his love for the sinner. It is no kindness to the weak and erring to make as though they were not in error, for error, if not corrected, will surely lead to disaster, and perhaps to ultimate destruction.

III

In the beginning of his first epistle, in one of the most eloquent and intimate statements, St. John declares the Incarnation of God the eternal Son: " That which was from the beginning, which we have heard, which we have seen with our eyes, which we have looked upon, and our hands have handled, of the word of life; (for the life was manifested, and we have seen it, and bear witness, and show unto you that eternal life, which was with the Father, and was manifested unto us); that which we have seen and heard declare we unto you, that ye also may have fellowship with us; and truly our fellowship is with the Father, and with his Son, Jesus Christ." He then goes on to give the warning against sin, a warning which is all the more terrible for the setting of love in which he places it.

In this first chapter we have three triads, closely woven together, but quite distinct, setting forth the reality, the guilt, and the evil and terrifying character of sin. The first triad is the statement of the case of the man who turns his back upon the loving revelation and service of the Incarnate God, whom the apostle has declared in the opening words of the epistle. It will be noted that this is no accusation which he makes against others. With all humility, he included himself in the warning, for no man, whatever the height of holiness to which he may attain, is free in this life from the peril of falling. Let us, then, look at the first triad, which embraces the other two.

> (a) " If we say that we have fellowship with him, and walk in darkness, we lie, and do not the truth."
>
> (b) " If we say that we have no sin, we deceive ourselves, and the truth is not in us."
>
> (c) " If we say that we have not sinned, we make him a liar, and his word is not in us."

These sentences thunder like an awful self-indictment promulgated before the judgment seat of God. Note the threefold repetition of the challenge, " *If we say.*" The implication is that few if any can deny the suggested guilt. The words fall again and again, like some some solemn knell of doom : " *If we say* that we have fellowship with him, and walk in darkness " ; " *If we say* that we have no sin " ; " *If we say* that we have not sinned."

The second triad goes beyond the stage of indictment. It is a verdict rendered. The sequence is startling, and the development of the thought is soul-shaking :

    (*a*) " We lie."
    (*b*) " We deceive ourselves."
    (*c*) " We make him a liar."

First, we are false to our own knowledge; for this is the true definition of a lie. Second, we persuade ourselves that a lie is the truth. Third, we commit the appalling blasphemy of making as though the God of eternal truth had spoken a lie. This second triad declares the facts of our sin, and sets it naked before us in all its hideousness.

The third triad shows the effect of sin upon the soul, and upon the character of the sinner. As a result of a course of sin :

    (*a*) " We do not the truth."
    (*b*) " The truth is not in us."
    (*c*) " His word is not in us."

First, we have failed to put into action that which we ourselves recognize to be the fundamental principle of our spiritual duty and privilege—" we do not the truth." Second, we expel the truth from our lives, for He who said, " I am the Truth," cannot dwell in the heart where evil is enthroned. We ourselves, by our deliberate failure, forbid in our hearts the indwelling presence of the divine Truth, of the Word which is Life.

As we who have sinned read and analyse these words, as we realize the significance of this ninefold inescapable self-condemnation, it would seem that all hope was extinguished. Can there be any forgiveness ? " Is there no balm in Gilead ? Is there no physician there ? " [1]

But the Beloved Disciple, the Apostle of Love, has not yet concluded his discourse. Thrice, in dramatic language, he sets forth the facts, the significance, and the dread consequence, of sin ; and the picture is a very terrible one. But the loving heart of St. John

[1] Jer. viii. 22

was too responsive to every beat of the loving heart of God to leave us thus to our despair. It is his love for the sinner which will not permit him to abate one iota of the truth concerning the peril which threatens the eternal safety of God's children. But in this setting forth there shine out the love and tender mercy of God. There is a fourth triad, for in every step in sin which he describes, the apostle triumphantly proclaims, in verses alternating with those of condemnation, the comforting assurance of the divine love for sinners. Let us study this charter of love:

(*a*) " But if we walk in the light, as he is in the light, we have fellowship one with another, and the blood of Jesus Christ his Son cleanseth us from all sin."

(*b*) " If we confess our sins God is faithful and just to forgive us our sins, and to cleanse us from all unrighteousness."

(*c*) " If any man sin, we have an advocate with the Father, Jesus Christ the righteous, and he is the propitiation for our sins." [1]

Following the first warning against walking in darkness, he hastens swiftly to reassure us as to the blessed consequence that will accrue if, by the help of the Spirit, we will set our feet in the way of light. Over against the possible denial that we are in sin, that we refuse to confess our sins, he shows the superabounding goodness and loving-kindness of God, which is ready, not only to forgive, and hold no more against us the sins we have committed, but, going beyond this, is eager to cleanse the soul from every stain or defect of unrighteousness that we have suffered as the consequence of our sin. How easily might it be thought that even the infinite love of God could not go beyond this; but the third promise lifts the whole case to the heavenly level where sin can be considered only from the standpoint of a perfect and infinite love. " If any man sin we have an advocate." We are not without a friend at court; we have one who pleads for us, and our advocate is none other than He against whom we have sinned so often and so grievously. What mean we by calling Him " the propitiation for our sins "? We do not say only that He made propitiation for our sins two thousand years ago on the cross; we say that He *is* our propitiation *now*. The propitiatory power of the Passion did not cease at three o'clock on the first Good Friday. It endures forever.

[1] The division of the chapters at this point is unfortunate. This verse should be in Chap. i, standing as it clearly does in apposition to the last verse of the opening chapter.

IV

We have thought already that definitions are intellectually economical. Let us see if we cannot construct a definition of sins which will make it clear what is meant by this worst thing in the world.

Sin may be defined as any thought, word, or action contrary to the known command of God, to which we give the consent of our will. It may be by commission or omission.

It were well for us, before proceeding farther, to consider what we mean by sins of omission, for they constitute a very special danger to the soul. It is of the gravest significance that in every one of our Lord's parables of condemnation, the sin condemned is a sin of omission. There is no exception in all His parabolic teaching. The guest at the wedding supper was cast out because he did *not* have on the wedding garment.[1] The five foolish virgins did *not* bring oil in their vessels with their lamps.[2] The man with one talent did *not* trade with it to his master's profit.[3] Dives did *not* minister to Lazarus, lying at his gate.[4] The unmerciful servant did *not* forgive the fellow-servant who owed him a paltry hundred pence;[5] and in the parable of the last Judgment, those on the left hand were cast into outer darkness, not because of any grave positive offence they had committed, but because " ye did it *not* unto one of the least of these my brethren." [6]

There is a good psychological reason for the special danger which attaches to sins of omission. If a man commits a definite act as a result of a reasoned purpose, he is not liable so easily to forget what he has done. The action makes an impression which enables him more readily to recall it, and more easily to repent of it. But the things we omit to do make no such impression. Perhaps at the time we did not even realize that anything was going wrong; because of our habitual selfishness, we are not conscious of failing God. This is showed by the sinners at the judgment, who, when accused of their delinquency, asked in surprise, " Lord, when saw we thee an hungered, and gave thee no meat? " They remembered nothing of it. They were so wrapped up in self that they did not even see the opportunity afforded them for a charitable ministry. Another point it were well to consider is that society about us takes little or no account of sins of omission, and therefore we are rarely reminded by public opinion of our failures in this sphere. The fact

[1] St. Matt. xxii. [2] St. Matt. xxv. [3] St. Matt. xxv.
[4] St. Luke xvi. [5] St. Matt. xviii. [6] St. Matt. xxv.

that we do not feed the hungry, that we neglect the poor and the outcast, that we are selfish and never sacrifice self for others, and a host of other sins of omission may go on for years, and society does not call us to account for them. It is easy, therefore, to think that all is right, for it is a strong point in our fallen nature to think that all is well so long as no one accuses us. We must therefore realize that there is a great social danger in sins of omission.

It will be noted that in our definition it is carefully stated that sin is the violation of the *known* will of God. In the Church's Litany we pray God to forgive us " all our sins, negligences, and ignorances," but, strictly speaking, there is no such thing as a sin of ignorance. If one does not know that an act is wrong, commission of that act in itself cannot be sin. If my ignorance is due to my failure to attend to the instruction which the Spirit of God offered me in times past, then the fault lies at my door. For the past failure I shall have to render an account, but, nevertheless, the act done in ignorance is not held against me as sin in itself. The sin lay in my previous neglect to follow the leading of the Spirit.

We speak of sin as the violation of a divine precept, but it is far more than this. It goes deeper than violating the letter of a law. It is a personal affront and wrong to God Himself, an offence against love. The penitent psalmist in confessing his sin makes this exceeding clear. He says nothing whatever about the law. " *Against thee, thee only*, have I sinned, and done this evil in thy sight," is his confession.[1] The Old Testament is filled with references to the law, with stern warnings against the violation of its sanctity; but in this psalm it might almost appear that the psalmist is unaware of any such code, so overwhelmed is he by the consciousness of the personal dishonour to God which his act has wrought.

Through the breaking of the divine law, we wound the loving heart of God. Sin is always personal in the strictest sense of the term. It is the violation of a personal responsibility on our part, and a blow at the infinite dignity of a Father who has given Himself to us in the bonds of an infinitely personal love.

v

Sin is never constructive. It is always destructive, a dishonour to God and man. It is a negation of the divine holiness. We were chosen before the foundation of the world to be holy. From all

[1] Ps. li. 4. See appended Note at the end of this chapter.

eternity God has called us to a place in the innermost unity of His Being. Sin denies that we are thus called, and so strikes at the dignity of human nature. There are those who, because man is far gone from righteousness, are loth to take seriously the dignity of his nature. They seem to think that in so far as they refuse to accord honour and dignity to fallen human nature, they are enhancing the honour of God, as though He could be honoured in the dishonour showed to His children. They forget that man was made in the image of God, after His likeness, and that this image, though sadly marred, is not wholly lost; and though we may have wandered far from our Father's house, we are still His children, the beloved of His Heart. Man is not wholly depraved, and those who believe in his total depravity propose that which is a philosophical impossibility, for if humanity were totally depraved, it would have no way of knowing that it was depraved at all. If I am conscious of sin either in myself, or in the human race as I observe its history, this is the proof that there is yet some good in me, that I am still able to form judgments from a standpoint of righteousness, for only by a comparison with the good that is within am I able to judge a thing to be bad. Those who take this position are not only guilty of a philosophical blunder, but they are also guilty of the grave moral error of refusing to remember not only man's divine origin, but also his divine destiny. The Saviour of the world is as truly man as He is God, and to refuse honour to humanity is to deny to Him that which is His due. In spite of the degradation into which sin has cast man's nature, God the eternal Son, in order to redeem His sinning creature, came " in the likeness of sinful flesh "; [1] " He did not abhor the Virgin's womb "; [2] indeed, the Holy Trinity " made him to be sin for us, who knew no sin, that we might be made *the righteousness of God in him.*" [3] Because of all this, man is to be honoured next to God Himself. Nothing in creation, not even the angelic spirits in the heavenly choirs, have such claim to dignity and honour. The yielding to sin is a denial of all this, and the result is that it ever produces a state of profound defect and disorder, a state in which there is an absence of the presence and work of the Holy Spirit, who " ordereth all things sweetly." [4] The soul is, as a consequence, devoid of any unifying force, and therefore is in a state of confusion and chaos. Sin offers nothing but dishonour, frustration, and unhappiness in this life, and eternal loss in the next.

[1] Rom. viii. 3.   [2] Te Deum.
[3] 2 Cor. v. 21.   [4] Wisdom viii. 1.

VI

The primary cause of all sin is the failure to abide in Christ. He Himself gives us this warning. He speaks of Himself as the True Vine, and of His disciples as the branches, and He goes on to say, " Abide in me, and I in you. As the branch cannot bear fruit of itself, except it abide in the vine; no more can ye, except ye abide in me. I am the vine, ye are the branches: he that abideth in me, and I in him, the same bringeth forth much fruit: for without me ye can do nothing." [1] Our Lord says, " Ye are the branches "; ye are now in grace, ye are in vital union with the source of life. To be apart from Him, then, necessarily involves an act of severance from Him.

Our Lord, in accord with His method of teaching, first puts the matter positively: " He that abideth in me and I in him, the same bringeth forth much fruit." Then He puts it negatively: " Without me ye can do nothing "; " If a man abide not in me, he is cast forth as a branch and withered." This failure to abide in Him, however, is not to be thought of as a merely negative condition. It is not the result of mere drifting. It is the deliberate, definite, positive creation, by the will of man, of a state of non-residence in Christ. It is the result of deadly sin, and there can be no deadly sin save through deliberate and wilful refusal in a serious matter to respond to the known guidance of the Spirit. It is this which gives its terrible character to sin. It is no mere negation of good, but it is ever to be recognized as a deliberate and positive renunciation of our allegiance to God, a renunciation of all goodness and righteousness and holiness, and an enlisting in the service of Satan. Nor dare we think of this only as a loss to ourselves, or even, appalling as that may be, as a dishonour done to God. It is more than these. It is the definite strengthening of the power of evil among men. " No man dieth to himself." [2] If I yield to temptation, and by my sin enlist in the ranks of Satan, it means that his infernal power is stronger; more than this, it means that by my deliberate act I weaken the hands of my brethren who, in the midst of mortal conflict day by day, need all possible strength. Who would dare to say that such a failure may not result in the final loss of some soul which the grace that God was intending to use through us in the Body of Christ might have strengthened? But when the soul needed that help, it was lacking, because of our infidelity.

Life is full of evil. We see it, we suffer from it on every side.

[1] St. John xv. 5.   [2] Rom. xiv. 7.

The world resounds with the tribulations of the people, with the perils of the nations, with the groans of prisoners, the miseries of orphans, the lamentations of widows, the necessities of strangers, the helplessness of the weak. Every mortal sin contributes to this desperate state into which the world is plunged. Every resistance of temptation in the power of the Holy Spirit is an amelioration of the awful condition in which the world lies. What choice shall we make? Shall we give our will and energies to the building up of the kingdom of God, the kingdom of righteousness and holiness; or, shall we use our power to lend force and endurance to the evil which is the cause, and the sole cause, of the horrors which in every age have stalked across the stage of human history?

Some have said, " I will not choose. I will not submit to this forced option." But to say this is only a futile effort, born of weakness and pusillanimity, to abdicate our function as moral beings; for a moral being is not only one who *can* make a free decision between right and wrong, but one who *must* make such a choice. Not to choose the right is to choose the wrong. There is no escape. It has been said that man's dream has ever been of liberty, but the practical question which confronts every soul from the cradle to the grave is, " Whom shall I serve? "

We have thought of our Lord's negative teaching—" He that abideth not in me, he is cast forth as a branch and withered." We do not need to look far into this divine teaching before realizing that these negative grammatical forms that appear so often in the New Testament not infrequently have a strong positive meaning. In the sermon on the mount He says that the salt which has lost its savour is " good for nothing " but to be cast out.[1] The word which we translate *good* is a verb and means *to be strong* and *efficient*. What a terrible thing is a strong, practical efficiency for nothingness in the Kingdom of God. So with this deliberate condition of " not-abiding " in Christ. By it we ignore and, therefore, dishonour Him, and make of no avail the work of infinite love which He wrought for us on Calvary. Indifference is often a greater wrong than hate. We do not hate the Lord Christ, but, careless of His love, we have so often hurt and offended Him. He whom we have put to scorn and crucified, He whom we, even now as He is in the act of pleading for us, wound daily by our selfishness, trading upon His love—He it is who offers to His Father on our behalf the very wounds which we have inflicted upon Him, and which are continually being inflicted upon Him in the house of His friends.

[1] St. Matt. v. 13.

O Crucified Lord, Thou wouldest crown me with mercy and loving-kindness, and my hands have crowned Thy Head with woeful thorns. O ever-loving Lord, Thou didst bear upon Thy back the awful burden of my sins, and I have scourged Thee with the biting lash. Thou didst stretch forth Thy hands to me in mercy, and I smote them through with cruel nails. My sins cry out against me ; Woe is me that I have crucified the Lord of Life.

NOTE TO CHAPTER XV

A distinction must be made between guilt and the consciousness of guilt. Guilt is an objective fact. One who *knowingly* violates the commands of God is guilty whether he feels a sense of guilt or not. It not infrequently happens that the most grievous and habitual sinners are the ones who have no consciousness of guilt. This does not argue a clear conscience. Rather does it indicate a calloused or drugged conscience. David had committed adultery with Uriah's wife and had followed it up with the murder of her injured husband, but he had no sense of guilt until Nathan declared, " Thou art the man," but he was none the less guilty. Those in the parable of the Judgment recorded in St. Matthew xxv were conscious of no wrongdoing, and in great surprise asked, " When saw we thee an hungered, and gave thee no meat? " But they were nevertheless cast out. If one persists in sin, and gives no heed when conscience speaks, it will require no long time for the conscience to become desensitized; it will be unable at all to react to the voice of God. Dr. Pusey says that by sin man " casts out grace, deadens his own ear until God's voice sounds fainter and comes seldomer, and at last there follows the stillness of death. It is heard no more. God leaves the soul, and it is dead." [1] This same great teacher quotes in another place St. Bernard's saying, " Perfect love casteth out fear, and so does perfect sin," [2] and adds his own comment: " He who blinds himself, fears not evil, for he sees it not till he falls into it. There are two ends in which men struggle not—when they are wholly free, and when they are wholly bound." [3]

It is the duty of every pastor and spiritual worker, indeed of everyone who is seeking to help souls to better their condition, to work to arouse in them a consciousness of the love of God for them, which will awake a sense of the guilt which lies upon their souls if

[1] E. B. Pusey, *Parochial Sermons*, Vol. II, pp. 247–248.
[2] St. Bernard, *De Grad. Humilitatis*, c. 21 ; Migne, P. L., Tom. 182, Col. 969
[3] E. B. Pusey, *Parochial Sermons*, Vol. II, p. 120.

they have committed serious sin. Such souls can be saved from the final fate of sinners only if they repent, and there can be no repentance unless there is consciousness of guilt; and *guilt is always primarily in relation to God.* " *Against thee, thee only, have I sinned,*" was the cry of the penitent David.

En route to a consciousness of guilt in relation to God there may be other right and legitimate forms and consciousnesses of guilt. I may have offended grievously against my parents, against my family, against the community in which I live, and against society at large, and I may have a real and necessary sense of guilt in relation to all these, with a profound sorrow that I have wronged them; and they may forgive me, and remember my offence against me no more. But if I have not taken God into consideration, and have not realized, with repentance, that I have sinned against man and society only through sinning against Him, that He, and He alone, is the source of all moral law and obligation, then neither my regret, nor the forgiveness which man accords to me, spiritually counts for anything. My guilt still lies upon my soul, and will lie there until I become reconciled to God through penitence, and if I am not made to realize this, I am lost.

The Holy Spirit was sent in order that He might " convince the world of sin," to give to the souls of unrepentant men a gnawing consciousness of having offended God, in order that they might be moved to repent, and be rescued from their perilous state. Those who would flatter themselves that the ones they are seeking to help are safe because they have no sense of guilt, are reversing the teaching of Christ, and are giving a denial to our Lord's declaration of the mission of the Holy Spirit. Pastors, teachers, and workers in the religious and social field who fail to reason with souls concerning sin, righteousness and judgment to come, with a view to awakening the sleeping conscience and producing godly repentance, are working to allay the symptoms only of spiritual and social disease, and their labours, as are all such labours, are pre-doomed to failure, and in this case the failure means the ultimate wreck of a soul. All this is, of course, meaningless to those who do not believe in the New Testament, and in the teaching of Christ. But to those who, in any sense, claim to be Christians, it presents a principle, and a fact, which cannot be ignored.

Then are we stirred of the Holy Ghost by contrition unto prayer and desire for the amending of our life with all our mights, to slacken the wrath of God, unto the time we find a rest in soul, and a softness in conscience. Then hope we that God hath forgiven us our sins: and it is truth. And then sheweth our courteous Lord to the soul—well-merrily and with glad cheer—with friendly welcoming as if it had been in pain and in prison, saying sweetly thus: My darling, I am glad thou art come to me: in all thy woe I have ever been with thee, and now seest thou my loving, and be oned in bliss. Thus are sins forgiven by mercy and grace, and our soul is worshipfully received in joy like as it shall be when it cometh to heaven.

MOTHER JULIAN OF NORWICH.

CHAPTER XVI

THE RESTORATION OF HOLINESS

I

WE have thought how impossible it ought to be for a soul which has had revealed to it the wonders of the divine love to turn against God in rebellion; and yet, impossible as it may seem, it is a dreadful and certain fact of human history that in every age men who have received this revelation of love have nevertheless thrown away the gift of holiness, have turned their backs on God, and given their allegiance to Satan.

But in spite of the sin of man, the love of God for sinners has never wavered. Indeed, as we read the divine revelation as contained in the prophets of old, and in the writings of those who, under the New Testament Covenant, have been taught directly by our Lord Himself, or by the Holy Ghost—and this teaching is one and the same—we see that as the sin of man made its horrid progress through history, paralleled with it always is the continuous and progressive revelation of the love of God for sinners. The increased sin of man seems always to have called out the love of God ever more powerfully. Consequently, it would be a violation of the lessons of God's historic dealing with sin for us ever to think of sin without at the same time thinking of the divine love.

It would do Him an added dishonour for us to think of our sins without immediately calling to mind how graciously God's love has ever worked in relation to the sin of man. We see above our city streets, or, it may be, on some lonely country road, a cross placed above a building. Let us never think of it merely as a sign that men are wont to gather there for the worship of God; but always must we take it as a loving call to repentance, as a silent proclamation to all who pass by of the pardoning love of God for sinners, while it speaks to us at the same time of the awful malice of sin, and of God's unswerving purpose to restore the sinner through the operation of His love, and to ensure to him again the heavenly destiny which has been prepared for him from the foundation of the world.

As always, God does His part perfectly. There can be nothing wanting to His work; but, as in everything else, we have to co-operate with Him in order to lay hold of the blessing of restoration and renewed strength which He has prepared for us.

II

Everywhere in the revelation of God we are taught that in order to lay hold of His restoring grace, in order to renew the hope of the divine destiny, we must repent. This is the condition which must in every instance be complied with. Repentance was the key teaching of all the Gospel. We find St. John Baptist, when he came to prepare the way for the Messiah, proclaiming as the first word of preaching, " Repent ye." [1] When our Lord began His ministry, He took this word from the lips of St. John, as it were, and, according to the account given us by St. Matthew, the first recorded word of His ministry was, " Repent," [2] and this was the continual theme of His message. The same teaching is found in the final evangelical praying from the cross: " Father, forgive them." [3] He prayed for His executioners that they might repent, and so become worthy of His forgiveness. On the first occasion of His appearing to His disciples after He had risen from the dead, His first words to them bore the same burden: " Whose soever sins ye remit, they are remitted unto them," [4] again showing the necessity of repentance, without which there could be no remission. And, finally, at the beginning of the apostolic preaching, on the first Christian Pentecost, to those who, " pricked in their heart," came to the apostles crying, " Men and brethren, what shall we do?" the reply was, " Repent, and be baptized every one of you in the name of Jesus Christ for the remission of sins, and ye shall receive the gift of the Holy Ghost." [5] All these occasions testify to the one way of restoration after sin, the way of repentance. Thus only can holiness be restored.

The way of repentance is the way of love. God's part is based on love, for while " the wages of sin is death," [6] yet " God so loved the world that he gave his only begotten Son that whosoever believeth in him should not perish but have everlasting life "; [7] and as St. Paul further declares, " God proveth his love for us, in that, while we were yet sinners, Christ died for us." [8] There is no death for the soul who repents.

[1] St. Matt. iii. 2. [2] St. Matt. iv. 17.
[3] St. Luke xxiii. 34. [4] St. John xx. 23.
[5] Acts ii. 38. [6] Rom. vi. 23.
[7] St. John iii. 16. [8] Rom. v. 8.

Man's part in repentance is also to be grounded in love. True repentance knows nothing of fear or selfishness, but is rooted in a godly sorrow for having offended One who loves us, and whom we realize to be all-lovable, and whom we seek to love.

The Greek word which is commonly used in the New Testament for repentance is one which means a fundamental change of mind (μετάνοια). Its scriptural use is explained as the "change of mind of those who have begun to abhor their errors and misdeeds, and have determined to enter upon a better course of life, so that it embraces both a recognition of sin, and sorrow for it, and hearty amendment, the token and effect of which change are good deeds." [1] This implies that the soul has, by God's grace, acquired a new point of view. There has been wrought a definite change of attitude towards God, towards the world, towards self. It has been given a new set of values. It no longer loves the world and the things of the world. It is no longer self-centred, or world-centred, but God-centred.

The motive that lies behind an act gives it its character. What is the motive of our repentance? Sorrow for sin may have its root in fear, remorse, or love. Fear thinks of the loss to self; love thinks of the wound inflicted by sin on the loving heart of God. Fear may include the terror of hell, or of the loss of worldly prestige; remorse may have its root in shame at having violated our own ethical ideals, or in the disgust we feel at having yielded to what we realize to be degrading. Love thinks only of the dishonour we have done to our loving Lord. The ethical condemnation of an action may make little or no impress on character. It may be comparable only to the realization of a damaging mistake a man may make in the conduct of his worldly affairs. Such self-condemnation takes on an interior spiritual quality only when we realize that it is a personal offence and wrong to one who loves us, and to whom we owe the fullest love and service. It does not affect our life and character until we are able to cry, "Against thee, thee only, have I sinned, and done this evil in thy sight:" [2] with the emphasis on the word *only*, for while our sin is a wrong to our fellow-man, it is so because it is first a wrong to the common Father of us all, a betrayal of the family honour. This is the expression of the true, godly sorrow which alone can work the repentance which brings pardon and restoration from God.

One test of the character of our repentance is the way we react to the humiliating knowledge of our sin and of our sinfulness. True

[1] Thayer, *New Testament Lexicon*. [2] Ps. li. 4.

penitence is always humble, because it results from seeing and valuing ourselves as we really are in the sight of God. It is a tranquil virtue, without excitement or vehemence. The true penitent is not surprised to find that he has sinned against the loving God. If he knows himself at all, if he realizes his weakness, his nothingness, rather is he full of a grateful wonder that the sin has not been tenfold greater than he discovers it to be. He who is angry with himself because he has sinned is giving expression to pride. I thought very well of myself; I was sure I would not fall in this particular way; and now I see how weak and worthless I am, and the realization of it is too much for me. As St. Francis de Sales says, " I am vexed at having been vexed, and angry because I lost my temper." [1] My pride cannot endure this exposure of my weakness.

III

If we would have true repentance, we must remember that it is a gift from God. We have no power in ourselves to repent. We must therefore pray earnestly and habitually for the grace of penitence. "Make me a clean heart, O God; and renew a right spirit within me" [2] is the prayer of the penitent David. "Create and make in us new and contrite hearts," are the words the Church places upon our lips on Ash Wednesday, and all through the great penitential season of Lent. The Church's liturgies are full of such prayers, and they are prayers directed to one end—namely, to teach us that only through sorrow for sin can we be made forgivable, that by the power of prayer alone can we lay hold upon this so necessary gift. We will see shortly that it is impossible even for God to forgive one who is not in a state of forgivableness.

Another point we need to keep in mind is that we do not, through sorrow for sin, however deep and true it may be, forgive ourselves by tapping as it were some great reservoir of pardon. We do not appropriate to ourselves the divine forgiveness, but by responding to His grace we are able to create the condition requisite for Him to do His pardoning work in us. So, the forgiveness is God's act, and He alone can forgive. In all this, love is the motive force. His part in this work has its root in love for man. "God so loved the world, that he gave his only begotten Son that whosoever believeth in him should not perish, but have everlasting life." [3] These were our Lord's own words long before He suffered

---

[1] St. Francis de Sales, *Devout Life*, III. 9.
[2] Ps. li. 10.
[3] St. John iii. 16.

on the cross; and St. Paul reveals to us another aspect of this love when he says, " God proveth his love toward us, in that, while we were yet sinners, Christ died for us." [1]

Man's part, as we have already seen, must be equally based on love. Not in any shame, or fear of consequences, not in any selfishness, but in love, must our sorrow be deeply rooted.

Without penitence it is wholly impossible for pardon to take effect. If absolution were pronounced over an impenitent soul it would have no more effect than if it were pronounced over an inanimate object; save that the inanimate object would not be affected at all, whereas a false or pretended penitence is one of the gravest of sins, hurting the soul grievously. It would be the sin of Ananias and Sapphira, to whom St. Peter said, " Thou hast not lied unto men but unto God." [2] Lest any soul be troubled at the thought of this peril, we must emphasize the truth that such a sin could only occur where one was deliberately and knowingly guilty of a lying pretence in the confessing of sins. Unless the undoubted and conscious intention was to deceive wilfully, there could be no room for fear in this matter.

IV

By penitence we create the condition under which the mercy of God is able to work, in order, (a) to cleanse us from all guilt, and (b) in addition to this cleansing, to make possible the bestowal of the special grace which God has prepared for those who truly repent, who confess their sins with firm purpose of amendment, and who are absolved. By penitence we enable God to act in His character as the perfectly just One. If He forgave one who was without penitence, He would be violating His own principle of justice, for, as we must note again and again, only the forgivable can be forgiven, and forgivableness is produced only by genuine sorrow for sin, a sorrow rooted in love. Perhaps we have had the experience of having some one generously forgive us under the impression that we were sorry for our offence when, as a matter of fact, we knew full well that there was no true penitence in our heart. Unless we have become hardened, such a situation brings with it a haunting sense of deeper guilt, a painful consciousness that we have added to the wrong done by accepting our friend's forgiveness when he should never have been allowed to take an attitude which was thus based on a totally false understanding.

What human experience thus shows us is confirmed by the

[1] Rom. v. 8. [2] Acts v. 4.

teaching of our Lord. Let us observe the repetitions in His commands to His disciples on this subject, repetitions as exact, and with such detail and emphasis as might be found in a legal document. " If thy brother trespass against thee," He said, " rebuke him; *and if he repent,* forgive him. And if he trespass against thee seven times in a day, and seven times in a day turn again to thee, saying, *I repent ;* thou shalt forgive him." This was indeed a hard saying. No wonder the apostles immediately cried out, " Increase our faith." [1] But in every instance the condition is made clear: one cannot be forgiven unless one repents. This does not mean that we are to hold against such an one any unkind or resentful thought. Indeed, we might even weep over the sinner, even as our Lord wept over impenitent Jerusalem, but could not forgive its sin, because it had not sought that repentance which alone could justify its being forgiven.

V

Another error regarding the meaning and application of penitence is that when a soul is forgiven by God it is simply " let off," as the saying is. Nothing could be more contrary to the truth, and nothing could be more definitely immoral. It is a natural law that where a wrong has been committed, compensation must be made. This holds good in the natural world, and also equally in the spiritual world. We find in the book of Exodus that God proclaims His Name to Israel, by which is meant that He sets forth to them the revelation of His character, the qualities which come into operation when He deals with the sons of men: " The Lord, the Lord God, merciful and gracious, long-suffering, and abundant in goodness and truth, keeping mercy for thousands, forgiving iniquity and transgression and sin." This may sound as though the sinner had before him a smooth and easy path. But he who thinks this reckons without the clause which follows, and which is the climax of this great revelation—" and that will by no means clear the guilty." [2] Guilt has to be taken away before the soul can go free. Atonement and satisfaction to the utmost must be made. Our Lord Himself testifies to the required extent of this satisfaction in the Sermon on the Mount, when He says to those who offend, that they shall not escape the judgment of God till they have " paid the uttermost farthing." [3] But we of ourselves are unable to make any atonement or satisfaction for our sins, to

[1] St. Luke xvii. 3–5.   [2] Exod. xxxiv. 5–7. See appended note.
[3] St. Matt. v. 26.

pay even one farthing of this debt. If it were left to our own
devices, hopeless indeed would be the outlook for time and eternity.
But we are not, praise be to God, dependent on our efforts alone.
Since of ourselves we can do nothing, Christ, the sacrificed Lamb of
God, has done all things for us. " By his agony and bloody sweat,
by his cross and Passion," He has made once for all the one full,
perfect, and sufficient satisfaction to His Father for our sins, and
for the sins of the whole world. If we, through the means which
His love provides, make ourselves one with Him, then will all His
atoning work be counted as though we ourselves had made the
satisfaction. " He is the propitiation for our sins." [1]

The work of penitence is the work which sinners are called upon
to do in order that they may lay hold of the great restoration. The
state of repentance is brought to pass by the divine love acting upon
the soul in such a way as to impel it to seek the restoration of holiness which has been prepared for it. Let us repeat that, as always,
God does His part, and man must do His part; and as God's part
in this great work is grounded in love for us, so must our part have
its roots in love for Him.

VI

The work of penitence, in its fulness, consists of five steps—
namely, Self-examination, Contrition, Confession, Satisfaction, and
Amendment. An understanding of this course will show us the
way of restoration to the holiness of God.

First of all, we must know what our sins are, or it will be impossible for us to have that true and godly sorrow for them which is
necessary if we are to receive forgiveness. This involves a careful
examination of our lives. I cannot be sorry for that which I do
not know. It would be impossible to confess it, or to make any
reparation for it; and it would manifestly be out of the question
to set myself seriously and intelligently to amend my ways unless
I knew in what particulars they were wrong. We need to go over
the years, if we have never done so, and try, as far as we can, to
recall the sins which, through the action of our wills, have come
between us and God. We need to see ourselves in some slight
measure as God sees us. Over the door of a famous academy of
philosophy in ancient Greece was the inscription, " Know thyself."
This would hardly be called a Christian primary principle, for the
first thing for us to know is God; but before we are through with
our preparation for the service of God, we must also have some

[1] 1 St. John ii. 2.

knowledge of self, and when we gain it we realize that it is a very
devastating knowledge. The story comes down to us from the
early days of the Jesuits of a young courtier who made a retreat
at one of the houses of the society. When he returned to the Court
his friends rallied him on his piety. " Did they make you see beasts
and monsters?" they asked. " No," he replied, " it was worse
than that: they made me see myself."

We are not to shrink from the ordeal. Some have thought of
it as a morbid proceeding, but there is nothing morbid in seeking
to know and realize my sins when it is for one purpose only—
namely, in order that they may be taken away forever. Morbidness must be avoided, or else the examination will be an inadequate
one. Morbidness always produces a want of proportion, a loss of
perspective. In so important a work it is necessary that one
approach it calm and clear-eyed.

But it has been asked, Are not these sins already done away
with? " Am I to try to recall the sins of my youth which I have
not committed in many years?" The answer to this question is
simple. The real point is not " How long has it been since these
sins were committed? " but, " Have I ever faced them honestly,
and repented of them?" There is absolutely no other way to be
rid of sin save that of penitence. It has been said, and that most
truly, that sins do not die of old age. If I have not repented of a
sin, what ground have I for thinking that God will overlook it?
Is His memory shortened because my violation of His love and
honour made so little impression on me that I have forgotten it?
Is it not better to go back and bring it up now, than to wait until
it is charged against me amid the thunders of the Judgment? Is
it not better to bring it to the light now in the presence of a loving
God, who is long-suffering and of great kindness, who wants me to
bring it to Him for no other reason than that He may forgive it,
than to wait the great accusation in the last day when the opportunity for forgiveness will be past?

We cannot flatter ourselves that we are free from the sins of the
past because we have not repeated those acts in many years. When
we make such a plea as this, we forget the absurd position in which
we place ourselves. It would be grotesque if a person of forty
engaged in the same sins as when he was a youth. It would imply
arrested growth, a stunted mentality. When youth is passed many
of the worst sins of youth have no longer any attraction for us. We
have ceased to commit them, but was it because we saw the evil
that was in them, and desired to avoid them for the love of God?

Was it because we were overwhelmed at the realization of how we had outraged His love and His majesty by them? Or was it only because we outgrew them, just as we outgrew our childish sports? " When I became a man, I put away childish things." [1] This was merely a natural, not in any sense a supernatural action.

Courageously facing what we have done, we seek God's loving forgiveness, not shrinking from doing our part in order to gain that knowledge of our sins which we must have if we would repent adequately. All this will be done for love of Him whose love for us wrought so mightily amid the agonies of Calvary that the divine pardon might be ours.

VII

Without contrition there can be no pardon. Sometimes we hear it said by ignorant persons that confessions are made without contrition just to get rid of the sin. Woe betide the soul who consents to such folly. The absolutions of all the priests in the world could not take away one sin without true contrition, and if I were deliberately to seek absolution without contrition, the absolution thus received would not only be invalid, but I would be doubly damned, for such a confession would add to my burden the deadly act of sacrilege, a greater sin perhaps than anything I might have acknowledged in my confession.

Contrition is defined as genuine sorrow of the heart and detestation of the sin committed, with a determination, by the help of God, never to repeat the sin. It is important to understand that this definition describes a condition which belongs not to the emotions, but to the will. True sorrow for sin may, and often does, involve certain emotional reactions, but these depend on the individual temperament. Persons possessing strong natural emotions are likely to shed tears under stress of any strong feeling. Love, hate, anger, pity, sorrow, fear, all these may produce emotional excitement, but this is temperamental. The seeming strength of the emotion is no indication of the reality that lies beneath it. We know that the most real and lasting love is often accompanied by little emotional expression. The deepest and most genuine contrition is often that which produces no excitement, but which proves itself in an effective and enduring determination not to repeat the acts by which we wounded the loving heart of God, and for which sorrow has been aroused.

Such attitude of the will has for its object both the sins of the

[1] 1 Cor. xiii. 11.

past and the possible sins of the future.   The sinner who with all his heart can say, " I abhor the sins which I have committed," and also, " I will never, by God's help, commit them again," is truly contrite, and if, for love of God, he holds fast to, and continues to act in accordance with, these purposes of the will, there will be nothing wanting to his work of penitence.

This contrition must be; (a) a genuine sorrow of heart and will, coupled with a firm purpose of amendment. (b) It must include as its object all the mortal sins that one can remember. It will not suffice for us to be filled with sorrow for some one sin only, the seriousness of which has suddenly been made clear; although such a circumstance might properly be the occasion of awakening the soul to realize the necessity of a general work of repentance. This one sin was the expression of the general condition of sin.   Sins do not stand in isolation.   They are the evidence of the interior character in every instance. (c) Contrition must be supernatural—that is, it must be inspired by love for God. It must be a grief arising out of the sense of having wounded the love of our Lord.   Mere remorse or sorrow, regret or dismay, because of some earthly loss, or embarrassment caused by sin, would be but the " sorrow of the world that worketh death." [1]   It would have no place in true penitence.   Fear of God's punishment, however, though it is the lowest motive of penitence, is a valid one. Even our Lord Himself appealed to it again and again in the Gospels.

But if we examine this ground of repentance we shall find that at bottom it has its motive in a desire to escape from making shipwreck of our life, even if at the time we do not recognize it as a life which we are meant to live for God's honour.   It is a flight from evil, from that which we know to be hurtful.   Here we can appeal to the principle which St. Augustine implies in his teaching. that the hatred of that which is evil is the first step towards loving that which is good.   To take the first step is necessary, but we cannot stop with this.   We have to hasten on in the course set before us, that we, cleansed and strengthened, may at last attain to Him who is the Author and Finisher of our faith, to Him who not only began the good work in us, but who alone can perform it until the day of Jesus Christ.

VIII

We have thought that the hatred of that which is evil is the first step toward loving that which is good, but more than the first step

_____
[1] 2 Cor. vii. 10.

must be taken in order to attain any objective. Mere interior sorrow for sin cannot stand alone. To shut up sorrow for sin in our hearts would only breed unhappiness, and lead to self-pity and frustration. All such motions in the heart and will must have expression. We have repeatedly had occasion to remark that the demands God makes upon the soul in the course of the Christian life are invariably in keeping with the instincts, and often with the necessities, of our nature. God Himself created this nature of ours. He knows what is in man, and He requires nothing of us save that which is consonant with our nature, that which will fit into it, arouse and stimulate the best that is in it, and bring it to perfection. The grace of God does not act contrary to our true nature. Rather does it work with it, and perfect it. This principle holds good at every step in the process of penitence.

If one is truly contrite, human nature being what it is, there will be an urge and desire to acknowledge one's sins. The truly contrite soul will not have to be importuned to confess. A penitence which persistently refuses to acknowledge the wrong done, gives evidence only of a counterfeit sorrow. If a child pretends sorrow for wrong-doing, but refuses sullenly to own to its fault, we decline to believe in its penitence.

So universally is this held, so consonant is it with human nature, that the public opinion of the world universally demands confession as an indication of sorrow for sin. Take the case of a criminal. He has been convicted, let us say, of a capital crime. The evidence is overwhelming, there is no doubt of his guilt. But he maintains a stolid silence, owning to nothing. Men feel that it is a strange and monstrous attitude, and they resent it. Such a man can command no sympathy from the public. But let the news run abroad that he has at last confessed, he has made a clean breast of it all, and the community draws a breath of relief. Base as the crime may have been, everyone feels that the man is not wholly bad. There is some good left in him yet, and he has gone a long way towards atoning for his act by his confession of it. So, even the natural sense of right and justice demands the confession of sin as the effective test of sorrow.

We are not to be distressed if we find the thought of confession repugnant. Our lower nature will naturally rebel against humbling ourselves, but if we keep before us the thought of the love of God whom we have wounded, these lower impulses will be overcome, and our better and nobler self will prevail.

There is a world of difference, however, between the confession of him who has broken the law of man, and the one who has violated God's law. The criminal confesses his deed. The sympathy of the community goes out to him, but the acknowledgment of his crime, the manifestation of sorrow for it, does not ensure him a pardon. He may still have to pay the dire penalty of his act. How different where the penitent soul humbly confesses his sin against God. " If we confess our sins, God is faithful and just to forgive us our sins, and to cleanse us from all unrighteousness." [1] Yes, this is the purpose of confession, that God in His pardoning love may blot out our iniquities, and remember them against us no more forever.

IX

Not only are these promises made, but God goes farther, and institutes in His Church a Sacrament by which not only is guilt taken away, and pardon bestowed, but through which the penitent receives a special power and gift in absolution which fortifies his soul against further sin as nothing else can do.

Let us make no mistake about what is meant by confession. St. John makes this clear beyond all doubt by the word he uses which we translate confess (ὁμολογῶμεν). This word means not merely to be willing to confess our sins, " but to acknowledge them openly in the face of men." [2] The Greek word can have no other meaning. In this first epistle St. John uses this word several times, and the context always shows that it refers to the confession which must be openly made to man. In the fourth chapter he says, " Every spirit that confesses that Jesus Christ is come in the flesh, is of God," and again, " Whosoever shall confess that Jesus is the Son of God, God dwelleth in him, and he in God." [3] The Greek word used in both these cases is the same as that which is used regarding confession of sins. No one would say that St. John in these passages meant to teach other than what our Lord taught when He said, "Whosoever therefore shall confess me before men, him will I confess also before my Father which is in heaven." [4] The Greek word used in all these cases is the same, and can have but the one meaning—open confession before men, whether it was to acknowledge one's allegiance to Christ, or to acknowledge one's sins.

It is no general confession of a state of sin which satisfies either God or one's own conscience. It is worth noting as significant,

---

[1] 1 St. John i. 9.
[2] Westcott, Comment. in loc.
[3] 1 St. John iv. 2, 15.
[4] St. Matt. x. 32; St. Luke xii. 8.

that in the verse we have quoted from St. John, the apostle changes from the singular number to the plural when he comes to speak of confession. If we deny that we are in a state of sin, we deceive ourselves, but, " if we confess our sins "—here it is plural—" God is faithful and just to forgive us our sins."   Over against the denial of sin, or sinfulness, the apostle sets the confession, not of sin or sinfulness, but of actual sins. The acknowledgment must extend to specific, definite acts of sin. The denial is in abstract form; the confession is personal and detailed.[1]

The penitent kneels in the presence of the priest; he confesses all mortal sins that he can remember committing, he declares his sorrow for them, and his intention to amend his life. The priest, speaking as God's agent on earth (as he does in every act of his ministry, whatever it may be), pronounces absolution. Not by any personal power which he may possess does he exercise this ministry. It is a power which God delegates to him, and in using it he is required to declare that it is so delegated. " By His authority committed unto me," he says to the penitent, " I absolve thee from all thy sins, in the Name of the Father and of the Son and of the Holy Ghost. Amen." With these words God has acted through the ministry of the priest, the burden lifts, the soul is cleansed in the Precious Blood; he goes on his way in peace, and, as the prophet declared to God's people, " none of the sins that he hath committed shall be mentioned to him." [2]

This confession must have certain characteristics. (a) It must be an accusation made by the sinner against himself, inspired by genuine godly sorrow for his sins. (b) It must be the confession of all one's mortal sins, committed since his baptism, or since his last confession, as far as he can remember. The sins of others are not to be referred to, nor has this sacrament anything to do with inherited original sin, the defect with which all men are born, for that was done away with in baptism. (c) The confession must be accompanied by a definite expression of sorrow, and (d) by a declaration of the purpose of amendment of life. Without these expressions absolution could not be given.

There are repeated statements in the New Testament which would have no meaning if this confession of sin were not taken for granted, and in at least one instance there is an account of sinners openly confessing their sins to the apostles, with no suggestion that it was anything unusual. When St. Paul and his companions preached at Ephesus " many that believed came, and confessed,

[1] See Westcott, *Comment. in loc.*   [2] Ezek. xviii. 22.

and showed their deeds." [1] It is also a fact that there has never been a time in the recorded history of the Christian Church when this ministry of absolution was not exercised, either privately or publicly. It is clear from his second epistle to the Corinthians that St. Paul regarded it as a normal function of his ministry. He writes concerning the penitent sinners at Corinth, whom he had rebuked so severely in his first epistle to that Church, " To whom ye forgive anything, I forgive also: for if I forgave anything, to whom I forgave it, for your sakes, forgave I it in the person of Christ." [2] This is to say, that it was a delegated ministry; he acted as Christ's authorized agent, empowered to minister pardon in Christ's stead, but with His authority—in short, to forgive sins according to the declaration He made to the disciples after He had risen from the dead. [3]

For some four centuries in the primitive Church, public confession of certain sins was compulsory. It was the merciful spirit of the Church, which, like her Lord, has ever been tender towards her erring children, that, in the fifth century, under the strong and gentle influence of St. Chrysostom, relieved sinners of this rule, which not only, in many cases, had caused grave scandal, and consequent hurt to the faithful, but which had been a burden which many sensitive souls found too heavy to bear. The Church retained her hold on the discipline of sinners, but the ministering of this discipline was delegated to the Bishop, or to a priest, and the penitent was protected by the seal of the confessional, one of the most solemn and binding obligations of secrecy ever known to man, for the sanctity of which not a few of God's holy servants have through the ages sacrificed their lives willingly.

The voice of the Church, speaking through her appointed pastors, repeats to penitent sinners the tender words of her Lord: " Neither do I condemn thee; go and sin no more." [4] Under the rule of the loving Spirit, no longer is the work of penitence a hard and painful thing. The tribunal of penance has become the mercy-seat of the divine love, a fount of sweet and gentle power, whence flow refreshing waters for the healing of the wounds of God's children. Well and joyfully did St. Paul proclaim the gracious tidings, " There is therefore now no condemnation to them which are in Christ Jesus." [5] Those who have sinned, but who have known the joy of absolution; those who have had experience of the loving-kindness of the forgiving Lord, can, out of their

[1] Acts xix. 18.   [2] 2 Cor. ii. 10.   [3] St. John xx. 21–23.
[4] St. John viii. 11.   [5] Rom. viii. 1.

experience, make their own the splendid protestation of the apostle: " For I am persuaded, that neither death, nor life, nor angels, nor principalities, nor powers, nor things present, nor things to come, nor height, nor depth, nor any other creature, shall be able to separate us from the love of God, which is in Christ Jesus, our Lord." [1]

O Saviour, merciful and tender, infinite object of all my love : whence is this to me that Thou dost so compassionate me ? Whence is this to me that Thou dost so lovingly pardon me ? Joy beyond all excess of joy, that Thou dost take away the burden of my sin !

NOTE TO CHAPTER XVI

The expression, " the wrath of God," in relation to sin and to sinners is one which has been much misunderstood. It is properly defined as " an energy of the divine nature, called forth by the presence of daring or presumptuous transgression, and expressing the reaction of the divine holiness against it." It is " the zeal of God for the maintenance of His holiness and honour, and of the ends of His righteousness and love." It is " in God the inflexible determination to uphold at all costs the interests of righteousness and truth." It " always appears in union with the idea of the divine holiness," and it " manifests itself in subserviency to the ends of righteousness and mercy." [2]

There are two words in the New Testament which are translated by our English word *wrath*. One of these is θυμὸς, which means a breaking forth of hot anger which arises suddenly, and later cools, perhaps to return. It implies an emotional state such as a fit of rage or temper. This word is used in all of St. Paul's epistles only five times, and always refers to the sinful wrath of man. It is never used in reference to God in the New Testament save once by St. John in Revelation, where it lends itself to the strong, apocalyptic expression characteristic of that book.

The other word is ὀργή, which denotes a righteous indignation which arises gradually, and always with good cause, until it becomes a settled attitude of mind. It is the attitude which every right-minded soul must have towards wrong. It is the interior state which constitutes righteousness in relation to sin. St. Paul uses

[1] Rom. viii. 38, 39.
[2] James Orr, Art. " Anger (wrath) of God," in Hastings' *Dictionary of the Bible.*

this word some twenty times, but not always in reference to God. Eight times his use of it refers to the anger of men.

It is significant that St. John, except in one instance, where he uses θυμὸς, quoting St. John Baptist, never uses either of these words save in Revelation, as noted above. Though he could be stern as befitted one of the " sons of thunder "—love is always a stern virtue—yet his mission was not to preach the wrath of God, save as that wrath was the expression of the divine love. He knew well that if the love of God could be driven home to the hearts and consciences of men, there would be no need to speak of wrath, for wrath has no place in the divine purpose concerning the children of God. " God hath not appointed us to wrath, but to obtain salvation by our Lord Jesus Christ " [1] through the love that is in Him. Love, not wrath, worketh salvation. Salvation through love is the divinely predestined end of man. God contemplates nothing else for the souls of men. He who becomes the object of wrath brings it upon himself.

[1] 1 Thess. v. 9.

Sorrow is repenting for something wrongly done; it is a longing to put right the evil and injury; it is determining that the like shall never happen again; and it is all from the motive of love. Sorrow springs from love or it is not sorrow; it is merely remorse, or disillusion, or self-blame, which, in the things that matter, bear no fruit. But sorrow that is born of love has in it the immortality of love and can never die; on the contrary, the more with time the soul's eyes are opened, and it sees what its sins have done, so much the more will it grow in intensity and in its effects.

ALBAN GOODIER.

CHAPTER XVII

LOVE AND SIN

I

GOD, who is love, speaking through the apostle of love, warns the soul of the peril of sin. This revelation is not to be construed as a threat. On the contrary, it is an essential part of the revelation of divine love, the loving Father pointing out the danger to His children. It is only another instance of the truth of St. Teresa's saying that " it is of the nature of love to work in a thousand different ways." [1]

We must bear in mind here that the separation from God, and from all that is good, which results from sin, is not the consequence of any action on God's part. Not for a moment has He ever receded, nor will He ever recede, from His eternal purpose of making man one with Himself. The aim of all His work for mankind is that we may be " with Christ in God " to the fulness of our capacity in this life, and in the completeness of His plan for our destiny in the life to come. But God being what He is—that is, perfect holiness—He can have no part in the soul that sins and repents not. Sin, both in Satan and in man, is the exact antithesis of the essential holiness of God. The two can have no commerce with each other. Sin and the holiness of God cannot dwell together in the same heart, any more than fire and water can occupy the same space. The separation of God and man through sin is the act of the sinner, never the act of God. By our deliberate act we break the bond of love with which God has bound us to Himself. We, by the stroke which we administer, sever ourselves, the branches, from Him who, as the true Vine, is the only source of life and love. Whatever the consequences of the acts of sin, it is the sinner who administers the punishment to himself; it is he who frames the decree of his own final condemnation.

II

We must not lose sight of the wholesome fact that punishment is a real and necessary element in the moral organization and discipline of the human race. Those who accept the divine revela-

---

[1] St. Teresa, *Interior Castle*, Man. vi, ix. 21.

tion realize that it is, in the true sense of the word, a settled principle of the Christian religion. Question is often made concerning the consequences visited upon men in this world for their sins. If one dared to express an opinion where so little has been revealed, it might be said that all penalty of whatever kind is the logical and natural effect of causes which we ourselves set in motion by our wrongdoing. "Thou hast commanded, and so it is, that every inordinate affection should be its own punishment," says St. Augustine.[1]

These words might be taken as a comment on St. Paul's saying: " Whatsoever a man soweth, that shall he also reap. For he that soweth to his flesh shall of the flesh reap corruption; but he that soweth to the Spirit shall of the Spirit reap everlasting life." [2] We must remember, however, that although every punishment may be accepted in such a way as to make it a salutary chastisement, we must not think of every chastisement as punishment. " Whom the Lord loveth, he chasteneth," declares the apostle, and he goes on immediately to say that this is done " for our profit, that we might be partakers of his holiness." [3] He is ever chastening His people. He sends or allows what the world calls misfortune as a discipline to detach souls from the world, that they, through the cultivation of patience and humility, might be bound in a close unity with Him, and attain to the loving destiny He has prepared for them. There would be no possibility of forming the character necessary for union with God if there were no discipline in human life, if everything were made smooth and easy.

Punishment, according to the Christian ideal, can have in it no element of retaliation. In its proper sense, the word implies nothing of vindictiveness. It is a testimony in action on behalf of righteousness, and against the evil that has been committed. It is the assertion of righteousness in the form of the chastisement of unrighteousness. Not to reprobate and to chastise would be to condone, and to condone an evil is to give consent to it. Those who wink at evil assume an attitude which is destructive of all spiritual integrity. God made man accountable for his actions, and all men recognize this accountability, and consider it as one of their prized prerogatives. No one wishes to be excused on the alleged ground of not being accountable. Rather would such an imputation be resented as an indignity. Therefore, justice and right, as well as the universal instinct of mankind, demand that an account be rendered for wrongdoing.

[1] St. Augustine, *Confessions*, I. 12; Migne, P. L., Tom. 32, Col. 670.
[2] Gal. vi. 7–8.   [3] Heb. xii. 6, 10.

Punishment, however, is more than a witness to righteousness in relation to a past unrighteous act. More particularly does it look forward to the beneficent effect upon the character of the transgressor, and thus punishment becomes an operation of love. All right punishment is a discipline of love, and has in view the bringing of the sinner to a realization of his guilt in relation to God, and to a consequent state of penitence. In other words, it is educative in relation to God, to the nature of sin, of penitence and of amendment, which is only another way of saying that it leads to God. The punishment that has any other than this loving object in view cannot, from the standpoint of Christian charity, be allowed. Of course, because of the hardness of men's hearts, it fails frequently to produce this result, but the principle holds none the less, and the purpose and object stand.

There are many instances where punishment sets in motion a power to discipline, to atone, and to sanctify. It may not work all at once. Time is often required to bring the sinner to a conviction of sin and of righteousness, and of the wholesome nature of punishment as affording an opportunity to make some amends for his sin. Those who have had to do with delinquents, guilty of either sin or crime (the two are not synonymous; there was a time when it was a capital crime to confess Christ, but a deadly sin to deny Him), know how frequent it is that the sinner humbly and gladly desires to bear his full punishment, welcoming it as an opportunity to make, in humility, reparation for his wrongdoing. In these cases the punishment is indeed a work of love, for it becomes a means of grace, and secures for the soul a life of righteousness. It becomes the remedial disciplinary agency of restoration which, in charity to the offender, it is intended to be.

III

Any teaching concerning hell is unpopular in our day; but the Christian aim must ever be to teach the truth as God has revealed it. Each soul accepts it or rejects it, through the use of his free will, and he will have to take the eternal consequence of his choice. It is truly said that there is " a degree of hardness and impenitence of heart which is fraught with everlasting evil to those who wilfully persist in it; and such obdurate sinners will ultimately be excluded from the vision of God, and condemned to a state of misery which knows no end." [1]

[1] James O. S. Huntington, O.H.C., *What is Meant by Hell*. Holy Cross Tracts, No. 16.

The punishment, so called, of hell is not, in the proper sense of the word, a punishment at all, as the world regards it. It is rather the natural operation of cause and effect. God who " will have all men to be saved " [1] is not responsible for the pains of hell. He who continues in mortal sin knowingly and deliberately is knowingly and deliberately instituting the cause of his own condemnation. There is nothing in this condemnation that is arbitrary, or, in any strict propriety of the word, inflicted. We think of death as the inherent and inevitable climax of mortal disease, not as an arbitrary consequence inflicted by one who resents the disease. In like manner, what is called the judgment of God upon sin is but the gradual, inevitable development of what sin inherently is. The whole progress of sin is a progressive alienation from God. The climax of such a progressive alienation is that essential incompatibility with God which we call hell. This St. James makes clear: " The lust when it hath conceived beareth sin, and when it is full-grown, bringeth forth death." [2] Nothing further is necessary for this dread and final consummation than that man, having identified himself wholly with sin, should be left by God altogether to his own will and devices.[3]

In the next world, whether in heaven or in hell, the souls of men will reach spiritual realizations and perceptions immeasurably beyond anything that can be known in this life. At the Judgment the soul which has wilfully rejected and dishonoured God will see in one awful blinding moment the beauty of that Face, the beauty which will haunt him through all the eternal ages, and yet with the certain knowledge that all hope is gone, that he has shut himself out forever from the Presence of Him for whom alone he was made, who alone can satisfy his longings; and that this fatal state is now irrevocable and irreparable. This is the veriest hell, and each man makes it for himself. God could have compelled his service, but in this event the kingdom of heaven would be peopled by a race of slaves, and He will have only the loving service of free men freely and lovingly given.

There are those whose wishful thinking has led them to deny the existence of hell, or to hold that it is a temporary condition which will come to an end after a period of time. If Christ intended to teach eternal punishment, could He have possibly found language plainer and more direct, or more awful, than that which He employed repeatedly? [4] If He did *not* intend to teach it, could He

---

[1] 1 Tim. ii. 4. [2] St. James i. 15 (R.V.).
[3] See R. B. Moberly, *Atonement and Personality*, pp. 15, 16.
[4] St. Matt. v. 29–30; xxv. 46; St. Mark ix. 43–49.

have possibly found words more deliberately calculated to mislead and to deceive?

Only those who wilfully persevere in mortal sin can find hell as their portion. No man slips into hell, as it were, by accident, or without knowledge of the end of the course he is pursuing. "This is a place that must be deliberately entered. A man must knock at the door perseveringly, demanding admittance, for no man can get into hell without the passport of his own actual mortal sin which proves that he has rejected God." [1] Full allegiance and confirmed loyalty to Satan, and to his evil kingdom, are required of those who enter hell. If God "will have all men to be saved," then we can rest in the assurance that no soul will be excluded from the company of His elect who can be reached by the utmost extension of His love and justice. Some have speculated concerning the number of those who will be lost from amongst men, but this is no question upon which the children of God need to waste precious time. The faithful, loving child is so engaged in rejoicing in the love of the Father that he has no time to concern himself with the dread of punishment. There is only one practical question that lies before us: "Am I living my life, am I using my opportunities, so as to work out my salvation, as the Holy Spirit commands, not as an alternative to the pains of hell, not as a mere escape, but because I know with certain knowledge that this salvation is the only destiny for which I was created, and that it consists in the ultimate and perfect oneness with God who loves me, a sinner, with an everlasting and infinitely tender love, a oneness in the joy of a unifying love which will grow and deepen through all eternity?" Can we not make our response to Him who asks so little, and gives so infinitely much in His transcending and forgiving love?

IV

After this extended but necessary digression for the study of the ultimate consequence of the sin which rejects and violates the divine love, let us now look at the conditions and meaning of sin as they are set forth in the warning revelation given us by St. John in his first epistle.

Few more startling expressions are to be found in Scripture than that which comes almost at the end of an epistle which glows in every line with the light and warmth of the divine love. The apostle has been repeating the assurances of the heavenly graciousness, and telling us of the ground of the confidence we have in Him.

[1] Farrell, *A Companion to the Summa*, Vol. IV, p. 451.

Seven times in the last nine verses of this epistle does he reiterate the word *know* to indicate the complete certitude and security which the soul enjoys in the divine promises. St. John would here by these repetitions call our attention to the philosophical truth that knowledge which is not absolutely certain is not knowledge. If I entertain even a trace of doubt, to say "I know" would be a falsehood. Six times the Greek word he chooses is one which means the acquisition of knowledge by reflecting on a subject. On the seventh and final occasion he employs another word which means to know, not by interior reflection, but by observation and personal experience: "He hath given us an understanding in order that (through the use of this understanding of circumstances and conditions) we may know him that is true."

The line of thought that the apostle is following is that we gain this divine knowledge by experience and observation, that we draw our conclusions from our own experience of the divine faithfulness and love. There is no one great blinding revelation of His love to the soul. It is a gradual unfolding as our capacity for knowledge deepens under the tutelage of the Holy Spirit. Our faith is to be fortified by a conviction that is based on reason, the whole process of God's revelation and of our own thought leading us to see the utter unreasonableness of doubting the divine goodness.

In the midst of this comforting consideration there seems to come to St. John a sudden and terrifying vision of the possibility of one of these souls, so precious to God, souls for whom the divine power and wisdom and love had wrought so amazingly, failing of the heavenly destiny. With this thought before him, he breaks off with swift abruptness to utter this loving, warning cry regarding sin as the only thing that can bring such loss to a soul: "If any man see his brother sin a sin which is not unto death, he shall ask, and he shall give him life for them that sin not unto death. There is a sin unto death: I do not say that he shall pray for it. All unrighteousness is sin, and there is a sin not unto death."

The apostle here makes a clear distinction between sins. "All unrighteousness is sin," he says, and there is a sin which utterly slays the life of God in the soul, a sin unto spiritual death; but there is also the sin which is not unto death. In order to evaluate aright the character of our sins, we must consider this distinction, and find an answer to the question concerning the difference between the two types of sin of which he speaks. Let us think first of the sin not unto death—that is, the sin which does not cut the soul off from God. But we note that St. John declares it to be really a sin, a violation of the all-loving will of our heavenly Father, even if His mercy does not allow us to be cut off from Him by it. These are sins of infirmity rather than of malice or of deliberate intent. They are the sins without grave or far-reaching consequences, and which are the result of impulse, those by which we are overtaken, sins of surprise, failures which arise because we did not stop to think.

These are venial sins—that is, sins which are in themselves pardonable (as the meaning of the word shows), without the formal arraignment of the soul in any sort of tribunal of penitence. As St. John tells us, they can be forgiven through prayer of any kind, whether a direct petition for pardon, or receiving Holy Communion, or any devout and faithful lifting of the heart to God. Such sins are not inconsistent with the way in which we are called to walk, provided they are committed only through frailty or surprise. They may retard our progress in the way of perfection, but they do not cause us to abandon this road that leads to God. They are comparable to the bodily indispositions which bring a certain degree of discomfort, but which the constitution, if it possesses a reasonable degree of vigour and health, can throw off of itself without the application of special remedies.

The case is different, however, if these sins are committed deliberately and habitually, and because we have an affection for them. To love that which is evil is in itself a perilous state of sin, even if it has not yet brought the soul to the forfeiture of divine grace. We shall see in our consideration of the effects of venial sin what the nature of this peril is. Let us first examine the negative characteristics of venial sin, and we shall see that there is little excuse for us in any event.

(a) Venial sins, we say, are not serious; they are only " little infidelities " against God. But can any offence against the love of God ever be a small and unimportant thing? The fact that it is a relatively small thing should fill us all the more with shame that we did not resist it.

(b) Venial sin means that we have, perhaps, only imperfect knowledge of the circumstances under which we fail. But why is the knowledge imperfect? Has not God given us every opportunity to learn His will, and to fulfil it? Has He failed us in this respect?

(c) There was, it may be, lack of thought, no real deliberation before we acted. " I did not stop to think," we say. But love which is thoughtless of the beloved is a false love.

While we are to distinguish carefully between mortal and venial sins, yet there is no proper comparison to be made between them, as they are in totally different categories. Venial sin has been called a curable wound in a living body, while mortal sin presents the spectacle of a dead corpse.[1] It will be seen at a glance that these two things cannot be compared.

For those of us who are, in any real degree of earnestness, seeking to serve God, venial sin is the danger. The tempter is altogether too wise to offer to a soul devoted to God the allurement to immediate mortal sin. He knows that in the first moment of realizing this peril such a soul would run swiftly to the feet of God for strength and protection; and this is precisely what he wishes, above all, to avoid. He leads the soul on, little by little, with suggestions of sin which lack the qualities of deadly sin; but which, if persisted in, will surely lead on to the weakening of the will, and, eventually, to serious falls. One who looks upon venial sin lightly is on the road to spiritual destruction.

V

Let us see in a definite way what are some of the positive effects of venial sin on a soul:

(a) Yielding to venial sin forms the habit of saying, "No," to God, and "Yes," to Satan, and, like all habits persisted in, it will eventually bind us.

(b) It strengthens the downward tendency of man's nature, the liking for, and inclination to, sin.

(c) It desensitizes the conscience, so that it is unable to give the alarm at the approach of temptation.

(d) It obscures the judgment, bringing doubt and perplexity, and leading to the breakdown of spiritual morale.

(e) It progressively saps the vigour of the will.

(f) It vitiates the spiritual taste, precluding a relish for the sweetness of God, and for His service and interests.

(g) As a result, love grows progressively cold.

(h) While no accumulation of venial sin can constitute mortal sin, yet it makes mortal sin possible, perhaps inevitable, through the depletion of the spiritual system. Anything can happen with a run-down constitution.

The consideration of these effects of venial sin makes it clear why the tempter is willing to go on with unfailing patience, if only he can lead the soul into habitual venial sin. He knows that in the end the victory will be his, to the ruin of the soul, and to the dishonour of God. He labours to weaken the soul little by little, so that he may be able in time, by some sudden, carefully planned,

[1] Vonier, *The Human Soul*, p. 144.

and devastating temptation, to precipitate it into some great moral apostasy. Satan's efforts do not always contemplate the immediate wreck of the soul. A low ideal in the life of the Christian often suits his purpose as well as does mortal sin; for in such an ideal he is able to dishonour God even if he cannot, at the time, cause the ultimate and complete ruin of one of God's children.

It is therefore of primary importance, using that adjective in its full and literal sense, for us never to yield deliberately to the temptation to venial sin. He who is alert to avoid venial sin, though he may fall occasionally, will never be in peril of mortal sin. There may be many failures arising from sudden impulse and surprise, from a lack of recollection, and from failure to realize what is going on at the moment the temptation assails us. But these are not of grave danger in their effects, especially if we make our acts of contrition at the first moment that we recognize what has happened. But to commit even the smallest violation of God's will deliberately, knowing what is involved, is exceedingly perilous. We do not put it to ourselves just in this way, but in substance it amounts to saying, " I know this is a sin; I know it will wound and grieve our Lord; I know it will weaken my own soul's strength to my hurt, and to His further dishonour. But it is not a mortal sin; it will not cut me off from God; I will take the chance. He is kind and forgiving; He will not hold it against me."

In short, we are deliberately trading upon the love of God. If it were a mortal sin, or if we knew that this sin committed, we should never be given another opportunity to serve Him, or even to find forgiveness, we would never yield. How long would a human friendship last under such conditions? If your supposed friend deliberately, and frequently, did that which he knew would wound and injure you, saying, " He is my friend, he will not hold it against me, he will overlook it," how long would you endure it? Shall we treat God with less of consideration and loyalty than we demand of an earthly friend? Is less owed to Him than to man?

VI

Let us now find an answer to the question, What is a mortal sin? What spiritual poison is it that lies in a certain act which quenches all grace and produces immediate spiritual death, while other acts of sin do not produce these dire effects?

A study of the question, comparing Scripture with Scripture, seems to show—and practically all Christian moralists agree in this—that a mortal sin must have three characteristics: first, it must be in itself a serious matter; second, we must have knowledge of its character; and third, it must be committed with deliberation, not on sudden impulse. If any of these marks be wanting, the act, though definitely a sin, is not a sin unto death. We must understand, however, that the distinction does not really lie in the nature of the sin itself; it is created only by the mercy and goodness of God, who knows the weakness of man, and does not ask more of him than he can give.

The results of mortal sin are obvious. The principal effects may be stated as follows:

(a) By such an act the soul severs itself as a branch from the True Vine; it deliberately becomes, by its own will and act, one of those of whom our Lord said, "It is cast out as a branch and withered."

(b) The commission of a mortal sin is not only a deliberate renunciation of allegiance to Christ; it is the giving of our allegiance to Satan. It is not merely a negative thing, but it is a formal enlistment in the armies of hell to fight against God and His righteousness.

(c) It means the forfeiture of all the merit that a soul may have gained by its past good life and works, of all the treasure it may have laid up in heaven.

(d) It renders the soul incapable of any act pleasing to God except the act of repentance.

Knowing these dread consequences, he who is capable of committing what he knows to be mortal sin, is indeed already far gone from righteousness. And he who, by the ready commission of venial sin, imparts to his soul the disposition to mortal sin, is reckless alike of his own safety, and of the divine honour.

It would be hopeless to attempt to describe the appalling change that comes over the soul of the child of God, adorned with all the moral and spiritual beauty which belongs to Him who is fairer than the children of men and altogether lovely, when he deliberately gives himself to the commission of mortal sin. In ancient days men believed in the existence of fabled monsters, horrible creatures which, bearing the form of man, had been half metamorphosed into some unclean beast. It is no fable in the spiritual life. The child of God, made in His glorious image and likeness, partaker of the divine nature and filled with the beauty of God, is made by mortal sin a member of Satan, a partaker of his infernal nature, is stamped with the hideous lineaments and form of the prince of darkness, and has become, by his own act, a spiritual monstrosity, from which the angels avert their eyes with shuddering horror. We shrink from such a description, but these sentences are weak and meaningless compared with the reality of the condition of him who gives himself, through mortal sin, to become the spawn of Satan. We are told in the legend of St. Catherine of Genoa, that God once gave her to see the effect of one venial sin on the soul, and the saint swooned away at the horror of the vision. How much more frightful are the effects of mortal sin upon the soul of a child of God!

VII

When we think of the awfulness of sin, it must be borne in upon us that it is of the utmost importance that we know something of this dread thing, that we learn how it makes its entrance into a human soul, in order that we may be able to recognize its approach, and, by watchfulness and prayer, make it impossible for it to invade the heart which God has prepared to be His own dwelling-place. Whether venial or mortal, all sin and all temptation to sin approaches the souls of men through the personal agency and antagonism of Satan, the enemy of God and man, and it is vital in this warfare to keep in mind that our foe is a skilled strategist. He has had an age-long experience in deceiving souls like our own. There is probably no type of human soul which he has not studied and vanquished. He lays his plans a long time ahead. He is tirelessly patient. He looks not for a passing victory, and is less interested in winning battles than in winning the war. If he can plan so as to win the last battle, he will achieve the final triumph over the soul. He who prays seldom or coldly, who receives Holy Communion infrequently, or with little preparation, who lives selfishly, and does not cultivate the spirit of penitence, leaves himself a narrow margin of safety, and can easily be thrust over the line into a state of serious and perhaps permanent rebellion against God.

There are three steps to sin—suggestion, pleasure, consent. The suggestion, at least in the beginning of sin, comes from without, and constitutes the work of temptation. Satan, or one of his evil spirits whom he assigns to the work of seeking continually to draw the souls of men away from God and into his snares, has the power to cast into the mind, as into a mirror, certain suggestions and solicitations to evil. But we must keep in mind that the suggestion to sin is not sin itself. In cases where we have in the past given encouragement to the tempter by agreeing to his temptations, and especially where the agreement with him has been so frequent as to form within us the habit of saying, "Yes," to him, it is very likely that temptation will arise out of our own interior; but, even so, the original temptation arose not out of our hearts, but was suggested from without. We shall later consider the consequences of denying the existence of a personal devil. It will not be necessary to go into this subject here, save to note the fact that such a denial does a grave dishonour to human nature in making it the source of evil. It does a still greater dishonour to God by asserting that when He saw the creation He had made, and pronounced it " very good," [1] He was in grave error, for man, whom He had made in His own image and likeness, was, in reality, an evil creation, with that within him which only required opportunity in order to develop into sin against self, society, and against God. It makes God, not man or the devil, ultimately responsible for the corruption and wickedness which have stained the history of mankind.

Whatever evil there is in the world, whatever evil there is in us, we can reflect with thankfulness that it did not begin with man. So far as we have any history of it, evil began with Lucifer and the rebel angels in heaven. Just as with the temptation of our first parents, our temptations are suggestions that we take a course contrary to that which we know to be the will of God. We may not be able to put them away, they may persist, they may return again and again, but they cannot constitute us guilty. We are always able to make a wholly effective, negative response, if we will.

The second step towards sin is found in the sense of pleasure we feel at the evil suggestion; but even this does not bring sin. Such pleasure arises out of our lower self. It is what St. Paul complained of as inevitable in himself—namely, a law in his members warring against the law of his mind. [2] I may feel a distinct pleasure, for example, in the thought of taking revenge upon one who has injured me; but if, when I realize this, I say, " Yes, it would give me pleasure, but it would be against the loving will of God, and, God being my helper, nothing will induce me to do this thing"—if we can honestly, in the presence of God, say this, then we are not only free from sin, but we have won a victory over the tempter, to the glory of God, to the strengthening, and to the further sanctifying of our souls.

There is nothing which can possibly make a soul guilty of sin save the consent of the will. If, by an act of my free will, I *will* to do the evil thing, then sin has entered in. But here we must be on our guard against one of the favourite deceptions of the devil.

[1] Gen. i. 31.   [2] Rom. vii. 23.

Where the temptation has persisted long, where we have had a hard and wearying struggle, and still the battle goes on, we have all had the experience of hearing, as it were, a taunting voice within, saying, "You do not realize it, but you have yielded, you have given your consent." There are many into whose hearts this temptation within the temptation strikes terror, and there have been many cases where, accepting this suggestion as true, the soul, despairing of its safety, ceases to fight the battle for God. But this is a lying voice. Turn upon the tempter with scorn. Charge him with his lie, and then, making a strong protestation to God of your desire, and of your unbending intention and purpose to be loyal and true to Him, cry out for His strong help. As long as the struggle lasts there is victory, continuous victory, a piling of victory upon victory, until the enemy be utterly put to flight. We must never count ourselves guilty unless we are wholly certain that we have deliberately given our wills into the keeping of Satan. The presence of the fear that we may have done this is one of the indications that our wills are still secure in the keeping of God.

VIII

It is of paramount importance that we distinguish between temptation and sin. Next to sin, the worst thing, so far as destroying our courage and morale and breaking down our whole line of defence is concerned, is for us to think that we have sinned. If there is doubt in the mind, give yourself, not the devil, the benefit of the doubt. You would regard it as a grave sin of injustice to accuse another of a crime unless you were entirely certain of your facts. That it happens to be against yourself in the present case does not make the accusation less unjust where there is still doubt as to the guilt. The fact that the thought of sinning makes you suffer is good evidence that God still holds your will and heart as His own.

Let us note, and note well, the following facts and principles, and apply them whenever temptation assails us.

(a) We are enlisted as soldiers in the armies of God. A soldier's one business is to fight. Temptation *is* the spiritual warfare. It is the normal experience in the life of the soldier. If we were rarely or never tempted, then should we be distressed and frightened. Why has God not honoured us by sending us forth to battle for Him? Why does He thus account us as unworthy to do hard service for Him?

(b) Temptation is a sign of Satan's enmity; he does not

attack those who have given him their allegiance. Therefore, his enmity is the indication that we are at friendship with God. Therefore, " count it all joy when you fall into divers temptations." [1] Temptation is our opportunity. " When the devils tempt us," says St. Augustine, " they are fashioning for us crowns of glory," and our temptations have been described as the raw material of the heavenly glory that will be ours.

(c) Temptation may bring suffering, but it can never bring sin into our lives save through our definite consent.

(d) The victory is ours whenever, and as long as, we say " No " to the temptation.

(e) In every occasion of temptation God's honour, the honour of the divine family of which we are members, is involved. He will have care for His own honour, and will make haste to help us.

(f) Keep ever in mind that temptation is a personal conflict. If we allow ourselves to think that it is some vague, impersonal influence working against us, there will be no way of organizing our plan of campaign. It will be like fighting a fog. In every temptation, as we have thought, three persons are involved—the tempting devil on the one side, and on the other side God and our souls. So long as the alliance between us and God holds firm, defeat is utterly impossible.

IX

When we think of all the goodness and love of God towards us, it would seem wholly impossible that we should ever turn our backs upon Him and enlist ourselves in the cause of Satan. But, alas, we can, and we do. We yield our consent, and the dread thing is done. The story is told of a group of visitors who had been shown over a famous monastery by a saintly old brother. On bidding him good-bye, one of them said, " You have been very kind to us; can we not give you something for yourself, in token of our appreciation? " " Oh no," was the reply, " we have nothing of our own except our sins, and they are our very own." Our very own because they are the creatures of our will. We speak them into being by the act of our will. It is as though we spoke the fiat, " Let there be sin," and there was sin. There is no material lying about in the path of man out of which the tempter can construct sin. On the contrary, every occasion and condition which might be used for sin can be employed for the building up of the kingdom of righteousness. Indeed, God permits these occasions and conditions just in order that they may be used for His glory, and for the breaking down of the kingdom of sin, Satan, and death, but we

[1] St. James i. 2.

too often pervert them to the base uses of him who is the adversary of God and of all that is good.

Consent once given, the act of sin follows. Just because we have done a thing once, it is easier to do it again; and so, by repetition of the acts, deadly habit fastens itself upon the soul. Then comes necessity. We have yielded ourselves so repeatedly that now, bound fast with the chain, we cannot choose but sin, unless we cast ourselves at the feet of God in sorrow, and cry aloud to Him for help. Unless we do this, spiritual death is inevitable. There is no hope save in Him, but in Him there is a sure hope that disappointeth not. " Him that cometh to me I will in no wise cast out." [1] But the death of sin is not only that which we prepare for ourselves in eternity, it is death here in this life, death to all that is good, to all that is high and noble and true, death to all that is Godlike.

X

Such, then, are the seven stages which lead to destruction—suggestion, pleasure, consent, act, habit, necessity, death. But no soul need run this fatal course. We have seen where and how we can call a halt, and by the grace and the ever operating love of God, secure certain and final victory.

Our safety lies in obedience to the divine command to love God with all our heart and mind and soul. If we love, we are safe. Love clothes us with the whole armour of God. " Love and do what you will," [2] said St. Augustine, for he knew well that if we love God, and as long as we love Him, there can be no desire or will to do aught that would offend Him, and therefore serious sin would be impossible. It was as though he were assuring us that if we hold fast to the fundamental motive principle of love, we can afford to move with the greatest and fullest freedom, for " where the Spirit of the Lord is, there is liberty." [3] Love will keep everything right; else there is no love, for love and sin cannot dwell together in the heart.

We have many limitations, but there is no limit to our capacity for loving. As the old Spanish mystic said : " Perchance thou canst not fast ; thou canst not bear the biting discipline, or labour much, or go on distant pilgrimage; but thou canst love. In every

---

[1] St. John vi. 37.
[2] " Dilige, et quod vis fac."—St. Augustine, *On St. John's Epistle*, Tr. vii. 8; Migne, P. L., Tom. 35, Col. 2033.
[3] 2 Cor. iii. 17.

place, in every season, thou canst love." [1]   And love is alert, eager, imperious; love will not be said nay in the service of the Beloved.

Armed by love and with love, we are equipped with all the power of God. The conflict is not, then, as we have said, between our souls and Satan, but between Satan on the one side, and our souls and omnipotent God on the other. If we co-operate with Him, defeat is impossible, for Satan is not stronger than God.

The Holy Spirit is ever working for our sanctification. His course follows the same steps as we saw offered in the progress of temptation. The stations, so to speak, on the road of life correspond with those which we find on the road to destruction. Here, too, we find suggestion, pleasure, consent, act, habit, necessity, death. The Spirit is incessantly, if we will but perceive it, suggesting holy thoughts and purposes. Let us find our pleasure in considering that which His tireless love suggests to our hearts. Let us give swift and joyous consent to every suggestion or call from Him. Let us hasten to translate the thought into action, and let us repeat the action again and again until it pass into a fixed habit of holiness which will bind us so fast in the bonds of the divine love that we cannot choose but love and serve Him. There will then be laid upon us the imperative necessity of loving God, and of expressing that love in all we think, or do, or say. Then will come the sweet and blessed death to all that is evil, to all that belongs to self and sin, to all that does not belong to love, and to the God of love. The alternative to this blessed death unto sin is death unto God. So St. Augustine says, " *Moriar ne moriar,* Let me die lest I die." [2] Let me die to sin lest I die to God, and out of this death to sin arises life, life unending, which is the very life of God Himself.

O Lord Jesus Christ, wounded by my transgressions, pierced by my sins, and yet loving me still : Thou in Thy mercy hast said, Come unto Me and I will give you rest. Lord, I come, I come. O Compassionate Lord, Thou in Thy mercy hast said, " I desire not the death of a sinner." Lord, I am that sinner. Lord, Thou knowest all things, Thou knowest that I love Thee.

---

[1] Diego de Estella, *Meditations*, lix.
[2] St. Augustine, *Confessions*, i. 5; Migne, P. L., Tom. 32, Col. 663.

So it is that, through the virtue of His Precious Passion, the flaming sword of the Cherubim that drove Adam out of Paradise, is now put away; and the endless gates of heaven are open to every man that will enter in thereto. For the Person of Jesus is both God and King of heaven in the bliss of the Father; and as Man He is the porter at the gate, ready to receive every soul that will be re-formed here in this life to His likeness. For now may every soul, if he will, be re-formed to the likeness of God, since that the trespass is forgiven, and the amends through Jesus is made.

WALTER HILTON.

CHAPTER XVIII

THE CROWN OF FORGIVENESS

I

WE have seen that the necessity of repentance for wrongs committed against another would seem to be a part of the earliest revelation of God to man. It is a universal human instinct, and the whole range of the revelation concerning sin, and the course which should follow upon sin, as we find it dealt with in the Church, would seem to be conformed to the instincts of man as God has created him. Men universally agree that wrongs should not be done either to God or man. There is equal agreement that where wrong is done, contrition should follow. All men require acknowledgment of sin as the necessary evidence of contrition, and that there should be a purpose of amendment, and a consequent work of reparation.

Further, it is a universal feeling that where real repentance exists, something is due to the penitent in the way of consideration, if not of full pardon. God responds to this instinct in man with the gift of the Sacrament of Penance. This is, as it were, a kind of ladder of repentance, leading the soul, step by step, up to God, and therefore to final release from sin, and from all its consequences in time and in eternity.

Although we may in some manner be able to analyse the work of forgiveness, yet we must ever approach the subject with an attitude of solemn awe, for we are here confronted with one of the deepest mysteries of the divine love. It has been said, " To the unseared conscience, the forgiveness of sin is a greater mystery than sin itself. We are, alas, too much at home with sin to be surprised at anything about it. Damnation is no mystery to the soul which feels separate from God. Darkness transelemented into light, hate transformed into love, ghastliness of sin transfigured into the beauty of holiness, deserved displeasure issuing in the overpowering, sin-forgiving, sin-annihilating love of God, this is the mystery of mysteries, which angels desire to look into, which man could scarcely dare believe." [1]

Spiritual penitence, however, is a different thing from re-

[1] Pusey, *University Sermons*, 1859–1872, p. 244.

pentance as it is generally regarded in the world. We find an indication of the universality of a belief in confession in the proverb that " an honest confession is good for the soul." Like most ancient proverbs, this expresses a truth, but true as it may be, it has nothing to do with confession as we regard it from a sacramental point of view. The object of the Sacrament of Penance is not to gain some general psychological good, some sense of release from the consciousness of guilt; nor is it to satisfy any merely human instinct, as in the case of one who may have wronged his neighbour or the community in which he lives. All these are indeed present, but the purpose of this confession goes deeper than this.

In sacramental confession the object, and the only essential object, is to secure absolution in the manner in which our Lord ordained, when, as the Church declares, He gave both " power and commandment to his ministers to declare and pronounce to his people, being penitent, the absolution and remission of their sins." [1] The only recorded occasion in our Lord's life which can be construed as one on which He delivered any such command or authority was on the first Easter night. The first time He appears to His apostles after He had risen from the dead, having given them the ordinary salutation which was the custom amongst people of that age and country, " Peace be unto you," He goes on immediately to say, " As my Father hath sent me even so send I you; receive ye the Holy Ghost; whose soever sins ye remit, they are remitted unto them, and whose soever sins ye retain, they are retained." [2] These words are used by the Bishop when he lays his hands upon a man to ordain him a priest. The form used in the Church is as follows:

" Receive the Holy Ghost for the Office and Work of a Priest in the Church of God, now committed unto thee by the imposition of our hands. Whose sins thou dost forgive, they are forgiven; and whose sins thou dost retain, they are retained."

With this ordination the power which our Lord gave to the Church in the persons of the apostles on Easter night is transmitted from generation to generation of the ministry through the ages. Men confess their sins to a priest, and their penitence is made evident. If they are sorry for their sins, and are willing to strive to amend their lives, absolution is given them, and they go on their way, cleansed, released, endowed with a new and special power to resist temptation, and rejoicing in the pardoning love of God.

[1] *Book of Common Prayer*, Office of Morning Prayer.
[2] St. John xx. 21–23.

On infrequent occasions it might happen that a man is not willing to give up some serious sin; or he may be unwilling to forgive another who has wronged him. When such unhappy conditions exist—and, thank God, they are rare—no absolution can be given, and the sins, though they may all have been mentioned in a form of confession, are retained, and the sinner cannot receive the forgiveness of God until he comes to a better mind.

All this means that the objective in the Sacrament of Penance is the receiving of absolution. It is the absolution that is sacramental. We do our part in our acts of penitence. We confess our sins, we declare our purpose to make satisfaction for the failures, and to amend our lives; but without God's act in giving us the grace of the Sacrament through absolution, what we do will not avail. The sacramental power lies not in anything that man does, but in the action of God. What we do in confessing our sins only creates the condition prerequisite to receiving absolution and the cleansing and strengthening grace that lies in absolution.

The spoken absolution is the outward and visible sign of the inward and spiritual grace of the Sacrament. When absolution is given, a very objective thing is done. Something actually happens. In the moment of absolution pardon is given, and there is also poured into the soul by the Holy Spirit a definite moral and spiritual force and power which enables it to go forward to a better service of God. It can now meet the temptations that beset it, and where formerly it had suffered defeat, it is now able to combat the temptation, and to win the victory over it.

II

Of course, if one is truly penitent, God forgives. But forgiveness is not the whole of God's work for the penitent soul. There is a special operation of grace secured in absolution which can be secured in no other way. He who doubts the necessity of receiving absolution, must ask himself the question, " Considering all that I have to contend with in this spiritual warfare, can I afford to leave unclaimed and unappropriated any grace which our Lord has prepared for me? It may not, in every case, be necessary for salvation, as when the sin is not mortal, but shall I deal so ungenerously with Him, who did so much for me, as to say that I will do nothing that is not absolutely necessary for my salvation, that I will gain heaven as cheaply as possible? " Is not the very fact that our Lord has ordained such an objective means of grace in His Church, the proof that it will be a help and a strength to me? Would He have ordained it so objectively and exactly had He expected it not to be taken advantage of and used by those who find themselves severed from Him by mortal sin?

What, then, are the definite effects of this absolution which seem to be of such great importance? They are many. We can list some of the more important of them, remembering that while these effects are not to be thought of chronologically, they present what really happens in the moment when the soul receives absolution.

(a) Absolution removes guilt from the soul, and procures for it the reconciliation to God, which our Lord purchased for it on the cross. So far as any further imputation of guilt is concerned, it is as though the sin had never existed.

(b) It imparts a special grace according to each soul's special need.

(c) It rebuilds spiritual tissue, broken down and wasted by sin.

(d) It knits us up again into the Heart of the divine love.

(e) It restores the grace, and the union with God, which were lost through our sin.

(f) It revives the merit which was lost through sin, and recovers the treasure we had laid up in heaven by our former good life, which was forfeited by sin.

(g) It infuses into us once more the human powers of Christ to think and to will, to love and to act, so as to be pleasing to the Father.

(h) The absolution is the outward and visible sign which gives us the assurance that these gracious spiritual happenings have actually taken place.

This is the blessed work which the Holy Spirit performs in the truly penitent soul, and the means by which this is done is the absolution we receive when we sorrow for sin with a truly godly sorrow.

III

What about our life after we receive absolution? Absolution removes guilt, but this is not the conclusion of the business. Faber has rightly said that " holiness has lost its principle of growth if separated from abiding sorrow for sin; for the principle of growth is not love only, but forgiven love." [1]

We must therefore practise the virtue of penitence. While the psalmist's practice of penitence was expressed in the words, " My

[1] F. W. Faber, *Growth in Holiness*, Chap. xix.

sin is ever before me," this was not the central theme of the psalm. His attitude was no morbid one, no brooding over his sins. On the contrary, he quickly rises to the expression of joy and gladness in his penitence, for there is no state of mind and soul which can so fully guarantee a life of joy. If I love God at all, and recall my sins in the light of the fact that God's overwhelming love and tenderness and mercy have created for me the opportunity to retrieve my soul, and to repair the dishonour done to Him, then it will be impossible not to be filled with a great and holy joy. The truly penitent soul is always the joyful soul. If joy be absent, it is certain that there is something wrong with our penitence. Can we imagine anyone more full of the radiancy of joy than St. Peter when our Lord on the seashore restored him to His favour, and entrusted him with the commission, " Feed my sheep "? [1] Was it not a reflection of his own state of heart when, nearly thirty years later, he wrote to his spiritual children concerning Christ, whom, he said, " having not seen, ye love; in whom, though now ye see him not, yet believing, ye rejoice with joy unspeakable and full of glory "? [2]

The habit of abiding penitence is that which will incline the soul to the continual expiation of sin, and to the continual rooting out of all the remains of sin, of all tendencies toward sin, and of all love for it. We will learn how to obey the apostolic injunction to " abhor that which is evil," and to " cleave to that which is good." [3] The abhorring is negative, but love is never content with a negative work. He who abhors evil because it wounds Christ whom he loves, will not stop with this. Love's work is positive, and such a soul will go farther, and cleave to that which is good. Indeed, the very act of hating sin constitutes the loving of that which is good, for the mind cannot be a vacuum in relation to spiritual things. Speaking of hatred of sin, St. Augustine says, " He who hates well, loves well." In so far as I hate the evil, just so far do I love the good.

This abiding sorrow for having wounded our loving Lord is manifested in a longing to make reparation for our sins, to fill up the measure of our unfaithful past. Absolution does not make reparation. It removes our guilt, but it does not give to God the honour He would have had from us had we, instead of sinning, served Him lovingly. Nor does it restore to us all at once that fuller measure of holiness which would have been ours had we given our hearts more completely to Him.

[1] St. John xxi. 16, 17.   [2] 1 St. Peter i. 8.   [3] Rom. xii. 9.

IV

The effects of this practice of the virtue of penitence are manifold. Let us recall some of them:

(a) It gives us a permanent, wholesome, supernatural dread of sin which will go far towards preventing its recurrence.

(b) It keeps us humble. The soul which has its sin ever before it will not easily fall into pride. It knows too well its own weakness.

(c) It is a great well-spring of purification, for penitence is a continual cleansing to the soul. It is our sorrowing more and more that enables God to cleanse us more and more.

(d) It is a source out of which will flow a spirit of generosity and self-forgetting. Penitence works continually for the mortification of self-will and self-pleasing.

(e) It imparts a full and eager spirit of renewed consecration to Him whom we are painfully conscious of having wantonly wounded.

(f) It is the greatest means and assurance of perseverance in the life of restored holiness.

(g) It will fill us with a longing for, and anticipation of, the blessed destiny that awaits us in the bosom of the Adorable Trinity, " with Christ in God."

The principle of abiding penitence, then, consists in much more than merely recalling our sinful acts. The psalmist said, " My sin is ever before me," but as we read the fifty-first psalm, we see that much the greater part of it is taken up with the contemplation, and with a joyful testimony, of the divine love and tenderness. His sins were ever before him, but there was no question in his mind that " Thou shalt make me hear of joy and gladness."

The essence of the matter lies in keeping fresh the memory of God's pardoning love which wrought so amazingly to take away our sin. I am not to dwell on my past sins in relation to the love of God; rather am I to dwell on the love of God in relation to my sins. This difference in point of view is fundamental. The thought of sin alone never brought penitence to any soul. It has brought despair to many. Judas hanged himself because he thought on his sin, and could not bring himself to think of the love of his Lord for sinners. The contemplation of the love of God is the panacea for every spiritual ill; for it fills the soul with tender, grateful, and lasting sorrow for having wounded one so dear and so loving, and powerfully stimulates to do the thing which makes amends for the wrong the sin has wrought to God, to our neighbour, and to self

As long as this abiding sorrow continues, no temptation can overcome us. We are safe, knit together " with Christ in God," in a loving and enduring union which no power can violate. This abiding sorrow for sin, if it has its root in love, will endure for eternity, and will be one of the fundamental causes of the joy which will be ours in the presence of the Lamb. Bernard of Cluny, in his " Hora Novissima," in which he set forth the truth and joy which belong to those who are " in Christ," expresses this for us in his radiant verse—we use Dr. Neale's translation. He is describing the flood-tide of happiness which engulfs the souls of those to whom it is given to see God face to face, the saints in heaven who are " the sinners who kept on trying ":

> " Their breasts are filled with gladness,
> Their mouths are tuned to praise,
> What time, now safe forever,
> On former sins they gaze.
> The fouler was the error,
> The sadder was the fall,
> The ampler are the praises
> Of Him who pardoned all."

V

True and abiding penitence will introduce the soul speedily to the next element in this work of repenting of its sins against God—namely, that of satisfaction. Satisfaction means simply that, in respect both to God and man, one does all that one can to repair the wrong committed. So far as it is possible, one must make restitution for the injury done. This is sometimes questioned on the ground that it seems to imply that there was something lacking, which we can supply, to the " one full, perfect and sufficient sacrifice, oblation and satisfaction for the sins of the whole world," which our Lord wrought upon the cross.

Those who raise this question, however, misunderstand the meaning of the term *satisfaction*, and have not carefully thought out what it involves. Nothing can be lacking to the satisfaction wrought by our Lord, and even if there were still something more to be done, a sinner would be utterly incapable of supplying it.

But the soul seeking to lay hold on salvation must do its part. Nothing is more clearly taught in the New Testament than this. " Lay up *for yourselves* treasures in heaven," [1] was our Lord's command. St. Paul enjoins St. Timothy to " Lay hold on eternal life "; [2] and St. Peter's exhortation is " to make your calling and election sure." [3] The fullest teaching in the New Testament on

[1] St. Matt. vi. 20. [2] I St. Tim. vi. 12. [3] 2 St. Peter i. 10.

the subject is found in St. Paul's description in the seventh chapter of his second Epistle to the Corinthians. Here he describes how " godly sorrow " wrought in the purpose and actions of the sinning Corinthians. " What carefulness it wrought in you," he exclaims; " yea, what clearing of yourselves, yea, what indignation, yea, what fear, yea, what vehement desire, yea, what zeal, yea, what revenge! " All this makes it clear how eager the penitent Corinthians were to do something to make satisfaction for their sin, and how joyfully the apostle approved their course.

All these expressions, and many others that might be quoted, give direct denial to the idea of our being passive in the work of salvation. We must have our part. This part is, indeed, utterly without force or effect if it be not in union with our Lord's work of satisfaction; but it is also true that His redeeming work is without force or effect in respect to us, unless we do those things that He has commanded in order to become partakers of His infinite work of satisfaction.

The law of making satisfaction for sin is not only a constant part of the New Testament teaching, but we have only to examine certain commonplace illustrations to see that it is in keeping with the normal instinct of right and justice which God has implanted in the natural heart of man. For example, one of us has treated another with rudeness. He is sorry, but this is not enough. He must make satisfaction by apologizing. Again, one has slandered another and injured his good name. No one would think it sufficient for him to refrain in the future from repeating the slander. He must repair the wrong done, and make satisfaction, as far as possible, by acknowledging the slander, and restoring the man's reputation. Once more, one has stolen another's property. He is repentant, but the repentance would be accepted by no one if the thief contented himself with resolving to steal no more, and refused to make satisfaction by restoring or replacing the stolen goods, so far as he could. All this is the work of satisfaction, of repairing, as far as it is possible, the wrong done by our sin.

Likewise, performing a penance which has been assigned by the priest presents one of the great principles of satisfaction. We can through no work of our own repair the dishonour which even the smallest sin does to God. But by some act given as a penance to be performed, the sinner, by outward expression, gives a pledge of his desire and intention of doing what he can to repair the wrong; and by this act, if devoutly and penitently performed, he becomes partaker of, and enters into, the satisfaction wrought by our Lord on the cross, and is made, as St. Paul expresses it, " accepted in the Beloved ";[1] not because of works of righteousness that he has done, but because the Father sees him in Christ, and accepts him accordingly.

The very slightness of the penance usually assigned in the confessional is a declaration of the inability of the sinner to do anything of himself to make satisfaction for his sins. If it were possible for us of ourselves to make satisfaction for them, then, considering the deep and far-reaching dishonour done to God, some great act would be required. But one may be told to say a simple collect or a psalm. This slight penance, because the dishonour done to God is infinite because His honour is infinite, is no less proportionate to our sin than would be a penance that would require the devotion of all our time and energy for the rest of our life in some labour of most painful self-sacrifice. It is of importance that we seek, as far as is possible, to make real and vivid to ourselves the truth that the greatest penance we might undergo would be utterly inadequate to counterbalance even the least sin that had been committed against the love and honour of God. Every sin is an infinite wrong against God. Absolutely nothing that we finite creatures can do, no matter how great, even the sacrifice of life itself, if done outside of Christ, can be of the least avail. No wise priest, therefore, gives a severe penance, for it would have a fundamentally false implication. On the other hand, the smallest act of penance, performed in union with Christ, with sorrow for our failure, and with trust in God's love, with firm resolve to try to sin no more, constitutes a successful pleading, a personal appropriation to ourselves, of the infinite satisfaction made by our Lord in His great atonement for our sins on the cross.

VI

The study of satisfaction cannot be complete without the consideration of the work of reparation. We know that the work of the God-Man on the cross was the full and infinite repairing of the Father's honour, which had been so grievously wounded by the sin of man. Nothing can be added to what He has done. But by His gracious condescension and love, He has given opportunity to men to have part in His work of reparation. For us He has brought to fulfilment the ancient promise that in the Messianic kingdom it should be given to God's people to " build the old

[1] Eph. i. 6.

wastes; they shall raise up the former desolations, and they shall repair the waste cities, the desolations of many generations." [1]

There is an interesting passage in the first chapter of the Epistle to the Colossians which bears on this subject. St. Paul speaks of his own sufferings as " filling up that which is lacking to the afflictions of Christ " (verse 24). Of course, the apostle could not have been referring to any lack in our Lord's atoning work, for that was the perfect sacrifice in which there could be no lack. But, as Bishop Lightfoot observes, " there is a sense in which it is quite legitimate to speak of Christ's afflictions as *incomplete*, a sense in which they may, and, indeed, must be *supplemented*." [2] His sufferings may be thought of from two points of view. First, He, as Man, made satisfaction to God for the sin of man, and corrected the deficiency in man caused by that sin. Thus He made it possible for men to become partakers of the divine holiness. Second, we think of His perfect conformity to the Father's will as offsetting the sin which violated that will, and as building up the kingdom of God. The God-Man alone could do the first. Man is utterly helpless, of himself, to lay hold of the holiness of God. Of all men, Christ alone was able to say, " I sanctify Myself." [3] This He could say, because He is the fount and source of all holiness. St. Luke tells us that Christ in His earthly ministry " began to do," [4] and every Christian soul by his good works, and by his life of prayer, must be continuing this work which Christ began. We offer ourselves as fellow-victims with Him. By the patient endurance of the sufferings which come to us in this life, in every pain of body or mind, if we bear it and seek not to be rid of it, are we enabled to share His cross and Passion, making ourselves one with Him in the great work He came to do of repairing the dishonour God has suffered through the sins of our fellow-men. There is a solidarity of the human race, and, while each must render an account to God for his own sins, we can by this work of reparation do something to repair the wrong the race has done to the Creator.

Every sin is an act destructive of the divine kingdom. Every holy action repairs that which sin has torn down. While Christ has fulfilled to the utmost His part of the work, His gracious love has left opportunity for men to do that which constitutes one of the highest and richest privileges that belongs to the Christian life. Not only does His love allow us to repair by penitence the wrong we have done to Him by our own sins, but He gives us the honour

---

[1] Isa. lxi. 4.   [2] See J. B. Lightfoot, *Commentary in loc.*
[3] St. John xvii. 19.   [4] Acts i. 1.

of making up to Him for the innumerable wrongs He and His people have suffered through the craft of Satan and of evil men. We are not only permitted to fill up the measure of our own unfaithful past, but to devote ourselves to offsetting the dishonours He continually receives at the hands of sinners.

The principle is admirably and very sweetly illustrated by the story told by Père Plus of two little girls whose mother had been badly treated by an elder son. They came to her and said, "Mother, don't feel badly about what our brother has done, for we are going to love you just twice as much because of it." Another practical illustration of reparation is found in the history of the Paris Commune in 1871. Archbishop Darboy and the priests who were martyred with him, after being taken to the place of execution, were subjected to a painful and humiliating delay before the firing squad arrived. While waiting, one of the communards made an insulting remark to the Archbishop. Instantly Père Alexis Clerc, a young priest who in a few minutes was to die with him, rose, and kneeling before the aged prelate, kissed his feet. Others might insult the servant of God, but he would make some reparation by doing him this signal honour.

The work of reparation does not always demand great labours; for the most part it can be carried out continually in a very simple manner. There are those who when they hear the Name of God used lightly or blasphemously, instantly offer Him a compensating act of love, or bow the head in loving reverence, or secretly make the sign of the cross. None of these things can take away the guilt of the sinner, but they counter the sin with an act of devotion to Him. Every creature in the world is created for the praise of God: "O all ye works of the Lord, bless ye the Lord: praise Him and magnify Him forever." But the world does not praise and honour Him. It is therefore our part and privilege to fill up this measure, to counter neglect with a fuller outpouring of love to Him; because men do not pray, to offer Him a richer measure of prayer, a measure beyond that perhaps which He demands of us as of obligation. All the day long one can thus make some amends to God for the hurt He receives from our brethren who are in the world. If we awake in the night, what could be better than to offer Him instantly an act of reparation for the sins which are everywhere seeking the cover of darkness, but which can never be hid from the eye of God?

If we love Him, we shall not find it difficult to pursue such a course. Indeed, we would find that our own natural instinct would drive us to it. We would be stimulated to a powerful activity in this field. We know how this works in ordinary human relationships. If we hear of a loved friend who has been treated with unkindness and contempt, how quickly do we hasten to him to assure him that though all others reject him, we are his loving and loyal friend; and if this act of reparation involves our entering into his suffering, how gladly do we bear it for love's sake. How much more should this principle find swift, spontaneous, and unceasing expression when the One who has been so deeply wronged and dishonoured is the dear Lord Christ who loves us with an everlasting love, and who spared not Himself that we might have the eternal joy and consolation of the love and presence of God Himself.

There can be no question that praise and prayer with this purpose and intention are more neglected than any other mode of worship. There are millions of earnest souls who are faithful and devoted in their continual practice of prayer, but to whom, through the want of the right knowledge, it has never occurred to offer to Him the service which our Lord asked of His disciples in Gethsemane when His soul was " exceeding sorrowful even unto death ": " Tarry ye here and watch with me." It was because of their neglect of this that He gave them His tender rebuke, " Couldst thou not watch with me one hour? " Thus did He testify to the longing and desire of His Sacred Heart for the sympathizing, compensating love of His children; although not a few Christian folk seem never to have heard of it. There is never a morning when the newspaper does not furnish us with unlimited material for prayers and acts of reparation, for most of the news is but the account of the evil done in the world, of the wanton wounding of our Lord.

Nor should we forget our responsibility to our brethren. St. Paul's great saying, " We are members one of another," [1] must also be ever in our minds as we think of the work of reparation. If my arm, through proper exercise, receives an increment of strength, every member and organ of my body participates in it, and the whole man rejoices in this increase. Likewise, in the Church, which is the Body of Christ, no one member can offer a prayer or do a righteous act without every other soul, whether in this world or in the next, having a share in the grace or glory which that action brings. We can keep nothing to ourselves in the Body of Christ. On the other hand, if we fail to give our love and service to Him, we hold back from every other Christian soul an unction of power and strength which God means him to have

[1] Eph. iv. 25

through our faithfulness, and which indeed he may sorely need. In our own personal lives, how many times have we failed our brethren, our fellow-members of His Body. Surely in both love and justice we need to make continual reparation to them, and so to God, for the unfaithfulness on our part from which even now they may be suffering.

Every Christian is called to take part in this work, but the great and continuous work of reparation is that which has been done in every age by contemplative and cloistered religious communities. The world about them, full as it is of cruel habitations, is busy by night and day with man's inhumanity to man, with its nameless infamies, its sordid money-getting, its selfish interests, its mad rush after pleasure at any cost of goodness, or of honour to God. But this evil is not allowed to go on without compensation to Him. By day and by night consecrated men and women cease not from their labour of loving praise in reparation. To them, as to all who seek the work of loving Him where others neglect or hate, come His words of old, " For the sorrows that I had in my heart, thy comforts have refreshed my soul." There is no hour of the twenty-four in which they are not, through their prayers, releasing the power of God for His glory and honour, for the assuaging of the wounds inflicted on Him by the sins of His people. No disturbing element is allowed to enter to draw these devoted servants of God from their *laus perennis*, their unceasing labour of praise and prayer that God may have the glory which must be His from the hearts of men, that the measure of His pleasure in His people may be the more full.

VII

What has been said has already introduced us to the subject of amendment. The work of amendment is that of carrying out day by day our resolution to do better in the service of God; but, simple as this may seem, not a little hurt and discouragement have come to souls from misunderstanding what this part of the work of penance means. In the first place, let us understand that amendment does not mean never again committing the sins of which we have repented. This is not the meaning of the word. Amendment means improvement, bettering the situation. Let us look at this very practically. A man might confess having lost his temper seriously a score of times within a week. He sets out, by the help of the grace of his absolution, to amend. Perhaps the next week he loses his temper only a dozen times. This is by no means ideal; but it is certainly a great improvement, it is a real achievement of amendment; and if he continues to strive earnestly in the power of grace, and to fight against this temptation, patient always with his own weakness, and not losing heart because he cannot break a habit of years in a few days, he will succeed, in time, in eliminating it altogether. We are not to be discouraged, however, if, in the course of this effort, the frequency of the sin seems to increase. It is in the nature of things that when by God's grace we become more sensitive to its presence, we are conscious of failures which formerly we had quite overlooked.

The work of amendment is a progressive work, and it is to last as long as we live. It is the real test of our penitence, of our good faith in the service of God, of how we are appropriating His renewed grace in our daily life. In the first place, we are to seek diligently to reduce the number of failures to do the will of God. We are not to expect perfection of ourselves, for we have no promise that we shall be perfect in this life. Sins will recur; but the faithful servant of God knows how to deal with the temptation, and also with the sin itself should he be so unfortunate as to fall again. Renewed penitence sets us once more upon our feet. Secondly, we work in the power of the Spirit to reduce not only the number of occasions, but the seriousness of the failures, even if we cannot wholly eliminate the acts themselves. If we persevere in this, there will be no question that in the end success will be ours.

There should be nothing vague or indefinite about our method of amendment. An excellent technique is to fasten upon some one bad habit, and, by special prayer and watchfulness, seek to correct it. The whole life of our souls, whether for good or evil, is so interwoven, is so much of one piece, that to weaken the power of sin at one point is to weaken it at all points, just as the cultivation of one virtue is the cultivation of all the virtues. It may be that we give way to a habit of impatience in little things; it may be the very common evil of exposing the faults of others unnecessarily. We know many conditions and circumstances which create the occasion of falling. Watch for these occasions. When they appear, the first step is to pray in that very moment for strength from God to defeat the tempter, for of ourselves we can do nothing. This done, we are then to set the will strongly against the sinful thing, and by a further act of the will seek to divert the attention from the evil thought that has been suggested to the mind. Compel yourself to think of something else. The mind can only deal with one thing at a time, and if it is kept busily engaged upon some good and holy purpose, nothing else can find place in it. Then, lastly, when old temptations recur, say to yourself—and it has a good psychological effect to say the words aloud if the circumstances make this feasible—" I promised God to do better in this very thing, and by His gracious help, I am determined not to break my promise."

An important part of this method of amendment is also to make a daily special examination of conscience regarding the evil thing we are fighting. At night we should look back over the day, and ask ourselves the searching question, Have I carried out my resolution in this matter? Have I used the means which I knew would bring victory over temptation? If not, why not? Let us thus summon ourselves before the forum of our own conscience, and demand of ourselves an accounting in this cause.

VIII

We have thought repeatedly that the service of God does not consist merely in casting out the evil, and we must at this point consider this truth again. The good must be brought in. We amend our way of life not only by putting away sin, but by bringing in that which is good and righteous. Therefore, let us also choose some one virtue in which we know we are weak, and seek to the utmost to cultivate it. Not only, for example, are we to be on guard against unloving thoughts, words, and actions, but we must set out resolutely and positively to do the thing that is kindly and loving. Not only should we not exalt ourselves in our pride, but humble ourselves deliberately, taking, for instance, the lowest place in some little thing, such as letting others speak before we undertake to express our opinion. It is best always that it be something which would not attract particular attention to ourselves, lest our very effort for humble amendment turn into an occasion of pride.

All this must be done according to a carefully and deliberately planned course. There must be nothing fortuitous about it, no depending on chance encounters for the opportunity and occasion of driving out the evil and bringing in the good. The issue is altogether too important to allow of such casual treatment. Perhaps we know that to-day we are going to meet certain people who provoke us to be censorious and resentful. We are to remember that *every occasion of sin is also an occasion of righteousness*. Forewarned is forearmed. We are to approach such an occasion with a resolution already made, by a strong act of the will to compel ourselves to think, and say, and do, that which is the expression of charity

T

and kindliness. If it be at great cost to our feelings, so much the more valuable the effort, so much the deeper impress will it make upon character, so much the more will the effort make us like unto our Lord.

Then we must make a daily particular examination regarding the Christ-like quality we are seeking to cultivate. The examination we made in respect to sin is the lesser half of this work of amendment. To do that which is righteous and loving is of greater importance than the mere refraining from that which is evil, for, as we have already said, the absence of sin does not constitute holiness. Have I actually loved God this day? Have I earnestly protested to Him that I love Him? Have I let my heart go out to our Lord, in warm and loving aspiration, reminding myself from time to time to speak to Him in my heart, not only protesting to Him my love, and my desire to love Him ever more and more, but asking Him to pour His love into my soul, for without Him in this matter I can do nothing? Have I tried diligently to show my love to Him, and to my fellow-men, by being kind and courteous, gentle and patient? Have I exercised these virtues especially in thought? Common decency and worldly politeness will keep me from being outwardly rude or unkind. But in the secret place of my heart has there been a kindly, sympathetic spirit, reaching out readily and sweetly to all whom I have met, and toward all those of whom I have been thinking?

If in any measure, however small, these blessed Christ-like things are finding place within me, then I am going forward indeed. Then am I steadily reducing within me the power of evil, and in the same measure deepening, by the help of the Holy Spirit, the presence and power of divine love in my life. In me is the principle being exemplified which the great teacher of love, St. Augustine, so constantly taught, that the increase of love constitutes the diminution of sin.[1]

This interior attitude and purpose, and the exercises that grow out of it, will constitute the practice of abiding penitence—that is the intelligent, loving sorrow which goes deep into our character transforming us more and more into Christ. This work on our part will move step by step with the abiding and continuous action on God's part, cleansing us more and more from our sins. It will bring to pass in us an ever-deepening participation in the divine holiness, not only restoring that which we had lost by our sins, but

[1] "Nutrimentum caritatis est imminutio cupiditatis."—St. Augustine, de divers Quæst., Q. 36; Migne, P. L., Tom. 40, Col. 25.

increasing our possession of this holiness in a measure which no man can estimate. It was the constant teaching of the Fathers of the Church that the soul was able to gain more grace by a true, lively, and enduring penitence than it had lost by the sin of which it was repenting. The energy of our penitent hearts, united with the energy of the infinitely loving heart of God, will converge upon specific lines of holy action, drawing us progressively into the inmost sanctuary of the life and Being of God, into an ever deeper partaking of His divine nature, every vibration of our souls pulsating in ever more perfect harmony with the ineffable purity of His divine life, and of His infinitely loving activity.

O most dear Lord, Give me vigilance of heart that nought of restless imaginings may lead me far from Thee ; give me a steadfast heart that no unworthy love may sever me from Thee ; give me a dauntless heart that neither pain nor suffering wear me down ; give me a righteous heart which no ill purposes may ever turn aside. Give me an eager and diligent heart to seek Thee, and wisdom to love Thee when I find Thee.

The Father and Son are drawn to one another by a common and mutual love: the Father is of such absolute perfection and beauty, the Son is so perfect an image of His Father! Thus each gives Himself to the other, and this mutual love which springs from the Father and the Son as from one source, is, in God, a subsisting love, a Person distinct from the other two Persons, namely the Holy Ghost. The Name is mysterious, but revelation gives us no other. The Holy Ghost is the ultimate term in the interior operations of the divine life: He achieves, if we may thus lisp in speaking of such mysteries, the cycle of intimate activity in the Holy Trinity. But, like the Father and the Son, He is God; He possesses like them, and with them, one and the same divine nature, equal knowledge, equal power, equal majesty, equal goodness.

COLUMBA MARMION.

CHAPTER XIX

THE HOLY SPIRIT (I)

I

WHENEVER we are dealing with the Christian religion we find ourselves continually recurring to the thought of the Holy Spirit.
When we read the New Testament, or any of the authorized
teachers of the Church in whatever age, we observe that the Spirit
of God is mentioned repeatedly. If we should make a reckoning
of them we should find that references to the Holy Ghost in the
Scriptures are quite as common as those to the Father and to the
Son. The uniform teaching of the whole New Testament is that
the Holy Trinity works nothing without the agency of the Spirit,
the third Adorable Person in the Godhead. This is inevitable, for
the reason that the Holy Ghost is equal to the Father and to the
Son in all things, and, as we have seen, the three Persons share
equally in all the attributes of the Godhead, and in all its activity.
Where one Person works, all work.

As is the case in all our thought of God, we find ourselves here
confronted by mystery. We are not to think this to be a strange
or novel thing. All life is shot through with mystery. There is
not a gay insect that dances in the morning sunlight, or a blade of
grass that springs at our feet, that does not present more of mystery
than of knowledge. Our Lord said to His disciples, " It is given
unto you to know the mysteries of the kingdom of heaven," [1] but
He did not say that they were to have an intellectual understanding
of them. We can have a clear knowledge of the existence of a fact
without understanding it. Let us note what we mean by a mystery
in religion. A mystery is a truth which we cannot fully understand, but which we accept on faith, nothing doubting, because
God has revealed it. We can understand only those things which
are inferior to us. I can understand the science of algebra, for
example. I can master it; I can go all around it; I can see it
from every angle, and in all its applications and relations. It is
not possible, however, for me to understand the divine mysteries
in this manner. The Infinite can understand and grasp the finite;

[1] St. Matt. xiii. 11.

the finite cannot understand the Infinite. If I could understand God He would not be God.[1]

So is it with the Holy Spirit, the Third Person of the Blessed Trinity. We can know much of Him as He reveals Himself to us, but we cannot encompass Him with our understanding. We can see the evidences of His presence, and of His work, but we cannot bring Him within the compass of our narrow intellect. Our Lord's first revelation concerning the Holy Spirit was made to Nicodemus, and the initial truth that He declared was that, although we can see the evidences of His work, and rejoice as the beneficiaries of it, we cannot understand it in the way we can understand certain things of the finite creation. He compared the Spirit to the mystery of the wind: "The wind bloweth where it listeth, and thou hearest the sound thereof, but canst not tell whence it cometh or whither it goeth. So is everyone that is born of the Spirit." [2] We can recognize the action of the Spirit, and rejoice in it, but how He works is beyond the range of human thought. Indeed, the "how" of the divine action is something we cannot inquire into save under peril of the grave sin of presumption. It was the unbelieving Jews of Capernaum who demanded to know, "How can this man give us his flesh to eat?" [3]

II

There are those in our time to whom the Holy Spirit is the "unknown God." There is often no formal intention on the part of these souls of denying the truth of the revelation of the Holy Trinity. Without hesitation they give a verbal acceptance to the creeds in which they declare their belief that there are three Persons in the one God; but when it comes to a definition, they refuse to agree to the truth that the Holy Ghost is a Person. We shall not discuss here the philosophical meaning of the word "person." For our purposes it is sufficient to say that the Christian believes the Holy Spirit to be a Person in the same sense in which we confess the Father and the Son to be Persons.

Such objectors would tell us that the Holy Spirit is merely an impersonal influence emanating from God, working in the hearts of men for righteousness. But this denial of the Personality of the Spirit is a denial of the revelation of the Trinity. Two Persons, plus an influence, cannot constitute a divine Trinity.

It is a curious circumstance that often the same minds that

---

[1] St. Augustine, *Serm.* cxvii. 5; Migne, P. L., Tom. 38, Col. 663. "Si enim comprehendis, non est Deus."

[2] St. John iii. 8.   [3] St. John vi. 52.

find difficulty in believing in the Person of the Holy Spirit, deny also the fact of the personality of Satan and of his evil angels. They reject the revelation concerning the Spirit who is sent to lead the souls of men into all the truth and on to the consummation of eternal life; and at the same time they deny the existence of the evil spirit who seeks to lead souls into error, and on to eternal death. Such souls do themselves a double disservice. They refuse to believe in any spiritual enemy, on the one hand; and, on the other hand, they deny the presence of the only power which can secure for them the victory in the conflict. He who shuts his eyes to the existence of any opponent in the warfare, and at the same time ignores the only source of reinforcement and spiritual supply, is inviting irretrievable defeat.

These errors are complementary to each other. They involve the belief, first, that the Spirit of God, without whom the apostles could take no step in their evangelical work, is nought but a vague, indefinable influence; and, secondly, that temptation to sin derives not from a power outside of the soul, but is the emergence of a so-called evil principle inherent in every man. The impossibility of this is shown by considering that in this event, the man who is tempted the most must have within him the most of inherent evil. But since Christ was tempted above all others, the necessary conclusion is seen to be an impossibility unless it is concluded that our Lord had inherent in Him more of evil than any other man who ever lived.

Of course, we are not undertaking to appeal to those who do not accept the Holy Scriptures as the word of God; or to those who so emasculate them in the interest of criticism as to make them worthless as anything more than a collection of ancient documents, without spirit or life. We are striving by the help of God to make clear the revelation that has been given, and we can address ourselves only to those who believe the teaching of the Church and of the Scriptures. With others there is no common ground upon which we can discuss the recorded revelation of God.

When we consult the Scriptures, we find expressions repeated everywhere which make no sense if the truth of the Holy Trinity is impugned by calling the personal existence of the Holy Ghost into question. It will not be necessary to do more than to examine the Scriptures to see that if He be not a Person, the sayings concerning Him are without meaning, and it would be just as irrational to believe in Him as an influence as to accept Him as a definite, living Person.

Let us consider the statement regarding the personal activities of the Holy Ghost in the Church and in the hearts of men. A few instances involving the historical activities of the Spirit will suffice. In giving the promise of the coming of the Holy Ghost our Lord declares that " when he, the Spirit of Truth, is come, he will teach you all things, and bring all things to your remembrance, whatsoever I have said unto you." He is also to " convince the world of sin, and of righteousness, and of judgement." This Spirit which the Father was to send, is to guide them into all the truth. He is not to speak of Himself, but " whatsoever he shall hear, that shall he speak: and he will shew you things to come. He shall glorify me, for he shall receive of mine and shall shew it unto you." [1] If we take these promises up one by one, it will be seen that little meaning can be found in them if the promised Spirit is a mere impersonal influence.

It will also throw the fullest light on the subject if we go on to see what was the office and work of the Holy Spirit after He came to dwell in the Church, as recorded in the New Testament. He was the author of the new birth: " Except a man be born of water and of the Spirit he cannot enter into the kingdom of God." [2] Was the soul to be born again through the agency of an impersonal influence? At Antioch did an impersonal influence say to the apostles and brethren gathered there, " Separate me Barnabas and Saul for the work whereunto I have called them "? [3] Did an impersonal influence speak to St. Peter, saying, " Behold, three men seek thee. Arise, therefore, and get thee down, and go with them, doubting nothing: for I have sent them "? [4] Could an impersonal influence instruct the apostles what to teach,[5] or where they should teach it? [6] What is meant by an impersonal influence making " intercession for us with groanings which cannot be uttered "? [7]

Again, let us look at the manner in which men might treat the Holy Spirit. Could a mere influence, flowing out from God, be vexed by the conduct of men? [8] Could an influence be tempted—that is, put to a test? [9] Could it be quenched? [10] Could it be grieved? [11] All these expressions, if they mean anything at all, must imply that we are engaged with a Person. References might be multiplied indefinitely, which would show that if language has any significance whatever, the work of the Holy Spirit, as outlined

---

[1] St. John xiv. 26; xvi. 7-14.   [2] St. John iii. 5.   [3] Acts xiii. 2.
[4] Acts x. 19, 20.   [5] 1 Cor. ii. 13.   [6] Acts viii. 29.   [7] Rom. viii. 26.
[8] Isa. lxiii. 10.   [9] Acts v. 9.   [10] 1 Thess. v. 19.   [11] Eph. iv. 30.

in the New Testament, is the work of a Person.   It is quite conceivable that one might reject the whole of the divine revelation of the Blessed Trinity, but to accept it at all, and then give it an interpretation which strips it of all meaning, is beyond the bounds of reason.

III

The Scriptures employ many expressions in describing the functions of the Holy Spirit.   He is called " the Spirit of God " [1]— that is, the Holy Spirit, the Third Person of the Blessed Trinity, who is God from all eternity, being of one divine, infinite substance with the Father and the Son, and equal to them in all things, both in His Being and in His activities.   This title is used by St. Paul in his great discourse on the Spirit in the eighth chapter of the Epistle to the Romans.   In the same verse the apostle calls Him " the Spirit of Christ," thus identifying Christ and God.   This latter title is applied to Him as the Spirit of the God-Man, of Him who is at the same time " perfect God and perfect Man."   Again, the same apostle calls Him " the Spirit of Jesus," [2] the One who guided the Sacred Humanity of Jesus of Nazareth in the days of His earthly pilgrimage, as we shall see when we come to consider the action of the Holy Ghost in the ministry of Christ.   The expression is used, " the Spirit of the Lord." [3]   The reference here is to the Old Testament, where the title is not uncommon.   In using this title, the apostle proceeds to declare the Deity of the Spirit, saying, " The Lord is that Spirit."   He then goes on to explain His relation to us: " we all, reflecting as a mirror the glory of the Lord, are transformed into the same image from glory to glory, even as from the Lord the Spirit."   It is to be noted that the change thus made in us by " the Lord the Spirit " is not superficial or accidental.   The passage means that we are actually transfigured from glory to glory into this image of the glorified Christ which is reflected in us as in a mirror.   By this transfiguration we undergo, in the power of the Spirit, a fundamental change of character and purpose, we, every moment, being carried on to an ever higher and more completely transforming plane of life in Christ.   What was at first a reflection of Christ in us as in a mirror is made a permanent quality in us by the Holy Spirit.   The verb used here is the same as that which both St. Matthew and St. Mark employ in their description of the Transfiguration of Christ on the mount.   What happens to us in our souls is analogous to that which happened to Him in His

---

[1] Rom. viii. 9.   [2] Phil. i. 19.   [3] 2 Cor. iii. 17, 18.

Body.   Our souls, through the action of " the Lord the Spirit," are transfigured.[1]

The same apostle writes to the Galatians of " the Spirit of His Son " [2] which comes into our hearts, enabling us to realize our sonship in God, endowing us with a filial relationship to Him, and more than this, giving us a joyous consciousness of this relationship, and teaching us to cry " Abba, Father."   This title, " Abba," was never used by men, but only by our Lord, and it was never used by Him in referring to the Father, but only in direct, loving, and intimate address to Him.   Our use of it is the expression of the realization of our oneness with Christ, in which unity we are given the privilege of speaking to the Father, even in the same manner as He speaks to Him.   The apostle implies that in teaching us to use this loving address, which before the coming of the Holy Ghost had never been used by men, but by the God-Man only, the Spirit bears witness to our intimate, organic union with the divine Son in the bosom of the Father.

In the contemporary Epistle to the Romans, St. Paul reverts to this same thought—an unusual thing for him, for he rarely repeats himself—and says, " Ye have received the Spirit of adoption " [3]— that is, the Spirit which characterizes and animates us who, having been sinners, and therefore aliens, are now adopted into the family of God, in the power of which Spirit we can, together with Christ, cry, " Abba, Father."   The title, " the Spirit of adoption," is closely allied in its implications to what underlies this " Spirit of Sonship," for the Holy Ghost is the agent who effects our adoption into God, and " beareth witness with our spirit, that we are the children of God, and if children, then heirs; heirs of God, and joint-heirs with Christ." [4]

This calls to mind St. John's profound and sweetly assuring declaration: " Behold what manner of love the Father hath bestowed upon us, that we should be called the children of God," and the apostle then adds the words which are unhappily omitted from the inadequate text used in translating our Authorized Version, *and we are*.[5]   It is not, then, merely through any condescending favour that this title is bestowed upon us, but having once been

---

[1] St. Matt. xvii. 2 ; St. Mark ix. 2. This word ($\mu\epsilon\tau\alpha\mu\rho\phi\delta\omega$) appears only four times in the New Testament—in the accounts of the Transfiguration noted above, in this present passage, and in Rom. xii. 2, where the faithful are enjoined not to be conformed to this present world, but to be transfigured by the renewal of their minds. This implies an essential and permanent change, " not external but internal, not of accidents, but of essence." See Trench *N.T. Synonyms*, § lxx.

[2] Gal. iv. 6.   [3] Rom. viii. 15.   [4] Rom. viii. 16, 17.   [5] 1 St. John iii. 1

made one with Him, we are in reality His children, and therefore must receive the name of children, since we are " partakers of the divine nature " [1] of our Father. Our Lord Himself spoke to His disciples of " the Spirit of your Father," [2] a title complementary to " the Spirit of His Son." St. Augustine discusses these titles with his accustomed clearness, and takes the relation implied in them to be one of origin, the Holy Spirit proceeding within the bosom of the Trinity, from the Father and the Son.[3]

The Third Person of the Trinity is also called " the Spirit of Life," [4] and " the Spirit of Truth " [5]—that is, the Spirit of Him who said, " I am the Truth and the Life." [6] While the title, the Spirit of Love, is not formally employed in the New Testament, yet in many passages there is the clear implication that He is the Spirit of Love, and we are bound to think of Him as such, and the title may be freely used. He is the agent through whom we receive the divine love which is essential to our life, for " the love of God is shed abroad in our hearts by the Holy Ghost which is given unto us," [7] and since " God is Love," [8] it is the very life of God Himself which is thus communicated to us. Likewise, He is " the Spirit of holiness." It is said of God " Thou only art holy," [9] and it is the coming into us of the Holy Spirit, who is very God of very God, and therefore Himself the perfect and essential holiness, which makes us to be holy.

In the epistle to the Hebrews there is a solemn warning given to souls who fall away from God, lest by their sin they do " despite to the Spirit of grace." [10] The word which is used here does not refer to the grace of God as given through the Sacraments and other divinely ordained means, but rather to the graciousness with which the Spirit deals with us. He is the Spirit of graciousness, and one commentator says that the expression is used to indicate " the personal, gracious nature of the power so wantonly insulted " by our sinning.[11] Archbishop Trench has a fine comment on the significance of the word grace, χάρις: " There has often been occasion," he says, " to observe the manner in which Greek words taken up into Christian use are glorified and transformed; they seem to have waited for this adoption in order to come to their full rights, and to reveal all the depths and riches of meaning which

---

[1] 2 St. Peter i. 4.   [2] St. Matt. x. 20.
[3] St. Augustine, in St. John, xcix. 6, 7; Migne, P. L., Tom. 35, Cols. 1888 and 889.
[4] Rom. viii. 2.   [5] St. John xiv. 17.   [6] St. John xiv. 6.
[7] Rom. v. 5.   [8] 1 St. John iv. 8.   [9] Rev. xv. 4.
[10] Heb. x. 29.   [11] Moffatt, Crit. Comment., in loc.

they contain, or might be made to contain. χάρις is one of these words." [1] Its adoption into the Christian vocabulary seems to have acted as an alembic to exalt and ennoble it, to purify it of the dross that may have attached to it in its common use. The word came to signify in Christian parlance " the grace embodying and uttering itself in gracious outcomings towards such as might be its objects." [2] What a hideous response is sin to these " gracious outcomings " of the Holy Spirit to the souls of men. The passage in Hebrews is one of the most terrible in all Holy Writ. The apostle speaks of those who despised the law of Moses perishing without mercy under two or three witnesses. He then goes on to say, " Of how much sorer punishment, suppose ye, shall he be thought worthy, who hath trodden under foot the Son of God, and hath counted the blood of the covenant, wherewith he was sanctified, an unholy thing, and hath done despite unto the Spirit of grace ? " [3]

Finally, the Holy Spirit is described as " the Spirit of glory and of God," [4] for it is He who makes us to be " partakers of the divine nature " of God, who inducts us into the life of grace which is the beginning of the life of glory which we shall share with our glorified Lord and Saviour in His completed kingdom. This Spirit of glory will lead us on in this life from grace to grace, from strength to strength, until we come to rejoice in the fulness of the Vision of God, and of His life of love and holiness, in the realization that every degree of grace here in this mortal life has a corresponding degree of glory in the life to come. Grace is the seed which is to be culti-vated and developed by every means which God appoints for us, that we may, through His goodness, be able to reap the eternal harvest. As the whole harvest which the husbandman gathers lies implicit in the seed which is sown, so the destined glory resides implicit in the grace which is bestowed upon the soul. The life in both is identical. As the life of the child of ten is the same as that of the fully matured man of twenty years later, so the life lived by the Christian way-farer here in the earthly pilgrimage is the same as that in which the saints in glory rejoice. The only difference is that the one is in the process of growth and development, while the other has attained to the divinely appointed maturity and perfection.

Glory and God—this is our destiny; and since God is not to be differentiated from His attributes (" *Quod Deus habet, hoc est*, What God has that He is " [5]), we say that this predestined glory *is* God.

---

[1] Trench, *N.T. Synonyms*, § xlvii. [2] Trench, *N.T. Synonyms*, § xlvii.
[3] Heb. x. 29. [4] 1 St. Peter iv. 14.
[5] St. Augustine, *De Civ. Dei*, xi. 10; Migne, P. L., Tom. 41, Col. 325.

When we attain to glory we attain to Him, and there is no glory save in attaining to Him. He is " the God of all grace, who hath called us unto his eternal glory in Christ Jesus," [1] not *by* Christ Jesus, as our Authorized Version has it; for while it is true that we are called by Him, yet this glory can be ours only in so far as we are " in Christ," and since Christ is God, to be in Him is to be taken up into God. Herein will lie the answer to His prayer " that they all may be one; as thou, Father, art in me, and I in thee, that they also may be one in us." [2]

A complete study of these titles, and of many others which are to be found in the Scriptures, brings before us in full review the nature and function of the Holy Spirit of God. They set forth the manifold aspects of the life and work of the Third Person of the Godhead in His relations within the Holy Trinity on the one hand, and with the souls of men on the other. They show us the work and, in large measure, the method of the work, of the Spirit in enabling the souls of men to become partakers of the divine nature, to have a participation in the holiness of God, and so to fulfil their destiny in taking their appointed place in the innermost life of the Most Holy Trinity.

IV

The primary study of the work and office of the Holy Spirit has to do with the interior life of the Godhead. In considering the Holy Spirit in the Trinity, we are to keep it clear in our minds that there are Three Persons in the One God, three Persons subsisting in one nature, and that these three Persons are in all things equal. Each of the Divine Persons possesses the totality of Godhead. There is no distribution or division of the divine life and nature and attributes amongst the three Adorable Persons. Each one is God in His absolute and infinite fulness. To quote the Athanasian Creed, " The Father is God, the Son is God, and the Holy Ghost is God, and yet they are not three Gods, but one God."

It is revealed to us that " God is love," [3] but this is not to say that He possesses love as men may be said to possess it. He *is* love in His infinite substance and essence. Since the Father is God, and the Son is God, each in Himself possesses the totality of love which is the essence of the divine Being. Now, love is a unifying virtue, and of its very nature it draws together the Persons of the Blessed Trinity in the unity of an infinite love. It is the office and unfailing prerogative of love to give, and the divine Persons of the

---

[1] I St. Peter v. 10.   [2] St. John xvii. 21.   [3] I St. John iv. 8.

Trinity, each being the fulness of essential love, give themselves to each other in an infinite donation of one and the same love. " And from this mutual donation of one and the same love, proceeds, as from one principle, the Holy Spirit who seals the union of the Father and the Son by being their substantial and living love. This mutual communication of the three Persons, this infinite, loving union between themselves, assuredly constitutes a new revelation of holiness in God; it is the ineffable union of God with Himself in the unity of His nature, and Trinity of Persons." [1] St. Augustine is explicit in his teaching on this point: " Love, therefore, which is of God, and which is God, is properly the Holy Spirit, by whom the love of God is shed abroad in our hearts, that love by which the whole Trinity dwells in us." [2]

The Holy Spirit has been called the ultimate term of the divine operations of the life of God in Himself. That is, the Holy Spirit, the third Person of the Indivisible Trinity, completes and closes the infinite cycle of the love which constitutes the life and essence of God. It is for this reason that in the economy of the Godhead that which is a work of achievement, of completing the divine operations, of bringing the divine activity to its full fruition, is attributed to the Holy Spirit. For example, He is the Sanctifier. He is the One who makes us holy. He is the One who teaches and guides us in the prosecution of the life of holiness even unto the end, when we shall, through His work in us, fulfil the vocation to which the eternal and infinitely loving Trinity has called us from the foundation of the world.

The three Persons are equal in all things, whether it be in their nature or in their work. We speak of the First, the Second, and the Third, Persons, but this is not to imply any priority either in time or rank. This may seem to present a paradox, but the humble soul accepts what is revealed, and does not ask for explanations from God. He honours us by revealing to us the mystery of the Holy Trinity, the divine Three-in-One. Out of His love for us He takes us, as it were, into His confidence. We receive the revelation, and bow down in loving adoration before the mystery in which lies our life in time and in eternity, but which is wholly beyond our understanding. We can do nothing but adore. Amongst other operations, the work of sanctification, as we have seen, is attributed to the Holy Ghost; but in all the process of making holy the souls of men—and let us renew our realization that this is

[1] Abbot Marmion, *Christ, the Life of the Soul*, pp. 11, 95 (4th ed.).
[2] St. Augustine, *De Trinitate*, xv. 18; Migne, P. L., Tom. 42, Col. 1083.

our only ultimate vocation and destiny, to be made holy in God—the Father and the Son have an equal part with the Spirit. Although they are three separate and distinct Persons, they so indwell each other that it is not possible for one Person to work without the others having an equal part in that work. This co-operation is such that each Person does the complete work, because there is but one nature in the Godhead. The divine activities are not parcelled out amongst the Divine Three. The Father is the Sanctifier, the Son is the Sanctifier, and the Holy Ghost is the Sanctifier, and yet they are not three Sanctifiers, but one Sanctifier. So is it in all the life and activity of the Triune God.

O Sweet Spirit of the Living God : O Spirit of the Living God, loving and tender : O Spirit of the Living God, tender and of great mercy : O Spirit of God, merciful and gracious : O Spirit of God, gracious and full of compassion : O Spirit of the Living God crowning me with loving-kindness. Thou art the ineffable Gift and the Giver of all gifts : I love Thee, be merciful unto me.

In resigning ourselves to the dominion of the Spirit of God, we shall have to accept the trials that accompany the period of transition. It is to be expected that when we begin to relinquish our natural habits and modes of action, and, on the other hand, have not yet attained to the habits and operations of the spiritual man, that we should betray a certain weakness in mind and heart. . . . This is but the natural result of unforming the old man, and not having yet formed the new man. . . . We have to see things in the light of God; to live, love, judge and act according to Him. In order to attain to this, we forego the loves and ways of the natural man. Thus our old nature is made weak and foolish because its former aliment is withdrawn from it. . . . We lose the natural life in order to gain the divine life. We leave that which is " according to man " in order to attain that which is " according to God."

H. REGINALD BUCKLER.

CHAPTER XX

THE HOLY SPIRIT (II)

I

THE Holy Spirit performs His infinite and unceasing function as the Third Person of the Deity within the mystery of the innermost life of the Holy and Indivisible Trinity, but He enters also into the sphere of time, and there He works the works of God.

We have to consider the activity of the Spirit in our Lord's earthly life, and also to study its bearing upon the corporate life of the Church, and upon the development of the individual souls who, along with Christ as the Head, constitute the Mystical Body which is His Church. These we shall have to consider together, as we cannot differentiate between the work which Incarnate God wrought through the Spirit in the days of His earthly pilgrimage, and that which He does through the same Spirit in His risen, ascended, and glorified life, for " it is the same God that worketh all in all." [1]

The supreme activity of the Godhead in the time-sphere lies in the Incarnate life of the God-Man. The work of God in creation, and in all the history of the human race, was preparatory to the work of Incarnate God. When in the fulness of time God became Man in order to redeem His people, it was through the Holy Spirit that the Incarnation of the Eternal Son was effected. When St. Mary of Nazareth was told by the angel Gabriel that she was to become the Mother of the promised Messiah, she asked by what means this great thing was to be accomplished. The reply revealed to her the ineffable plan in the purpose of God: " The Holy Ghost shall come upon thee, and the power of the Highest shall overshadow thee: therefore also that holy thing which shall be born of thee shall be called the Son of God." [2] When St. Joseph was troubled at these strange and, to him, unaccountable happenings, the angel reassured him, saying to him, " That which is conceived in her is of the Holy Ghost." [3]

The originating cause of the Incarnation was God's love for man. " God so loved the world that he gave his only begotten

---

[1] 1 Cor. xii. 6.   [2] St. Luke i. 35.   [3] St. Matt. i. 20.

Son." [1] In this familiar passage we must not fail to interpret the word *God* aright. It means not the Father, or any one Person of the Trinity, but the fulness of the Triune God, Father, Son, Spirit, for there is but one love in the Holy and Indivisible Trinity. Where one Adorable Person loves, the totality of the love of the Trinity is poured out in that act, for the Three Divine Persons love and act as one.

The Holy Spirit created the human body and the soul of Christ and united it by a mysterious union to the Second Person of the Trinity, the Divine Word. In effecting this union He filled this body and soul without measure with sanctifying grace. But we must think first of the uncreated grace and holiness which our Lord's sacred Humanity possesses in virtue of its union with the Second Person of the Trinity which was effected once for all in the act of Incarnation. This is what is called the hypostatic union— that is, the union of His Humanity with the full essence and substance of the Deity as it resides in the Second Person of the Godhead. This grace is unique. It is wholly incommunicable. If another human being were to receive this grace it would mean that in Him also would the Word be Incarnate, and there cannot be two Incarnations.

This unique and incommunicable uncreated grace must be distinguished from the created sanctifying grace which the Spirit inused into the human soul of Christ in the first moment of the Incarnation, and which is transmitted continually from Christ to the souls of all the children of God who are one with Him, and who hold faithfully to their divine heritage. It was of this sanctifying grace that the apostle spoke when he said, " Of his fulness have all we received." [2] Sanctifying grace is that endowment of the Humanity of Christ which enables it to work in a manner befitting the union it has with the divine Word. Let us keep in mind that the human soul of Christ is not different in its essential nature from the souls of other men. Both are human, both are created, both are finite. But the soul of Christ is perfect, without any inheritance of sin or weakness such as handicaps our souls. The entail of sin and all consequent moral and spiritual weakness, or tendency to evil, were cut off in Him. His Humanity is the perfect norm which God had in His mind in the beginning when He took counsel in the bosom of the eternal Trinity, saying, " Let us make man in our image, after our likeness." [3]

It is His purpose to conform all men to this norm, and such

[1] St. John iii. 16.   [2] St. John i. 16.   [3] Gen. i. 26.

the awful responsibility and power of man's free will, that nothing else in the universe can stay or frustrate this divine purpose. It is a frightening thought that the will of fallen man is free to choose, and to do, only that which is evil. He has no power to choose or do that which is good, save by the help of the Holy Spirit. " Free will is of itself," says St. Augustine, " sufficient for evil, but as respects good, it is capable of doing nothing without the assistance of the all-divine Goodness." [1] Our Lord established this truth when He said, " Without me ye can do nothing." [2] Independence confers on man only capacity for evil. He is sufficient unto Himself only for co-operating with Satan as against God. No wonder a saintly soul, affrighted at this most dangerous gift of freedom, prayed, " Give me to practise that supremest liberty of will, which is to strip my will of every liberty." [3]

II

Not only was the Holy Ghost the agent in this work of Incarnation, but everywhere in the Gospels we learn that the activities of our Lord's Humanity were directed throughout His earthly life by the same Spirit who presided over the Incarnation.

On the occasion of His baptism, the Spirit gave an outward and miraculous manifestation by which He revealed to St. John Baptist that this was the very Christ, the only begotten of the Father, made Man. Indeed, the Blessed Trinity, the divine Three Persons, each had His part in this manifestation. It was the first open and direct revelation given of the Trinity. The Son of God, the Second Person of the Godhead from all eternity, stood visible before men, clothed in human form, to receive the divine witness to His mission and work. The Holy Spirit, the Third Person, descended upon Him in the form of a dove, and the voice of the Father proclaimed, " This is my beloved Son in whom I am well pleased." [4]

Immediately after His baptism, " being full of the Holy Ghost," [5] " He was led up of the Spirit into the wilderness to be tempted of the devil." [6] The temptation being ended, He returns to Galilee " in the power of the Spirit." [7] He preaches to His own fellow-townsmen at Nazareth, and selects the passage from Isaiah lxi: " The Spirit of the Lord is upon me," and to the astonished and

[1] St. Augustine, *De Corrept. et Gratia*, xi. 31 ; Migne, P. L., Tom. 44, Col. 935.
[2] St. John xv. 5.
[3] Juan Falconi, *Compendium Breve*, xi, in Peers, *Studies of the Spanish Mystics*, Vol.i i. 392.

[4] St. Matt. iii. 17. [5] St. Luke iv. 1.
[6] St. Matt. iv. 1. [7] St. Luke iv. 14.

scandalized congregation He declares that it was of Himself, the village carpenter, that the prophet had spoken these words seven centuries before. He testifies that " the Lord hath anointed me to preach good tidings unto the meek; he hath sent me to bind up the brokenhearted, to proclaim liberty to the captives, and the opening of the prison to them that are bound." [1] In short, in the power of the Spirit He is to initiate the Messianic kingdom.

He attributes all the details of His ministry to the working of " the Spirit of the Lord " which is " upon me." He chooses the Twelve and sends them forth to preach the Gospel, assuring them that " it is not ye that speak, but the Spirit of your Father which speaketh in you." [2] Later in His ministry He declared that He " with the finger of God cast out devils." [3] This expression, " the finger of God," was one of the titles of the Holy Ghost. When He came to the supreme work of His earthly life, it was " through the eternal Spirit " [4] that He offered Himself without spot to God on the cross. Every phase of His Incarnate life was dependent upon the Spirit. Every step in carrying out the great work of Redemption was performed through the powers of His Sacred Humanity, wrought upon by the Holy Spirit of God.

III

Christ was under the direction of the Holy Spirit in all that He " began both to do and teach." [5] The emphasis in this sentence from St. Luke's prologue to the Acts of the Apostles should fall on the word *began*. Not only in His own personal labours was He directed by the Spirit, but when, through the apostles whom He had chosen, He continued the work and teaching which He had begun, this, too, was through the Holy Ghost. He had promised them the Spirit of God, who was to abide with them forever, [6] who was to teach them all things and bring all things to their remembrance whatsoever He had said unto them. [7] The Spirit was to assist them in all their evangelistic work. He was to be with them, convincing the world " of sin, and of righteousness and of judgment." [8] He was to guide them into all the truth. [9]

This last promise of our Lord's requires some special considera-tion. The passage, as St. John records it, is an emphatic one. If we translate the words as St. John gives them, they will read, " He

---

[1] Isa. lxi. 1.   [2] St. Matt. x. 20.   [3] St. Luke xi. 20.   [4] Heb. ix. 14.
[5] Acts i. 1.   [6] St. John xiv. 16.   [7] St. John xiv. 26.   [8] St. John xvi. 8
[9] St. John xvi. 13. ὁδηγήσει ὑμᾶς εἰς τὴν ἀλήθειαν, πᾶσαν.

will guide you into the truth, all of it." As we look at the sentence
the question suggests itself, what did our Lord mean to promise
them? Was it that they should be guided into truth in a general
way, or was His emphasis on the fact that the Spirit was to give
them a knowledge of the complete and full body of divine truth
such as men had never had before? They already had much of
the truth. The Old Testament revelation afforded His people a
deep, even if partial, knowledge of God and His mysteries. But
here our Lord foretells the guidance which they shall have into the
truth, and then, as though it were an emphatic afterthought, to
guard against their not grasping the fulness of the promise, He
adds: " All of it." The faith was to be delivered once for all to
the saints.[1] It was no longer to be foreshadowed in type and
symbol, but in its organic fulness it was to be revealed—" the
Truth in all its parts," and every part co-ordinated with every
other part, full, rich, life-giving.

Several other thoughts challenge us in this promise. Christ
does not say that this revelation of the Truth was to come to each
individual in a full and overwhelming gift in an instant of time. He
says we are to be guided into the truth. To be guided implies
that we have our part to play. We are given a divine leading, but
we have to follow it—that is, we have, under the Spirit, to use our
judgment and reason, and all the faculties which God has bestowed
upon us, in order to reach that to which the Spirit is guiding us.
He does not take us up and carry us. The word *guide* in the original
is a verb from corresponding with the noun meaning a *way*. We
go along a way; we do not stand still in it. We are given to see
more and more of the truth as we progress under the Spirit's
guidance along this way. Every moment we gain a fuller grasp
of the length and breadth, the depth and height, of these divine
things. We see them in ever-growing completeness; we see them
in all their relationships, both Godward and manward.

In this same discourse, only a little while before, our Lord had
said, " I am the Way, the Truth, and the Life." [2] Now He says we
are to be guided into all the Truth, into the complete knowledge
of, and union with, that absolute and personal Truth which is
Christ Himself. Christ is the Way by which men are led into
Himself, who is the Truth. This was a constant and favourite
theme of the Fathers. St. Augustine repeats it in more than one
of his works. He says, " He is the home, whither we go, He is the
Way whereby we go: go we by Him to Him, and we shall not go

---

[1] St. Jude 3.   [2] St. John xiv. 6.

astray " [1]; and again: " Christ, as God, is the home whither we go; Christ, as Man, is the Way by which we go." [2]

The Spirit can guide only those who will follow His leading. He guides them into the Truth which is the domain upon which they are to enter, and in which they will find their true inheritance. The Truth is not that which is to be viewed from a distance and admired.[3] It is the sum and substance of the Christian life. Thomas à Kempis gives a beautiful commentary on these words of our Lord: " Without the Way there is no going; without the Truth there is no knowing; without the Life there is no living." [4] In short, without Christ there is nothing, and only in Him shall we find anything that will endure.

In whatever way the Spirit was to do His gracious work in the souls of men, He was not to take the place of an absent Christ. On the contrary, He was sent specifically to make the presence and power of the risen, ascended and glorified Christ real and practical to men. " He shall glorify me, for he shall receive of mine, and shall shew it unto you." There is a solemn emphasis in this expression, if we translate it literally: " He shall declare it unto you." Three times are these words repeated in three successive verses.[5] They present the objective of the Holy Spirit in all His work for men. He has come to interpret God and the things of God. The modes of demonstration and interpretation may be various, but the aim never falters. He is to bring the souls of men to their appointed destiny, which is to be " with Christ in God." [6] The Spirit is the agent for the fulfilment of the promise, " Where I am there shall also my servant be." [7]

IV

We have seen something of the work of the Spirit in the instruction which He gave to the apostles, His demonstration to them of

---

[1] " Factus est quem fecit, ne periret quem fecit. Homo verus, Deus verus, Deus et homo, totus Christus. . . . Ipse est patria quo imus; ipse via qua imus. Per Ipsum adipsum eamus et non errabimus."—St. Augustine, *Serm*. xcii, 3; Migne, P. L., Tom. 38, Col. 573.

[2] " Deus Christus patria est quo imus: Homo Christus via est qua imus. Ad illum imus, per illum imus: Quid timemus ne erremus? Non recessit a Patre et venit ad nos. Ubera sugebat et mundum continebat. In præsepi jacebat, et angelos pascebat. Deus et homo, idem Deus qui homo, idem homo qui Deus. Sed non unde homo, inde Deus. Deus quia Verbum: Homo quia Verbum caro factum est. Et Deus manendo, et hominis carnem assumendo. Addendo quod non erat, non perdendo quod erat."—St. Augustine, *Serm*. cxxiii. 3; Migne, P. L., Tom. 38, Col. 685.

[3] See Westcott, *Comment. in loc.*

[4] Thomas à Kempis, *De Imitatione Christi*, iii. 56.

[5] St. John xvi. 13, 14, 15.   [6] Col. iii. 3.   [7] St. John xii. 26.

the things of Christ and of God. Let us now go on to see how His office was fulfilled in the external ministry of the Church. Before He ascended into heaven, our Lord gave to the Church, in the persons of the Twelve, the great commission to go forth and teach all nations; and He assured them of the signs and wonders which should accompany their words. He empowered them to make men the children of God in baptism; to forgive the sins of the people, being penitent; to consecrate the bread and wine to be His Body and Blood for the spiritual sustenance of the faithful; and He promised them many extraordinary gifts, such as healing the sick, and even raising the dead. But as all His ministry was under the guidance of the Spirit, so should theirs be, for their work was really His work. And not only during their apostolic ministry, but in the work of the Church through all the ages, His words are true: "Without me ye can do nothing" [1]; and they were to undertake none of these things until the promise of the Father, the Holy Spirit, was come. Christ, now working in them, was still to be under the guidance of the Spirit.

He told them that they were to be witnesses unto Him both in Jerusalem, and in all Judea, and in Samaria, and unto the uttermost part of the earth, but they should not depart from Jerusalem, but wait for the promised Spirit. They knew not how long this delay was to be, but, faithful to their Lord, they waited. They did not attempt to teach any soul, they celebrated no Sacrament, until the Holy Spirit came on Pentecost. Then, in the new power, what marvels were wrought. Peter, the Galilean fisherman, unlearned and ignorant, who but a few weeks before had been so intimidated by the taunt of a servant-girl that with oaths and curses he denied his Lord, now went out into the streets and preached with such commanding power that three thousand souls were added to the Lord. The whole apostolic band, which had been timid and fearful, went forth and converted the world. Only in the power of the Spirit could they do anything. They realized that they were dependent on Him, and that without Him they could do nothing.[2]

As we read the New Testament we see that the apostles were intensely conscious of the presence and the guidance of the Spirit in all the details of their work and ministry. Whether this same guidance was intended also for us, and has been lost by our faithlessness, we know not; but it is certain that with us the power of the Spirit is a feeble thing compared with what the Christians of

[1] St. John xv. 5. [2] Acts i and ii.

the early Church were able to employ; and the issue proved that their confidence was well justified.

In the work of evangelizing the world, from the very beginning until now, it is the power of the Holy Spirit which lies behind all that the Church does and says, because only the Spirit, as our Lord had indicated, could convince men of the fact of sin, sin in the world, sin in their own lives, and of the power of Satan amongst men; only He could convince them of the possibility of righteousness, and of the certainty of judgment to come. Without this conviction there can be no repentance, no conversion, no illumination through divine truth.

The Spirit not only taught them the facts and principles of the Faith, but, in ways we know not of, He directs where they are to preach. St. Paul essays to go into Bithynia, but the Spirit suffers him not, and forbids them to preach the Word at that time in Asia.[1] He also dictates what shall be the content of their preaching.[2] He makes known His will as to who is to be entrusted with certain offices and missions.[3] He appoints Bishops to oversee the flock of God.[4] The apostles are conscious of being made the instruments of the divine purpose " through mighty signs and wonders, by the power of the Spirit of God." [5] Where great principles of faith and practice are involved, they are assured of His direction of their course, and they give their decisions as He indicates to their minds and consciences. In all things they proceed with a definiteness which eliminates all doubt. " It seemed good to the Holy Ghost and to us," is the ground of complete certitude upon which they base their decrees in the first of the Church's councils at Jerusalem.[6]

Time would fail us to recount all the work which the Spirit accomplished through His direction of His servants, but we know that in the founding of the Church, and in the preaching of the Gospel throughout the world, they undertook nothing save in and through Him. These early Christians knew that they were the sons of God, and as such they yielded themselves to be led by the Spirit of God. St. Paul asserts this when he says, " As many as are led by the Spirit of God, they are the sons of God "—they and they only.[7] They looked to Him to teach them, to guide them into all the truth, and into all the ways and methods that He willed them to use. They had no will of their own, no self-devised plan for the building of the kingdom. In everything they depended on Him.

[1] Acts xvi. 6, 7.   [2] 1 Cor. ii. 13.   [3] Acts xiii. 2.   [4] Acts xx. 28.
[5] Rom. xv. 19.   [6] Acts xv. 28.   [7] Rom. viii. 14.

V

As the apostles and the great teachers of the Church in all ages have found their strength and enlightenment in their union with, and submission to, the Holy Spirit, so is it with the whole Body of Christian people throughout the world in every age. The whole life of the Christian depends on the Spirit of God. One can discern in this a kind of hierarchical order. Our Lord did nothing without His Father: " The Son can do nothing of himself but what he seeth the Father do." [1] We see the Spirit dependent on the Son: " He shall not speak of himself, but whatsoever he shall hear, that shall he speak "; [2] " He shall receive of mine and shall declare it unto you." [3] Again, all the people of God, in their service of Him, must look to the same Spirit for guidance and instruction. It is not only the truths of the Faith that the Spirit is to teach the Church, nor is it guidance only in greater things, as we may conceive them, for which we must look to Him. Everything in the life of the Christian, without any exception whatever, depends on the teaching and inspiration of the Holy Spirit. We must again recall that the Christian life is the life of the God-Man functioning within us, and since all that the Incarnate Son does is through the Spirit, that which He does in us is also done through the Spirit. Our Christian life, both within and without, is a part of the life and activity of Incarnate God. " Without me ye can do nothing," He declares. Christ works through His mystical Body; what the Body or any member of it does, He does. If my hand pens a letter, I say, " I wrote the letter." If a member of Christ performs a certain good act, Christ says, " I performed that act "; and what He does is done through the Spirit of God. Here, as in everything, we can apply the saying of the seraphic virgin of Siena of a saintly soul: " If you speak to Christ, and say, ' Who is this soul,' He will make answer, ' It is another Myself, made so by perfect love.' " [4] There is not a prayer said, there is not a good or dutiful action performed, even the commonplace things of our routine daily work, be it in shop or office, at desk or at the bench, that is not dependent for its worth on the Holy Ghost. No heart was ever lifted up in aspiration to God save through the Spirit. Every good and holy suggestion of which we are aware comes directly or in-directly from Him. In the perplexities which arise concerning the things of everyday life and duty, the Spirit is at hand to guide and

[1] St. John v. 19.   [2] St. John xvi. 13.
[3] St. John xvi. 14.   [4] St. Catherine of Siena, *Letters*, cxxix.

direct. Well do we pray, " Grant that Thy Holy Spirit may in all things direct and rule our hearts." [1] In the midst of our weakness, of our natural infirmities, our temptations; yea, in the midst of our sins, the Spirit is unceasingly alert to prompt us with good and holy inspirations, and since life is made up of little things, it is in the little and seemingly inconsequential happenings that the Spirit gives us His chief guidance, through conscience and judgment. Hence we pray that we may through the Spirit " have a right judgment in all things." [2] The Holy Spirit can be left out of nothing. If we wait for the great things before hearkening what the Spirit will say, He will have small place in our lives. The great events in any life are few and far between, whereas the common warp and woof of daily and hourly life are made up of that which may appear unimportant, but which offers with every thought, word, and action opportunity either to honour God by our loving, humble, and Spirit-directed service, or to dishonour Him by refusing to hear His voice speaking within us.

The guidance of the Spirit is not, however, to be ordinarily looked for as an unusual thing, nor is such guidance given in any unusual way. The normal procedure, even in the lives of great saints, is the use of the God-given endowments of reason and judgment, these powers being employed under the direction of the Holy Ghost in the grace that comes with prayer.

A wise and thoughtful teacher has said, " Intellectual illumination, in the strict acceptance of the term, is rarely given by the Holy Spirit directly. It was given to the apostles because they were apostles. It is given to many apostolic men as the world goes on, to great doctors and saintly pastors. But ' teaching ', as regards the greater number of souls, results rather in the firm and luminous grasp of conclusions than in the gift of proving such conclusions. It means the gift of being right, of loving what is right and of enjoying what is right. It means wisdom rather than understanding." [3]

VI

The Holy Spirit not only guides the judgment and conscience of His people, but He is also the active agent who produces the working of the Sacraments, and makes them to be realities in themselves, and effective in the lives of His people. He is the

[1] Collect for XIX Trinity.
[2] Collect for Pentecost.
[3] Hedley, *A Retreat*, p. 187.

minister of every Sacrament, and without Him there can be no transmission of grace. This is taught everywhere in Holy Scripture, and the Church has ever held to it in her practice of the Sacraments.

The relation of the Spirit to baptism, which is the initial Sacrament, without which no other Sacrament can be of effect, was declared by our Lord Himself in one of the earliest revelations He gave of His truth. He declared to Nicodemus that the new birth in baptism, without which no man could enter the kingdom of heaven, consisted of being " born of the Spirit." [1] St. Paul carries on this teaching when he says, " By the one Spirit are we all baptized into the one body." [2]

On the first Easter night, when the Risen Lord appeared to the disciples in the upper room, He ordained them to their priesthood and to the apostolate, and by the one action instituted both the Sacrament of Penance and that of Holy Order. But before He gave them their priesthood, and bestowed upon them the power and authority to forgive sins, He solemnly invoked upon them the power of the Holy Ghost: " Receive ye the Holy Ghost: whosoever sins ye remit, they are remitted unto them; and whosoever sins ye retain, they are retained." [3] The exercise of this gift, of course, lay in abeyance until the coming of the Holy Ghost at Pentecost. The power was conferred, but not until they were touched with the fire of the Spirit could it become effective.

In the Sacrament of Confirmation our union with Christ, which was once for all effected when we were baptized, is so deepened and intensified, that we are made more than ever before sharers in the grace of Christ and in the Gifts of the Holy Ghost. As we shall have occasion to notice again, it is a matter of grave significance that there is nowhere in the New Testament any mention of the Gifts of the Holy Ghost as such. They are enumerated only in the eleventh chapter of Isaiah, and they are there described as the endowment of the Messiah who is to come. These gifts belong by right and nature only to the Sacred Humanity of our Lord Christ, but they are transmitted to us through our union with Him, which union is effected, and strengthened, by our reception of the Sacraments. By being made one with Him we receive what He has, and thus does He share with us the Gifts of the Spirit. In Confirmation the Spirit clothes us with the fulness of the Christian state, and makes the divine endowments of our Incarnate Lord our very own. By the work of the same Spirit within us, these Gifts

[1] St. John iii. 5.   [2] I Cor. xii. 13.   [3] St. John xx. 22, 23.

can, and must be, employed to carry out the purpose and will of God. It is our part to yield ourselves to Him, and He is then enabled to do this great work within us, for our perfecting, and for the divine glory.

Likewise, in the Holy Eucharist, according to the constant teaching of the Church, it is the Holy Spirit who, descending upon the bread and wine, makes them to become the Body and Blood of the Risen, Ascended, and Glorified Christ. In the Eastern liturgies this is made explicit by the direct invocation of the Holy Ghost at the time of the consecration of the sacred species. The ancient liturgy of St. James gives us one of the typical forms of this invocation:

> " Send down the same most Holy Ghost upon us, and upon these holy Gifts, that coming upon them with His holy and good and glorious presence, He may hallow and make this bread to be the Holy Body of Thy Christ, and this Cup to be the Precious Blood of Thy Christ."

It will be noted that this invocation is not a prayer for a good Communion, as are certain of the forms of invocation in the Anglican liturgies, but it is a definite praying down upon the bread and wine of the Holy Spirit, that He may change these species into the Body and Blood of our Lord Christ.

VII

When we come to examine the great fundamentals upon which the Christian life and power are based, we find that here, too, nothing can be accomplished without the Holy Spirit. The first condition required for the gaining of eternal life is a full faith in God, in Him personally, and because of a belief in Him, a consequent belief in all that He has revealed; but without the Holy Ghost there can be no effective faith. We may give an intellectual assent to certain historical truths concerning God, what He is, and what He has done for His people; but this belief would be a vain thing, with no validity for salvation, unless it was given to us, and sustained within us, by the action of the Holy Spirit. The fundamental thing, the one without which all Christianity fails, is a sound belief in the Deity of our Lord Jesus Christ; but St. Paul warns us that this belief is no mere natural intellectual acceptance of the fact. He declares that " No man can say that Jesus is the Lord but by the Holy Ghost." [1] The Spirit infuses into us the power of believ-

[1] 1 Cor. xii. 3.

ing that which we call the Faith, and it is He also who works within us to increase and develop our belief. We are utterly unable to believe unto salvation unless the Spirit works within us to give us the supernatural power of belief. Therefore, our continual prayer must be, " Lord, increase our faith." [1]

Not only in respect to believing, and in practising the use of the Sacraments, is the work of the Holy Spirit indispensable, but in the daily living of the Christian life nothing can be done save through the Spirit. Self-denial—the mortification and discipline of the body and also of the inner man—is a necessary part of the Christian life, and the apostolic teaching follows that of our Lord in its insistence on such mortification and self-discipline. It is quite possible to mortify the body for a merely natural end, as when the athlete denies himself many things, but only that he may have a better chance of winning in the contest. St. Paul shows us the difference between the natural mortification and that which is supernatural when he says, " If ye, through the Spirit, do mortify the deeds of the body, ye shall live," [2] but without the Spirit no mortification will avail.

Again, we are taught that the life of prayer, which is an essential part of the life of the Christian, is impossible without the Spirit of God. " We know not what we should pray for as we ought, but the Spirit itself maketh intercession for us with groanings which cannot be uttered." [3] It is clear, then, that when we find prayer difficult, we should have immediate recourse to the Holy Spirit, asking Him to bestow upon us the power to pray, since He presides over all prayer, and there can be no prayer save " in the Spirit." [4] Even when prayer does not seem difficult, we dare not put any dependence on what might seem a natural capacity for drawing near to God. We can secure the true value of prayer only by conscious dependence on the Holy Ghost, by calling upon Him to teach us to pray. We are dependent on Him in our entire inner life as completely as we are on the electric current for furnishing light, or power, or heat. We may have all the necessary apparatus, every required fixture and appliance may be in its proper place, but until the current is turned on, it is dead and lifeless. In like manner, there can be no spiritual life without the Spirit.

Above all else, it is the Holy Spirit who enables us to receive and practise the virtue of love to God and to our neighbour, which is the first essential of the life in Christ, for if we have not love we

[1] St. Luke xvii. 5.   [2] Rom. viii. 13.
[3] Rom. viii. 26.   [4] Gal. v. 16, 25; 1 St. Tim. iii. 16.

are none of His. How does this love come to dwell in us? The apostle answers the question: "The love of God is shed abroad in our hearts by the Holy Ghost which is given unto us." [1] Our Lord sends to us His Holy Spirit, and that Blessed Spirit having come to us, and He being God, and God being essential love, it follows inevitably that the love of God which is His very being, since "God is love," [2] is bestowed upon us, and abides in us, for "he that abideth in love abideth in God and God in him." [3] The love of God can dwell in us in no other way. When St. Paul would commend the Colossian Christians, he speaks of their faith, and of their hope, but, above all, of their "love in the Spirit." [4] He is careful to emphasize that it is "in the Spirit," for without the Holy Ghost there is, and can be, no love, and without love the soul is dead.

VIII

As God the Holy Spirit, in the act of the Incarnation, raised the Humanity of Christ up into the Godhead, so by grafting us into Christ, the same Spirit likewise raises us up into the Godhead, into the current of the divine life and love, for if we are one with Christ, we must, of necessity, be where He is. St. Paul expresses this very literally and very beautifully when he writes to the Ephesians, "God who is rich in mercy, for his great love wherewith he loved us, even when we were dead in sins, quickened us together with Christ, and raised us up together (with Christ), and made us sit together in heavenly places in Christ Jesus." [5]

This "quickening" and "raising up" refers to Christ's resurrection. When we were baptized, God caused us once for all to know "the power of His resurrection." [6] We then entered into, participated in, the resurrection life of the Eternal Son. Christ, now that He has risen from the dead, possesses in His Humanity no life except His resurrection life. This is His only life, the life from the dead. He can give us no life save that which He now lives at His Father's right hand. Into His risen, ascended, and glorified life we have entered, because we have entered into Him and He into us. We must note the powerful significance of the three "togethers" in St. Paul's declaration to the Ephesians. We are never alone, but always "together with Christ." But we note a change in the close of the sentence—"in heavenly places *in* Christ Jesus." No longer *with*, but *in*. No longer as though we were

---

[1] Rom. v. 5. [2] 1 St. John iv. 16. [3] 1 St. John iv. 16.
[4] Col. i. 8. [5] Eph. ii. 4–6. [6] Phil. iii. 10.

merely accompanying Him in the heavenly places, but we are made wholly one with Him, recalling the Easter Epistle, " Your life is hid with Christ in God " [1] in the bosom of the ever-Blessed Trinity. This is the mighty work of the Holy Spirit.

O Eternal, Loving Spirit : Thou who dwellest in the high and holy place : Thou who dwellest also with them that are of a humble and contrite spirit, make me to drink of Thy pleasures as out of a river. O Loving, Gracious Spirit of God, bearing with me in the might of Thy love : strong and patient, yet provoked every day, let me no more desire aught save Thee, and only Thee.

[1] Col. iii. 3.

The grace of Christ is the mysterious renewal of our humanity by the infusion of the substance of His glorified Humanity. That glorified Humanity brings, of necessity, along with it the Gifts of the Holy Ghost wherewith it is glorified. The Holy Ghost, the bond of the Eternal Trinity, the Spirit of Life, is the glorious principle by which the Body of Christ lives. Thus by the grace of our Lord Jesus Christ, the members of His Body are partakers of " the fellowship of the Holy Ghost," the Spirit of life in Christ Jesus.

RICHARD MEUX BENSON.

The soul of man is a principle of action, and the will has an originating power to initiate its natural action. But the perfection of the soul consists in two things—the action of the Holy Spirit of God upon it; and a voluntary, and perfect and prompt conformity, and response of the will, to that operation of grace. As you cultivate the intelligence and the heart and the will of a child by constant and watchful education, so the seven Gifts cultivate the soul.

CARDINAL MANNING.

CHAPTER XXI

THE GIFTS OF THE SPIRIT (I)

ONE of the mysterious workings of the divine love towards men is seen in God's use of multiplied, and sometimes seemingly cumulative, if not repetitive, means for bringing His people the more surely to that state of holiness which is necessary in order that through union with Himself they may attain their destiny in Him. We have seen that the Holy Spirit makes us partakers of Christ's own endowments of sanctifying grace—" of his fulness have all we received " [1]— and that He infuses into the soul at baptism the theological virtues of faith, hope and love. We have considered how these work for the perfection of the soul. But there is an ever richer superabounding activity in the love of God. He, in the great love wherewith He loves us, seems never content with what He has done for us. In His divine eagerness to hasten us along the way of holiness He is ever devising new means and instruments for bestowing upon us spiritual beauty, grace, and perfection.

When we see how mightily grace, and the virtues of faith, hope and love work within us for our sanctification, it would seem that nothing further could be required to bring us to the ultimate destiny which His love has ordained for us. But the divine urge to do still more for His children is in continual operation. St. Teresa's saying that " it is of the nature of love to work in a thousand different ways," [2] applies pre-eminently to the love of God for man, for in Him love finds its completest and most varied expression, beyond the knowing and understanding of the human mind. His love is not satisfied with transmitting to us even the riches of the sanctifying grace with which He filled the sacred Humanity of His Incarnate Son; He is not content with endowing us with the virtue whereby we are able to exercise our faith in Him and in all that He has revealed to us of Himself and of His loving purposes. His love is not content with giving us through hope a share in the imperturbable security which He Himself enjoys in His Triune life; or with enabling us through the virtue of love to conquer all

---

[1] St. John i. 16. [2] St. Teresa, *The Interior Castle*, Man. vi, ch. ix. 21.

things that would militate against our complete oneness with Him. In addition to all these, He has prepared for us gifts which the Holy Ghost bestows upon us, first in baptism, and still more abundantly in confirmation, and which He, through the Sacraments, and through other means which the infinite ingenuity of His love is unceasingly devising, continually exercises and develops within us to the ever fuller perfecting of our souls. In the great Collect in the Office of Confirmation the Bishop prays for the candidates upon whom a few moments later he is to lay his hands. The prayer runs as follows:

> "Strengthen them, we beseech Thee, O Lord, with the Holy Ghost, the Comforter, and daily increase in them Thy manifold gifts of grace: the spirit of wisdom and understanding, the spirit of counsel and ghostly strength, the spirit of knowledge and true godliness; and fill them, O Lord, with the spirit of Thy holy fear, now and forever."

These are the seven gifts of the Holy Spirit by which He is able to work in us His loving will, meeting through these gifts every exigency of life. It is thus made possible for us to yield ourselves to the urge of the Spirit in our every faculty and impulse, even as the ship responds in its every part and movement, from keel to masthead, when the sails are thrown to a favouring gale.

Let us try to secure a clear view of the significance of these operations of the Spirit and their relationship to each other. The highest of all these divine donations made to the soul by the Holy Spirit are the theological virtues. Next in importance and dignity are the gifts of the Holy Ghost which act upon the virtues, and make them to function in a more excellent way. The supernatural moral virtues stand next in rank. These are the gifts of justice, prudence, fortitude, and temperance, embraced and lifted up to the supernatural plane by the theological virtues. As a result of all this work of the Holy Ghost in the soul, we are able to bring forth the fruits of the Spirit, which are acts of virtue performed by a soul which has so yielded itself to the rule of God that it is able to produce them with ease and sweetness. Finally the soul thus living under the divine guidance enters into the joy of the beatitudes. " The operation which proceeds from the virtues and is made perfect by the gifts of the Spirit, is called a beatitude," [1] which is the state of blessedness which our Lord in the Sermon on the Mount promised to His faithful people.

[1] St. Thomas, *On Isaiah*, ch. xi.

II

No list of the gifts of the Holy Spirit, as we have seen, is to be found in the New Testament. But as these gifts belong to Christ, they belong also to us if we are in union with Him. He said, " I am the Vine, ye are the branches," [1] and the branches participate in whatever properties are possessed by the vine, to the limit of their capacity.

Of our Lord it was prophesied: " There shall come forth a rod out of the stem of Jesse, and a Branch shall grow out of his roots: and the spirit of the Lord shall rest upon him, the spirit of wisdom and understanding, the spirit of counsel and might, the spirit of knowledge and of the fear of the Lord; and shall make him of quick understanding in the fear of the Lord." [2] What was here prophesied of Him was prophesied also of those who were to be one with Him.

It will be observed that in this passage there seems to be no mention of the gift which we call piety, or sometimes true godliness, while fear is mentioned twice. The Church finds her solution of this seeming difficulty in the ancient Jewish traditional interpretation of the word *fear* in the second verse of this chapter. This interpretation is made clear by the translation given in the Septuagint Version, where this word is rendered by the Greek word εὐσέβεια, which means a loving, reverent, filial attitude towards God, which is just what the Hebrew word implies. [3] When St. Jerome made his Latin Vulgate translation in the fourth century, he used the tender word *pietas*, meaning filial love and devotion of the soul to our heavenly Father. From this version we get the word Piety, which is often used for this gift. [4]

[1] St. John xv. 5.
[2] Isa. xi. 1–3.
[3] The learned rabbis of Alexandria in the third century B.C. translated the Jewish Scriptures into Greek for popular use, and this translation became the Authorized Version for Jewish use for many centuries, including the first ages of the Church. It is still the authorized version of the Greek Church. The prophet uses the same Hebrew word twice. In verse 2 the rabbis translated it, as we have said, by εὐσέβεια, which means a loving, tender, veneration. In verse 3 they render the same Hebrew word by φόβος, which implies a reverence and due respect, akin to awe.
[4] Trench, *N.T. Synonyms*, § xlviii. One of the most unhappy instances of the degradation of a fine word is found in the popular use of the English word *piety*. It is one of the most beautiful derivatives in the language, but it has been made to connote all that is contemptible in religious cant and hypocrisy. *Pietas*, devotion to a parent, was regarded by the ancients, especially by the Latins, as one of the supremest virtues which could adorn the character of a man. Virgil's " pius Aeneas " has become a proverb in every land where Latin literature is valued.

III

What is the character of these gifts of the Holy Ghost? The teachers of the Church, by a careful comparative study of the references to them in Scripture, agree on the definition that they are certain infused, not acquired, supernatural habits, permanent qualities, which are communicated to the soul by the Holy Spirit, and which incline the soul to respond readily to the divine leading and inspiration.[1] They are not transient aids given by the Spirit from time to time as we may have need of His help, but they are permanent endowments, the power and effectiveness of which can be diminished or destroyed only by sin.

Man, being what he is in his nature, must possess habits if he is to lead an orderly life and attain to any definite objective. One who has no habits at all lives without plan, or unity, or objective, and achieves nothing. Men naturally acquire habits by the constant repetition of certain acts, and the habit, being thus formed, reproduces these acts as the occasion requires. But since the gifts of the Holy Ghost are necessary to our salvation, this divine issue is far too important to be allowed to depend on our action for the doing of the work which will produce the formation of those habits that make for the glory of God, and for the final sanctification of our souls. Therefore, God, in His love and goodness, does not wait for us to form these habits by the laborious repetition of the necessary acts, which are difficult for us, and therefore likely to be neglected. He comes to the rescue of our weakness, and infuses into us, ready to hand, the habits which are imperatively required if we are to attain to the glorious destiny which His love has prepared for us from the foundation of the world.

These gifts endure not only in time, but for eternity. They have their place in the souls of the redeemed in heaven. In that beatific life they will work in a wholly positive manner, for the negative activities of the gifts belong to this world only. No longer, then, will there be fear or anxious apprehension lest our weakness lead to a wounding of the Father whom we love, but none the less is holy fear the mainspring of the devotion and worship of the heavenly host. It is the overwhelming sense of the reverence and honour and love due to the Triune God that impels the great multitude of all nations, and kindreds, and peoples, and tongues to fall before the throne, crying with angels and archangels, " Blessing and glory and wisdom, and thanksgiving and honour, and power

---

[1] St. Thomas, *Summa*, 1.2, Q. 68, Art. 2.

and might, be unto our God forever and ever." [1]   All that God asks of us in this great eternal enterprise is that we yield ourselves to the leading of the Spirit, that we interpose no obstacle of self-will.   This done, the eternal purpose of His love can never fail. We give ourselves in utter abandonment to the omnipotently loving action of the Holy Spirit within us.   Then shall we be caught up into the current of the life of God Himself, then shall we find our appointed place in the secret deeps of the divine nature, where all the gracious springs of life and love have their never-failing source.   The gifts are the sources of our power to respond to the demands of the Spirit.   At the same time they render us docile and passive under the hand of God, and we are enabled through the operation of these same gifts to give ourselves more earnestly to the active service to which we are called.

These gifts are conferred upon every soul in baptism, and they continue to exist in the soul as long as it is in a state of grace.   Their possession can be forfeited only by the commission of mortal sin, and even then an act of true repentance will restore their force and activity.   Like the virtues of faith, hope and love, these gifts lie dormant in the soul until the Holy Spirit calls them into action. Our spiritual teachers speak of all these endowments as residing in the soul at first in germ.   They are like the seed sowed in the ground.   We have already thought that the seed contains within it the germ of all the gracious harvests which in the future years are to develop from it.   But as the seed requires good ground in which to grow, and air, and rain, and sunshine, and cultivation, in order to be brought to the fullest fruition, so do all the gifts of God require analogous conditions in order to develop as God has ordained.

Certain of the soul's endowments we can cultivate by acts of the will.   By deliberate courses of action I can develop the powers of faith, hope and love.   There are other gifts, in the operation of which God Himself must take the initiative.   Amongst these are the gifts of the Spirit.   Here He asks us only that we give Him all our faculties that He may work through them His own divine and sanctifying purposes.   But in every case we have the sinister power of baulking the will of God.   He forces nothing upon us.   His constant call to us is, " My son, give me thine heart," [2] and upon our response depends all that we can do, or all that God can do within us.

Four of the gifts of the Spirit, wisdom, understanding, knowledge

<hr>

[1] Rev. vii. 9–15.   [2] Prov. xxiii. 26.

and counsel, operate to enlighten the mind, to make perfect the work of the intellect in matters pertaining to our spiritual progress, and to our final union with God in the bosom of the Blessed Trinity, where our ultimate destiny awaits us. These four gifts develop faith, and operate to perfect all our power of knowing and of judging the things of God. The gifts of holy fear and piety act upon the affections, as does also fortitude, strengthening and directing the will. All these operations have in view our supernatural end.[1]

IV

It will contribute to our understanding of the life of the Spirit within us if we consider the relation of His gifts to the other spiritual endowments which the divine love confers upon us.

First, we might profitably consider their relation to the sanctifying grace which dwells in Christ, and which, being received from Him, becomes the basic factor in our spiritual life. Grace is related to the gifts of the Spirit as the possession of sight and hearing is related to the disciplined development of these faculties. Whatever grace we have within us, the gifts strengthen and perfect it, and bring it to maturity. It is as though a man with weak eyesight had his vision strengthened by certain exercises recommended by the oculist; or as one might cultivate a keen and discriminating ear for music. The gifts are seven powers, or springs of action, whereby indwelling grace is excited to activity, and is thereby increased. As the eye can be trained to a precision and delicacy of perception that seem almost like another sense, so, under the working of the gifts of the Spirit, the graces in the soul are stimulated, expanded, and directed on their appointed course. Through the action of the gifts one gains a clearer knowledge of truth, a keener intuition for penetrating the secrets of divine revelation, and a realization through supernatural discernment of the true values of our relationships, both to God and to man.

We have seen how love dominates everything in the spiritual life. No exception can be made to this rule in respect to the gifts of the Spirit. St. Francis de Sales gives us an illuminating analysis of the gifts in relation to love. " These gifts are not only inseparable from charity," he says, " but they may be called its peculiar properties. The gift of wisdom is nothing more than love which has discovered by experience how sweet the Lord is. Understanding is a love which attentively considers the truths of faith, to penetrate

[1] F. J. Hall, *Dogmatic Theology*, ix (" The Sacraments "), p. 54.

he depths of their sweetness, and to fathom the abyss of the divinity,
lescending afterwards from the knowledge of the Creator to that
of His creatures.   The gift of knowledge is a love which we apply
o the knowledge of ourselves and creatures, as conducive to the
:nowledge of the Almighty, and tending to impart a correct idea
of the homage due to Him, by the consideration of His perfection
:nd our extreme misery.   The gift of counsel is a species of love
oy which we vigilantly seek the best means of serving God perfectly.
"he gift of fortitude is also the strength which love communicates
or the execution of whatever has been suggested by the gift of
ounsel.   Piety is likewise love which alleviates suffering and
abour by inspiring a filial affection, and a joy in performing such
.ctions as are pleasing to our heavenly Father.   Finally, the gift
of fear is evidently love, since it urges us to avoid all that is dis-
oleasing to God." [1]

In relation to the virtues of faith, hope and charity, the gifts of
he Holy Spirit are the forces which call the virtues into action.
"hey do not produce results in the soul peculiar to themselves, or
ndependent of the effects secured by the virtues.   The gifts are
1ot superior to the virtues, but are ancillary to them, facilitating
oowerfully the practice of faith, hope and love.

The operation of the gifts is a part of the hidden interior activity
of the Holy Spirit, who is compared by our Lord to the wind, which
' bloweth where it listeth, and thou hearest the sound thereof,
out canst not tell whence it cometh or whither it goeth." [2]   For
his reason it is not infrequently difficult to distinguish the action of
he gifts of the Spirit from that of the virtues of faith, hope and love.
3ut we do not have to make such distinction.   Let us rather with
1umble and thankful hearts rejoice in the simple truths that God
1as, in His love, made known to us.   We may not understand the
vorking of the Spirit within us, nor is it required that we under-
tand it.   We can experience it, we can rejoice in it, with an ever-
:rowing faith and love which will open to the eyes of the soul ever
vider vistas, and more profound depths, of the divine love and
:oodness.

The chief difference between the virtues and the gifts lies in the
1anner in which they are used by the Spirit to carry out the work
f God.   While always supernatural in their activities, because
1ey can be exercised only in those who are in the Body of Christ,
1e virtues operate according to human methods.   That is to say,

[1] St. Francis de Sales, *The Love of God*, Bk. xi, ch. xv.
[2] St. John iii. 8.

I can by an act of my will, after giving consideration to the matter through my natural reason, determine, and carry out my determination, to perform some definite act that is loving. I can likewise, deliberately and consciously, do some definite act which is the expression and exercise of hope or of faith. Not so with the gifts of the Spirit, for here the illumination of the Holy Ghost takes the place of the light of reason. The gifts are divine intuitions, lights and inspirations. They have been well described as " seven divine qualities inbreathed," " seven radiations of divine light, flowings of spiritual unction, breathings of power, that attract and draw the will to comply with the inspirations of the Holy Ghost," and they " give a higher perfection to the faculties than the grace of the virtues is able to give, raising our spirit to higher things, and rendering it prompt, vigorous and readily responsive to the divine influences." [1]

Amongst the spiritual masters the exercise of the theological virtues, taken by themselves, has been commonly compared to the progress which can be made by labouring heavily at the oars. By their persistent use we can arrive at the haven where we would be; but with how much less of toil, with how much greater freedom and swiftness, can one voyage who spreads also his canvas to the winds, by the use of the will, keeping a careful eye to the trimming of the sails, and a steady hand on the helm. Such is the effect of the working of these gifts of the Holy Ghost.

V

In thinking of both the theological virtues and the gifts of the Spirit, we would fall into fatal confusion if we thought that any one of these could be possessed and exercised by itself. They constitute an organic unity. They operate as an organism, and as an integral part of the greater organism which is made up of sanctifying grace, along with the virtues and the gifts. For the convenience and necessity of our human understanding, we treat these things as though they were separate entities; we talk of their effects and fruits as though each gift and virtue produced an independent and separate result. But no organism functions in such a way as this. An organism is made up of interdependent members and we are not to think of such members as separate from each other, even though they be co-ordinated. It is not a matter of mere co-ordination. They work together, and if one member fails

[1] Ullathorne, *Christian Patience*, pp. 164–165.

all fail; the organism then ceases to function. Let one vital organ of the body cease to function, and soon the body perishes. As this is true of the equipment of the bodily organism, it is equally true of the complex endowments of the soul.

If these gifts exist in a unity, then we are to think of them as acting together, simultaneously. One does not perform its functions and then make way for another. There is no chronological order about them. Some may be developed more fully than others, but in order to exemplify the law of the organism, they must act together. If one of these gifts should be lacking, this lack would mar the perfection of all the others. In like manner the lack of the development of one mars the fulness of the others. So, in order to protect these gifts, and to insure their right functioning in our souls, there must be no slackening of our purpose to give our hearts to the Holy Spirit in such a manner that He may do His fullest work within us.

By means of the virtues of faith, hope and charity, assisted always, of course, by divine grace (for of ourselves we can do nothing), we guide, as it were, ourselves. As we have just said, the human reason and will are operative in these acts of the virtues, but by the gifts of the Spirit we are led and guided. " The soul is not the mover, but it is that which is moved." [1] Reasoning and consideration do not play a part here. Committing ourselves to Him, we are led by the Spirit, as befits the sons of God, and we do not stop to examine the grounds, or to weigh the reasons why He guides us as He does. We are acted upon rather than acting. " For the movement of reason, man is prepared by the virtues; for the movement of God, by the gifts of the Holy Ghost." [2] When we have once cast ourselves upon the Lord, He " lovingly caresses the soul, stirring with such heavenly sweetness its knowledge and love, that it seems rather led and sweetly urged by Him than moving of itself; rather breaking forth into acts passively under Him, than producing them of its own accord." [3] Indeed, faithful souls who have yielded themselves to the leading of the Spirit are often quite unconsciously directed in their course through the work of these " divine qualities inbreathed," these divine habits which have been infused into them.

The passage above quoted may seem merely rhetorical unless we look with care to its meaning. The action of the Holy Spirit

---

[1] St. Thomas, *Summa*, 2.2, Q. 52, Art. 2.
[2] Farrell, *A Companion to the Summa*, Vol. II, p. 140.
[3] Joan a Jesu, *Theolog. Myst.*, Ch. 6. Quoted by Buckler, *The Perfection of Man by Charity*, p. 195 (2nd ed.).

in stirring our knowledge and love is a very practical proceeding. How often in ordinary earthly concerns do we need to recall our knowledge of a subject, to renew it. We say we have grown " rusty " on a certain branch of learning which we are called upon to employ, and we brush up our knowledge of it. This is what the Spirit does for us in respect to the heavenly knowledge. Likewise is it with love. A friend comes to me in trouble. He places before me vividly the difficulty he is in, and pleads with me to help him. My love is deeply stirred, and I rise up resolutely to throw myself into his cause, without regard to my own convenience, ready in my awakened love to make much sacrifice on his behalf. Thus does the Spirit stir us up in our knowledge and in our love in the service of God.

There is another expression in this passage from Joan a Jesu which needs our attention for a moment, lest it seem to involve a contradiction. He speaks of " acting passively." Action and passivity are generally contrary to each other. By passivity in this context, however, we mean the state in which by strong, persistent force of the will we maintain ourselves in a receptive attitude in order that God the Holy Ghost may work in us His holy will without hindrance from us. As St. Thomas says, " Man submits to the action of the Holy Spirit, but in such a manner that the man himself acts because he is free." [1] The soul in this life never comes to the place where its liberty of will is interfered with. Without this liberty nothing the soul could do would be meritorious. It is our freedom to reject God that gives merit and spiritual validity to our act when we choose to serve and follow Him.

VI

Like all gifts, those of the Spirit must be cultivated. But the method of cultivation is different from that used in developing the virtues. We have already seen that we can, by an act of the will, practise love. We cannot practise wisdom. One can say, " I will now perform this act of love," and can carry out this resolution effectively to the strengthening of the force of love within him. One cannot say, " I will now perform an act of wisdom." This is something which the Holy Ghost does within us. The only part we have in it is to keep the way open for the Spirit, to avoid such sins as would retard, or make His work in us difficult or impossible; and, on the other hand, to do resolutely and persistently, those

[1] St. Thomas, *Summa*, 1.2, Q. 68, Art. 3.

good and holy things which conform us more and more to the likeness and nature of God.

While in the exercise of the gifts we are acted upon rather than ourselves acting, nevertheless we must prepare our souls in order that this work may be done within us by the Spirit. The soul who yields habitually to sin, even though it be only venial sin which does not destroy the power of the divine grace within us, cannot expect this delicate work of the Holy Spirit to be carried on within it with facility, or to any great advantage. The soul that desires to be wrought upon by the gifts of the Spirit must be on constant guard against temptation, swift to give a strong negative to every solicitation of the tempter, letting our unfailing prayer to God be, " Deliver us from evil."

But the resistance of temptation is not enough. One must also discipline and tame the passions, and suppress all evil impulses, by the help of God. This is to be done by cultivating with diligence and perseverance the virtues which are contrary to the evil which tempts us, not only the theological virtues, but the cardinal virtues of prudence, justice, fortitude, and temperance. There must also be a steady development of the virtues which normally should grow out of the cardinal virtues—that is to say, the virtue of religion, which leads to the due reverence and worship of God; obedience, which means the mortification of self-will, which is the root of every sin that was ever committed; chastity, which means not only purity of body and mind, but spiritual orderliness, the whole man being so disciplined that everything will function as it should, without clash or interference, remembering St. Augustine's defini-tion of peace—" the tranquillity of order." [1] Humility and meek-ness must follow. By the cultivation of these last two we shall more and more have a true estimate of ourselves, seeing and knowing ourselves as we really are, and somewhat as God sees us and knows us.

He who seeks to practise these virtues consistently will prepare the way for the ever fuller indwelling of the Holy Spirit, and the Spirit, once having taken possession of our hearts, will, through the operation of His gifts, fulfil His great and gracious work within us.

O Holy Spirit, The Light of every soul, the Strength of every heart, the Source of every virtue, the Life of every virtue : Thou very God of very God, the Eternal Love of the Father, the Eternal Love of the Son, binding the Godhead into One : I long for Thee alone, I desire Thee alone.

---

[1] " Pax tranquillitas ordinis." St. Augustine, *De Civ. Dei*, xix. 13; Migne P. L., Tom. 41, Col. 640.

Our Lord having been conceived by the Holy Ghost in the womb of the Blessed Virgin, willed to be guided in all His actions not only by the Person of the Word, but also by that of the Holy Spirit in order to teach us that, as this Divine Spirit is the principle of our spiritual regeneration in baptism, He must also be the principle of our conduct; that He must govern us in all things, and that we must depend absolutely on His direction, since the members must be animated with the same Spirit as the Head.

LOUIS LALLEMANT.

CHAPTER XXII

THE GIFTS OF THE SPIRIT (II)

FOLLOWING the method of St. Augustine, we shall consider the gifts of the Spirit in an ascending scale,[1] beginning with fear, which is the lowest of the gifts, as wisdom is the highest. In Holy Fear is set the mainspring of all the other gifts, as it is also the guardian of them all. St. Augustine and St. Thomas Aquinas agree in this teaching. We begin with the gift of fear, says St. Augustine, and passing step by step through the intermediate gifts, we reach their consummation at last in the gift of wisdom.[2] As we have already noted, this is not to say that these gifts operate separately or in any sort of chronological sequence. We commonly speak of them as gifts, but rather is the expression which is employed in the ancient hymn, *Veni Creator*, the more accurate—" Thy sevenfold gift." There is no moment when the soul does not need the full benefits of the operation of all the gifts, nor is there a moment when the love of the Spirit is not working in the fullness of His omnipotence to supply every such need.

I

The word fear is used in the New Testament in various senses, but more often its meaning is good.[3] Fear, as a gift of the Holy Ghost, has always a good significance. When St. John speaks of perfect love casting out fear [4] he is, of course, not referring to the gift of the Spirit. This gift has nothing to do with being afraid of God, for it has its full operation only in the souls of God's faithful children who love Him and trust Him. Those who are not in union with God cannot have the gifts of the Spirit.

Holy Fear would seem to have, in certain measure, a negative office, and to be an exercise of the purgative way. Through its action we are warned against the things which are contrary to the divine Spirit, and which, if consented to, would stain the soul with sin, and do dishonour to God. The Greek word used in the

---

[1] St. Augustine, *Sermon on the Mount*, Lib. I, Cap. 4; Migne, P. L., Tom. 34, Col. 1234.

[2] St. Augustine, *De Doctrina Christiana*, Lib. II, ch. vii; Migne, P. L., Tom. 34, Col. 39–40. See St. Thomas, *Summa*, 1.2, Q. 68, Art. 2.

[3] Trench, *N.T. Synonyms*, § x.   [4] 1 St. John iv. 18.

New Testament (φόβος) has *flight* for its first meaning, the fleeing from the object which we fear. We are never in this life able to leave the way of purgation wholly, for we must ever be cleansing ourselves more and more from sin, and from the consequences of sin. To this end, in union with whatever other gifts the Holy Spirit may bring to our aid, the operation of fear is to be a continuous help. " Happy is the man that feareth alway." [1]

Much of what we know of the gift of fear we learn from the Old Testament, particularly from the book of the Proverbs of Solomon. We learn there that " The fear of the Lord is the beginning of knowledge " [2]; " The fear of the Lord is to hate evil " [3]; " The fear of the Lord is the beginning of wisdom " [4]; " In the fear of the Lord is strong confidence " ; [5] " The fear of the Lord is a fountain of life " [6]; " The fear of the Lord tendeth to life." [7] While all the gifts of the Spirit are not referred to here, an examination will show that, directly or indirectly, they are all involved in these sayings of the Wise Man, and that none of them can be effective if separated from holy fear. Upon reverence for God they are all built up. St. Anselm sums up this gift in these words: "The fear of the Lord is the beginning of the divine gifts, and the Holy Ghost gives this fear as a foundation on which to build all the other gifts." [8] It is a filial and reverential fear. It is " the chaste and venerating reverence that flows from the touch of the Holy Spirit on the will, moving the soul to revere our heavenly Father with ease and promptitude, and to dread offending Him." [9] " Under the name of pure fear is signified that will whereby we must needs be averse from sin, and avoid sin, not through the constant anxiety of infirmity, but through the tranquillity of charity." [10]

The prophet speaks of the fear of the Lord as the endowment of the Messiah, and the question might quite legitimately be asked, how would it be possible for the gift of holy fear to be exercised in our Lord's humanity? He was God, He had no sin, and could have no sin, since God cannot sin. Knowing He could not sin, how could He entertain a fear lest He sin? This is a serious question, and to it we must find a serious answer. Of course

---

[1] Prov. xxviii. 14.   [2] Prov. i. 7.   [3] Prov. viii. 13.
[4] Prov. ix. 10.   [5] Prov. xiv. 26.   [6] Prov. xiv. 27.
[7] Prov. xix. 23. In all these passages from Proverbs the Hebrew word is the same as that in Isa. xi, and in the Septuagint they are all translated by the word φόβος.
[8] St. Anselm, *De Similitudinibus*, Cap. 130; Migne, P. L., Tom. 159, Col. 680.
[9] Ullathorne, *Christian Patience*, p. 171
[10] St. Augustine, *De Civ. Dei*, xiv, ix. 5; Migne, P. L., Tom. 41, Col. 416.

there could be in our Lord no servile fear, no vigilant anxiety regarding possible spiritual loss. The gifts and virtues operate in different souls in different ways according to the temperament, and to the nature and needs of each. While holy fear works against possible sin in the case of the ordinary man, its operation is by no means confined to this. All holy reverence has its root in holy fear, and in this respect the working of this gift of the Spirit finds its highest perfection in the human soul of our Lord. In Him, as it will be with us in the end, the gift of fear was purified of all doubt and painful anxiety. No soul ever had so profound a reverence for God as the human soul of Christ. Herein lies the difference between the work of holy fear in Christ and in us. His human course goes straight forward, steadfast and serene, while we, because of our weakness, must walk circumspectly lest sin cause us to fall, to the dishonour of God whom we revere and love. First of all, in His humanity, veneration and worship of God existed in the highest possible perfection. Nothing could show this better than His high-priestly prayer in the seventeenth chapter of St. John. Secondly, there was in Him an absolute dependence upon God. "The Son can do nothing of Himself, but what He seeth the Father do. . . . I can of myself do nothing . . . I seek not mine own will, but the will of Him that sent me." [1] Lastly, there was a perfect submission of His will to the will of the Father: "Not my will, but thine, be done." [2] These three elements, worship, deference, and submission, are the essential constituents of holy fear.

The saints in glory, being perfectly at one with our Lord, enjoy the same operation of holy fear in themselves. At the moment of death the faithful are permanently confirmed in the possession of grace, and can never forfeit it. This gift of the Spirit, therefore, ever produces in them an increasing sense of loving awe and reverence, enabling them, along with the whole company of heaven, to cry continually, "Holy, Holy, Holy."

Holy fear is the sleepless sentinel that stands at the door of the heart, and sounds the alarm to warn us of the approach of any evil thing that might wound or offend our Lord. It is the guardian and protector of all the other gifts, and, indeed, of everything that God bestows upon us which is to be used for His honour. We should pray continually for the deepening of the spirit of fear. 'The less you have of this fear, the more cause to be afraid; the more you have of this fear the less reason you have to be afraid.

[1] St. John v. 19, 30. [2] St. Luke xxii. 42.

If you fear lest you should offend God, lest you should be cast out of His sight, lest you should lose the vision of His face in eternity, such a fear is the beginning of love. No man fears to lose that which he does not care for. That which we prize we fear to lose, and we fear to lose it in the measure in which we love it. Therefore, a great fear of losing God is a sure sign of a great love to God. And that love will ripen and grow, for God will increase it, and will bestow upon you the gift of fear purified of all doubt and pain." [1] In short, the gift of holy fear, when at its best and highest, is exercised in us in some degree approaching the manner of its exercise in the Sacred Humanity of our Lord, the God-Man.

II

Holy fear is close akin to the gift of piety, which the New Testament calls True Godliness.[2] Piety might be said, in a sense, to be the reverse side of fear, the latter having reference, as we have suggested, more to the purgative aspect of the soul's life, while piety is positive rather than negative. While fear, as it works in the souls of sinners, puts us on guard against evil that should be avoided lest we wound a loving Father, piety is the gift which fills us with a loving, child-like devotion to God, stimulating us to love, honour, and worship Him, and to find our joy in Him and in all that honours Him. It is this gift which enables us to say, " I have loved the habitation of thy house, and the place where thine honour dwelleth." [3] Hugh of St. Victor gives us an account of the work which this gift does in our souls, an account so full of sweetness and unction, and at the same time so practical in its assurance of the Spirit's blessed work through piety for our sanctification, that we might do well to commit it to memory, recalling it from time to time, and using it as a test of our faithfulness to God. He says: " This piety urges us to leave off despondency; the love that is included in it draws us away from self-will; the mercy in it calms our irritability; the cheerfulness in it gives us a sense of security; its affability leads us to an intimacy with God, and this intimacy reveals to us the divine secrets. When these divine secrets are opened to us, our friendship with God is cemented, and we are joined to the Lord in one spirit." [4]

[1] H. E. Manning, *The Internal Mission of the Holy Ghost* (London, 1875), pp. 225–226.
[2] See 1 St. Tim. iv. 7–8; vi. 3–6; 2 St. Peter i. 3, 6; iii. 11.
[3] Ps. xxvi. 8.
[4] Hugh of St. Victor, *De Claustro Animæ*, Bk. iii. 5; Migne, P. L., Tom. 176, Col. 1092.

Piety fills the heart with a sweet refreshment from God, with a warm and comforting consciousness of His tender love to us, with a realization of His presence, of His friendship, of what we owe to Him in return, and it fills us with joy and gladness as we go forward to pay the debt. It makes us see the truth of the saying of Dame Gertrude More, " To give all for love is a most sweet bargain." [1] It enables us to make Mother Julian's gracious colloquy our own: " Wouldst thou learn thy Lord's meaning in all His sweet approach to thee? Learn it well: Love was His meaning. Who showed it unto thee? Love. Wherefore did He show it? For love's sake only." [2]

III

Fortitude, or as it is sometimes called, Might, or Ghostly Strength, is the gift of the Spirit which perfects the natural virtue of so-called fortitude by infusing into the will an energy and a courage which will enable it to meet and conquer the difficulties and obstacles of the Christian life. These difficulties may be interior, as temptation to sin, or meeting the demands which God may make upon us for our own perfecting, such as continuance in prayer and good works when it is pain and grief to us. They may include the endurance of the mortification of our desires, or the contending against the spirit of the world which ever presses so hard upon us all, recalling the words of the apostle, " We have received, not the spirit of the world, but the spirit which is of God , that we might know the things that are freely given us of God." [3]

While the greater part of the Christian warfare has the interior of our souls as its arena, there are also many external difficulties and obstacles against which we are to contend with the gift of fortitude. It may be physical suffering which we are called upon to endure patiently, or persecution, calumny, hate, or any of the innumerable afflictions which were visited upon our Lord, who endured them all for us, setting His face like a flint, and never once flinching from the agony of it, and calling us to share it with Him. It was the power of fortitude which enabled Him to suffer what no man had ever before been called upon to bear. " For the joy that was set before him, he endured the cross, despising the shame." [4]

We shall be able to endure to the end if we keep in mind St. Paul's repeated boast—his holy boast—that while of himself he

---

[1] Dame Gertrude More, *Confessions*, 28.
[2] Julian of Norwich, *Revelations of Divine Love*, Chap. lxxxvi.
[3] 1 Cor. ii. 12.   [4] Heb. xii. 2.

Y

could do nothing, yet, " I can do all things through Christ which strengtheneth me." [1]

The strength bestowed upon us in this gift of fortitude constitutes a sharing in the strength of God, and His strength is nothing less than the omnipotence of the Triune Godhead Itself. It is not any gift outside of Him that I am called upon to use. " The Lord is my light and my salvation: whom then shall I fear? The Lord is the strength of my life: of whom then shall I be afraid? " [2] This is the great psalm of fortitude, the lesson of which we must make our own. Not only the gifts of God, but God Himself dwells within us, and His gifts are ours only because He is ours. All the occupations of His omnipotence take place within us, for where God dwells there His omnipotence works continually. Unless the devil be stronger than God, it is impossible for us to fail if God be on our side.

" What is man? Who is he that he should undertake to scale heaven, and to do this mighty feat in the face of all these enemies? His nature, his name is weakness. Measure the grandeur of his undertaking by the weakness of his nature, and the difference between them represents the divine force of which he stands in constant need." [3] This force is supplied by the gift of divine fortitude which the Holy Spirit bestows upon us.

IV

We have thought of holy fear, piety, and fortitude, which are the three gifts of the Spirit which act upon the will, stimulating it to greater service and love. We must now go forward to examine what is involved in the gifts of knowledge, of counsel, of understanding, and of wisdom, which operate to enlighten the mind and judgment of God's people.

We shall think, first, of the gift of knowledge, and it is necessary at the beginning of our consideration that we understand what we mean by this word. Like many words in our language, it has several meanings, and we have to explain what we have in mind whenever we use it. When we are speaking of the gift of knowledge, we are not speaking of the intellectual knowledge which we acquire by processes of study, observation, or experimentation. Nor do we mean the knowledge which is gained by applying the reason to the facts of the Faith which God has revealed to us. We

[1] Phil. iv. 13.   [2] Ps. xxvii. 1, 2.
[3] Ullathorne, *Christian Patience*, p. 177.

mean the knowledge which we derive from a life of association with God. It will be interesting to note here how through the Christian ages the words *theology* and *theologian* have changed their meaning. In the early days of the Church the words had no reference to scholarly erudition in the science of religion. Theology, according to the Fathers, indicated a knowledge acquired not by study, but by prayer; and a theologian was one who had acquired an intimacy with God through contemplation, rather than through the investigations of reason.[1] St. Gregory's fine characterization of St. Benedict illustrates well what is meant. Of the great patriarch of Western monasticism, who had no scholarship in our modern sense of the word, he says he was " Learnedly ignorant, and wisely unlearned." [2]

Let us make clear our definition of knowledge. This gift is such a participation in God's own knowledge of created things as enables us to see them somewhat as He sees them, and to be able to adjudge them, and, on the basis of a right judgment, to use them accordingly. It gives us the power to know the true values of created objects and relationships, and to employ them in such a way that they will prove to be guides which will lead us to God. Knowledge shows us God in His creation. St. Paul says, " The invisible things of him from the creation of the world are clearly seen, being understood by the things that are made, even his eternal power and Godhead." [3]

Knowledge produces spiritual detachment from created things, enabling us to look at them objectively, to see their true place and value, especially in their uses for the salvation and sanctification of men. By this same gift we learn the true nature and significance of human relationships, how to employ them that they may lead us, and those with whom we are associated, nearer to God. It gives us the right view of the work of the Church on earth, it makes men wise in the administration of the Church's spiritual affairs. It enables us to evaluate society, and to judge concerning the

---

[1] Two quotations will suffice to show the older use of the words. St. Ephrem the Syrian (A.D. 373) writes, " Let us apply ourselves to the spiritual life in order that we may become perfect. Only thus can we become learned in theology." (*De Virtute*, ch. x.) St. John Climacus (A.D. 606) says, " Those may rightly be called theologians, who in prayer are penetrated and inflamed with a fire which is sacred and all divine." (*The Ladder*, 28th Degree.) See Lamballe, *Mystical Contemplation*, p. 15. A like meaning persisted for a thousand years or more in the use of the expression *mystical theology*, which implied not a course of intellectual study but a curriculum of prayer. John Gerson, in the fifteenth century, said, " The object of mystical theology is experimental knowledge of God acquired in the unifying embrace of love." (*Considerationes*, xxviii.)

[2] " Scienter nescius et sapienter indoctus." St. Gregory Magnus, *Dialogue*, Bk. ii. 1; Migne, P. L., Tom. 66, Col. 126.

[3] Rom. i. 20.

validity of its demands upon us, and to seize hold upon it, and use it for God's glory, and for the building of His kingdom. Amid the chaos of affairs which besets us, knowledge shows us how to arrive at prompt and wise judgements as to the courses to be followed. " The natural man receiveth not the things of the Spirit of God, for they are foolishness unto him : neither can he know them, because they are spiritually discerned ; but he that is spiritual judgeth "—perhaps the better translation would be, discerneth— " all things, yet he himself is judged of no man. For who hath known the mind of the Lord that he may instruct him? But we have the mind of Christ." [1] The gift of knowledge imparts to us the mind of Christ, that we may know and judge all things as Christ knows and judges them. This gift enables us to participate, in our measure, in the right and infallible thinking of Christ, and therefore gives us a right judgment in all things, enabling us to plan our lives according to His will.

V

Counsel, in general, is defined as an exercise of prudence by which we learn what is the means to be chosen for attaining an end. Thus the gift of counsel has to do with the direction of particular actions. It is a light by which the Holy Spirit shows what we ought to do in the time, place, and circumstances in which we find ourselves. What faith, wisdom, and knowledge teach in general, the gift of counsel applies to particular cases. It is easy to perceive the wisdom and the necessity of a certain course, but it is not enough to know that a thing is good in itself; we are also to judge whether it is good under the existing circumstances, whether it is better than some alternative that is suggested, and more likely to attain the object at which we are aiming. This kind of knowledge we acquire through the operation of the gift of counsel.[2]

Counsel, as we have said, is closely allied to the moral virtue of prudence. Indeed, counsel is nothing less than prudence raised to the supernatural plane. St. Thomas tells us that counsel guards and perfects the virtue of prudence,[3] or rather one might say, it embraces it, and makes it its own, spiritualizing the natural virtue, and placing it in the realm of the supernatural.

Counsel is akin to the virtue of discretion which St. Anthony the Hermit declared to be the guide of all the virtues, without which

---

[1] 1 Cor. ii. 14–16.
[2] See Lallemant, *Spiritual Doctrine*, Princip. IV, Ch. iv, Art. iv.
[3] St. Thomas, *Summa*, 2.2, Q. 52, Art. 1.

none of them, not even love, would be able to operate effectively.[1] Even our love needs to be enlightened, directed, and rightly applied. One may easily, with the most loving intention and purpose, act unwisely and hurtfully, if discretion be wanting. In all our actions we need light as well as love. While love is the form, the animating spirit, and the motive of all the virtues and of their operation, yet it needs regulation and direction, and this it receives through the gift of counsel, under the guidance of that discretion which St. Anthony pronounced to be " the mother, the guardian, and the mistress of all the virtues." [2] Counsel, like discretion, may be said to be " the light of the Spirit of God in the mind resulting from the love of God in the heart. . . . When discretion has brought the soul under the habitual influence of the Spirit of God, governing through charity, it belongs to her further, amidst the great variety of charity's operations, to show the precise thing that has to be done in the particular circumstances in which we find ourselves, being aided therein supernaturally by the gift of counsel; and not only is it her work to show the right thing, but to lead us actually to do it. For to fail in the *doing*, says the Angelic Doctor, is, above all, contrary to discretion, because ' as the end is the main point, so a failure in the end is the worst defect of all '." [3]

We have seen that the gifts of the Spirit are not to be exercised actively by our wills in the manner in which we exercise the virtues of faith, hope and love, but rather are we passive, while their exercise within us is carried on through the directive work of the Holy Ghost. In a degree perhaps greater than with any other of the gifts, our yielding ourselves to the leading of the Spirit increases the power of the gift of counsel within us. We can develop more and more a right judgment, and by the work of the Spirit, He using the gift of counsel as an instrument, attain to a better judgment in carrying out our moral and spiritual duties and exercising our spiritual privileges. The more faithful we are in making our response to the Spirit, the greater our facility in serving Him rightly and wisely.

When the Spirit of God suggests to the conscience a certain course of action, it should be followed swiftly, and resolutely to the end. The generous spirit does not wait for the spur of obligation. Indeed, out of sheer love, it will rise up quickly, and do what the interior moving of the Holy Spirit indicates to be right. It is a joy to a teacher to instruct the pupil who is willing and eager to

---

[1] Cassian, *Conferences*, ii, Ch. 2; Migne, P. L., Tom. 49, Cols. 526–27.
[2] Cassian, *Conferences*, ii, Ch. iv; Migne, P. L., Tom. 49, Col. 528.
[3] Buckler, *The Perfection of Man by Charity*, pp. 243–247 (2nd ed.).

learn. Thus does the Holy Ghost find His joy in leading the soul who is glad to follow.

We do not gain perfection of judgment all at once. It is a development, and it may transpire that in some matter in which we acted conscientiously, we nevertheless made a mistake of judgment, we read the Spirit amiss. God will not hold this against us, but vacillation and hesitation, when action is due, are a sin against the gift of counsel. There are weak, untrusting souls who are unwilling to take any step lest they should make a mistake. This attitude has its root in pride. We can have no mathematical, or even logical, certainty that we are always on the right course, but we are to trust the Holy Spirit to overrule our blunders, and supply our inadequacies, which He will surely do if we have sought His guidance, and have sincerely done the best that in us lay. The Spirit will teach us through our mistakes often more effectively than through our successes.

Though we must serve God with a generous spirit, care must be taken lest we mar our service by over-eagerness and impetuosity. There is always time enough and strength enough to accomplish the divine will, and many a soul has been led into sin by an over-eagerness to do something for God. The prudent soul does nothing with precipitancy. The working of the gift of counsel fills us with a spirit of patience, of calm, which indicates that we know that the strength of God is our own. We are willing to tarry the Lord's leisure.[1] Our faith in Him will permit of no apprehension of failure. " Thus saith the Lord God, Behold, I lay in Zion for a foundation stone, a tried stone, a precious corner stone, a sure foundation: he that believeth shall not make haste." [2]

This gift belongs to every Christian, but more especially to pastors and teachers, and to those who are called of God in any field of work to direct others. These require this gift not only for their own sanctification, but in order to guide souls wisely in the way of salvation. Everyone should pray earnestly and continually for the increase of this gift, but this should weigh especially upon the consciences of spiritual directors and pastors and teachers, because any failure they may make is likely to work spiritual hurt to the souls committed to their charge. Perhaps the most terrible saying of our Lord's in the very rare condemnations that He pronounced, was His words to the pharisaical lawyers: " Them that were entering in, ye hindered." [3] Souls can be as really hindered by an ignorant direction as by one which leads to the wrong road.

---

[1] Ps. xxvii. 16.   [2] Isa. xxviii. 16.   [3] St. Luke xi. 52.

VI

When we speak of the gift of understanding, we must distinguish it from the intellectual faculty which bears the same name. This gift is the one which enables the soul—not necessarily the intellect—to gain a continually deepening insight into the divine truths which have been revealed to us. As the gift of knowledge has to do with the true evaluation of created things, the gift of understanding opens our minds to the right appreciation of the uncreated things of God. This does not mean, of course, that we are given a natural comprehension of the mysteries involved in the revealed truths. This would be impossible, for the finite cannot compass that which belongs to the infinite sphere of God.

The Holy Spirit is able to act through the operation of this gift for the enlightenment of the soul in proportion to the love which it possesses. This divine charity is not only the bond between the soul and the Holy Spirit, but it is the means whereby the Spirit communicates His light. The apostle says, " that, being rooted and grounded in love, ye may be able to comprehend." [1] " If, therefore, we wish for much light, let us have much love. Then by means of divine love we shall understand divine things. ' His unction teacheth you all things.' " [2]

St. Thomas Aquinas, eminently practical as he always is, out-lines certain definite ways in which the Holy Ghost, through the gift of understanding, enables us to penetrate the truth of God.

First, the work of the Spirit discloses to the soul the realities which lie beneath outward appearances. To use philosophical terms, this gift shows us how to recognize the substance which lies hidden beneath the accidents. Perhaps the most practical and constant operation of this gift is seen in the realization possessed by even the simplest and most ignorant minds of the presence of our Lord Jesus Christ under the species of bread and wine in the Eucharist. A vivid instance of this is found in the 'oft-repeated story told in the biography of the Curé d'Ars. The saint observed an ignorant peasant who used to kneel long before the altar, absorbed in devotion. He asked him, " What do you say to our Lord as you kneel so long before Him? " " I don't say anything at all," was the reply; " I just look up there at Him, and He looks down here at me." The peasant would have been bewildered at a theological definition of the Real Presence, but the gift of under-

[1] Eph. iii. 17.
[2] Buckler, *The Perfection of Man by Charity*, p. 341 (2nd ed.).

standing made the reality of Presence of his loving Saviour vivid beyond all question.

Second, the gift reveals to us the meaning of the Scriptures, as well as that of other forms of revelation which had been hidden from us. Marked instances of this are found in St. Luke's account of our risen Lord's walk to Emmaus after the Resurrection with the two disciples whose " eyes were holden that they should not know him "; and in His instructions to the Ten and those who were with them on Easter night. The evangelist says, " He opened their understanding that they might understand the Scriptures," as He taught them the things " concerning himself which were written in the law of Moses, and in the prophets, and in the psalms." Though the Holy Spirit had not yet been given, our Lord enabled them to see the true meaning of the ancient Scriptures, by means of what seemed to have been, by anticipation, a direct operation of the Spirit, as they had never before been seen even by the greatest of the prophets. No wonder they said one to another, " Did not our heart burn within us while he talked with us by the way, and while he opened to us the Scriptures? " [1]

A devout commentator has said of this event:

> " This is in all probability as stupendous a miracle as any in our Lord's history. That men should in a moment receive a power of mental comprehension which they had not before, and that this power should enable them to see the true import and meaning of a book which had hitherto been closed to them, seems greater than any acts of healing, or feeding of multitudes, or stilling of tempests. It implies divine power over our spiritual and intellectual nature such as God only can exercise. And yet it is the commonest of all miracles, and the one which survives amongst us. The opening of the mind and heart to the things of God is now constantly going on. To many—we may say to all—who submit their wills and understandings to God, the Scriptures are unlocked, a new light is shed upon every part of them, especially upon the works and words of the Lord. This power of a risen Christ we claim every time we put up to God one of the most familiar of all our prayers, that ' by patience and comfort of thy Holy Word we may embrace and ever hold fast the blessed hope of everlasting life ' in Jesus Christ." [2]

Third, through the gift of understanding we grasp the significance of outward signs and actions. We are able, for example, to realize the meaning of the outward and visible signs of the inward and

---

[1] St. Luke xxiv.   [2] Sadler, *Comment. in loc.*

spiritual grace in the Sacraments.   When our Lord gave the great
Eucharistic discourse in the synagogue at Capernaum,[1] His disciples knew not what it meant.   When the Holy Ghost, with His
enlightening gifts, came upon them, they then realized well its
significance, and they proceeded to celebrate the Eucharist daily,[2]
and to teach its meaning, as St. Paul did so cogently to the Corinthian
Christians.[3]

Fourth, St. Thomas teaches that the gift of understanding
enlightens us to see the hand of Providence in the events of history,
and in the ordinary external happenings of every-day life.   It
shows us how to interpret these events, and to see how God uses
men and nations for the fulfilment of the purposes of His kingdom.

Again, it is the gift of understanding which imparts the power
to unfold the often-unsuspected truths which lie hidden in some
great saying of the Holy Spirit.   We are told that the whole of
the revelation of the Incarnation, with all its manifold amazing
and glorious implications, is contained in the one sentence, " And
the word was made flesh, and dwelt among us." [4]   But only as the
great saints and Fathers studied these words on their knees was
their fulness revealed.   It is not only to great saints and Fathers
that the Scriptures are thus opened by the use of this gift of understanding.   How often have we, sinners though we be, while reading
some familiar passage in God's word, been startled as there seemed
to spring out of the page a new and rich interpretation of some
phrase, of which we had never before dreamed.

By the exercise of this gift within us, the Holy Spirit shows us
how to relate one truth of revelation to another, and to realize that
the revealed faith is an organic whole, made up of mutually interdependent parts.   It makes us to see the oneness of the faith, and
to understand that there can be no such thing as a half-truth, or a
partial acceptance of the divine revelation, any more than a human
body can be divided, and retain its full life and vigour.[5]

VII

Before we pass on to the consideration of the gift of wisdom, it
will be well to note that while wisdom and understanding are

[1] St. John vi.   [2] Acts ii. 42, 46.   [3] 1 Cor. xi. 23–29.   [4] St. John i. 14.
[5] " Truly it has been said that men do amiss to speak of mysteries of revelation.
For all is *one* mystery; all is one mysterious whole, of which you cannot detach
part from part, without deforming the whole.   As well detach, if it were possible,
one of the prismatic colours, and think that the light would remain the same, as
think to sever from the rest one truth of God, the Father of lights, and think that
the other truths would remain harmonious."   E. B. Pusey, *University Sermons*,
1859–1872, p. 339.

closely allied, there are certain fundamental differences of which account must be taken. With the gift of understanding, it is the intellect which is called into action by the Spirit. In the exercise of the gift of wisdom it is the heart that undergoes a spiritual experience. So these two gifts are complementary to each other. " One is light, the other is love, and so they unite and complete each other. Wisdom, withal, remains the more perfect gift, for the heart outranges the intellect, it sounds greater depths, and grasps or divines what reason fails to reach." [1]

When we come to study the gift of wisdom, we arrive at the climax of all the Spirit's work through these mysteries and gifts. Wisdom is the subtlest and most commanding of all the gifts, the one without which no other gift can be effective. In relation to the other gifts it stands as love stands in relation to the other virtues, being the necessary accompaniment without which no other gift can be of effect. " The Holy Spirit accumulates this gift upon His other gifts," says St. Anselm, " when He infuses wisdom into the soul, enabling what is rightly known through the gift of understanding to be sweetly relished through the gift of wisdom, in virtue of which from a motive of pure love we are able to follow after that which is excellent." [2]

Wisdom is a supernatural habit infused into the soul by the Holy Spirit, by the use of which He enables us to discern, as by intuition, as by an interior and spiritual sense of taste, God and the things of God, and to delight in them accordingly. Wisdom to the soul is like the sense of taste to the body. Indeed, the Latin word *sapientia* derives from *sapere*, to taste. This gift enables us, as soon as a thing is presented to us, to judge whether or not it be of God, whether it is to be rejected or accepted. " Wisdom," says St. Francis de Sales, " is simply love which tastes and experiences the goodness and sweetness of God." [3] If wisdom, then, be so near allied to love, it follows that all love is wise, and all wisdom is loving. This is but one of the many illustrations we might find of how the universal quality of love insinuates itself into everything; and wisdom possesses much of the same universal character. Love permits nothing to escape her dominion, and wisdom floods all with her illuminating light. They take the whole of life, divine and human, for their province. The exercise of wisdom leads straight to God, who is the divine love. St. Augustine says all

---

[1] Tanquerey, *The Spiritual Life*, No. 1350.
[2] St. Anselm, *De Similitudinibus*, ch. cxxxii; Migne, P. L., Tom. 159, Col. 681.
[3] St. Francis de Sales, *The Love of God*, Bk. xi. 15.

that is necessary to say in his aphorism, " *Summa sapientia est caritas Dei*—The summit of wisdom is to be found in the love of God." [1]

St. Thomas guards the definition of wisdom by reminding us that this gift does not consist so much in the mere taste for divine things, as it does in the judgment we are able to make intuitively as the result of the tasting.[2] By the exercise of wisdom within us at the hands of the Holy Ghost we form spiritual judgments, not based upon argument or external evidence, but upon the sense of spiritual taste, somewhat as a connoisseur can in a moment distinguish a rare wine from a baser vintage. The soul is able to decide in a manner and with an accuracy which makes it possible for us to go straight forward to God. As we persevere in yielding ourselves to the moving of the Spirit, our inner taste grows more and more refined and discriminating. Again, it might be compared to the gift of right criticism in art. There is a subtle, intangible quality, for example, in a certain painting which declares it, to him who has eyes to see, to be from the brush of a particular artist. The critic perhaps cannot tell you what these signs are, but he knows with a certainty which admits of no question.

Wisdom does more than enable us to judge intuitively of the character and value of things. One might recognize a thing to be good, and acknowledge it to be such without doubt, and still find no relish or satisfaction in its use. By the gift of wisdom we not only realize the excellence of a thing, but we go on and find our delight in it. If we find no relish in prayer, no joy in the sweet and ennobling companionship of God and His saints, we need then to call on the Spirit to strengthen within us the power of the gift of wisdom. There are those who find their pleasure and satisfaction in the frivolities of life, in cheap and flippant conversation, which are the amusement of weak minds. These are they who lack wisdom, who need to " ask of God that giveth to all men liberally." [3]

Our part in this gracious and transcending work is to yield ourselves continually to the inspirations of the Holy Ghost, training ourselves to be docile to His leading in all things, " for as many as are led by the Spirit of God, they are the sons of God." [4] In order to deepen our spiritual life, a simple faith and trust in the divine guidance is required. Nothing obtains this so surely as constant prayer for faith and illumination. " Lord, increase our

---

[1] St. Augustine, *Epist.* cxl 18; Migne, P. L., Tom. 33, Col. 558.
[2] St. Thomas, *Summa*, 2.2, Q.45, Art. 2.
[3] St. James i. 5.
[4] Rom. viii. 14.

faith "; [1] " Lord, I believe, help thou mine unbelief "; [2] " Give me understanding that I may learn thy commandments." [3] These prayers and many others, like them, may be used. If they are in the very words of Holy Scripture, all the better. It is well to speak to the Holy Spirit in the exact language of the Holy Spirit. By doing this we are less liable to blunder in our prayers, less liable to pray presumptuously. If we approach every subject with a divine confidence, and an eager expectation that God will show us wonderful things in His righteousness, there will be no limit to the light that He will throw for us on the mysteries of His loving revelation.

O Spirit of the living God, loving and tender :
O Spirit of the living God, tender and of great mercy :
O Spirit of God, gracious and full of compassion :
I love Thee ; be merciful unto me.

---

[1] St. Luke xvii. 5.   [2] St. Mark ix. 24.   [3] Ps. cxix. 73.

Things I previously fled from, I now seek; things once my bugbear are now the objects of my delight. Poverty, meekness, mourning, the hunger and thirst after justice, cleanness of heart, the making of peace, mercy, the suffering of persecution for justice's sake. . . . These things are beatitudes to me. . . . To be ever pursuing now peace and sorrow, and, at whatever cost, justice, is an energizing state of life which is due entirely to the new perception of the value of these things. . . . But not only are they actions, they produce as an effect joy in the heart . . . even here on earth a foretaste of the bliss of final happiness.

BEDE JARRETT.

CHAPTER XXIII

THE GIFTS AND THE BEATITUDES

HAVING understood that the theological virtues and the gifts of the Spirit operate together for the soul's sanctification, we must understand something further of the consequences of this inter-relation between them. The working of the gifts upon the virtues produces the beatitudes, and each gift is related to one or more of the beatitudes. Through the development of the power of the gifts of the Spirit we are led on into the unitive way, which culminates at the end in the Vision of God which is our destiny.

I

Our Lord pronounced eight beatitudes in the Sermon on the Mount. They present certain aspects and varieties of the blessed-ness which the faithful soul is to enjoy in this life in anticipation of the beatitude of the life to come. The number eight is symbolical, not literal. According to ancient numerology, the number eight symbolized the heavenly perfection. It is not necessary to suppose that our Lord had this in mind when He gave the eight beatitudes, but it is none the less interesting, if not significant, that these states, which are a foretaste on earth of the heavenly blessedness, should be set forth in the number symbolizing heavenly perfection.

There are many beatitudes to be noted in both the Old and New Testaments. They do not, of course, connote complete beatitude such as is enjoyed by the saints in heaven. Nor do they imply the joy which is felt in an emotional way in the earthly life. These beatitudes are objective states of the soul, blessings in the sense of divine favours conferred, which, if used faithfully, will lead on eventually and inevitably to the full joy of the life of the blessed in the presence of God. They are states of which the soul may not be conscious; or, if we are conscious of them, we may, through ignorance of true values, regard them as anything but blessings. For example, few regard poverty as a blessing, and yet in the teach-ing of our Lord, as recorded by St. Luke, a special beatitude is pronounced upon the poor.[1] Again, few of us would regard tears

[1] St. Luke vi. 20.

and mourning, and still less persecution, as blessings; but our Lord categorically declares them to be such. Those who find themselves in these conditions, and recognize in them the cross, and who follow His command to take up the cross, and bear it patiently, and not try to get rid of it—the bearing of the cross is the absolute condition laid down by our Lord for being His disciple [1]— are those for whom the everlasting beatitude is reserved. The apostles did not misunderstand this. They were arrested, and thrown into "the common prison"; they were haled before the court, and although they were acquitted of any charge, nevertheless they were stripped and publicly whipped; after all this injustice, this public humiliation and suffering, we are told that " they departed from the presence of the council, rejoicing that they were counted worthy to suffer shame for his name." [2] They realized the objective blessing of what they were enduring. The world to-day explains away all this teaching, but in doing so, it is trying to explain away Jesus Christ; it explains away and repudiates the blessedness of the sacrifice and suffering involved in His service. Those who accept poverty, meekness, purity, humiliation, and suffering, for Christ's sake, whenever and under whatever conditions it be the will of God to send them, are in the way of the beatitudes. They are in union with God, and are making swift progress along the way that leads to the glorious culmination of the highest union with Him.

The first two beatitudes have to do with the purgative way of life, the way of avoiding all that is not consonant with the loving will of God. The third speaks of a strong and gentle tenderness towards all men. The fourth and fifth belong to the active life of the Christian. The sixth and seventh are exercised in the unitive life of contemplation, while the eighth shows the operation of all the gifts of the Spirit.

II

The first beatitude—the blessedness of being poor and humble in spirit—lies in being detached from the world, and from the things of the world. The gift of holy fear enables us, as we have seen, to walk circumspectly, humbly, and always fearful lest we wound our Lord by entering into the spirit of the world. The soul need fear no fall so long as it walks in lowliness and poverty of spirit, assuming nothing to itself, but depending on God in all things. The Holy Scriptures offer a special beatitude to those who are continually

---

[1] St. Luke ix. 23.   [2] Acts v. 26–42.

governed by the spirit of holy fear—" Happy is the man that feareth alway." [1] The working of the gift of holy fear produces in us this beatitude of lowliness. He who truly fears with a godly fear cannot, so long as he maintains this attitude, possess a heart lifted up by pride. He depends on himself in nothing, and on God in everything. He flees to God in every exigency, as does the little child to a father. In this humble dependence on our heavenly Father, and in this absence of dependence on self, lies our blessedness. " Confide in God; diffide in self," is the command given in the fine and regrettably obsolete phraseology of an ancient English teacher.

III

The second beatitude proclaims the blessedness of those who mourn. Our Lord did not mention any special object of this mourning, but we know that in order to mourn aright, we must have a sense of true values. Men often grieve when they should rejoice, and contrariwise. Those who grieve for worldly things cannot expect comfort from God. Those who have a knowledge of real values will mourn primarily for sin, for their own sins, for the sins of the world, and above all, they will be full of grief at the dishonour which they see continually done to their Lord by the sin of those who should love and serve Him.

The gift of knowledge shows us the worthlessness and the evil of the things of the world, when used apart from God. The working of this gift enables us to see our own failure, and incites us to sorrow for having joined the world in its rejection of the divine love and service which are so richly offered us by the Holy Spirit. It enables us to understand the cry of crucified Love, " Is it nothing to you, all ye that pass by? behold, and see if there be any sorrow like unto my sorrow." [2] As we hear these words, the sight of His sufferings becomes a powerful stimulus to a life and work of reparation to Him who for the joy that was set before Him, the joy of bringing His banished ones home again, " endured the cross, despising the shame." [3] He who, through the working of this divine knowledge, gains a realization of the truth that God made the world that it might be used for His honour, cannot but mourn as He sees the things that should be for the divine glory prostituted to the service of that which is evil. He who thus mourns is blessed of God, for he has the sure promise of the divine comfort.

The thought of being comforted is presented here with some

[1] Prov. xxviii. 14.   [2] Lam. i. 12.   [3] Heb. xii. 2.

Z

what striking significance. The words, "shall be comforted," are the Greek verb form of Paraclete, which is one of the principal titles in the New Testament of "the Holy Ghost the Comforter." He it is who comforts the hearts of those who mourn, and, better still, who takes away the cause of their mourning. If we allow Him to deal with us as He wills, which means if we follow with stern resolution every dictate of conscience, "the Spirit of the Lord God will comfort all that mourn," will "give unto them beauty for ashes, the oil of joy for mourning, the garment of praise for the spirit of heaviness." [1]

IV

The third beatitude—the blessing of meekness—is enjoyed by those who have not merely in word, but in profound reality, renounced the world, the flesh, and the devil. But we must not be misled, as has been most of the English-speaking world, by the word which our translators have used. The evangelist's expression has in it none of the sense of weakness, or shrinking, which our word *meek* so often implies. One commentator tells us that the word "never did at any time, or in any passage of any author, signify *meek*. Further, the virtue of meekness is already commended in the first beatitude—'the poor, that is, the lowly in spirit.'" [2] A better rendering would be *gentle ;* and it must be kept in mind that gentleness, in its true meaning, implies strength, chastened and disciplined by tenderness.

Gentleness which is not strong is a poor quality, and honours neither God nor man. Gentleness which is strong and patient possesses great power to affect others. The psalmist acknowledges the effect of the gentleness of God on him: "Thy gentleness hath made me great," he says. [3] True gentleness in man is "an inwrought grace in the soul, and the exercise of it is first and chiefly towards God." [4] It accepts His discipline in the humble knowledge that we both need and deserve His discipline. At the same time it enables the soul to meet all rebuffs and injuries with a sweet and

---

[1] Isa. lxi. 3.
[2] W. J. Hickie, *Greek-English Lexicon, in loc.*
[3] 2 Sam. xxii. 36.
[4] Trench, *N.T. Synonyms*, § xlii and xliii. A word which in meaning is akin to this word, and which is commonly translated *lowliness, humility*, is ταπεινοφροσύνη. It was never used by any classical Greek author, for it implies a trait which the pagans regarded as contemptible, mean-spirited, and slavish. The idea of meekness and humility as a virtue had its origin in the divine revelation of the Old and New Testaments. The Greeks would not tolerate it as a virtue any more than does our world of today.

humble, but very strong, patience, because it knows true values, and suffers these things with a sure conviction that they can neither hurt nor hinder, but will always help the soul that is " in Christ." Such a soul realizes that it is the discipline of Him who said, " Learn of me; for I am meek and lowly in heart." [1] It is not easy to refuse anything to such a spirit, and therefore it is these strong, gentle, and disciplined souls who shall win the earth for Christ, and the " new heaven and new earth, wherein dwelleth righteousness," [2] shall be theirs.

This " inwrought grace " of gentleness is the result of the gift of piety working in union with the virtues of faith, hope and love. The " divine infusion of piety softens the hardness of our nature, enlarges the soul by the ardour which it enkindles, sweetens her with unction, and draws her with tenderness towards God." [3]

V

The beatitude which those enjoy who hunger and thirst after righteousness is full of the possibility of suffering. This hunger is not only for the righteousness which we desire to make our own, but for the setting up of the righteous kingdom of God in the world; but the world will not tolerate His kingdom. All history shows a continual battle of the world against that for which we hunger, and against those who would set up the kingdom amongst men. There are obstacles innumerable, and persecutions, not only external, such as those endured by the martyrs, but interior torments, with the temptation to lose heart in the struggle. Here the soul needs the fullest operation of the gift of fortitude to strengthen it against all the fears and dreads of the difficulties which lie in the way. We need to be animated by the power of the Holy Ghost, to be made " strong in the Lord, and in the power of his might," [4] that we may find our calm and confidence and courage in the assurance that " great are the troubles of the righteous, but the Lord delivereth him out of all." [5] The happy assurance of this deliverance, and of the final triumph of righteousness, is the beatitude which God pledges Himself to give us.

When our Lord said that they who hungered and thirsted after righteousness should be filled, He did not mean that this satisfaction should be theirs all at once. The word has in it a pastoral quality,

---

[1] St. Matt. xi. 29. [2] 2 Peter iii. 13.
[3] Ullathorne, *Christian Patience*, p. 172.
[4] Eph. vi. 10. [5] Ps. xxxiv. 19.

and contains the implication of the daily leading of the flock out to graze. There is a sweet suggestion in it of " green pastures," [1] and of " waters of comfort.' As the continual recurrence of hunger and thirst is the indication of a healthy body, so the soul which continually hungers and thirsts after righteousness will grow up more and more into Christ, the Good Shepherd, who continually feeds His flock.

VI

The beatitude of the merciful has reference to a wide area of service. Works of mercy fall into two categories—corporal and spiritual works, both of which are commanded as a necessary part of the Christian duty. The corporal works are those of feeding the hungry, clothing the naked, sheltering the homeless, ministering to the sick, and to those in trouble. The importance of corporal works of mercy is set forth clearly in the Scripture. The works mentioned in the great parable of the judgment, for which some were condemned for omitting, and others accepted for performing, were all, without exception, corporal works of mercy.[2]

The beatitude of the merciful is obviously connected with the gift of counsel. There are many souls whose sympathies are easily aroused, and who quickly respond to the call of distress, but who show little judgment as to how mercy should be exercised. They earnestly desire to do all that mercy asks, but their ministrations are often ill-judged and ill-timed, and do as much harm as good. Their charity needs to be guided, and the gift of counsel shows not only what ought to be done, but the wise and discreet way in which to do it.

The spiritual works of mercy are to instruct the ignorant in religion, to correct offenders for their soul's good, to counsel those in trouble, to comfort the afflicted, to suffer injuries with forgiving patience, and to pray for the living and the dead. The faithful performance of these duties of mercy brings the blessing of mercy poured out upon us by God.

Some commentators consider the sequence of the beatitudes in the Sermon on the Mount as of significance, and they connect this beatitude with the one that goes before it. The zeal for the kingdom of God, and for the spread of His righteousness into all hearts, has at times in the history of the Church been perverted

---

[1] The noun form of this word means *pasturage, grass*. It is used in St. Matt. xiii. 26, in the parable of the tares, for the fresh young blades of the wheat.

[2] St. Matt. xxv.

by some into a bitter zeal against those who oppose the truth, whether in faith or conduct. One of the chief characteristics of our Lord was His tenderness towards sinners. He did not break the bruised reed, or quench the smoking flax. He was infinitely patient with those who opposed themselves to His divine teaching. On the two occasions when He pronounced heavy woes against confirmed and obdurate sinners, He could not speak the word of condemnation without at the same time giving them one more tender, loving call to repentance. He pronounced a terrible judgment on the cities of Galilee, but concluded with the cry, " Come unto me all ye that labour and are heavy laden, and I will give you rest. Take my yoke upon you, and learn of me; for I am meek and lowly in heart, and ye shall find rest unto your souls." [1] He uttered dread woes upon the rulers of Jerusalem, but ended with the heartbroken lament, " O Jerusalem, Jerusalem, thou that killest the prophets, and stonest them which are sent unto thee, how often would I have gathered thy children together as a hen gathereth her chickens under her wings, and ye would not! " [2] His was the infinitely merciful spirit, whether to friends or enemies, and beatitude can be found only in an imitation of His tenderness. By our mercy or by our severity we are daily preparing the terms of our own judgment at the end. We write our own condemnation or our acceptance by God, and He, respecting the freedom of will with which He has endowed us, will ratify our choice when we come to stand before His tribunal.

VII

The two beatitudes which follow belong to the life of contemplation. " Blessed are the pure in heart, for they shall see God." Blessed indeed are they who, having the hope of God in their hearts, purify themselves in the power of the Holy Spirit even as He is pure. Through the operation of the gift of understanding, they have been able to catch some glimpse of the divine beauty, which, though dim and fleeting in this life, ravishes their souls, and gives them a longing and desire to enter into the courts of the Lord, like St. Paul's desire " to depart and to be with Christ." [3]

The gift of understanding enables them to see ever more clearly, and to appreciate ever more deeply, the ultimate and absolute values that lie in God and in the things of God. As a consequence, they desire to purify themselves more and more, that they may

---

[1] St. Matt. xi. 28.   [2] St. Matt. xxiii. 37.   [3] Phil. i. 23.

enter ever more deeply into that blessed vision. We cannot, as finite creatures, rise to a complete knowledge of His infinite value, but we know that where with all our hearts we desire God He counts us to have attained to Him. The longing and desire for the perfection of Christ are credited to us as perfection. God takes the will for the deed.

This purification is a continual process, not a swift and instant answer to our longing. It is the objective of all the work of the Spirit through the ages in the Church and in the Sacraments, in the good desires and thoughts He puts into our hearts, and in the prayers and good works He inspires us to offer to God.

The purity of heart which the Holy Spirit achieves in us is extended progressively and simultaneously to every department of our being. The whole man is purified. From the soul is banished every movement which could tend to arouse the passions and appetites to God's dishonour and to our hurt. Indeed, we are enabled to have no desire or taste for aught else save God and the things of God. Once, through this purity of heart, we have caught the vision of God, naught else can satisfy us. It consecrates more and more the will, enabling it to govern the affections, that we may be able to love only those things which could win the all-pure human heart of our Lord. It clears the mind of all error and false belief, of all misunderstanding, and of the lack of judgment which might baffle or lead us astray.

The imagination—that impetuous and many-coloured faculty, which so often drives us headlong into perilous ways—is calmed and controlled through the divine work of purification. It becomes the obedient servant, and is no longer the master. It does the bidding of the Holy Spirit, presenting to the mind only those images which reflect the presence and goodness of God, and brings them at just the right time, and in the right relationships, so that they become the means of light and grace and strength to us, rather than will-o'-the-wisps leading us into spiritual quagmires. Every earth-born cloud dissolves and disappears, until at the end of the way the final, and never-to-be-lost, vision of God breaks upon our en-raptured sight.

VIII

The second of the beatitudes of the life of contemplation is that of the peacemakers: " Blessed are the peacemakers, for they shall be called the children of God." This beatitude we are able to enter into through the working of the gift of wisdom, and the wise man tells us that "sweetly doth she order all things."[1] We are reminded of St. Augustine's definition, "peace is the tranquillity of order."[2] Order means that everything is in its appointed place, all things co-ordinated, the many parts of this complex human nature and life of ours working together without friction, or interference.

The world longs for peace, but there is no peace save the peace of God, and in the heart where He abides there abides peace, for He is the God of peace. Where He dwells, there He rules. St. Augustine declares, "In Thy good will is our peace."[3] They who in the power of the divine wisdom seek after peace shall most surely find it in obeying the divine will, and once having found it, they will be able to communicate it to others. This is a natural, as well as a supernatural, law. We know how the companionship of one who is full of a strong calm, who is at peace, imparts peace and calm to others; and thus are the possessors of peace able to be the makers of peace, true emissaries of the Prince of Peace.

IX

The last of the beatitudes is not counted as a separate blessing, because it is the confirmation and manifestation of all the others: ' Blessed are they which are persecuted for righteousness sake, for heirs is the kingdom of heaven: Blessed are ye when men shall revile you, and persecute you, and say all manner of evil against you falsely for my sake; Rejoice and be exceeding glad, for great is your reward in heaven." This is nothing less than our Lord's confirmation, here in the very beginning of His ministry, of the truth that had been repeated again and again, and which was to be one of the foundation truths of His kingdom, that " all that will live godly in Christ Jesus shall suffer persecution."[4] A few hours before He endured the supreme persecution of men on the cross, He said to His assembled disciples, " These things have I spoken unto you that in me ye might have peace "; and then He added, " In the world ye shall have tribulation; but be of good cheer; I

---

[1] Wisdom viii. 1.

[2] " Pax est tranquillitas ordinis."—St. Augustine, *De Civ. Dei*, xix. 13; Migne, P. L., Tom. 41, Col. 640.

[3] " In bona voluntate tua pax nobis est."—St. Augustine, *Confessions*, xiii. 9; Migne, P. L., Tom. 32, Col. 848. Migne omits *tua* in this passage. The Knöll text, which is used by Mr. Rouse in the Loeb Library, retains it. See an interesting critical correspondence in the *Times Literary Supplement* in December, 1943, involving Dante's possible familiarity with St. Augustine's saying when he wrote his well-known line, " E'n la sua volontade è nostra pace."

[4] 2 St. Tim. iii. 12.

have overcome the world." [1] In this beatitude of suffering, of pain, and of shame for His Name's sake, all the gifts of the Holy Spirit are to be called into action for the protection and for the sanctification of God's people. He is to show them how to find joy in suffering, and to give them the realization of the blessing of the kingdom in this life, and the consummation of its joys in the life to come, where all will be swallowed up in the completeness of beatitude in the vision of God face to face.

We meditate with joy and gladness upon the beatitude which God has offered, and is continually offering to His children, and rejoice in the hope of it; but we are never to forget that the true destiny of man lies not in beatitude, not even in the beatitude of God, but in God Himself. "I am thy exceeding great reward." [2] We look not for any gift of His, however precious; we look for Him.

O loving, risen Saviour : Without Thee I can do nothing : with Thee I can do all things. Let Thine omnipotence bless me ; let Thy wisdom teach me. Only in Thee can I serve Thee well. Grant, therefore, that Thy sweetness and goodness may draw me, and unite me to Thee forever, that experiencing Thy blessing in time, I may rejoice in Thy Beatitude in eternity.

[1] St. John xvi. 33.   [2] Gen. xv. 1.

Devotion is neither private nor public prayer, but prayers, whether private or public, are particular parts or instances of devotion. Devotion signifies a life given, or devoted, to God. He, therefore, is the devout man, who lives no longer to his own will, or the way and spirit of the world, but to the sole will of God; who considers God in everything, who serves God in everything, who makes all the parts of his common life parts of piety, by doing everything in the Name of God, and under such rules as are conformable to His glory.

WILLIAM LAW.

If thou canst not ask, are the hands of God tied that He cannot give? If thou hast no words wherewith to give Him thanks, give Him thine heart.

JUAN FALCONI.

CHAPTER XXIV

PRAYER: ITS NATURE AND PRACTICE

THERE is an ancient maxim which philosophers in every age, whether consciously or unconsciously, have made the basis of their investigations and labours—" Before all things the end is to be considered; and according to the end our course is to be directed." [1] Nowhere is the principle set forth in this maxim of so much importance as in the spiritual life; and nowhere in the spiritual life is it of greater importance than in the consideration and practice of prayer.

I

Prayer is the breath of the Christian. It has been said that one could as readily find a living body which did not breathe as a living Christian who did not pray. If we were cut off from the surrounding atmosphere, in a few minutes the body would die. Should we cut ourselves off from prayer, the life of the soul would quickly perish. Christianity involves a system of belief and a code of conduct, but with these alone our religion would be a sterile thing. Christianity is an inner life to be lived, a life of the soul, and prayer is the breath of this life. It has been most truly said that every soul that has ever been lost was lost because it did not pray; and every soul, since the beginning of time, who has been saved, was saved as the result of the fact that it did pray. There is no possibility of salvation without prayer; with prayer there is no possibility of a soul being lost. Dogmas and institutions, ceremonial rites and ideals of behaviour, are necessary elements in Christianity, but in the prayer-life alone can we find the essence of our religion. Religion is a personal union with God which cannot be effected by merely conforming to codes of conduct, or accepting articles of belief. There have been those who gave an intellectual acceptance to the faith in its fulness, or whose code of outward conduct coincided with Christian requirements, but who were not Christian in the true interior sense because they lived no life of union with God in prayer. A thoughtful and devout writer

---

[1] " Ante omnia considerandus est finis; et secundem finem dirigendus est cursus."

has expressed it well: " Prayer," says Girgensohn, " is a perfectly accurate instrument for grading the religious life of the soul. Did one only know how a man prays, and what he prays about, one would be able to see how much religion that man has. When a man without any witnesses, speaks with his God, the soul stands unveiled before its creator. What it has then to say shows quite distinctly how rich, or how poor, it is." [1]

II

The misconceptions of prayer, and the objections often raised to it, grow out of a misunderstanding of its nature, and particularly of its objective. Prayer of whatever kind, whether it be vocal, meditative, ejaculatory, affective, or contemplative, has but one ultimate aim—namely, to give glory to God through the attainment by the soul to participation in His beatitude in heaven. This is the apex of all human evolution, for a theory of evolution which does not apply to the inner spiritual man as well as to the outer physical man, is a poor, inadequate thing which fails to take account of the best and highest in the nature of man, and deals with him as though he were only another species of the brute. It ignores the one thing which constitutes his kinship with the divine. It ignores the only enduring element in man, and concerns itself only with that which is ephemeral, and which will pass away in a brief period of time and be forgotten. Such a theory is an affront to the dignity of humanity. The physical is but the instrument and vehicle of the interior man. The work of all prayer, of whatever kind, must converge upon this one objective of eternal oneness with God, or it will cease to be prayer.

Prayer aims at oneness with the Father through the Son, in the power of the Holy Ghost. But we do not pass through Christ to the Father, leaving Christ behind us. He is, it is true, the Way— " No man cometh unto the Father but by me " [2]—but He is also the Truth and the Life. He is both the means and the end, the Way and the goal. As the progress that we make in and through Him is a never-ending progress in virtue of His grace and merits, so we shall never leave Him, the Way, even though we have entered into Him, the Truth and the Life, in the most intimate degree

[1] K. Girgensohn, *Addresses on the Christian Religion*, quoted by Fr. Heiler in *Prayer* (tr. by S. McComb), pp. xv, xvi.
[2] St. John xiv. 6.

possible in the very bosom of God. It is always, whether in time or in eternity, " with Christ in God."

Prayer has been described as " God's created image seeking union with the Divine Original." [1] In prayer, as in all things else, the Holy Spirit is the mover, and every motion sponsored by Him, in the soul, looks to the complete union of the soul with God ultimately. Indeed, every such movement in the soul is a summons to a further step in this union with God which is the final destiny prepared for man. To every moving of the Spirit man is to respond, and the work of co-operation between the soul and the Spirit effects the oneness of our prayer with the heavenly intercession of Christ. Rather might we say that the Holy Spirit makes our prayer to be the pleading of Christ. This is what is implied in praying in His Name. When He lends His Name to our prayer, He makes it His own, as I make a petition my own when I sign it on behalf of another person. In all this is set forth the dignity and Godlike majesty of prayer. The activity of the whole Godhead is called into operation with every lifting of the heart to God by the humblest Christian soul.

To realize this glorious truth we have only to look at the processes of prayer. First of all, we are moved to pray by the Holy Spirit; the prayer is offered in unity with the heavenly intercession of the Incarnate Son, and in dependence upon His merits; and it is directed to, and accepted by, the Holy Trinity, as our reasonable and obedient service of love. If these conditions are fulfilled, it is impossible for our prayer to fail, because it is in reality an activity of the Blessed Trinity. When we pray, we are caught up into the triune activity of the three Divine Persons. We are lifted up to God on the current of our Spirit-inspired praying, which is made divine in virtue of its origin in the Holy Ghost, of its union with Christ, and of its acceptance by the Father.

Every aspiration of prayer is, therefore, a proclamation on our part that God alone is our objective. Every elevation of the heart to God is a forward step in our progress, not *towards God*, for if the divine grace be in us in any degree, we are already in Him when we pray; but it is a step in our progress *in God*. It is a more secure anchoring of the soul " with Christ in God."

We need to recall here our consideration of the truth that our relation to God is not only that of union, but of communion. It is a mutual affair. God gives Himself to us in order that we may be able to give ourselves to Him. In this communion God indwells

[1] Ullathorne, *Christian Patience*, p. 185.

the soul. "God is love; and he that abideth in love abideth in God, and God in him." [1] He fills the soul with Himself; it is permeated through and through with the very Being of God. Filled with the God-given spirit of penitence, no longer do we stand like the publican in the parable afar off, not lifting up so much as our eyes to heaven.[2] Just because we are penitent through love, we are able with strong confidence to look up, and lift up our heads, and to stand with Christ in the very Holy of Holies.

In the temple at Jerusalem, the Holy of Holies, where was the Ark of the Covenant and the Mercy Seat, was a place of awe and darkness. It was separated by the veil beyond which no man could pass save when, on the great day of atonement, " went the high priest alone, once every year, not without blood, which he offered for himself, and for the errors of the people; the Holy Ghost this signifying, that the way into the holiest of all was not yet made manifest." [3] But now the way has been made clearly manifest. Our great High Priest does not enter alone, but whenever we pray we stand within the sacred precincts of the Holy of Holies with Him, for every day for the Christian is a day of atonement, when, in company with Him who bears in His hands the offering on our behalf of the Precious Blood of Calvary, we can come " boldly unto the throne of grace," [4] offering in union with Him the all-atoning Blood of the Everlasting Covenant.

This was the precise significance of the startling incident on Good Friday, when, at the moment that the great and final Atonement was once for all consummated by our Lord on the cross, " the veil of the temple was rent in twain from the top to the bottom," exposing to all the multitude the place which was the holiest of all, into which through fifteen centuries of time, no Jew had dared to look. Three of the Gospels mention this incident specifically, and with significant detail. We are told that it was " rent from the top to the bottom," a complete exposure of the Holy of Holies.[5] It was a happening of the profoundest importance, proclaiming, as it did, a wholly new dispensation, under which no longer were the faithful to be held back from the most intimate personal communion with God, but were to be made one with Him, even as the Son of God is one with the Father—" as thou, Father, art in me, and I in thee, that they also may be one in us." [6] In

---

[1] 1 St. John iv. 16.   [2] St. Luke xviii. 13.   [3] Heb. ix. 7, 8.   [4] Heb. iv. 16.
[5] St. Matt. xxvii. 51; St. Mark xv. 38; St. Luke xxiii. 45. St. John's Gospel does not mention the incident as his purpose was not to duplicate, but to supplement, the narratives of the other three evangelists.
[6] St. John xvii. 21.

short, the only place where the Christian can stand is in the inner-most sanctuary of the Godhead, within the very cycle of the life of the Adorable and Indivisible Trinity—" with Christ in God." Not to stand there is to forfeit every privilege as a Christian.

Being " in Christ," we are organically one with God, as the engrafted branch becomes one with the vine. We become inte-grated with Him, and He with us. This is what our Lord meant when He prayed, as we have just noted, " that they all may be one, as thou, Father, art in me, and I in thee, that they also may be one in us." This is the divine integration, Christ one with the Ever-Blessed and Indivisible Trinity, and we, because we are one with Him, also being one with this adorable Godhead. Within this state of oneness with God we are continually progressing, for while, as we have thought, there are different degrees in this state of union, the obligation of souls is to use the divine gifts so that we shall ever be going forward to higher things within this state, until " complete in him," [1] filled with the holiness of God, we shall attain to the destiny which His love has prepared for us.

III

If we believe prayer to be the loving communication of the soul with God, we shall see that in these considerations we are touching the very essence of prayer. The Spirit of God, St. Paul declares, now prays within us with groanings which cannot be uttered.[2] This is to say that we know not how to pray as we ought. We are spiritually inarticulate, we can only groan within, not knowing how to fill our helpless yearnings after God with any meaning. But we are upheld by the Holy Spirit, who makes our dumb aspirations His own and gives them force and point and expression, and converts them into an offering worthy to be presented to the living God.

If we allow His Spirit to draw us with Christ into the current of the divine activity, life will become one unbroken prayer. It will become a state of prayer as distinguished from mere acts of prayer, for if the divine love dwells within us, love prays con-tinually. Thus does prayer become not only a lifting up of the heart to God, but it becomes a life-in-God, love praying without ceasing even when the direct attention is engaged with external affairs. More than this, we can say that, sleeping or waking, we are ever in communication with God—" I sleep, but my heart

[1] Col. ii. 10.   [2] Rom. viii. 23–26.

waketh " [1]—and therefore we are ever engaged in prayer. Prayer does not have to be a continuous, conscious advertence of the mind to God. If we are in reality partakers of the divine nature, God abiding in us and we in Him, our union with the God-Man in the bosom of the Father must consist of prayer, everything becoming prayer because every motion of our being will be a communication with God. " The essential element in prayer is the supernatural contact of the soul with God whence it imbibes that divine life that is the source of all holiness." [2]

If we accept this as the ideal of prayer, it will be seen that the word must be taken in its highest, widest, and most comprehensive sense. Prayer will then be regarded as a living, vivid, spiritual state rather than as an act, or series of acts. Acts of prayer are, of course, requisite in the Christian life, but they can never rise to their highest plane, or be brought to their true and full value, until they become the expression of an interior permanent condition of union with God the Holy Trinity. There is an interesting analogy to this in the 109th Psalm, where the psalmist, speaking of his enemies, says, " For the love that I had unto them, lo, they now take my contrary part; but I give myself unto prayer." The Hebrew original in the last sentence consists of just two words— " I, prayer." He has completely identified himself with his prayer. The act expresses not his emotion or desire, not even his aspiration. It expresses his entire self. He is prayer. In our union with God, and therefore in our communication with Him, we are transformed into living prayer.

Christian prayer, therefore, cannot consist of isolated acts, however frequent they may be. It must be the overflowing of an interior reservoir of divine life and power. It will be the manifestation of the life-movement of the indwelling God, the normal expression within us of the divine nature of which we are partakers. This life-movement must, from the nature of it, be continuous. If the life of the soul ceases for a moment—and it can cease only through sin—we are spiritually dead, and only a resurrection through the action of God, made possible by our repentance, can restore the life. Lest this thought give discouragement to some, let us remember that where the grace of God dwells at all there life always exists. It may be a feeble thing, but wherever the seed lies, there is the possibility of growth and harvest. God, in His goodness, is employing the infinite fulness of His omnipotent love

[1] Song of Songs, v. 2.
[2] Marmion, *Christ, the Life of the Soul* (4th edition), p. 307.

in doing everything, if we will permit Him to do His work within us, to bring our life to a rich fruition of that holiness which must be ours.

God alone can create a state of prayer in the soul. The disciples realized this when they said, " Lord, teach us to pray." [1] His action depends, however, as in all else, on the development of the spiritual life, on our co-operation with Him. By continually praying, we make it possible for Him to work within us, and to produce the state of prayer which is necessary. This is why the Scriptures so constantly urge upon us the duty of prayer. It is not that single acts of prayer, taken alone, are of the highest value, but that he who is obediently mindful of our Lord's word that " men ought always to pray and not to faint," [2] and of the command of the apostle, " Pray without ceasing," [3] will, without doubt, form, through the help of the Holy Spirit, and in the course of no long time, a habit and state of interior prayer which will express itself constantly, and produce an unbroken life of prayer which will go far to securing the sanctification of the soul, and its progress towards its final destiny " with Christ in God."

IV

Keeping in mind these general principles, it will be profitable to go on to see what the great Christian teachers through the ages have handed down to us concerning the practice and life of prayer. There are almost as many definitions of prayer as there have been wise and holy men who have spoken of it. One of the oft-quoted definitions, one of the best because one of the simplest, is that of St. John of Damascus, who flourished in the eighth century. He defines prayer as any elevation of the soul to God.[4] This corresponds in general with the definition that prayer is any loving communication of the soul with God. The word *elevation* here demands attention. It is, of course, a principle of natural philosophy that every motion involves a double action, the receding from one position and the approaching another. A lifting of the soul to God implies, of necessity, a drawing away from the world and the things of the world. Prayer is, therefore, not only an effort to reach out after God, but, unless it is an act of bad faith, it is a formal renunciation of the world, and of all the things that are not of God. It will be of great benefit if we keep this idea alive in our hearts in

---

[1] St. Luke xi. 1.   [2] St. Luke xviii. 1.   [3] 1 Thess. v. 17.
[4] St. John of Damascus, *De Fide Orthodox.*, I, i. 24; Migne, P. G., Tom. 94, Col. 1090.

A A

all our praying. It will save us from the unhappy fate of being numbered amongst those presumptuous souls who, while ready enough to fly to God for succour in their trouble, have no definite accompanying resolution of giving up self, and sin, and the follies and evils of the world.

St. Augustine has given us many definitions of prayer in his voluminous writings, and perhaps none is better than the one which reflects the loving spirit which we find always in him. Although one of the greatest intellects the world has ever known, he is never merely intellectual. He is ever tender, warm, and loving. " Prayer," he says, " is the soul's affectionate quest after God." [1] William of St. Thierry, having in mind the state of prayer of which we have been thinking, says, " Prayer is the loving union of the soul with God, a tender and familiar converse, and a repose of the spirit, which, illuminated by the light of grace, enjoys the divine sweetness." [2] St. Teresa gives us a similar conception of prayer when she declares that it is " an intimate friendship, a frequent converse, heart to heart, with one whom we know to be our Lover." [3]

A more general definition of prayer, embracing its various aspects, is that prayer is a lifting up of the soul to God, in order to offer Him our homage, and ask His favours, in order that we may grow in holiness for His glory. The important point in this definition lies in the last clause, where the real purpose of praying is said to be indeed our own growth in holiness, but only in order that God may in this growth be the more glorified. Self is never an ultimate objective. It may be used as a stepping-stone to higher and nobler things, but the final aim is always God and His glory. Our holiness, indispensable as it is to our salvation, is an objective only as being instrumental to the divine exaltation and glorification, the hallowing of His Name for which we pray continually in the Our Father.

Definitions might be multiplied, and in every case, in one form or another, they imply the union with God which we have seen constitutes the Christian life, and without which, indeed, there is no Christian life.

Prayer is the normal and ordinary mode of intercourse between

---

[1] " Oratio est namque mentis ad Deum affectuosa intentio."—St. Augustine. *Sermo*, ix. 3. So quoted in Tanquerey, *Precis de Théologie Ascetique et Mystique*, 6th Ed. No. 501.

[2] This definition is from a letter long supposed to have been written by St. Bernard to the monks of the Mons Dei Monastery in France. It is printed in the saint's works. See Migne, Tom., 184.

[3] St. Teresa, *Life*, vii. 7.

the soul who dwells in God and God who dwells in the soul.   When we are " in Christ," our work of prayer is merged in the current of the eternal communication between the three Adorable Persons of the Holy Trinity.   But we are not to think that it is by prayer that we learn to communicate with God, but contrariwise, by communicating with Him we learn to pray.   Contact with God must be established before we can pray, just as the electric connection must be established before we can send a message.   We have no power of ourselves to make the contact with God, but He holds always the initiative, and through His kindling touch enables us to do our part, and to do it adequately.   Christ must be in us and we in Him before we can pray as Christians, and our praying is the normal functioning of the members of the Body of Christ, members instinct with the divine life which He lives within us.

Christ and His baptized members are bound together in a indissoluble unity.   When we say it is indissoluble, we do not mean that it is never dissolved.   It is, alas, too often dissolved by sin. We mean that in the nature of it there can never be any violation of the bond between God and the soul save where sacrilegious violence rends asunder the God-created bond between us and Himself.   In the creation of this bond it is never contemplated, either by God or the soul, that it will ever be severed.   It is no temporary or trial alliance.   God gives Himself to the soul, and the soul gives itself to God.   This mutual donation is for eternity.

The life of the Body of Christ into which we enter at baptism is not manifold; it is one life—that is, the life of the risen, ascended, and glorified Christ as He exercises it in the bosom of His Father today.   Of this life we all partake.   We have thought repeatedly of the truth that when one Person of the Holy Trinity acts, all act. The prayer-life in the Body of Christ is analogous to this life of the Godhead.   Where one member of the Body of Christ prays, all pray.   The members of the Body act together under the power of the Head, which is Christ.   Christ, the Head of the Mystical Body, transmits to His every member His own power of life and action, and this not by means of any gift apart from Himself, but by an extension of Himself through all the Body, dwelling in every member, and in every member living His own life.

v

In human affairs the motive force in all action is desire.   Spiritual desire may be defined as a movement of the soul, resulting from the action of God on the will, towards some good which we are conscious of lacking, and which is necessary, or contributory, to our spiritual progress. The measure of the gift of God is according to the measure of our desire. St. Augustine says, " His gifts are very great, but we are small and straitened in our capacity of receiving. In proportion to the simplicity of our faith, the fulness of our hope, and the ardour of our desire, will we more largely receive."

In prayer the desire for God and for the things of God is the impelling motive. Whatever the character of the prayer, desire is the necessary factor. It would be folly, and, worse still, it would be hypocrisy, to approach God in the words and attitude of prayer, and not sincerely to desire Him and the blessings He gives so generously to all those who come to Him in their quest after the perfection which is required of each one of us in the end. Prayer is the foremost and most powerful agency which makes for this perfection, and without it we could not take even the first step toward this so necessary goal.

Desire, in order that its steadfastness and efficacy be maintained, must be ever on the increase. The natural, as well as the supernatural, way of inflaming desire is to dwell upon the objects of desire, to meditate upon them, representing to ourselves vividly the advantage and joy of possessing them. This will produce a conviction of the value of these objectives in themselves, and of their desirability in our lives.

In supernatural affairs it is also necessary to pray earnestly to God for the grace of desire. It is a gift which He alone can bestow, for it is from Him that " all holy desires do proceed." [1] " Covet earnestly the best gifts," [2] and " desire spiritual gifts," [3] are the commands. The soul who thus prays for these graces of desire, and meditates frequently upon the glory and beauty of the heavenly life, upon the companionship of God, and upon the blessing and beatitude of participating in ever-increasing degree in His joy and love, cannot fail to find its desire and longing for God inflamed more and more.

It is a psychological truth that an idea impressed upon the mind tends to produce action. When an idea is accompanied by desire, the tendency to action is stronger, for the desire in itself constitutes a formulated act of the will which is necessary to set our faculties in motion. " To desire perfection is to tend towards it, and to tend towards perfection is to begin to attain it. To desire to love

---

[1] The Collect for Peace (Book of Common Prayer).
[2] 1 Cor. xii. 31.   [3] 1 Cor. xiv. 1.

God is already to love Him since God sees the heart, and takes into account all our intentions." [1]

Applying this principle to our consideration of prayer, we see that the desire to pray is to pray. St. Augustine, interpreting St. Paul's exhortation to "pray without ceasing," says, "when we cherish uninterrupted desire along with the exercise of faith, hope, and charity, we pray always." [2] If, as our Lord taught, the desire for sin is the same as though we had committed the act of sin,[3] much more is the desire for goodness accredited by God to us as goodness.

It is evident, therefore, that desire, as we are considering it in the spiritual sphere, is not an emotion, or a passing aspiration. It is a practical moral and spiritual power and force which, as a gift of God, operates to carry us forward in the essential work of prayer. It is indispensable to the life of prayer, and, therefore, to the life of holiness to which we are called. In the exercise of this gift we shall find God. There can be no question or doubt about the success of this divine quest, for our Lord has promised, " He that seeketh, findeth." [4] But without desire we can do nothing. God gave the promise of old, " Open thy mouth wide, and I shall fill it." [5] It has been said that God has greater regard for adverbs than for verbs. That is, He is more interested in how we do a thing than in the mere doing of it. In the command which God gives through the psalmist, this unqualified condition is laid down: " Open thy mouth *wide*." We must treat with God as a generous God; we must look with a sure expectancy for great things from Him, and prepare ourselves to receive them, and they will be ours. Through His prophet of old, He has given us this assurance: " Prove me now herewith, saith the Lord of hosts, if I will not open you the windows of heaven, and pour you out a blessing, that there shall not be room enough to receive it." [6]

VI

Every prayer is an exercise of the three great supernatural forces, or virtues, of faith, hope and charity, which exercise is of the essential substance of the Christian life, and without which we can have no life in Christ. The exercise of these virtues involves a degree of knowledge of God. If we did not know Him as our Father, it is not likely that we would be moved to honour Him, or to appeal to Him at all. It is perhaps the most natural thing in

[1] Tanquerey, *The Spiritual Life*, No. 418.
[2] St. Augustine, *Epist.* cxxx. 18; Migne, P. L., Tom. 33, Col. 501.
[3] St. Matt. v. 28. [4] St. Matt. vii. 8. [5] Ps. lxxxi. 11. [6] Mal. iii. 10.

all human relationships that a child should speak with trust and confidence to a father. The fact that the child of God speaks to his Father in confidence, necessarily implies an attitude of faith in His revelation, and a basing of all life on that faith. Likewise, unless we had hope in God, unless we had a serene and steadfast expectation of the fulfilment of His promises, knowing they could not fail, there would be no reality in our prayer, and an unreal prayer is a contradiction in terms. Again, every prayer is an act of love to God, for it is quite impossible to have a genuine, super-natural faith and hope in Him without our hearts going out to Him in love.

It is not only the three theological virtues which find their expression in every sincere prayer, but there can be nothing in all the range of the virtues which is not embraced in prayer. How many times in the Church's liturgies and prayers do we find humility, which is the seed-ground of every other virtue, either expressed or taken for granted. When we come before God in penitence, the Church exhorts us that we " humbly confess our sins unto Almighty God." We pray Him, " Look upon the hearty desires of thy humble servants," [1] and " Let thy merciful ears, O Lord, be open to the prayers of thy humble servants." [2] Nor can we express our gratitude for His mercy and loving-kindness without offering Him " our humble and hearty thanks." These instances could be multiplied indefinitely to show that every virtue finds place in prayer. Unless this be so in all our devotions, we may be saying prayers, but we are not praying. Prayer is the universal practice of all the Christian virtues.

In communicating with our Father in heaven we also make an act of conformity to His will, for, either explicitly or implicitly, every prayer is an act of filial submission whereby we place ourselves wholly in His hands. There can be no real prayer which does not in substance embrace the principle expressed in our Lord's words in His supreme hour of prayer: " Not my will, but thine be done." [3]

The crowning element in all prayer is that, in itself, it is the expression of a definite desire for perfection, for certainly no soul would come to God in sincerity who did not in his heart desire progress in Christian perfection, and St. Bernard assures us that an earnest desire for the perfection of Christ, and a humble eagerness

---

[1] Collect for III Sunday in Lent.
[2] Collect for X Sunday after Trinity.
[3] St. Luke xxii. 42.

to participate in His perfection, is accounted to us by God as perfection itself.[1] Prayer is, therefore, not only a desire for the state of spiritual perfection, but it is an act by which we definitely enter more fully into that state. The way of prayer is the way of perfection, and the practice of prayer is the practice of perfection, and a continual progress in that way.

VII

Prayer, as we use the word in the religious sense, can be made only to God. To pray to anyone else would be idolatry. It is not always clear, however, in the minds of Christians what is meant by God. There are Three Persons in the one God, three distinct divine Persons, subsisting in one nature. Each of these Persons possesses the totality of the Godhead. The Son and the Holy Spirit have the same fulness of Deity as the Father, and, therefore, prayer can, and should, be addressed to each of the three divine Persons since each of them is very God.

Amongst most Christian people in our day, prayer is made habitually to the Father, less frequently to the Son, and practically never to the Holy Spirit. There is in such a method of praying an almost inevitable loss of the sense of the relationship which exists between the three divine Persons in the Godhead, and also a measure of loss from our lack of consciousness of the nature of the God to whom we pray. The dangerous effect of this is frequently observed in the fact that those who do not pray to the Son and to the Holy Ghost are vague in their faith regarding these three divine Persons, often to the point of a practical, though in many instances quite unintentional, denial of the divinity of Christ. Also these are they who deny the Personality of the Holy Ghost, and by so doing, overthrow belief in the truth of the Holy Trinity. *Lex orandi, lex credendi*, the law of praying is the law of believing. As a man prays, so he believes, and inadequate or erroneous prayer, in the end, will produce inadequate and erroneous belief, which, in its turn, reacts disastrously upon the prayer life.

The Church in her liturgies throughout the world prays freely to the three Persons of the Trinity, but it must nevertheless be kept in mind that prayer to one Person is prayer to all three, for the equality of the Persons in all respects makes this inevitable. Just as whatever one of the divine Persons does all do, and whatever one possesses all possess, likewise, whatever one receives in the way

[1] St. Bernard, *Epist.* ccliv. 3; Migne, P. L., Tom. 182, Col. 460.

of homage and love and prayer, is received equally by all. He who prays to the Father, prays also to the Son and to the Holy Spirit, but if he does not know that he is doing so, or does not recognize these two Persons as those to whom he should pray, he will suffer grave spiritual loss, and his prayer will lack the fulness and richness which belong to all true prayer.

Further, he withholds, even though unconsciously, from the Divine Three that which is due to each of them from every soul. We have just thought that he who gives honour and homage to one Person of the Trinity, gives honour and homage to the Divine Three. But, on the other hand, he who withholds honour from one Person withholds it from all. One who does not believe in the divinity of Christ, or of the Holy Ghost, may offer prayer with much earnestness to the Father alone, but such prayer will not be made to the Christian God, but to a God who is the creation of his own erroneous thinking. If such an one prays in ignorance of the triune God whom our Lord Christ came to reveal, but with sincerity, God will not be unmindful of his sincere offering, but none the less will he direct his prayer to a God who has no existence, for there is no Deity who is of one Person. There is but one God, and He is the eternal Three-in-One, Father, Son, Spirit. No one of these exists without the others. To deny any one of them is to deny the existence of the Trinity, which is, of course, a denial of the only God who has a real existence.

VIII

A method of prayer to the Ever-Adorable Trinity which has been used by many with profit, is to offer an act of love, for example, to the Father, then the same act to the Son, and then to the Holy Ghost. The Church teaches us this mode of prayer on many occasions. In the Litany of the Church, we are taught to offer the prayer, " Have mercy upon us, miserable sinners," first to " God the Father of heaven "; then the identical petition is addressed to " God the Son, Redeemer of the world "; then to " God the Holy Ghost, proceeding from the Father and the Son "; and finally, to the " Holy, Blessed, and glorious Trinity, three Persons and one God." And since it is the revealed Faith that " we worship one God in Trinity, and Trinity in Unity," [1] and are given " grace, by the confession of a true faith, to acknowledge the glory of the eternal Trinity, and in the power of the Divine Majesty to worship

[1] The Athanasian Creed.

the Unity,"[1] the same petition may rightly be addressed as an act of worship to the Divine Unity.

The *Kyrie Eleison*, which from primitive days has been a universal devotion of the Church in practically all of her public services, presents the same mode of worship. Whether it be the threefold or the ninefold form, the worship is the same—first the cry for mercy to the Father, " Lord, have mercy upon us "; then to the Son, " Christ, have mercy upon us "; then to the Holy Spirit, " Lord, have mercy upon us." The ninefold form is an intensification of the cry for mercy, being addressed thrice to the Father, thrice to the Son, and again thrice to the Spirit of God. We have the same principle presented in the *Gloria Patri*, and in all other doxologies of whatever form; and the Sanctus, taken directly from the scriptural accounts of the heavenly worship,[2] which has its place in every Christian liturgy, gives us the expression of the praise of the holiness of the three Divine Persons.

In their great mystical commentary on the psalms, Neale and Littledale have furnished us at the end of each psalm with an edifying elaboration of the *Gloria Patri*, the material being skilfully drawn from the psalms under discussion. This method is to be commended for our private prayers. Anyone with a little imagination can elaborate the great doxology for himself, making of it acts of praise, adoration, thanksgiving, reparation, petition, and including the varied expression of all the virtues the Christian is called upon to practise. For example, at the close of Psalm lxxxv they give us, " Glory be to the Father, who speaketh peace unto His saints; and to the Son, in whom mercy and truth are met together; and to the Holy Ghost, the Loving-kindness of the Lord." The expression of praise at the end of Psalm lxxxix, which Dr. Neale calls " this noble psalm," is as follows: " Glory be to the Father, the Lord God of Hosts; and to the Son, His First-born and Anointed, higher than the kings of the earth; and to the Holy Ghost, the Light of the Countenance of God, and the holy oil of His elect." The great psalm of praise, Psalm ciii, is concluded with: " Glory be to the Father, who pitieth His own children; and to the Son, who hath prepared His seat for judgment in heaven; and to the Holy Ghost, who healeth all our infirmities." One more will suffice to show us the method we may use for ourselves in making such devotions. In connection with Psalm cxviii, we have: " Glory be to the Father, whose mercy endureth forever; and to the Son, the Corner-stone, the King who cometh in the

---

[1] Collect for Trinity Sunday. [2] Isa. vi. 3; Rev. iv. 8.

Name of the Lord;—and to the Holy Ghost, who hath shewed us light."

The *Gloria in Excelsis* falls into practically these same divisions, according to the titles of the three Divine Persons; and the *Te Deum*, which for fifteen centuries, next to the Holy Eucharist, has been perhaps the Church's chief expression of worship and adoration, contains like separate acts of praise to " the Father of an Infinite Majesty," to " Thine honourable true and only Son," and to " the Holy Ghost, the Comforter."

It is not only in the liturgies and prayers of the Church universal that the three Divine Persons are thus addressed, but in the authorized and prescribed hymns the same practice prevails. St. Bernard's universally used hymns, such as *Jesu dulcis memoria* ("Jesu, the very thought of Thee "), are prayers addressed to our Lord. St. Thomas Aquinas gives us such devotions in the *O Salutaris Hostia*, and in the *Adoro Te devote*, both of which appear in most Anglican hymnals. The same principle is seen in the ancient hymns to the Holy Spirit, *Veni Creator*, and *Veni Creator Spiritus*. Other such hymns, both modern and ancient, deriving from both the Western and Eastern Churches, are almost without number, and can be found in any collection of sacred hymnody.[1]

IX

If we accept the universal witness of the Church and the Scriptures, there can be no doubt that the revelation of the Holy and Indivisible Trinity calls for the constant worship and adoration of the three Divine Persons. But the essence of prayer does not consist in words, or even in the innermost and most loving thoughts of the heart towards God. Prayer is the essential objective unity of the soul with God; this state of union constitutes the state of prayer. Life " in Christ " is life in God, and life in God is prayer. Life does not consist in the mere expression of that which is within;

---

[1] The so-called " liturgical movement " in the Roman Catholic Church, as interpreted by its distinguished theologian, Dr. Karl Adam, opposes addressing direct prayers to the Son, or to the Holy Ghost. He condemns St. Athanasius, St. Basil the Great, and St. John Chrysostom, for encouraging the practice which had been employed in all Christendom since the days of the Apostles. (See Acts vii. 59, 60; Rev. xxii. 20.) During our Lord's life on earth He was repeatedly prayed to for favours which it was only possible for God to grant. (See St. Luke xvii. 5; St. John xiv. 8, etc.) Dr. Adam arrives at the strange conclusion that praying thus to the Son and to the Holy Ghost has resulted in Christianity becoming " variously a weary, wilted, morose Christianity, and not a victorious and glad Christianity." (See *Christ, our Brother*, chap. iii.) These views are curiously like certain elements in the heresy of Bishop Colenso which produced such a battle for the faith in the Anglican Church in the mid-nineteenth century.

life *is* that which is within. We know not how to express the life of God, but God Himself, the Holy Spirit, gives the expression of Himself in and through us in what manner He wills, provided we yield ourselves wholly to Him. To this eternal, rich, and gracious inheritance we are called, an inheritance which human thought cannot conceive, nor human speech describe. We can only stand in dumb awe and adoration in the presence of the things that God has prepared for those who love Him.

Father, Son, Spirit : Subdue the turmoil of my heart, that in the unifying calm of love, where thought is hushed to rest, all may be stilled for the sweet and silent intercourse of love. Make me to dwell so wholly one with Thee that I be wholly lost in Thee ; that I no longer be myself, but of one soul with Thee, my own, my Well-Beloved.

Let the ship take what course it will, let it sail towards the east, west, north, or south, by whatsoever wind it may be driven, yet its compass always points towards the fair polar star. Let everything turn upside down, not only around us, but even within us; let our soul be sad or joyful, in sweetness or bitterness, in peace or trouble, in light or darkness, in temptation or repose, in dryness or tenderness, still let the needle of our heart, of our spirit, of our superior will which is our compass, unceasingly turn towards the love of God, its Creator, its Saviour. Who shall be able to separate us from the love of God!

St. Francis de Sales.

CHAPTER XXV

THE WARFARE OF PRAYER

ONE of the universal consequences of the blight of sin upon man's nature is seen in the fact that the attainment of holiness is difficult, while the pursuit of evil requires little or no effort. This presents a condition which is found in every sphere of human life. It is easy to neglect a duty; it calls for effort faithfully to perform it. Perseverance involves a wearing and often laborious constancy; to slacken in a purpose means only to relax, and let things fall as they will of their own gravity. This obtains markedly in the practice of prayer. It is, therefore, of importance that we examine some of the difficulties of prayer, and consider how they are to be met.

I

Perhaps the most universal difficulty in prayer is that which has to do with distraction, with the wandering of the attention from God, and from the subjects of prayer. Yet we are not to think of distraction as sin. It is the result of the infirmity of our nature, and in distraction itself is involved nothing which is inherently wrong. It arises from infirmity, and is not confined to the spiritual sphere, but is found in every activity of the human mind. It is rare that anyone can keep his attention wholly fixed on any subject for any great length of time, whether it be in reading, study, conversation, or prayer.

Distraction and wandering thoughts in prayer do not constitute sin, unless we deliberately yield ourselves to them. If when we are conscious that the attention has wandered, we withdraw it by an act of the will from the distracting subject, and apply it once more to our prayers, not only has no sin been committed, but by such withdrawal we have won a victory over our infirmity, and, it may be, over a direct temptation of Satan. The distraction may come again after a brief interval, but if we deal with it again in the same manner, again we have gained a victory for the glory of God, and for the strengthening of our own souls. If we persevere in this we shall soon learn the habit of concentration in prayer which will prevent any serious failure. Let it be understood that distractions that are not voluntary, and which are not deliberately yielded to, in no way diminish the value, or the fruit of prayer. God does not penalize us for our infirmities. All He asks is that we use reasonable diligence to combat them, and employ the appointed means to strengthen the weak points in our spiritual fortifications. St. Basil, one of the four great doctors of the Eastern Church, says, " If you cannot pray with wholly fixed attention, hold your attention as best you can, and God will overlook your defects, because it will not be through negligence, but through frailty that you cannot keep yourself in God's presence as you ought to do." [1]

The peril from distractions depends altogether on how we deal with them. They should never be taken too seriously. Often they arise from a mere mechanical association of ideas, and their presence may have no spiritual significance. The soul, eager to hold fast by God, is on guard against everything that would dishonour Him, and when one is guarding against a peril, the thought of it is sure to recur to the mind from time to time, and these recurrences should cause no distress or alarm.

While we are to be continually on guard against him, and his deceptions, we should not attribute too much to Satan. Many interior states which may make prayer difficult are only the result of physical and nervous reaction on the mind, and have in their own nature no more of spiritual significance than an aching tooth, although by our unwise handling of them, hurtful spiritual consequences might be produced.

One of the most effective ways of dealing with distractions is to ignore them. In ordinary daily affairs everyone makes this a continual practice. We are writing a letter, or reading a book; someone comes into the room, or some unusual noise is heard. It produces a momentary diversion, but almost instantly the mind swings back to its employment, and no more attention is paid to the cause of the interruption. Think how absurd it would be if we deliberately suspended attention to our work, and went about in some formal way to deal with every such distraction. We would never get anything done. The use of the same method and principle in our devotions would secure for us an effective habit of prayer which would lift our spiritual life to a higher plane, and maintain it there.

[1] St. Basil, *Constitutiones Monasticae*. cap. 1; Migne, P. G., Tom. 31, Col. 1334.

II

There are some distractions, however, which are of a more persistent and aggressive character, and which cannot be so easily ignored. But to think about a distraction is, in itself, another distraction, so that a double obstacle to our prayer is erected. We must in no case entertain any anxiety about the matter. Such anxiety is often a more serious enemy to prayer than the distraction itself. By an act of the will let the attention be withdrawn from the object which has interposed itself, and let the heart be set steadfastly upon God and the things of God, and the distraction will perish through want of nourishment. There are few of us who do not have to repeat this again and again during our periods of prayer, but the recurrence of distraction is only the recurrence of opportunity for victory and grace.

In withdrawing the attention from the distracting thought, one must take care to do this with gentleness. A vehement wrenching of the attention from a distraction, or wandering thought, is apt to upset the calm and poise of the mind, and we may not be able to recapture it. Such a circumstance would prove far more disastrous than the original distraction. The mind must be firmly, but quietly and gently led back to God, so that it can take up the prayer where it was left off, without any disturbance to its tranquillity. Rather than be distressed at the continued temptation, we should, as the apostle St. James enjoins us, " count it all joy " [1] that the adversary regards us as so formidable an enemy to his cause that he has to be continually attacking us lest our faithfulness work harm to his plans of warfare against souls, and against the honour of God.

The habitual practice of patience will prove a great help in this work. If we ordinarily allow ourselves to be annoyed and irritated by little things, this will grow into a habit which will certainly intrude itself seriously into our prayers. We bring to our prayer the kind of mind we have. If the mind is undisciplined, and therefore dissipated, prayer will suffer accordingly. If we assiduously cultivate calmness of spirit, we shall arrive in time at that happy condition where our service of God will be given " with a quiet mind." We cannot expect, nor does any generous soul desire, in this life to be freed from the spiritual warfare which presses upon us, especially when we seek to draw near to God; but we are assured that if we do our part, the conflict can never bring

[1] St. James i. 2.

anything else but victory, with its ever-deepening inflow of the divine grace, which is the assurance of the progress which will issue in the end in gaining for us the crown of life which our Lord has prepared for all those who love and serve Him.

III

We need always to watch against the occasions and circumstances which produce distraction, and to study how to avoid or control them. One of the most fruitful sources of distraction is the body itself, its natural restlessness, its tendency to fatigue, its slight indispositions, which often show themselves only in producing difficulty in thinking, or in concentrating for any length of time. Prayer and meditation should not be left until periods of the day when both mind and body are fatigued. It is a mistake, for example, to defer one's evening prayers until the last wearied minutes of the day. It means poor prayers, and deliberately to do this borders on irreverence. Any prolonged effort in prayer should be made at times when both body and mind are alert. The early morning is usually the best time, as there is less liability to interruption, although there are those who find it difficult to apply the mind seriously to anything until they have had the stimulus of a certain amount of bodily activity.

Bodily posture has much to do with mental attention. We hear much in our day of the influence of mind on matter. We do not consider sufficiently the influence of matter on mind. There are certain physical attitudes which contribute directly to mental sloth, while others induce an alertness of mind which makes for concentration. A soldier at attention in the presence of his superior officer, awaiting orders, is in a very different mental state from that which is produced by taking his ease in an arm-chair. The psalmist, good psychologist as he was, was well aware of these reactions: " As the eyes of servants look unto the hand of their masters, and as the eyes of a maiden unto the hand of her mistress, even so our eyes wait upon the Lord our God until he have mercy upon us." [1]

Experience teaches us that certain practices produce closer attention, such as kneeling in an erect position, with the hands folded, a special guard being always kept over the eyes, lest through these " windows of the soul " distraction find entrance. It is well, in any event, never to look about when one is praying. There is

[1] Ps. cxxiii. 2.

always distraction enough in any case without deliberately providing this further opportunity for it. It is, again, often a help, when the mind is difficult to control, to use a book of prayers for a time. Not infrequently the reading of prayers for a few minutes with very close application to the words will steady and focus the attention, and dissipate the mental numbness. Sometimes those of a nervous physical temperament find it wise to concentrate the attention by bodily action. The late Bishop Moule, of Durham, was said always to make his early morning devotions walking up and down his room, experience having showed him that attention would be more difficult to maintain if he were quietly kneeling. The rhythm of such physical action takes up the restiveness of the body which is so often a cause of distraction. Each soul must, through his own experience, learn, under the guidance of the Holy Spirit, what is most profitable for himself, and will govern himself accordingly. All this is to be done in a quiet, self-possessed, common-sense manner, without strain, or violence, or panic. If we deal with them aright, we have nothing to fear from distractions.

IV

Another of the inevitable incidents of the search after holiness is that absence of emotional pleasure in prayer which is commonly spoken of as spiritual dryness, or aridity. It is the dulness of spirit which often quenches the sweetness of prayer, and demands the greatest exercise of fortitude in order to continue its faithful use. This involves, of course, the emotions, and we are not to make the mistake of despising the emotions. They are a gift from God for our help, especially in the beginning of any hard spiritual adventure. But to use them to launch us on some spiritual campaign is a different thing from depending on them during the whole progress of the conflict. The soldier goes off to the wars with bands playing and banners flying, but it requires more than this initial thrill to sustain him in the weariness of the forced march, and amid the shock of battle. The first emotional enthusiasms soon evaporate, and it is then seen if he has in him the stuff of which veterans are made.

This kind of experience is universal in the Christian life. It is no theory of ascetical theologians, but a plain matter of history. It appears everywhere in the record of Christian spirituality, and it is significant that it besets only those who are really making a serious effort to scale the heights of sanctity. Lukewarm Christians

B B

are puzzled at the very name, and they have nothing in their experience to give them a clue to what the faithful servants of God mean when they speak of it. Nor is it found amongst the earnest seekers after the higher ideals which may be set forth in certain non-Christian religions. It is a distinctive experience, belonging to the religion of the true God as He has revealed Himself in the Old and New Testaments. All the saints have had their repeated and painful bouts with it, these sometimes lasting for years, calling out to the fullest their fortitude and devotion, their willingness to suffer these interior trials for the love of God with an unshaken conviction that, dark as the way may be, God is none the less their light and their salvation.

It is not, however, confined to the higher ranks of the saints. All who set out to give a really consecrated service to God sooner or later will be called upon to endure it, and unless they are fore-warned, grave consequences may be produced. Nowhere in the Christian life is the gift of fortitude needed more than when, on occasions of prayer or Communion, God seems very far away, the heart as dry as dust, and the words of prayer seem to get no further than our lips.

It is quite probable that there has never been a human soul who was seeking earnestly after God along the paths that He has revealed, who has not had this difficulty to meet. The record of it begins in the Old Testament. In Psalm xxiii David tells us that he found the valley of the shadow of death lying directly across the path of righteousness into which the goodness of God had led him. He gives us the highest example of the courage and faith which are necessary in meeting such an experience. In the valley he feared no evil, for he knew that God was with him. His comfort and support lay in God's "rod and staff," which mystical interpreters of the psalms have taken to be the two beams of the cross which God has promised to every soul, and from which, if resolutely taken up and borne, without seeking to escape it, will be derived strength, joy, and glory.

Again, in Psalm lxiii the psalmist cries, " O God, thou art my God, early will I seek thee; my soul thirsteth for thee, my flesh also longeth after thee." And where is this seeking, this longing, which will not cease? " In a barren and dry land where no water is." The psalmist goes on to declare, " Thus "—that is, in the midst of the thirst and longing in the barren and dry land—" have I looked for thee in holiness." He demanded no consolation, no mere emotional satisfaction. He was humbly content to wait on

God, content with whatever God might give or withhold, supported by the unswerving conviction that so long as he could say, " O God, thou art my God," so long as he hoped and looked for God even in the midst of his weak striving after holiness, all would be well. And then comes, as in God's good time there will always come, the cry of triumphant joy: " My soul shall be satisfied even as it were with marrow and fatness when my mouth praiseth thee with joyful lips." This joy was not because of the consolation he received, but on account of God Himself, of whose presence and love he was assured, whether it was in the darkness or in the light.

Many other psalms give expression to this suffering from spiritual dryness, notably x, xiii, xxii, lxxxviii, cii, cxxx, and cxl. But there is never absent from them the confident expression of the goodness and mercy of God in such time of trouble, with the firm conviction that no good thing will be wanting to him if he holds fast and does not yield to discouragement.

Of course, the supreme instance of a human soul in darkness and aridity is that of our Lord in His Passion. In the garden of Agony, he said, " My soul is exceeding sorrowful, unto death," [1] and on the cross He made the cry of the psalmist His own: " My God, my God why hast thou forsaken me? " [2] This cry on the cross offers the highest consolation to our souls when they are engulfed in the gloom and desolation of a seeming desertion by God. God had not forsaken the human soul of Christ. He Himself had declared to His disciples only the night before, " Ye shall be scattered, every man to his own, and shall leave me alone: and yet I am not alone, because the Father is with me." [3] Moreover, since He Himself was very God of very God, it was not possible that He could be forsaken of God. He could not forsake Himself. So is it with the souls of men. Often our eyes are holden that we do not know Him, but He is ever with us, for He has said, " I will never leave thee nor forsake thee," [4] and His promise must come true. So we wait patiently, sharing with Him the cross, knowing that " the disciple is not above his master, nor the servant above his Lord." [5]

V

It would be rash indeed to attempt to discover the causes of spiritual dryness. God may send it to us as a test of our love and faithfulness. It may arise from our own past unfaithfulness in not

[1] St. Mark xiv. 34.   [2] Ps. xxii. 1; St. Matt. xxvii. 46; St. Mark xv. 34.
[3] St. John xvi. 32.   [4] Heb. xiii. 5.   [5] St. Matt. x. 24.

responding on occasions to His holy calls and inspirations. With a soul inexperienced in prayer, possessed of zeal, but not according to knowledge, it might come from an indiscreet overstraining in devotion. But more often one can hope that it arises from certain psychological or physical conditions—weariness, ill-health, often from some bodily indisposition which shows itself in no other way than in a mental lethargy which prevents us from being mentally alert about anything. But whatever the cause, the remedy lies in setting the will like a flint against yielding one whit to the pressure on the soul. We must go forward courageously, remembering that He is none the less our light though our eyes are holden that we should not know Him.

Under these conditions we cannot too often remind ourselves that the value of prayer is not to be found in terms of pleasure, but in terms of struggle. If there be no struggle, if there be no eclipse of spirit, no " dark night of the soul," no abiding in " a barren and dry land where no water is," one would need to fear that there is no vital oneness with God in prayer. Why should He not deal with me as He has ever dealt with His faithful servants?

Those who always expect to find joy in prayer, and repine when they are plunged into some degree of spiritual gloom, have misunderstood the character of union with God. The objective of the life in God is not happiness, but God Himself. He who finally attains to God will indeed possess happiness beyond all human understanding, but the happiness is secondary, and results only from union with, and possession of, God. If the mercy of God gives joy and consolation in prayer, the soul will receive them thankfully, but it is neither to seek them, nor to place any dependence upon them when they are given. Dryness of soul, utter dulness of the inner spirit, are indications neither of spiritual delinquency nor of God's disapproval. All the great saints endured these things to the most painful degree. To think that we are cut off from God because we do not have an emotional consciousness of the joy and brightness of His presence, is what St. Francis de Sales calls " a terrible mistake." [1] This great teacher tells us that the soul which desires to walk the way of the divine will " by the road of pleasure " is in constant peril of the grave sin of " loving the spiritual pleasure more than the will of God." [2]

Those who measure their spiritual condition by the pleasure they find in it are falling into spiritual Epicureanism, and are in

---

[1] St. Francis de Sales, *Treatise on the Love of God*, Bk. I. 12.
[2] St. Francis de Sales, *Treatise on the Love of God*, Bk. VI. 10.

danger of wrecking their spiritual life by a constant and unwhole-
some examination of the state of their emotions. St. Francis says,
" There are those who are not content to be content unless they feel,
see, and relish their contentment. . . . If God grants them the
sacred repose of His presence, they voluntarily forsake it to note
their own deportment, to examine whether they are really content,
disquieting themselves to ascertain whether their tranquillity is
really tranquil, and their quietude quiet, so that instead of sweetly
occupying their will in tasting the sweets of the divine presence,
they employ their understanding in reasoning on the feelings they
have. . . . There is no small difference in occupying oneself with
the God who gives contentment, and amusing oneself with the
contentment which God gives. . . . He who loves it too much
loses it; the right rule for loving it well is, therefore, not to love it
too anxiously."

If the teaching of St. Francis be true, then it follows that those
who yield to sadness and discouragement because of the absence
of emotional sense, are in danger from many quarters. This sense
of sadness may easily be a temptation, in which case we can make
ourselves safe by refusing to yield to it, remembering that one might
easily *feel* depressed and discouraged without *being* depressed and
discouraged. As with all other temptations, we can turn it into
victory by refusing to consent to the inner urge. Only our deliberate
consent can produce the sin of actual discouragement, however
strong the feeling may be. Let us keep this comforting truth always
before us.

If anyone really gives way to this temptation he shows that he
lacks faith in God's word, for He has promised, " I will never leave
thee nor forsake thee." [1] He is making God, who has given this
promise, false, as though He were deceiving the soul. He is refusing to accept our Lord's promise, " In the world ye shall have
tribulation, but be of good cheer, I have overcome the world." [2]
This tribulation has to do not only with temporal suffering, but
embraces the far more crucial pain of the soul. Such a soul needs
to be mindful of the warning given in the Imitation, " There are
many who follow Jesus as far as the breaking of bread, but few to
the drinking of the cup of His Passion." [3] Moreover, those who
actually yield consent are denying all Christian experience, for in
every age, and in every rank of the servants of God, this situation
is to be found. Indeed, as we have seen, this sense of spiritual

---

[1] Heb. xiii. 5.   [2] St. John xvi. 33.
[3] Thomas à Kempis, *De Imitatione Christi*, II, xi.

desolation is one of the invariable marks of the earnest Christian. If we never had to suffer from this buffeting of Satan, the validity of our Christian consecration would be definitely in question.

VI

Those who allow their resolution in prayer to lag because of spiritual dryness are guilty of a fault which is exceeded only by the fault of those who pray long and fervently only and for no other reason than that they experience an emotional delight in it. The former attitude is spiritual sloth or cowardice, but the latter is sheer selfishness, the prostitution of one of the holiest of exercises to the base uses of their own selfish pleasure. Nothing can be more important than for the soul to realize the folly of depending in its relations with God upon " the changing and treacherous emotional content of his consciousness. *Without* an experience of a particular kind, he supposes himself to be deserted by God, void of religion, and without hope in the world; *with* that experience (or something which he mistakes for it), he may only too easily regard everything else—morality, self-discipline, love of the brethren—as irrelevant and superfluous." [1] " To depend upon anything so transient, arbitrary and irresponsible, as a recurrent feeling or ' experience,' as the mainstay of life, is obviously a counsel of despair." [2]

In dealing with these dangers, we are to remember that nothing depends on the emotions. These may be evidences only of a passing psychological condition which comes and goes as the result of influences, not infrequently purely physical, over which we have no control; but everything depends on our resolute will and intention. The wise Christian prays no more earnestly because he seems raised up to heaven, and no less resolutely if he seems cast down to hell. Prayer, if it be true prayer, exists on a plane far above all these evanescent influences. Our objective relation to God our Father is too profound, it is too eternally important, to be affected by the ebb and flow of such tides of transient feeling. One should keep the will alert to pray steadfastly, whatever these conditions may be. There is only one difference in method to be noted: when the mind is sluggish, it were well to set the will Godward with more vigour than at other times, for the reason that under this condition wandering of the attention is naturally more likely to occur.

---

[1] Kirk, *The Vision of God*, p. 104.   [2] Kirk, *The Vision of God*, p. 199.

VII

We would, however, be going contrary to the teaching of all the great spiritual leaders of the Church, and to the testimony of the saints, if we did not agree that there are times when our spiritual lethargy is so great, and goes so deep, that any active prayer whatever, in the ordinary sense of the word prayer, is impossible. So profound a saint as St. Teresa recognizes in herself this condition, but she has a remedy which keeps the soul very closely united to God in the midst of the darkness, and, after all, is not this the very highest form of prayer? At such times, she says, " We must not show ourselves as labouring after spiritual consolations. Come what may, to embrace the cross is the great thing," [1] that is to accept the dryness of heart as the will of God, and to seek to love it as the precious cross which He is laying upon us that we might be the more sanctified through becoming like unto Him in bearing the cross. Even if we cannot think or speak, we can in the silence of the soul adore Him.

Let us sum up with one more quotation, from a spiritual master who has for three centuries been a guide to many saints. Scaramelli explains that " if a man finds himself in prayer as dry as the desert sands, he has but to resign himself to God's will, and, humbling himself in God's presence, to persevere without flinching, and in the midst of dryness still to form the resolutions, the petitions, the desires, which he was wont to make with much feeling, and former sweet and delightful meditations. This is the time of real and solid devotion, although we may think ourselves entirely bereft of it. Indeed, these dry meditations are more full of merit, generally speaking, if we only do our duty, than many others made with great unction, and filled to the brim with spiritual consolation: because to submit in painful prayer to the will of God, to make acts of real humility and self-oblation, to pray earnestly and perseveringly, conjuring the Almighty Lord, and using many industries of supplication, is, of necessity, to do great violence to self in the struggle to overcome the repugnance of nature, when left in aridity and desolation. Now this is what truly makes the acts of the will (in which resides the marrow of merit and of devotion alike) grow in strength, intensity and worth. And thus in the meditation which we make in seasons of aridity, the soul waxes stronger, even if the body grows weak; and if the animal man be exhausted, the spirit of man finds new vigour, fresh increase of power." [2]

[1] St. Teresa, *Life*, xxii. 15.   [2] Scaramelli, *Directorium Asceticum*, I. 187.

We must ask ourselves continually, What is the aim and object of our spiritual effort? Is it to find comfort and pleasure, or is it to find God? The answer to this question should set us right.

O True, Supreme Peace, speak to my soul, vexed and harried by many fears : Say, " Peace be unto thee "—what words more joyful that the ear can hear ? " It is I "—what possession of the soul brings richer peace ? " Be not afraid "—what words can speak a deeper peace ? " Lo, I am with you alway "—what surety brings sweeter peace from everlasting unto everlasting ?

EPILOGUE

" *Caput et membra, unus Christus*, The Head and the members constitute the one Christ." Not the stock alone, but the stock and the branches make the vine. We are baptized, as St. Paul declares, " into Jesus Christ," [1] and in the development of the regenerate soul it " grows up into him in all things, which is the Head, even Christ." [2] The engrafted branch partakes of the life of the Vine, and as its participation in His life grows and increases, it becomes not only more and more like unto Him who is the source of its life, but there is realized more and more its identity with Him, as the branch is identified with the vine.

But the Blessed Christ, with whom we are one, is not the Christ of the days of His earthly pilgrimage, for now that He is risen, ascended, and glorified, there is no longer a Christ who is compassed about with infirmities, no longer a Christ who can suffer, a Christ who can die. " Christ being raised from the dead dieth no more; death hath no more dominion over him. For in that he died, he died unto sin once, but in that he liveth, he liveth unto God." But he took not this life from the dead for His own behoof, or benefit, but for ours. Therefore, the apostle goes on to say: " Likewise, reckon ye also yourselves to be dead indeed unto sin, but alive unto God through Jesus Christ our Lord." [3] The emphasis here falls on the words " likewise," and " also." His Manhood is risen, ascended, and glorified in the bosom of the Ever-Blessed Trinity. In like manner are we also risen, ascended, and glorified with Him. This has not yet reached its perfect consummation indeed in us, but since we have entered into Christ, so we have part in His Resurrection life, the only life which He now possesses. We have partaken of the divine nature in our measure, even as His Humanity has, without measure, partaken of the divine Nature, of the divine holiness. Being one with Him, we, along with Him, are made one with the Ever-Adorable Trinity, and in this oneness we participate in that knowledge and love which are the continuous and infinite activity of the blissful Godhead.

We recall the great Easter epistle: " If ye then be risen with Christ, seek those things which are above, where Christ sitteth on

---

[1] Rom. vi. 3. [2] Eph. iv. 15. [3] Rom. vi. 9–11.

the right hand of God. Set your affection on things above, not on things on the earth. For ye are dead, and your life is hid with Christ in God." [1] The apostle passionately exhorts us to seek our rightful place, the only place possible for us if we make not eternal shipwreck of the life to which God, from the foundation of the world, has called us in order " that we should be holy." [2]

We are heirs of God, and joint-heirs with Christ. His inheritance in the Godhead is our inheritance. Whatever He possesses in His glorified Humanity we share because we are members of that Humanity. Let us not make the mistake of thinking of this relationship as some vague, symbolic thing. If we are " in Christ," we live on a plane where symbol and figure are done away for ever. We have left all types and foreshadowing behind us, and we have passed into the realm of ultimate fulfilment and reality.

We cannot, however, think of ourselves as, in any sense, isolated members in the Vine which is Christ. The engrafted members become not only His members, but they become members one of another, and share with one another the eternal life which has been transmitted to them, and all the gifts that accompany that life.

Whether in the Church Militant, in the Church Expectant, or in the Church Triumphant, we all partake of the life of the divine Head, and we all share it with one another. Each soul participates in the life of every other soul in the Body of Christ, and whatever gifts, graces, or glory one receives, all receive, each in his appointed measure. " If one member be honoured, all the members rejoice with it," [3] because the gifts of life and love, of grace and glory, made to one, flood every soul who abides in the same Mystical Body. Every increment of glory in which the saints in heaven rejoice is the increase of the God-life to every soul in Christ. On earth every prayer and aspiration addressed to God, every good Communion made, every holy action performed, releases the further power and love of God for the benefit of all. A little child half-way round the world offers a simple act of praise or prayer, and each of us, even the saints in heaven, has an integral part in that act, and is stronger in the Lord, and in the power of His might, because of it. Far away some soul, beset by temptation, tottering on the brink of the abyss of sin, is, by every exercise of the divine life in the humblest member of Christ, strengthened to stand the more stiffly against the assaults of the adversary, and to win a victory for the honour of God and the kingdom.

Thus, in unbroken co-operation with God and with each other,

[1] Col. iii. 1–3.   [2] Eph. i. 4.   [3] 1 Cor. xii. 26.

in mutual participation in every divine gift, the mighty ranks of the armies of God move on with steady front in ever-ascending progress to ever higher planes of love, and of life and service in God. The final destination will be found amid the innermost mysteries of the Holy and Indivisible Trinity. There shall we enter upon the ultimate state of perfection for which we were created, within which state we shall go on for all eternity ever moving on from great things to greater. There the soul is permeated with God, immersed in Him, plunged in the unfathomed and unfathomable depths of the divine life, possessing Him wholly, and possessed wholly by Him and in Him.

Yet in this supreme unity with the divine there is no subversion of the powers of the soul. On the contrary, every faculty—intellect, will, heart, imagination, all else—is raised to the highest power of conscious efficiency and perfection, to a degree passing the comprehension of human thought; and this condition is at once a profound repose in God, and a participation in the infinite activities of Divinity. Its length and breadth, its depth and height, are limited only by the finiteness of man and of his nature.

It belongs to the nature of man to find the reward of satisfaction and joy in work well done. If this be so in the halting labours, and in the poor ephemeral achievements of the earthly life, how unspeakably greater will be the reward of the heavenly life. In that life there is no lack. There every activity is crowned with the joy of a perfect and complete consummation; there every labour is infinitely congenial; there every power employed will be a perfect instrument for the fulfilling of the holy purposes of Him whom we love, in whom we have our being, and for whom we are given to accomplish a perfect labour in the joyousness of a love which embraces all things, a love which can never know a moment's frustration, a love which can never fail.

It is this for which God has destined us for eternity. In union with Him, with a complete oneness with His infinity of love, our created powers will be merged with His uncreated and essential life. To the utmost bound of the possibilities of our finite nature, we shall share in all that He is, in all that He has. Saving only that man cannot become God, that the finite cannot be the Infinite, our capacities and potentialities will be as deep as the abyss of the divine Love, and as wide and limitless as God's own omnipotence and omniscience. For this the divine Love has brought us into being. For the accomplishment of this all heaven waits. If the angels rejoice over one sinner that repenteth, over one soul who takes only the first step towards God, how much more will there be joy in heaven over one who reaches the final goal, who attains to that splendid and irrevocable destiny which was prepared for him from everlasting.

This destiny fulfilled, in that everlasting kingdom there will be the performance of the rich and precious promise, " And his servants shall serve him." [1] There shall we find labour without toil, service sweet and unwearied. Upon that kingdom of peace and love rests the untroubled light, there broods the calm of God, there saints are at rest; beauty withers not, and love does not grow cold. There will the soul find sweet, supreme security, for there shall we look for evermore upon the Face of God.

> *Amen, amen, amen, so let it be !*
> *O tender, gracious Father ;*
> *O Son of God, sweet and infinitely loving :*
> *O Spirit of Love, pitiful and compassionate ;*
> *O gracious Trinity, Three-in-One,*
> *So let it be, So let it be.*

[1] Rev. xxii. 3.

INDEX

ABSOLUTION, withholding of, 261; produces objective grace of penance, 262; effects of, 262; removes guilt, does not make reparation, 263

Adam, Dr. Karl, opposes prayers to Son and Spirit, 362; condemns St. Athanasius, St. Basil, St. Chrysostom, for permitting it, 362

Adoption, nature of divine, distinguished from human, 83 ff.

Affinity between God and man, 144

Alford, Dean, on " power " to become sons of God, 100

Amendment, necessary to penance, 271 f.; progressive and lifelong, 272

Anselm, St., on holy fear, 318; on wisdom, 330.

Apostles, ordained by Christ, 299

Athanasius, St., purpose of Incarnation, 38, 59; Karl Adam on, 362

Atonement, 75 ff.; basis of, in Incarnation, 80; effected by Christ's life and work, 75; reversed fall of man, 81

Attributes of God, varied manifestations of His love, 168; totality of, possessed by each divine Person, 169

Augustine, St., on peace, 205, 215; identity of God with attributes, 3, 38, 101, 113, 132; necessity of command for perfection, 19 f.; purpose of Incarnation, 38; Eve and B.V.M., 36; action of divine love, 39; dying to self, 52, 256; desire and prayer, 54 ff.; all love to be referred to God, 69; processes of grace, 90; on light of faith, 113; on passions, 137; mode of exercising love, 155 ff.; loving and liking, 157; love of neighbour not altruism or philanthropy, 158; the new commandment, 158; union with God secures love of neighbour, 158; unitive love, 159; communicative love, 160; humility, 191; sin its own punishment, 242; love and sin, 255; on Holy Ghost, 283, 286; man free to do only evil, 291; gifts of Spirit, 317; holy fear, 318; on wisdom, 331; definition of prayer, 354; on praying without ceasing, 357; quoted,

47, 73, 79, 104, 138, 143, 144 f., 166, 172, 197, 255, 274, 278, 294, 343

Baptism, effects of, 65, 86; necessary to salvation, 77

Basil, St., on humility, 195; on attention in prayer, 366

Beatitudes, 335 ff.; result from gifts of Spirit working with theological virtues, 335; not emotions, but objective states of soul, 335 ff.; foretaste of Beatific Vision, 335.

Bernard, St. of Clairvaux, action of God's love, 18; on God as end and reward, 19; dignity of human soul, 47; desire for perfection credited as perfection, 56; grace and free will, 74; identity of God with love, 10, 142; on hope, 126; love and reason, 140; God alone the soul's reward, 145; four degrees of love, 147 ff.; mode of loving God, 155; unitive love, 159; communicative love, 160; humility, 194; humiliation necessary to humility, 195; quoted, xi, 18, 19, 22, 24, 139, 146, 147, 148, 149, 157, 159, 160 ff., 168, 169, 179, 194, 195, 199, 210, 220, 359

Bernard, of Cluny, quoted, 265

Berulle, Père, on acts of virtue, 27

Body, use of in mental concentration, 368

Boëthius, love and cosmic harmony, 90

Bossuet, Jacques Benigne, grace and Beatific Vision, 189

Bright, William, on Eucharistic Sacrifice, 78

Buckler, O. P., H. Reginald, on discretion, 325; quoted, 313, 327

Camus, Jean Pierre, quoted, 68, 181, 193

Cassian, John, on discretion, 325

Catherine of Siena, St., on God possessing the soul, 89; Christian another Christ, 297

Christ, glorified, the only Christ, 377 ff.; man's union with Holy Trinity in Christ, 377; Christ's heavenly inheritance we share, 378; Deity of, supreme essential in Faith, 114;

Printed and Bound in Great Britain by
Richard Clay and Company, Ltd.,
Bungay, Suffolk.

4528
1R